A NEGOTIATED LANDSCAPE

A view to the Ferry Building through the Financial District and the Embarcadero Center. Photograph by author.

A NEGOTIATED LANDSCAPE

The Transformation of San Francisco's
Waterfront Since 1950

Jasper Rubin

CENTER FOR AMERICAN PLACES AT COLUMBIA COLLEGE CHICAGO

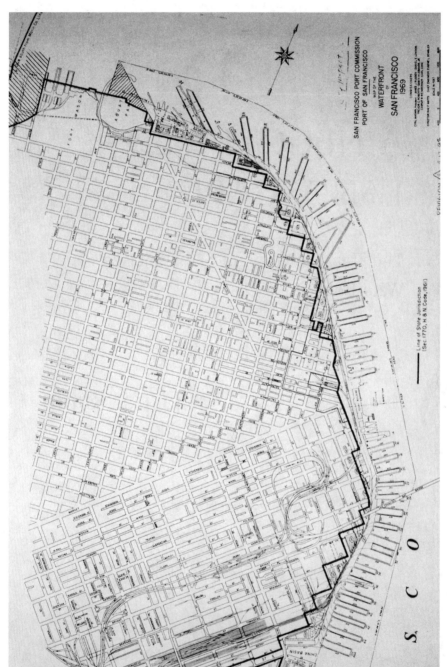

San Francisco Port Commision Map of San Francisco, 1969. Courtesy Port of San Francisco.

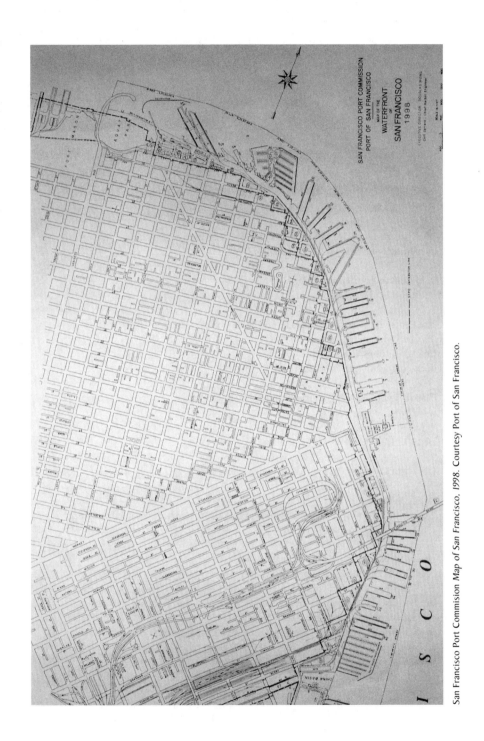

San Francisco Port Commision Map of San Francisco, 1998. Courtesy Port of San Francisco.

Published in 2011. First Edition.
Published in the U.S.A. on acid-free paper.

The Center for American Places at Columbia College Chicago
600 South Michigan Avenue
Chicago, Illinois 60605-1996, U.S.A.
www.colum.edu/centerbooks

Distributed by the University of Chicago Press
www.press.chicago.edu

20 19 18 17 16 15 14 13 12   1 2 3 4 5

Library of Congress Cataloging-in-Publication Data

Rubin, M. Jasper.
 A negotiated landscape : the transformation of San Francisco's waterfront since 1950 / M. Jasper Rubin. — 1st ed.
    p. cm.
 Includes bibliographical references and index.
 ISBN 978-1-935195-28-3 (acid-free paper)
 1. Waterfronts—California—San Francisco—History. 2. Harbors—California—San Francisco—History. 3. Landscapes—California—San Francisco—History. 4. Social change—California—San Francisco—History. 5. City planning—California—San Francisco—History. 6. Architecture—California—San Francisco—History. 7. San Francisco (Calif.)—History. 8. San Francisco (Calif.)—Social conditions. 9. San Francisco (Calif.)—Politics and government. I. Title.
 F869.S357R83 2011
  979.4'61—dc23
                        2011018494

To Leonard,
dearest father and mentor

Contents

List of Abbreviations

ADL	Arthur D. Little, Inc.
BCDC	Bay Conservation and Development Commission
BSHC	Board of State Harbor Commissioners
BZC	Blythe-Zellerbach Committee
CAC	Citizen Advisory Committee
CEQA	California Environmental Quality Act
CWC	Citizens' Waterfront Committee
FWAP	Fisherman's Wharf Action Plan
NEWAC	Northeastern Waterfront Advisory Committee
NEWP	Northeastern Waterfront Plan
NWP	Northern Waterfront Plan
OSH	Ocean Shipping Handbook
PFEL	Pacific Far East Lines
PSF	Port of San Francisco
SAP	Special Area Plan
SFC	*San Francisco Chronicle*
SFPA	San Francisco Port Authority
SFRA	San Francisco Redevelopment Agency
SFPD	San Francisco Planning Department
SFT	San Francisco Tomorrow
SLC	State Lands Commission
SPUR	San Francisco Planning and Urban Research Association
TDP	Total Design Plan
WPAB	Waterfront Planning Advisory Board
WTC	San Francisco World Trade Center Authority
WTPO	Waterfront Transportation Projects Office

Acknowledgments

THIS BOOK, like many such projects, is not the result of work done in isolation. It evolved with the help and support of many people. I owe great thanks to Noreen Ambrose, formerly general counsel for the Port of San Francisco and ever guardian of its history, and to Diane Oshima, the Assistant Deputy Director of Waterfront Planning, whose help and patience with my questions were invaluable. They pointed me to rooms full of books and binders and welcomed me into their offices. Many thanks to Mark Paez for boxes of research material and to Dan Hodapp for maps and drawings. David Beaupre and Phil Williamson have also generously answered my pesky questions in the most gracious manner. I am very grateful for tales of the port set to paper so thoughtfully and generously by Mr. Don DeLone, a past public relations director for the port.

The San Francisco History Center at the San Francisco Main Library is a wonderful resource, but it would be nothing without its helpful, knowledgeable and professional staff. I also extend my gratitude to Mr. Rick Romagosa at the *San Francisco Chronicle* for permission to reproduce images.

This project began as a dissertation (more years ago than I care to think about), which I completed while still a planner at the San Francisco Planning Department. Not only were friends and colleagues there patient with my distraction, but their dedication to their work and heartfelt concern for the city was a constant source of psychic nourishment. While in some way or other everyone in the Citywide

Policy Planning section deserves my thanks, several people were particularly instrumental to my survival through the process of working and writing. David Alumbaugh, John Billovits, Teresa Ojeda, and Ken Rich are the kinds of professionals—and people—that every city needs. More than consummate planners, they hold a progressive and enlightened approach to how a bureaucracy should function. While no longer at the SFPD, special thanks goes to Scott Edmondson, whose undying encouragement and enthusiasm for wide-ranging discussions were inspiring at just the right times, and to Miriam Chion, who led by example and is the best planning-trained geographer I know.

The faculty in the Department of Urban Studies and Planning at San Francisco State University made the transition from professional planning life to the university smooth and welcoming, and the parallel progression from dissertation to book would have been far more difficult otherwise. I could not ask for more supportive and patient colleagues than Professors Ashok Das, Richard LeGates, Ayse Pamuk, and Raquel Pinderhughes. The larger institution of the university has also been very supportive. The Vice President's Assigned Time Award, administered through the Center for Teaching and Faculty Development, was particularly helpful in making the final push to completion. A travel grant from the university and Joel Kassiola, Dean of the College of Behavioral and Social Sciences, is also much appreciated.

I will always be grateful to Richard Walker for his willingness to befriend and encourage a young (ish) professional with academic aspirations, and for introducing me to the California Studies Association, whose members both intimidate and amaze with their seemingly endless knowledge of the golden state. I hope that I reveal something in this book that CSA members do not already know.

This project found life as a book because of three people in particular, Ted Muller, who read the rough-around-the-edges dissertation, George Thompson, who has supported this project over its extended life and despite exploding page counts, and Brandy Savarese, Editorial Director of the Center for American Places at Columbia College Chicago. Throughout the whole process Brandy has been encouraging, professional, and patient.

I cannot say how much I appreciate Geoff Buckley's untiring encouragement. His long distance prodding and easy-going humor were at times a life line. Ed, Monica, and Henry put the there there, despite being neither geographers nor planners, something I hold dear.

Lastly, I am deeply grateful to my wife, Rebecca. She has seen me through this project and, despite my bouts of crotchetiness, has been my unswerving best friend and ally—proven by the occasional swift kick in the pants. To our wonderful little beasties, Adrienne and Calder, I say "OK, now let's play monster—rawr!"

A NEGOTIATED LANDSCAPE

Introduction

Approaching the Local

In 1958, Matson Line's *Hawaiian Merchant* was the first container ship to leave San Francisco Bay and head for open seas. As it slipped past the Golden Gate Bridge, few recognized that its voyage heralded a dramatic change in course for San Francisco's storied waterfront. By the early 1970s, while increasing numbers of massive container ships sailed on a regular basis from Oakland's growing port, San Francisco's cargo operations had slowed to a trickle, and much of the once-bustling waterfront became moribund. Shipping and maritime-related industry are to this day secondary, nearly invisible, features of the city's urban waterfront. Over the course of the last fifty years, much of San Francisco's waterfront has been transformed from an exotic and often dangerous place of work into a place of leisure, distinguished by beautiful public spaces and entertainment facilities that attract visitors from around the world. Slender, obelisk-like historic markers punctuate a well-used public path—named for the late local columnist Herb Caen—explaining the obvious to curious visitors, that San Francisco's waterfront is not what it once was.

The waterfront's revitalization was not as quick as its decline and in fact is still underway. Decades of obsolescence and disuse passed before it formed new and different connections with its city. Even as the adjacent downtown reoriented itself, straining skyward and expanding outward with the forms of the new postindustrial economy, the waterfront lay largely stagnant, struggling to find a purpose. The eventual transformation of San Francisco's urban waterfront was not the result of a smooth or methodical shift to a new morphology, guided by a well-coordinated, purposeful bureaucracy, a steady administrative regime, and a compliant public. Rather, the port and its governing commission were caught off guard by the difficulties of competing for business in a new age of transportation technology and the sudden decline in shipping activity that resulted. Over the years, a mixture of governmental hubris, poor strategic decision making and, most critically, complex development politics hampered San Francisco's ability to reinvent its waterfront. Early attempts to promote new uses were fitful and largely unsuccessful, despite the tremendous potential value of waterfront real estate. Some proposals were misguided ideas that faded on their own, but others were prevented by successful resistance from neighborhood activists, environmentalists, organizations of varying stripes, and an accumulation of land-use and zoning restrictions. Indeed, partly because the port is so much a part of the city's identity, deciding what to do with it has been at the center of many rounds of impassioned debate among San Franciscans.

At first, in the mid-twentieth century, when officials began to think that portions of the port could be put to new use, unrestrained modernist visions predominated. By the 1960s, battles over development proposals were joined across multiple strata of San Francisco's political structure. Apart from a few exceptions, such as the opening of Pier 39 in Fisherman's Wharf in 1978, it was not until the 1990s that little by little major changes began to take place. Some of the most significant projects, for instance the renewal of the Ferry Building, have occurred only relatively recently. Much of the San Francisco waterfront is a stretch of urban space that has shifted in use from production and industry to consumption and recreation. This kind of change can be seen as physical evidence of a switch in the functioning of a capitalist economy and the advent of new transportation technology. Tourism and entertainment, for instance, provide new fuel for the engines of capitalism; the energy that shipping provided is mostly spent. But it also reflects the demands, expectations, and limitations related to the locale, that is, to the political, social, and cultural peculiarities of San Francisco as well as the city's geographical site and situation.

So, while this book is about the evolution of the San Francisco's port over roughly half a century, from 1950 to the turn of the millennium, it is also an examination of the processes and circumstances that have influenced that transformation. Of particular importance in this regard has been how planning and regulation, and generally the planning process, have affected this physically and symbolically important part of San Francisco. In essence, the evolution of planning during the fifty years covered here, especially land-use policy and environmental regulation, is articulated in the transformation of the waterfront. The waterfront is not just a creation of the free hand of capitalist development, assisted by a retreat of public agencies from their civic responsibilities.

Much urban research has focused on broad forces of change—*grand narratives*, they are sometimes called—in its approach to urban transformation. Whether developed within the urban literature or adapted from various disciplines, grand narratives are held to have broad explanatory capacity, capturing both meta- and microphenomena within their sweep. The grand narrative is usually based on a primary organizing concept, such as a theory of space, or social structuring, or political economics, to which almost everything else in the field of view is rendered peripheral. Cultural practices, for instance, may be treated as an epiphenomenon of capital.[1] Put somewhat differently, the interest of many urbanists has been in forces that operate on larger scales, that swirl around and permeate cities and which, in their ebb and flow, do not necessarily seem to relate to the particularities of place. Within this expansive range of analysis, certain foci have come to predominate: theories of capital, an engagement with postmodern urbanism, and the processes and conditions of globalization. These kinds of conceptualizations can be deeply revealing, helping us understand the complex and often obscure phenomena that influence the nature of cities and their roles in our world. Yet one consequence of their elaboration is that the local often seems to be powerless, rendered little more than a spatialized instance of the varying character of those larger forces and their interactions. Phenomena at the scale of the street, wharf, neighborhood, or even city are often read as evidence of forces that act beyond, and irrespective of, the local context. Everyday life loses any nektonic quality as people and communities, especially if fractured by identity politics, become subject to powers beyond their control. Moreover, globalization, advanced capitalism, and the patterns of consumption related to them, are seen to cause the urban world to suffer from a creeping genericness that threatens to overwhelm many of the complexities of material culture, social relations, and the variations and vagaries of urban forms and functions.[2] All too easily, cities and the neighborhoods that comprise them become undifferentiated or anonymous, or are given a postmodern branding as they are broken into bits and pieces, represented in abstract maps and diagrams with labels like "ethnoburbs," "command-and-control centers," "blue-blood estates," and "festival settings."[3] Cities, along with the grand theories that explain them, become abstractions. The locality is smeared into the background of the theoretical canvas. Yet, as geographer Richard Walker reminds us, "local difference is of more than parochial interest. . . . Local differences may provide clues to unevenness within larger geographies of capitalist development . . . they can bear witness to resistance against the whirlwinds of capitalism . . . and to the persistence of oblique ideas and ways of life in the face of homogenizing forces of modernization."[4]

The basic premise of this book, then, is that local conditions and local power contribute in essential ways to the set of influences that interact to create and recreate places. So, to understand fifty years of a changing urban waterfront requires cognizance both of larger, overarching forces and of the role of the local and particular. In some ways, this may be thought of in the "top down" and "bottom up" conceptual framework occasionally employed to characterize forces that effect change. While such a structure may be useful conceptual shorthand, it is critical to recognize the complexities that more accurately reflect forces of change. For our purposes, top-down forces are of three sorts. The first are grand and expansive, such as the ability of capital to cause development or disinvestment, the effect of technology on the arrangement of shipping routes and the location of production, or the impact of globalization on urban hierarchies and city structure. Related to these, the second set are external forces embodied by, for example, businesses and investors who may come from outside a locale to engage in development, likely bringing with them sources of capital tapped from global financial flows, or members of the "transnational capitalist class" who influence the creation and design of the built environment.[5] The third sort take the form of policy and regulation established by state or federal government, especially as imposed on specific places with little local input. All of these have influenced San Francisco's waterfront. From the other direction, the bottom up or local can include powerful actors, local government agencies and the regulations and policies they administer, and interest groups. More specifically, powerful gatekeepers may be agency heads or commissioners, local real estate magnates, local business groups, civic leaders, neighborhood and environmental organizations, or experienced activists.

What is particularly important in the top-down/bottom-up schema is the implication that top-down forces such as containerization or the restructuring of the urban economy do not act as unchecked powers: they must contend both with local conditions, such as the fundamental geographical qualities of site and situation, and with bottom-up forces. The converse is also true; local actors may have to tap into larger forces to effect an agenda for change. Local conditions include other elements as well, such as the general political, cultural, and social characteristics that differentiate places. San Francisco's history as a politically progressive city, its status as a charter city, its strong-mayor form of local government (less strong after recent initiatives), its cultural cache, its ability to produce innovation, and its strong identification with its neighborhoods, are examples of local characteristics that influence the various forces of change.

It is important to recognize the variations in the ways top-down and bottom-up forces interact. First, they are not always in opposition, although frequently portrayed as such. For instance, if any development is to proceed, it requires willing developers, the availability of capital (or substantial public funding), and local entitlements. Second, their relationship can vary over time. A top-down force may create a condition to which local actors take some time to react, and some local conditions develop that require top-down forces to adjust. The different ways they interact create different environments for opportunity, or of constraint. Starting our story from an earlier point in time and working forward reveals shifts in the balance between forces—one or the other may be prevalent at any given time—and how different elements of either may be the "force of the moment." Third, not only are the host of local actors and agencies part of the local power structure that contends with outside pressure but they also struggle with one another over development issues and some may even be a point of focus for external agents. Their collective nature and roles can be kaleidoscopic. Some actors or agencies may be both top down and bottom up, making it difficult to adhere rigorously to the duality inherent in this framework. This last point emphasizes that the historical geography of a place does not necessarily fit easily into the ready comfort of a duality that fails to capture the complexity of the interplay of forces, how their relationships change over time, and the dual roles that some actors and agencies play.[6] The devil, as they say, is in the details.

LANDSCAPE

Urban researchers have not, of course, overlooked the local—geographers, especially, are concerned with place and landscape, both inherently local.[7] This book is about a waterfront landscape, one of great importance to San Francisco. Indeed, it was once observed that the story of San Francisco is the story of its waterfront.[8] I invoke the concept of landscape because it embodies two aspects of the world that are essential to understanding urban places—the material, in particular the built environment, and the processes of its creation (or destruction). First, at one level, as John Frasier Hart has said, the landscape is "the things we see."[9] Here, that is the built environment—the physical, visible aspect of an urban landscape with which one may interact. An urban waterfront is a built environment comprised of piers, buildings, container terminals, roads and pathways, open spaces and other physical elements. Particularly notable is its contrast to the waterfront's natural, aquatic setting and its immediately identifiable functions. The built environment tells us in a general way where we are and what kind of place we are in: port or seaside resort, suburb or downtown financial district, old neighborhood, new loft enclave, slum.[10] Built spaces, including waterfronts, are made by and populated with people and thus reflect a multitude of both personal ambitions and structural impulses. Thus they can also be symbolic: skyscrapers can represent power, crumbling and rotten piers can reflect the faded past of a maritime era, and derelict neighborhoods can symbolize the failure of a socioeconomic system.[11] And for most of us, our daily lives occur in and around buildings and streets. The built environment frames the space for and influences the character of many interactions and relationships.

Conversely, some writers have made the point that a landscape is not *what* one sees but is, rather, a *way of seeing*, an ideology, and one based on an act of appropriation. A painter, for instance, depicts a familiar scene but incorporates into it aspects that represent relationships among people, serving to assert certain societal roles above others. Or the way a landscape is depicted can indicate a particular, often class-based or socially structured, conception of the relationship between humans and nature.[12] In another vein, real landscapes hide the conditions of their creation, as Don Mitchell has tellingly portrayed in *The Lie of the Land*, wherein he reveals that the ordered and pleasant agricultural landscapes of California have been the result of "ugly processes" typified by a capitalism that traps migrant workers in an oftenwretched system of abuse. In both cases, whether it is the *idea* of landscape as it may be represented in a painting or map, or its *physical character*, they are held to be beguiling or deceitful.

The potentially misleading nature of the physical aspect of landscape is underscored when one considers that not everything important about a place shows up materially. Reading the landscape from material arti-facts alone runs the risk of starting from an incomplete text.[13] What is not present in the landscape can be as essential to understanding the nature of the place as what is there. For example, the defeat of a proposal for an urban freeway could be an important substantiation of the effectiveness of civic activism that might be missed if one began with the physical evi-dence available in the built environment (if there is no freeway to observe, how does one know a struggle over its construction occurred?). Things that did not happen also have important implications for the future. There would be little space along San Francisco's waterfront for its current, rela-tively publicly minded renaissance had proposals for development in the past been successful.

But landscapes may be more than a lie. At any given moment, they may represent the conclusion of a struggle, the assertion of class or economic power, a stalemate over development policy, a victory for preservation-ists, a moment of transition between cultural trends, or a combination of many things. The built environment, then, is a starting place for inves-tigating the urban landscape. It is the material manifestation, not neces-sarily in obvious ways, of cultural and social practices and of an economic system.[14] Viewed over time, it provides signposts marking underlying shifts in a set of forces and their interplay. So, for coming to grips with a landscape, it is doubly true that what is out of sight should not be out of mind. Borrowing from Denis Cosgrove, we must be wary of falling into an "argument of the eye."[15]

This brings us to the second important aspect of landscape, that it is more than the visible, material character of a place; it is also the often-invisible processes and conditions that shaped it. For the purposes of this book, those processes are embodied in the interplay of top-down and bottom-up forces. One must also recognize that the built environ-ment—the visible landscape—at the moment of encounter offers only a brief window of perception, an incomplete set of clues for understanding a place. Thus to see a city—or a waterfront—as a landscape often requires a historical approach. If a landscape is partly a process, then it is something that can only be properly perceived as existing through time. And so this volume looks at the past fifty years or so, a span sufficient to ferret out the processes most relevant to explaining how San Francisco's waterfront came to be the way it is and "to make visible, to bring out of conceal-ment, what is not visible in today's landscape."[16] Many forces generate urban transformations and determine the character of change; a shift in the built environment influences the next set of interactions among forces and how they may resolve themselves. Thought of in this way, landscape in this book can be understood as a form of dialectical landscape, which Don Mitchell argues is "crucial to understanding how the landscape *works* (emphasis in original)."[17]

PLANNING

A concern for bottom-up or local influences on urban landscapes leads us to city planning. Urban change is deeply influenced by the practice of planning, which has been an accepted, albeit controversial, bureaucratic and administrative function of American society for the better part of the last century. In fact, rooted in the police power and supported by the courts, federal enabling acts, and state legislation, planning is one of the most important sources of local power. Urban planning has as its focus the built environment, its character and functions, how it is shaped, and for whom. The San Francisco Planning Department expresses this loftier role in its mission statement, which is to promote "the orderly, harmo-nious use of land and improved quality of life for our diverse community and future generations." Planning, in the form of policy (as expressed in plans), codes, and regulations, provides local jurisdictions with the ability to exert significant control over development, the provision of infrastructure, and the distribution of resources and public amenities. Planners, and the institution of planning, are at a nexus of government, politics, law, and economics.

Planning can also be thought of as a process, a series of decisions made over time in a more or less mediated and structured fashion. This pro-cess can create many ethical and moral difficulties, especially for plan-ning staff. Allan B. Jacobs, former director of planning in San Francisco and author of *Making City Planning Work* advised that one ought to keep one's bags packed—meaning, basically, be ready to leave if the ability to maintain professional and ethical standards are threatened. To greater or lesser degrees, this process has become one that unfolds in a system that includes public participation, the nature and success of which varies by place.[18] In this regard, the planning process is both the primary mechanism for and the arena of most struggles over urban land use and development. Therefore, it provides one of the most direct ways to engage forces from beyond the city and county line and to influence or even determine the nature of urban growth and change.[19] It is also where opponents within a locality square off against one another. This happens in obvious ways at commission or board hearings and community planning meetings, and through less obvious, sometimes even sub-rosa means, for example, in closed-door meetings or in attempts to influence elected officials and staff in how to approach problems or reach decisions. If the process is seen to fail a particular party, the ultimate recourse is to place propositions on the ballot, a strategy that many planners and planning advocacy groups find frustrating, but one that has been used effectively in San Francisco by anti-growth activists.

City planning is largely a locally situated practice, and how it works or does not work is very much, though not entirely, a reflection of the community it serves.[20] Where planning is in fact part of the everyday life of a city it is embedded in the workings of the place and is produced and reproduced by myriad actors, agencies, and structures all across the city. Political activists, the mayor and mayoral offices, councils and boards, business organizations, developers, and neighborhood groups all tug and pull at the planning process, creating pressure to promote outcomes that benefit their particular interests. As we shall see, activist-minded populations can ensure that decisions made during the planning process reflect more than purely bureaucratic, political, or narrow economic purposes and can be successful in realizing very specific, even neighborhood-centered goals.

Much of the potential strength of planning is in the quality of the tools available to staff, members of the public, and decision makers. The primary mechanism is the general plan, also called a master or comprehensive plan, which sets forth a vision for the future of the community. The general plan is intended to guide growth and development based on written objectives and policies using maps, illustrations, and quantitative information that address subject areas such as housing, transportation, open space, and environmental quality. In many jurisdictions, general plans provide policy direction for other agencies.[21] Zoning codes and maps are used to implement general plan policies as they relate to the built environment through the regulation of heights, building bulk and setbacks, parking requirements, and so on. They can also enable exactions, implement the transfer of development rights, support historic preservation, and require various public notification procedures and requirements.[22] Neither general plans nor zoning codes provide absolute surety in a course of action. Planning policy is especially susceptible to interpretation because the language used in policy statements can be one of conditional tenses and weak exhortations, such as "the city should encourage," and because policies can contradict one another. Nevertheless, at a minimum, general plan policy makes relatively clear to the public how a project or development relates to official policy, revealing much about the decision-making process. At their most effective, which is usually when implemented though specific zoning codes and other regulatory mechanisms, general plans set a course for growth and change that considers social and economic issues as well as equity. However, we should be mindful that, as noted by Michael Neuman, "plans are powerful because they are built into the power structure."[23]

The failures of planning are legion and often painfully apparent. Most egregious are those associated with urban renewal and sprawl, although smaller-scale problems riddle the built environment, from allowing construction of market-rate lofts in working-class neighborhoods to poorly designed plazas and public spaces. It is, ironically enough, sometimes difficult to identify the successes of planning if gauged only by the built environment. Of course, the definition of *success* depends on the perspective of the parties involved and any number of measurements, from fiscal soundness to legislative victories and even to enforcement. Generally, though, the point of planning is at least to curb market impulses enough to ensure that public needs are not ignored and to make certain that critical political or bureaucratic decisions about land use, development, and related subjects, are not made in isolation, entirely out of public view. To some degree, then, planning successes must be evaluated on that basis and the results can be hard to see, especially when they are in the form of exactions from developers or negotiated public benefits. Nonetheless, they are there. One cannot discern the unbuilt office tower or easily perceive design features enforced to protect light and air or to prevent shadowing of public parks. Nor is it possible to pick out the affordable units required as part of a new housing complex or to recognize patterns of height limits designed to protect public views. To some, these are marginal victories in the face of persistent social justice issues and the inequities of a rapacious market system; for others, they represent ill-directed government interference in the natural course of urban growth and change.

One theme in this book is the fate of public access to the waterfront. Public space and the right to the city—intrinsically related concepts—are the subject of a burgeoning literature made rich by critical perspectives and insightful analyses.[24] However, serious treatment of the role of planning in creating or destroying public space, in ensuring that public space is public for all, and in mediating the right to the city is, for the most part, strangely absent. City planning is, for better or worse, a critical part of establishing constraints on property rights (or perpetuating them) and maintaining the public realm (or degrading it). It directly handles issues of inclusion and exclusion that are embedded in a democratic, though often fallible, process. In fact, one may argue that it is impossible to have public space absent a democratic process in its making. Planning has had, or can be made to have, a pivotal position in this regard. People have a voice and wield influence over what happens in a city by becoming involved in the planning process.

An examination of the transformation of San Francisco's waterfront through the lens of planning and regulation reveals important aspects of how local conditions interact with larger forces of change and how local actors interrelate, and so leads directly to the main agencies, gatekeepers, activists, and development interests involved. Furthermore, through planning's dual roles as a local force countervailing external pressures and as an institution mediating among various interests, we will come to see San Francisco's waterfront as a negotiated landscape.

An Overview of Waterfront Transformation

Many people are fascinated by ports—or at least the sites of what were once working waterfronts. Old waterfronts have an especially alluring quality. They are often in cities' older sections and their bits and pieces, from piers to historic ships, are easily recognized, making them a visible part of local history. They suggest the excitement and bustle of shipping and related activities even after they have moved elsewhere. This is partly because, as in San Francisco, some ports manage to retain a few of their traditional activities or features, even if those features are just docks for tugs or fireboats, a few commercial fishing vessels, a passenger terminal, or the shells of old brick warehouses or food-processing plants. Especially in the United States and Europe, a number of cities have used these remnants to help re-market their waterfronts, which have become newly important parts of the traditional city center. Often as part of efforts to claim world-class status, cities play up the natural setting and historical depth of place particular to waterfronts, emphasizing new educational and recreational opportunities, seen in historic ship tours or aquariums, for example, along with residential and commercial development. Certainly, visitors, new residents, and other businesses are attracted by buildings and activities related, even if tenuously, to what occurred there in the past.

As part of what creates the image of a city, urban designers also note the importance of a waterfront's location at an edge, in Lynchian terms.[25] An edge at once joins and separates two different areas of activity, two different aspects of the physical landscape, in this case, land and water. So, waterfronts are also themselves edges, and they are unusual because they do not always form hard transitions, like that made by the buildings lining Central Park in New York. San Francisco's finger piers, for instance, disrupt the edge. Indeed, waterfronts are as much an interstice as an edge. They are also untypical because to move from one side of the edge to another requires a special conveyance. So the water is also a boundary—one that hinders movement.[26]

But a watery frontier is also evocative. The sounds of seabirds, the smell of saltwater, and the view across a bay or out to sea can make the routines of an urban life seem less quotidian and may conjure up images of faraway places. This kind of effect may be what helps to romanticize waterfronts so easily, hiding a past reality filled with labor struggles and violence, smuggling, racketeering, and dangerous work. Clearly, most people today do not experience waterfronts as places of work, as nexus points for the global distribution of goods, or even as centers of passenger movements. Many cities that were established as ports and grew up around their waterfronts have long since lost those functions. Contemporary shipping areas have been relocated away from the centers of cities and people use cars and bridges rather than ferries. Recent concerns with terrorism have made it even more difficult to experience firsthand what a cargo terminal is like. So, for the general population, old waterfronts provide only hints of the activities that once occurred there and that now continue in some other place—removed from experience in space nearly as much as in time. Yet, the appeal of these vestiges of a colorful past, and of the water itself, remains.

WATERFRONT DECLINE

The decline of waterfronts is generally due to the influence of top-down forces on port functions.[27] In particular, changes in transportation technology and other large-system factors such as economic restructuring have been of major importance. During the last half century, the most significant and probably most apparent force behind the loss or relocation of cargo operations was the advent of new transportation technology.[28] For many ports, the result has been abandonment and disuse, turning what was once a vibrant connection between city and water into a deserted no-man's land. Most ports that floundered, including San Francisco's, started to do so in the late 1950s and early 1960s, when containerization revolutionized the shipping industry. Site and situation played a major role in whether ports could adopt the new technology and remain competitive. Even if a port authority or other entity could absorb the tremendous capitalization costs to develop the specialized facilities needed to handle and move containers, they often simply did not have the space available. And, because container ships require deep channels, ports found themselves having to pay for dredging—an expensive project and today a very sensitive environmental issue. A host of related problems arises from trying to convert old port facilities to new ones, the most salient being that urban infrastructure adjacent to old ports usually cannot absorb the additional activity, particularly truck and rail traffic, associated with containerization. New technology and its requirements quite quickly rendered the older port morphology of finger piers and storage sheds obsolete.

International cycles of growth and recession and the influence of political-economic groups such as the European Union are also important to the fate of ports, especially as they relate to globalization.[29] The effects of globalization manifest in the reorganization of world trade networks in response to new patterns of national and international development. New manufacturing capacity and infrastructure development can redirect shipping routes and thus affect shipping lines' choices of home and destination ports.[30] As national economies have gained strength in parts of Asia, ports in the Bay Area, for instance, have found themselves in stiff competition with more northern ports in Seattle and Portland, which are at the end of shorter routes from the Far East or which have better access to inland destinations. Given the massive and frequent relocation of production facilities by transnational corporations, it is easy to imagine resulting shifts in the world web of shipping lanes. Shipping lines are by nature international and may react to national policy formation in one place by redirecting services and operations to another.

Insofar as economic restructuring is a hallmark of globalization, it should also be noted that recent changes in capitalism have affected the role that capital plays in the decline of waterfronts. To minimize the use of variable capital (labor, as distinct from fixed capital, such as factories) corporations both promote the internationalization of the labor pool and encourage the introduction of laborsaving technology. Furthermore, industrial capital is invested overseas to take advantage of lax pollution regulation, cheap labor, and various economic incentives to build production facilities, such as foreign trade zones. Waterfront areas thus become deindustrialized as productive infrastructure is relocated, and waterfront communities become generally derelict as the workforce is marginalized.[31]

National and state events or conditions also generate the top-down forces that cause decline or perpetuate disuse. Relocation and closure of U.S. Navy bases, for example, have reduced the viability of some waterfronts. In San Francisco, the impact was felt by the ship-repair business, which for years had prospered maintaining naval vessels. Furthermore, when military bases are closed or other federal holdings are slated for transfer to local authorities, federal real estate policy becomes an important issue in waterfront development planning. Federal interpretation of public interest can differ from that articulated by local agencies or groups, significantly affecting the potential for and character of revitalization. Moreover, federal procedures and budget limitations may prevent or significantly delay the reuse of former naval sites because of the cost and difficulties of cleaning up what have often become intensely toxic sites.[32]

In a very different vein, regulations contained in the 1920 Jones Act require, essentially, that foreign flagged vessels make only one U.S. port of call. Since all major cruise lines are now foreign-owned, many U.S. port cities have lost passenger-based business, and thus find little reason to devote much time and money to passenger-terminal upkeep. San Francisco saw most of its cruise ship business disappear because cruise lines have preferred to make their one U.S. stop at Los Angeles. On the other hand, San Francisco has recently become home port to an increasing number of "go nowhere" entertainment cruises. Passenger ships load, take a turn about the ocean beyond U.S. territorial waters (thus avoiding federal restrictions on gambling and wagering), and then come back to port. San Francisco is also a good base for trips to Alaska.

State fiscal policy, legislatures, governor's offices, and regulatory agencies can also influence waterfronts. This has been of particular importance in California, where for many decades the state controlled the Port of San Francisco.

WATERFRONT REVITALIZATION

Starting at the beginning of the 1960s, and coming into full force by the early 1980s, cities around the world have made efforts to reuse the land at the water's edge.[33] By the late 1970s, waterfront revitalization in the United States had become such a common urban issue that federal and national agencies began to produce guides and reports to address the trend.[34] Revitalization appears in many forms and at many scales and can include upgraded shipping and maritime-related facilities, new industrial growth that is not necessarily water-related, mixed-use commercial projects, new recreation opportunities, and residential development.

While top-down pressures have been the main reason for the decline of waterfronts, they also exert a significant influence on revitalization. Some waterfronts have benefitted from changes in shipping technology because they have such advantages as deep-water channels, ample backlands, or efficient intermodal connections, again emphasizing the role of site and situation. Federal funding for highway construction and programs such as ISTEA (Intermodal Surface Transportation Efficiency Act, now TEA-21) influence the geography of transportation infrastructure, which translates into advantages for those port cities whose intermodal connections improve. Also, federal grants have been awarded directly to port authorities; Oakland's port, across the bay from San Francisco, benefitted greatly from such cash infusions. Of course, capital has had a tremendous impact on waterfront redevelopment. In fact, the success of waterfront redevelopment projects can be tied to increasingly service-oriented economies. Economic restructuring requires new built spaces, and derelict waterfronts can provide the much needed acreage in what are otherwise built-up urban cores. Similarly, there has been a movement of capital away from the production process into fixed assets, especially the built environment. Waterfront redevelopment is in part a response to economic cycles that encourage businesses to switch capital into the secondary circuit.[35] As a result, many urban waterfronts are now bejeweled with dockside office towers for the service and information labor force, up-market housing for the increasing ranks of the well-heeled, and wharves of distraction for globe-trotting tourists.

Waterfront revitalization has also been a process of homogenization. It has been observed that the postindustrial economy has supported a "Manhattan-like development style adopted all around the world."[36] One can quickly point to the "Rousification" of waterfronts—Baltimore and Boston stand out—and the important role that a few large international development and architectural firms play, for instance, Canada's now defunct Olympia and York and Australia's Lend Lease. Indeed, developers' drive to create the most profitable scheme possible results in similar land uses being replicated, not just at ports within a given country, but across international borders. Of this kind of waterfront renewal perhaps the most common are tourism-related "festival" and "heritage" developments, which are often at the forefront of broader discussions of urban redevelopment.[37] Such projects mix and match office towers, passenger terminals, apartment or condominium blocks, retail development, and new, primarily nonindustrial commercial ventures, but they are perhaps best known for their food courts, waterside malls, and adaptively reused warehouses. Even their design and architectural character are inscribed with a certain sameness. Examples include New York City's Battery Park City, London's Canary Wharf, Toronto's Harbour Square, and of course, San Francisco's Fisherman's Wharf—the apotheosis of the festival/heritage waterfront.

For the most part, waterfront redevelopment projects serve to privatize the waterfront. Less common in revitalization schemes is the provision of open spaces and expansive areas for passive and active recreation along waterfronts. Even in areas where access to the water or to waterside recreation is provided, designs discourage their use by the general populace.[38] The transformation of San Francisco's urban waterfront, while it now has some of these features, has been slower and has produced a somewhat different morphology. At this time, the port has no office towers, housing has been built in only two places, and hotels are absent. Its recent reconnection with the city has been not just as an extension of downtown or as an elite bastion. Instead, the waterfront is characterized by modestly scaled development, is laced with open space and publicly oriented uses, and it has an emphasis on public access to and movement along the waterfront.[39] These qualities reveal a resistance to the privatization that often threatened, making its present form and function very different from early visions for its revitalization. It seems to be more and more a place in which civic life is carried out. Indeed, the emphasis on public space along San Francisco's waterfront is a dramatic contrast with what has happened at other waterfronts, for instance in London's Docklands, where gated housing estates and a suburban mentality have created some very asocial spaces, and Toronto, where the public space on the waterfront has been "inscribed by disenfranchisement."[40]

As much as the scale, mix of uses, and social orientation of projects proposed by the Port of San Francisco were for many years in the modernist mold, the (so far) successful countervailing discourse could be characterized as one of postmodern resistance. Using a different lens, if a neoliberal landscape is one that bears the imprint of deregulation, devolution, and the concomitant expansion of the private sphere into the public realm, then our story can be seen as one of at least a partially successful struggle against neoliberal tendencies that have affected the rest of San Francisco, as evidenced in the spread of business improvement districts, public-private partnerships, and more generally, rollbacks in government programs. One critical factor in this regard is that port land is public land. The waterfront then is a kind of spatial frame onto which all manner of forces adhere, and within it, we can place the story of contestation over the use of a public resource threatened with commercialization and privatization.[41]

But much has yet to be resolved, and the struggle over waterfront development in San Francisco embodies a key issue that the port and city continue to face—What and, therefore, who is the waterfront for? Commerce and industry or consumption and recreation? Residents or tourists, workers or pleasure-seekers? Or put slightly differently, echoing social theorist and urban thinker Henri Lefebvre—Who will have the right to the waterfront? Will only members of the middle and upper classes be welcomed, or will skateboarders, pamphleteers, the homeless, and the variegated "other" be tolerated, if not embraced? Will exchange value trump use value?[42] Will private enterprise ultimately dictate the fate of a public resource? Or can such an important urban amenity accommodate many, often competing needs and desires?

The Chapters Ahead

The book is arranged essentially chronologically, with the exception of Chapter One. To answer the most basic question—How did the waterfront get the way it is?—we need to start with a description of what the waterfront is like today. This includes not just the built environment but the nature of the port itself and its relation to other governmental bodies. The chapter ends, and the main narratives begins, with the state of the waterfront in the 1950s. Chapter Two begins to answer our primary question in earnest by delving into the primarily top-down causes of the port's decline. Even before the wave of containerization washed away its shipping business San Francisco's port was beset with problems, some of its own making and some the result of external pressures that were starting to reshape the city across from its docks. Chapter Three finds the port reacting to the slipping away of its maritime activity with misbegotten ideas for a reimagined modernist waterfront. But concerns about development in areas of the city across from the port resulted in the first locally imposed restrictions on development of port land along its northern waterfront.

Nevertheless, encouraged by consultant advice about what to do with its property, the port entered the 1960s set on the pursuit of massive real estate ventures. Chapter Four documents the clash between the port's vision for the waterfront and the one being established by new plans and the creation of a new regional agency charged with protecting San Francisco Bay. The port's proposals caused a reaction among environmentalists and the general public that initiated more limitations on development on port land. By the end of the decade, the port found itself in a very different political and policy context.

Chapter Five describes how the 1970s ushered in an entirely new stage in the port's evolution. After a century, the port was reclaimed by San Francisco, but its transfer from state jurisdiction back to the city did not ease its problems; rather its status as a local agency exposed the port to powerful local interests. Chapter Six continues this theme. Even as large-scale economic transformations gripped the city's downtown, a spate of new plans and regulations were put into place as a result of the efforts of bottom-up forces. This had the effect of stalling nearly all development on much of the waterfront for years. Yet as Chapter Seven details, the waterfront of the 1970s and 1980s did not remain completely unchanged. Policies that applied to the port's property allowed for the birth of a new, consumer-oriented waterfront. The port's attempts to exploit a loophole, to build hotels, again generated a strong public response, this time forcing the port to come up at long last with a plan for its future. As described in the concluding chapter, this, along with an earthquake, helped shift the port onto its current path, one paved with good civic intentions.

1

Oceans Apart

The San Francisco Waterfront Now and Then

WATERFRONTS ARE COMPLEX places, and San Francisco's is no exception. Its scale is large enough that to form a mental picture of its entirety can be difficult. And because the waterfront is used in many different ways, it can be a challenge to conceptualize in an ordered fashion. So, our inquiry begins with the key question: What kind of place is San Francisco's waterfront? The answer begins with a description of the contemporary built environment—the physical qualities and various activities that characterize San Francisco's port—and then moves to some of the basic aspects of how the port functions as a local government agency. However, the more fundamental question is: How did the waterfront become what it is? To answer that question requires knowing a little of the port's origins, and, more important, what it was like around the time that it began its metamorphosis in the 1950s. This is addressed in the second part of the chapter.

The Contemporary Port

The focus of this book is San Francisco's urban waterfront, an area nearly entirely under the jurisdiction of the Port of San Francisco (Figs. 1.2 and 1.3).[1] It is roughly a seven-mile stretch of San Fran-

Bay Area Counties

1.1 San Francisco Bay Area counties. Map data from the San Francisco Planning Department.

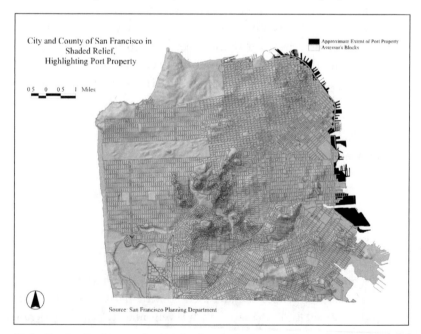

1.2 San Francisco Bay Area counties. Map data from the San Francisco Planning Department.

cisco on its bay side running from Fisherman's Wharf on the north to India Basin on the south. For the most part, our focus will be on the area above China Basin Channel, as that is where the most dramatic change has occurred. In this book, "Port of San Francisco" or simply "the port" is the name of the city agency, but also refers to its land and its governing commission. The port, through its commission, has responsibility for about 730 acres of property. Port property, also referred to as "land" throughout this book, comprises a thin band extending inland at most for several blocks, and then in only a few places. Its largest parcels are made either of bay fill or piers. Fill is dredged material, excavation waste, or earth and rock taken from nearby hills that literally extends the city into San Francisco Bay.

Port lands include some of the most valuable real estate (at least potentially) in California, if not the country, and consist primarily of piers, roads, and seawall lots, and contains a variety of structures that, together, cover about 20 percent of the port's area.[2] One of the port's most notable features is the Embarcadero, a wide public access roadway that runs along the northern half of the waterfront. Piers include not just the traditional long wharves (finger piers) that extend into the bay, but also "marginal wharves" that run parallel to the shoreline or seawall, usually designated by ½ as in Pier 1½. Piers to the north of the Ferry Building area are odd-numbered, and piers to the south are even-numbered. Many of the wooden and concrete finger piers that for so long characterized San Francisco's waterfront, of which fewer and fewer remain, were built between 1912 and 1930, primarily to service ferryboat and shipping activities. Technically, piers are pile-supported structures, although the term *pier* is also used for more modern concrete slab structures that are usually built on bay fill. Covered sheds or warehouses are found on many.

Waterside property, which includes piers and pier-related structures, comprises a little more than half of port land.[3] Most port property on the land side, that is most anything that is not a pier, consists of seawall lots and roads. Seawall lots were created by filling in the area of water that ran between the seawall and adjacent embankment and the original shoreline; it was much like a channel, but of fetid water. As the street grid extended to meet this newly filled land, the seawall lots were divided into many oddly shaped parcels, especially in the northern areas. Over the years, a variety of structures has been built on many of these seawall lots; the future uses of a few are currently the subject of considerable debate.

There are many different structures in the port's jurisdiction besides piers, including container cranes, grain elevators, and a few hundred buildings including warehouses and, most notably, the Ferry Building. Some of the most impressive structures are bulkhead buildings, which demarcate the entrance to a pier, much like a portcullis.

The port's narrow geography is characterized by a variety of primarily water-related uses and activities including cargo shipping and related support services, such as rail and truck access and warehousing, ship-repair, small craft marinas, passenger terminals, maritime-related offices, commercial and recreational development, open space, and miscellaneous industry that either indirectly relates to port activities or benefits from a waterfront location but is not water-dependent. Not all businesses that lease space along the waterfront are water-related; among them are some office tenants, warehouse users, and industrial firms.[4] Most of the port's commercially leased space (especially restaurants), its cruise ship and historic boat moorings, and commercial fishing facilities are located in the northern part of the waterfront, while its remaining industrially oriented maritime activities, including cargo handling, are located in the southern areas of the waterfront, below China Basin Channel.

Equally important to establishing the character of the port's built environment is understanding the port as an agency of local government. Coming to informed conclusions about how the waterfront evolved without basic knowledge of the port's authority and powers, and the limits thereof, is almost impossible and not something that can be derived soley from observing the physical landscape. Indeed, the waterfront's transformation is intimately tied to the nature of the port as an agency, and whose evolution is traced through the book.

The range of the port's operations is reflected in the agency's internal organization, which includes a number of divisions: maritime, real estate, engineering and maintenance, operations, and planning and development. The port does not run its facilities; all commercial and industrial facilities and their operation, from warehouses to restaurants to container cranes, are leased to private firms. The port purchases equipment, such as container cranes, but they are operated by stevedoring companies or shippers that lease a pier and its facilities. The port does provide maintenance and, through city departments, police and fire protection. The Port of San Francisco is not a typical San Francisco city agency in that it is quasi independent. The port neither receives money from nor contributes money to the city's general fund. Rather, it is an "enterprise agency" that depends on revenues from shipping and shipping-related activities, commercial leases, other income-generating activities (such as filming), and revenue bonds to continue operations, maintain facilities, and pursue improvements. Until very recently, the city did not support general obligation bonds to address port financial needs. The port's fiscal disassociation from the city has sometimes translated into more general separatist inclinations—port staff member's e-mail addresses even have ".com" extensions, not the ".org" used by the rest of the city.

The port's decision-making body is the five-member San Francisco Port Commission. The mayor appoints members, subject to approval by the city's legislative body, the San Francisco Board of Supervisors. The commission does not have an entirely free hand in running the port. The board of supervisors approves its budget and leases of more than ten years or that would generate more than $1 million.[5] The full extent of the board's authority over the port is a little unclear and has been subject to city attorney opinions and occasional court cases. The San Francisco Planning Department (SFPD), ultimately through its commission, has some regulatory authority over port lands through the San Francisco *General Plan* and *Planning Code*.[6] However, the planning department generally does not become deeply involved if a proposed use or development or other activity that requires approval is maritime, is sanctioned by California's doctrine of public trust (explained below), or is in an industrial zone. However, the planning department has one seat on the Waterfront Design Advisory Committee, a body that reviews projects to ensure their compliance with the *Waterfront Design and Access* element of the port's planning policy document, the *Waterfront Land Use Plan* (WLUP). Otherwise, the planning department has three direct methods of regulating port property: first, proposed development on port property must comply with the planning department's land-use designations (zoning); second, and related, the planning department must approve conditional-use permits; third, building height and bulk must comply with the planning department's height and bulk districts, as indicated in its zoning map.[7] However, as a practical matter of coordination, the SFPD and other city agencies are involved in policy review, design analysis, and implementation of port projects.

The port commission cannot be directly affected by a city voter initiative unless the initiative required another agency with some jurisdiction over the port to do something that would affect the port.[8] For instance, when local ballot initiative Proposition H passed in 1990, it required the San Francisco Board of Supervisors to request that the port initiate a planning process. Port activities are also constrained by various federal agencies including the U.S. Coast Guard and the U.S. Army Corps of Engineers. More important, however, are state agencies, state legislation, and regional governing bodies, as we shall see later. Of these, the Burton Act and the public trust are key. The 1968 Burton Act and accompanying Transfer Agreement transferred control of the port from the state to the city. The transfer took effect in 1969. The city was thereby required to create its own port commission "to use, conduct, operate, maintain, manage, regulate, improve and control the port within the requirements of State law."[9] Even though jurisdiction over the port was transferred to the city, the land is held as a trust grant, and the state legislature has retained the right to revoke the transfer. Most port land is, therefore, actually held in trust for the people of California, and is subject to oversight by the California State Lands Commission (SLC).

When California joined the Union in 1850, it became the owner of all land underlying navigable waterways, including tidelands, to be held in trust by the state for the benefit of the people of California. Because of the particular geography associated with the public trust, it is sometimes referred to as the tidelands trust (or sometimes just "trust land"). Port land consists primarily of tidelands that the state filled in to build docks, wharves, and whatever else was needed to promote commercial activity in San Francisco's harbor. The SLC is the agency that regulates the use of trust lands, which, again, include most of the port's property. The SLC regulates trust land according to the public trust doctrine, which is based in common law and embodied in the California constitution. In turn, public trust doctrine defines the allowable uses of submerged land and tideland areas, filled or unfilled, public or private. The state constitution prevents lands in the public trust from being sold. In the 1980s, restrictions on the use of trust land would become very important to the development of the waterfront.

The Waterfront from North to South

The port divides the waterfront into five sub-areas: Fisherman's Wharf, Northeastern Waterfront, Ferry Building Waterfront (northern water-

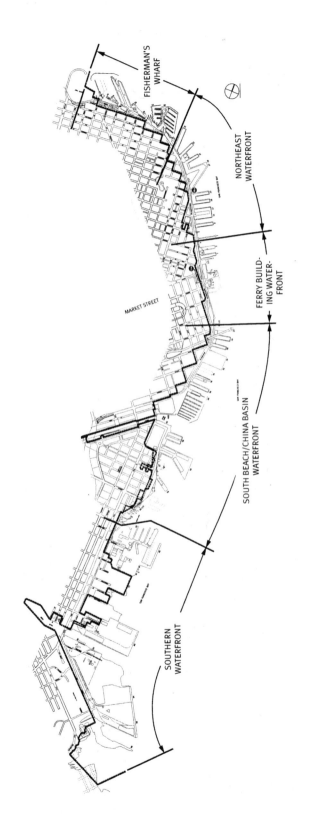

FISHERMAN'S WHARF

NORTHEAST WATERFRONT

FERRY BUILD-ING WATER-FRONT

MARKET STREET

SOUTH BEACH/CHINA BASIN WATERFRONT

SOUTHERN WATERFRONT

1.3 Waterfront Land Use Plan sub-areas with the port's property line. Port of San Francisco, *Waterfront Land Use Plan*, 2000.

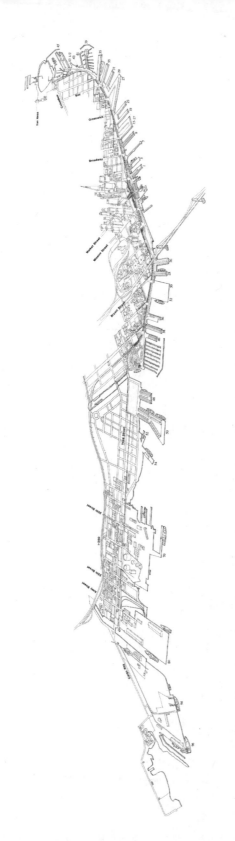

I.4 Axiometric rendering of the waterfront. Courtesy of the Port of San Francisco.

front), South Beach/China Basin (central waterfront), and the southern waterfront. For the most part, reference will be made to the three generic designations—northern, central, and southern (Figs. 1.3 and 1.4).

THE NORTHERN WATERFRONT

The northern waterfront extends from Fisherman's Wharf to the Bay Bridge. It is notable for its finger piers, bulkhead buildings, and the recently redesigned Embarcadero roadway. The city's historic streetcar line runs along this part of the Embarcadero; farther south it contains the alignment for the light-rail system. Its median is adorned with $10,000 palm trees carefully selected and transplanted from Los Angeles neighborhoods, where they are also not indigenous. The Fisherman's Wharf area, which extends a little under a mile from just inside Aquatic Park on the north to Pier 39 on the south, is characterized by recreation, tourism, and a vibrant fishing industry. Many of the things that are commonly associated with Fisherman's Wharf are actually outside of the port's jurisdiction, including Aquatic Park, the Cannery, and Ghirardelli Square. The latter two are indoor-outdoor malls poured into the shells of old industrial buildings as "adaptive reuse."

Hyde Street Pier, the port's northernmost, is home to the San Francisco Maritime National Historic Park, which has the largest concentration of historic ships in the United States. Moving south one finds a collision of tourists and the still active fishing industry. Street performers, artists, and homeless people line the sidewalks, creating an uncomfortable contrast between carnival-atmosphere fantasies and the reality of urban impoverishment.

Nestled between the Hyde Street Pier and Pier 45 is the fishing fleet itself—once hundreds of boats strong but now much diminished (Fig. 1.5). Tourist attractions and throngs of visitors conceal the presence of the fish-loading, fish-packing, and fish-processing operations that are semi-hidden in the sheds on Pier 45 and in Fish Alley, the historic center of the wharf's fishing industry. According to the port, Pier 45 houses the largest concentration of commercial fish processors and distributors on the West Coast. The facilities here, some worse for wear, serve fishermen from well beyond the bay—millions of pounds per year of crab, salmon, herring, shrimp, squid, abalone, mackerel, and halibut, pass through Fisherman's

1.5 View of the fishing fleet at Fisherman's Wharf. Photography by author.

Wharf.[10] The last significant feature of the area is Pier 39, at the southern-most end of the wharf. This famed "festival mall" attracts more visitors per year than any place in California, Disneyland excepted. California sea lions (sometimes incorrectly called harbor seals) have taken up residence in its west basin. Overall, the wharf is a place of spectacle, of opportunities for shopping and entertainment that surround a small bastion of working-class San Francisco.

Gazing down from the wealthy aeries atop Telegraph Hill, one can follow the curve of the waterfront from Pier 35 nearly all the way to Pier 7, about three-quarters of a mile. This is the Northeastern Waterfront, an area that for the most part lies sandwiched between the base of the hill and the bay. Although in the last stages of its metamorphosis, the area is still in transi-tion. The most notable facility is Pier 35, not because of the structure itself, but because of the giant white cruise ships that berth here. More frequently of late, these blocks-long ships disgorge passengers into the port's outmoded and somewhat shabby passenger terminal. The piers and bulkhead buildings here are home to a variety of businesses, from a tug and barge operation to a chocolate maker. The southernmost pier in the area is Pier 7, an award-winning 900-foot public strolling and fishing pier dedicated in 1990.

On the other side of the Embarcadero, the port has a sizeable amount of land in seawall lots facing the piers. Here are found Fog City Diner

1.6 Bulkhead buildings at Piers 31 and 33. Photograph by author.

and the historic Belt Line Roundhouse; the latter was converted into an office building in 1985. Commercial buildings and parking occupy much of the rest of the area. Across from port land are Levi's Plaza and the Golden Gateway. These developments extend several blocks inland and form a neo-neighborhood of condominiums and brick warehouse spaces converted to office use where once much maritime-related industry and commerce thrived.

Finally, perhaps the most striking feature of the area is the impressive series of bulkhead buildings that line the waterfront from Pier 35 to Pier 9 (Fig. 1.6). These imposing structures are part of the recently adopted Port of San Francisco Embarcadero National Register Historic District.[11] Their historic importance derives not just from their architectural quality but also from their role in the social and economic history of the port. For the most part built before World War II, they stand now as silent witnesses to a waterfront that often flared with strife, something that few of the skaters, strollers, or bikers are likely to reflect upon as they stream past them along Herb Caen Way. In fact, recreational activities are probably more noticeable to the casual observer than any traditional maritime uses, past or present.

From around Pier 5 to the Bay Bridge the downtown presses close to the water. Underscoring their new role in contemporary San Francisco,

Piers 1½, 3, and 5 have been recently renovated by developers of a new restaurant and office complex. For many years, neighboring Pier 1 was used
for little more than ferry and excursion boats, and its large shed was used
for parking. But it too has been renovated, its historic character documented in photographs displayed in a public hallway marked by rail tracks
that once served the pier. In 2001, it became home to the port's offices.

The focal point of this area, and of the waterfront itself, is the Ferry
Building (Fig. 1.7). The towered, neoclassical, Beaux Arts building designed
by Arthur Page Brown has been a beacon on the waterfront for one hundred years.[12] Originally called the Union Depot and Ferry House, it is an
imposing structure consisting of a 600-foot-long, 160-foot-wide base centered on a 240-foot-tall clock tower, prominently placed at the foot of
Market Street, the main artery through downtown. The Ferry Building
once saw 170 ferries a day and 150 million passengers a year, for a while
second only to Charing Cross in London in passenger throughput. Now,
though only a fraction of the commuters pass through it, the Ferry
Building has a new lease on life.

The Ferry Building has recently undergone a historic transformation, including a restoration of its magnificent interior atrium and walk-
through. For years, it had been devoted to office space primarily for port
staff and the World Trade Center; now it is home to specialty food shops,
restaurants, a weekly farmers' market, and new ferry docks. It is a tremendously successful public space even if the plaza in front, an island between
lanes of Embarcadero traffic, is not. The Ferry Building and the former
Agriculture Building just to the south are listed in the National Register
of Historic Places. From here to the Bay Bridge are a series of public open
spaces including Pier 14, a public pier completed in 2007, a wide promenade, and Rincon Park, a modest public green open space with two upscale
restaurants developed on old seawall lots. A Claes Oldenberg sculpture
marks the spot.[13]

CENTRAL WATERFRONT (SOUTH BEACH/CHINA BASIN)

The central waterfront extends for roughly two miles and comprises two
distinct parts: South Beach and China Basin. South Beach extends south
from Pier 22½ to the China Basin Channel and the China Basin area
reaches south from the channel to Seawall Lot 345, near 18th Street. The

1.7 The Ferry Building, looking north. Photograph by author.

central waterfront is home to Fire Engine #9 and two fireboats, *Guardian* and *Phoenix*. Piers 26 and 28 are used for storage, some fish-handling operations, and short-term uses such as laydown areas for construction contractors. For some years now, the large expanse that is Piers 30–32 has been used for layover berthing, concerts, and events like the X-Games. It was recently the site of a proposed cruise terminal project and mixed-use development; all that was built, however, was the Watermark, a condominium tower next to the Bay Bridge. Between Piers 40 and 46 is South Beach Harbor for pleasure craft, built in 1986.

Implementation of the redevelopment plan also resulted in a residential area, now essentially complete, that contains about 2,500 housing units. The project incorporated three port seawall lots across from Piers 36 and 40. Seawall Lots 331 and 332 are home to the nonprofit Delancey Street, which includes a rehabilitation center and ultra low-income housing, and the Steamboat Point Apartments, an affordable housing project, occupy Seawall Lot 333. Opened in 2000, the new Giants baseball stadium occupies port property between Third and King streets (now lined with large chain stores such as Borders) (Fig. 1.8). The stadium helped recast this entire section of the waterfront, and with it, part of San Francisco. What

1.8 AT&T Park, home of the San Francisco Giants. Photograph by author.

was once the site of the infamous longshoreman strike of 1934, and the place where the events of Bloody Thursday unfolded, is now the center of a booming neighborhood and an urban recreational wonderland.

Across the historic Lefty O'Doul Bridge at 3rd Street and past the houseboat community in the China Basin Channel, the main port road becomes Terry A. Francois Boulevard, named for the city's first African-American member of the board of supervisors. The bridge has been renovated as part of the 315-acre Mission Bay project, and is being transformed from a rather informally designed street that served mostly commercial traffic into a more genteel thoroughfare to serve the new University of California-San Francisco medical campus, which has risen up out of abandoned rail yards. The scheme for the Mission Bay site is utterly transforming the old Southern Pacific property and the vacant land across from the port into housing, offices, commercial and retail space, and a major hotel.[14]

Yet there are maritime activities here, and they are a little more industrial and cargo-related than the primarily support-oriented maritime activity found north of China Basin Channel. Pier 48 has a ferry maintenance facility. Pier 50, a massive 20.5-acre facility, houses maintenance operations (machine shops, welding facilities, sheet metal, and woodworking) and harbor services (tugs and barges), and provides storage and warehousing space. In this part of the waterfront, the absence of buildings becomes notable. Around here, a little farther from the downtown core, open storage and marshaling areas replace pier sheds and bulkhead buildings. Also located in this somewhat out-of-the-way part of the waterfront, next to Pier 52, is the port's only public boat launch. Below condemned Pier 64 there is an unlikely park, Agua Vista, and just to the south of that scrubby patch of open space are a couple of restaurants with outdoor seating. The weather is good in this part of town, the fog shies away from here and there are worse things than sitting in the sun with a drink, watching small boats being repaired and big ships being hauled into dry dock, just down the way.

THE SOUTHERN WATERFRONT

As far south as China Basin Channel, the waterfront has a definite spine; that is, it is connected to the Embarcadero, which feeds into Terry A. Francois Boulevard. In the south, however, Terry A. Francois runs into

1.9 Aerial photograph of the Pier 70 area in the Southern Waterfront c. 2002. Courtesy of the San Francisco Planning Department.

Illinois Street, and the water's edge begins to retreat. The southern waterfront, which extends for several miles from 18th Street and Illinois at the Central Basin and across Islais Creek, is irregular and disorienting. This is a place of open backlands, marshaling yards, container cranes, and scattered, aging industrial structures. In fact, most of the port land in this area is used by industrial businesses dealing in, for example, sand, gravel, cement, and recycling. There are few piers here, and their sheer size seems to make them seem part of the land mass; the city and its waterfront are not as intimately pressed together in this gritty part of San Francisco.

Perhaps the most dramatic feature of the waterfront here is the dry dock at Pier 70, currently used by the national ship repair firm BAE Systems (Fig. 1.9). During San Francisco's early years, this area was called Potrero

Point. Already in the 1850s, it was crowded with shipbuilding and man-ufacturers of blasting powder, cord, steel, and locomotives, and Potrero Point would rank as the West Coast's most important industrial and heavy manufacturing center for more than a century. Pier 70's real shipbuilding life began at the end of the nineteenth century, when Irving Scott brought Union Iron Works to the Point. The business was eventually bought by Bethlehem Steel, which, when shipbuilding disappeared, sold off the dry dock and shipyard to the port in 1982 for one dollar. The dry docks here and at Hunters Point to the south, the latter outside of port land, pro-duced many ships for the Pacific fleet.

The last ship produced at Pier 70 was commissioned by the navy and was completed in 1965, but repair and maintenance operations have con-tinued since, though sometimes haltingly. After years of losing business as a result of naval base closures and competition from Asian shipyards (cheaper labor and less restrictive environmental standards can make it less expensive to send a ship across the Pacific for repair), things have been looking up for the local shipbuilding industry. The dry dock itself, which is owned by the port but run by BAE Systems, is the largest such facility on the West Coast, and it services an increasing number of cruise ships because of the rise in popularity of Alaskan and Mexican routes (which favor San Francisco as a port of call). It is now part of the oldest continu-ally operating civilian shipyard in the United States, which also includes a collection of brick offices, machine shops, warehouses, and old gantry cranes that some people consider the most significant concentration of historic industrial structures in the western United States.

Many San Franciscans are unaware that modern cargo facilities exist in the city and continue to move goods through the port at Pier 80 and Piers 94–96, albeit in small amounts. Most of the business is bulk, "neo-bulk," oversized shipments, and rolling stock—things that do not fit in containers. Ironically perhaps, these piers are most notable, and probably most noticeable, for the decades-old giant grain elevator that stands across from them on Islais Creek—unabashedly big and vertical in an era of hori-zontal industry (Fig. 1.10).

A trip through the southern waterfront reveals an inversion in the port's spatial distribution of activities. Where the port is most inte-grated with the city is where it least serves its original purpose—to move cargo—an activity that once connected it so intimately to San Francisco, physically and functionally. Where cargo passes through the

1.10 View of Islais Creek in the Southern Waterfront. Pier 80 and its gantry cranes are to the left and the old grain silos are to the right. Photograph by author.

port today is an area of the waterfront least connected to the city. It is a place in San Francisco's backwater, though not very likely for much longer. In the northern waterfront, at Fisherman's Wharf particularly, San Francisco's global connection is through the national and international flow of tourists and money. This is completely different from the southern waterfront, where the (tenuous) global connection is more traditional: as the destination of ships moving goods along sea-lanes from faraway places. Yet even were the port to experience a dramatic increase in cargo business, container facilities and even specialty bulk operations do not have the same intimate link to the city as finger piers, and moving containers is qualitatively and quantitatively different from handling goods in crates or sacks. Goods moved by containers are not packed and unpacked at dockside or sent to nearby processing plants. They hide their contents and, after a pause in the flow of goods just long enough to attach container to rig, are moved on to their final destinations. They do not help create the same intimate sense of place, and of connections to other places. While being more global, in the sense that they represent the time-space compression that characterizes contemporary advanced capitalism, they are less of the world, of the everyday realm of the senses.

Instant City/Instant Port

The city and port of San Francisco can attribute much of their success, past and present, to a basic geographic quality—site. San Francisco occupies the head of a dramatic peninsula at the mouth of an expansive bay, and the port, which stretches along the northern and eastern sides of the city, has one of the deepest natural channels in North America. The American flag was raised over the customs house in 1846 and the first pier to jut out into bay water was constructed in 1848, just one year after the city was renamed from Yerba Buena to San Francisco.[15] The port and city's phenomenal growth began the next year, famous as the start of the Gold Rush. In fact, San Francisco has been called an "instant city," and that description fits the port equally well.[16] The burst of population and industrial development associated with the extraction of gold and silver from the hills of the Sierra Nevada made San Francisco the preeminent city in California, if not the American west. The port became the main artery for pumping trade, commerce, and culture into, through, and out of a vast regional hinterland; it served vessels that sailed from China and the East, that rounded Cape Horn from the west, and that plied the Sacramento River. San Francisco's role expanded from regional economic center to communication hub and melting pot. In 1860, it was in third place among U.S. immigrant centers, and was described at the time as a modern Babel.[17]

The state took a keen interest in the port's growth and development because it was essential not just to San Francisco but to California. San Francisco's burgeoning waterfront was key to the general expansion of California's commerce and industry. The waterfront also contributed directly to the state treasury through the sale of tideland lots to real estate speculators, commercial enterprises, and homestead associations. Indeed, because both the state and the city profited from the disposition of waterfront land, the demarcation of the waterfront line between local and state jurisdictions was a matter of some contention. The waterfront line, that is, how far out into the bay the city's jurisdiction extended, was established by an 1851 legislative act.[18] A few years later, under pressure from speculators, the state assembly passed a bill extending the waterfront line 600 feet into the bay in an attempt to increase substantially the number of water lots that could be sold off.[19] This would have had the effect of turning what was then waterfront property into inland property and would have rendered a number of wharves useless. Not only would businesses and entrepreneurs have lost out but ships also would have been forced to berth farther offshore, exposing them to wind and tide action. The outcry from numerous businesses and the city, which would have had to implement expensive infrastructure improvements, was loud enough to convince the state senate to defeat the bill, if narrowly. Federal courts eventually finalized the permanent boundaries of San Francisco, including the waterfront line, in 1865. The city had laid claim to all land above the high-water mark of 1846, which the courts confirmed; the state retained all of the tideland and water lots below that line. The state's tidelands would eventually become part of the jurisdiction of the California SLC when that body was established in 1938.

While state and city boundaries and land titles were being settled, both government entities pursued the lease or sale of property.[20] San Francisco sold beach and water lots in a series of auctions between 1847 and 1852 to help pay for the city's administration and governance. In 1851, the state granted leases for land created out of portions of Yerba Buena Cove and Mission Bay and in 1855 began to make homestead grants and grants to industrial concerns, including railroads, to support the city's, and thus the state's, economic development. The surveying and sale of beach and water lots also created a pattern of submerged streets. The city leased these submerged rights-of-way to entrepreneurs who in turn constructed wharves that reflected their alignment.[21] This early form of public-private partnership was not without its problems. As leases started to expire, wharf owners began to look for ways to guarantee their profitable enterprises. To this end, they attempted to leverage the need for a new seawall, a costly public endeavor, into a bid for the permanent privatization of public land. They did this by forming an association of wharf owners who lobbied the state and offered to pay for the construction of the seawall if the legislature would grant them control of the waterfront for fifty years.[22] The wharf owners pushed a bill through the corridors of the state capitol in Sacramento, but their maneuvering was vocally opposed by the public and the bill was eventually vetoed by Governor John G. Downey.

The contention between public and private interests over the disposition of public waterfront land that marked the formation of San Francisco's waterfront in its earliest, ascendant years prefigured some of the key debates that would occur after the onset of its decline a century later. It also shows that relationships among the state, private capital, and public interest that have shaped the contemporary waterfront have been around in one form or another since the port was founded. Of course, as economic, technological, and social conditions have changed, the actors and their roles, interactions, and motivations have also shifted. The personifications of capital interests in the waterfront, for instance, evolved from individual commercial entrepreneurs, speculators, and industrialists into real estate moguls, land developers, bankers, and even the port itself. And the public's concerns would shift from maintaining equitable control of the waterfront's commercial potential and a balanced distribution of interest in real property to ensuring that commercial activities would not contribute to the further environmental degradation of the bay, or prohibit public access to and enjoyment of the water. The state of California's involvement was essentially reversed after one hundred years, and the line between the port's role as a public agency and its need to function as a kind of commercial enterprise would become blurred.

Sometime during the 1850s, apparently frustrated by their failure to privatize the waterfront legally, wharf owners turned to other, shadier, methods to line their pockets and limit their expenses. Corruption spread, and investigations into the city's inability to pay for a new seawall led to the discovery that officials had been skimming from freight revenues.[23] Graft and collusion along the waterfront, along with poor maintenance, caused the state to intervene in the city's (mis)management of the port. San Francisco's port was far too valuable and important for the state to let it slip into neglect or to allow criminal activities to disrupt the flow of money and commerce. Thus, in 1863, Governor Leland Stanford signed a bill, known as the Oilton Law, that placed control of San Francisco's waterfront under the jurisdiction of the Board of State Harbor Commissioners (BSHC). As the port grew, the board became the governing authority of one the most significant ports in the United States, at least through World War II. The board retained authority over the port until 1969, when the city regained control, an important event discussed later. The Port of San Francisco has been the only major port in the state of California not directly administered by and responsible to the local jurisdiction for any substantial period.

The board's first major task was to construct a seawall, which was partially completed in 1869. The seawall's serrated edge trapped silt, forcing wharf owners to pay for expensive dredging. Parcels of land created by fill were also compromised by inadequate protection from the bay, so a new seawall had to be built. This required acquiring all property along the waterfront between Fisherman's Wharf and China Basin Channel, which meant waiting for leases to expire as well as buying back some tidelands and submerged lots the state had sold off earlier.[24] Construction of the second seawall began in about 1878 and was essentially finished in 1915. Of this endeavor, the board said, "it behooves us to be alive to the situation and the consequences that may follow our failure to provide, in advance, accommodations of the most modern and improved character."[25] How different the board's attitude would be fifty years later, when there was little evidence that it felt the need to be forward-looking in the face of increasing competition for cargo.

The great seawall, as it became known, lay two hundred feet off the waterfront line established in 1851 and ran for two-and-a-third miles, roughly from Fisherman's Wharf to China Basin Channel. Even as the seawall was being completed, the area between it and the older shoreline was being filled in and paved over to accommodate construction of the San Francisco Belt Railroad (also called the State Belt Line), a series of switching and shunting tracks that connected each pier with the young intercontinental railway system. The belt-line project was begun by the board in 1890 and was an essential part of the creation of the Embarcadero, a wide right-of-way that remains one of the port's most important assets. Together, the great seawall and the Embarcadero lend to the port its distinctive curvature and they form the spine from which San Francisco's famous piers and wharves spread out like ribs. They are the physical foundation of San Francisco's modern urban waterfront.[26]

Although the growth of the port and city were bound together in their early years, their fates have not always been completely entwined. For instance, while the city was all but destroyed by the earthquake and conflagration of 1906, the port sustained little damage. Conversely, the often-militant International Longshoreman and Warehouse Union (ILWU) strikes of the 1930s affected the city at large, but were particularly significant for the port. Nevertheless, brimming with activity, port and city together reached the early post-WWII years as a metropolis of international significance. But if the initial rise of San Francisco and its port was instant, the port's decline was almost as fast. The hubbub of activity that had defined the waterfront for years dissipated quite quickly, and the various sights, sounds, and smells that had piqued imaginations fast faded along with it. By the 1950s, many of San Francisco's famous finger piers settled into a state of decay and disuse, and the destiny of the port began to separate from that of the city.

The Waterfront on the Eve of Decline

The shipping lanes of the world lead directly to every pier in this mag-nificent harbor.[27]

—Board of State Harbor Commissioners, 1952

As did the rest of the nation, San Francisco reacted jubilantly to the end of World War II and the promise of postwar growth. The city had been a major base for deployment and a center of industrial activity during the war, roles that seemed to mature the port, relegating to the past its sometimes frontier-like nature and a darker history, which included kid-napping, corruption, violence, and crime. Indeed, the postwar period was a time when the port could easily be romanticized. Then, the port was a place where one's senses and imagination could be led from the immediate and mundane to the distant and exotic: "Pick out by the street light the names of the pier sheds. 'Java,' they say, and 'Singapore' and 'Hong Kong' and 'Pago Pago.' Repeat them and look to the dark west and know that all America is at your back. You're at the end of the continent, and the water you hear whispering under the wharf has whitened the sands of Tahiti and tossed the ice floes in the Bering Sea. The spices you smell are from Cathay."[28]

The ships were not the only things that created a sense of being some-where unusual, almost dreamlike. In the late 1940s, the Embarcadero was lined with pier sheds, warehouses, cold storage, and places to buy everything from grappling hooks to accordions. The waterfront was a cacophony of sounds coming from foghorns, locomotives, passenger ships, ferries, and stevedores; it smelled of saltwater, engine oil, copra, coffee, and other pungent odors issuing from sacks and pallets piled with boxes. Such an engagement of the senses was joined by a mass of movement:

Even before the eight o'clock wail of the Ferry Building siren, the Embarcadero comes violently to life. From side streets great trucks roll through the yawn-ing doors of the piers. The longshoremen, clustering in groups before the pier gates, swarm up ladders and across gang-planks. The jitneys, small tractor-like

conveyances, trailing long lines of flat trucks, wind in and out of traffic. . . .
Careening taxis, rumbling underslung vans and drays, and scurrying pedestrians suddenly transform the waterfront into a traffic-thronged artery.[29]

Although at the end of an era, San Francisco's urban waterfront still
pulsed with activity in the 1950s. The waterfront was a place of hard work
and people from many walks of life—a sailor town at the edge of the city.[30]
The working waterfront was not quite yet a place to idle and contem-
plate nature and the importance of the bay as an ecosystem, or a place
to spend leisure time or pursue recreation. Consumption would come to
replace production in later years, but at the time, the finger piers that
lined the waterfront from Fisherman's Wharf to China Basin Channel were
well used, though many were in need of repair. Stevedoring companies
and chandlers had plenty of business, and warehouses and cold-storage
facilities were full. Thousands of tons of coffee, newsprint, and copra, the
largest imports at the time, moved from ship to shore. The engines clacked
along the Belt Line Railroad shunting tracks that ran the length of the
Embarcadero and a multitude of trucks added to the motorized bustle.

Perhaps the port's most identifiable feature was its collection of aging
but busy finger piers (Fig. 1.11). About forty-two piers and twenty-eight
docks and wharves, almost all public (that is, owned by the port and leased
to private enterprise) extended into the bay to create a comb-like edge
along the waterfront from Fisherman's Wharf to China Basin Channel.
South, beyond China Basin Channel, the finger piers gave way to a more
chaotic and less evenly developed waterfront, where most of the privately
held docks and piers were located. None of the twenty or so private docks
was used for moving general cargo; most of the private wharves were
owned and operated by oil companies or other industrial businesses.[31]
Most of the port's seawall lots were used by the Belt Line Railroad, served
by six diesel engines owned by the state and operated under the auspices
of the BSHC, which provided switching services to three major rail lines:
the Southern Pacific; the Western Pacific; and the Atchison, Topeka, and
Santa Fe (Fig. 1.12). Only the Southern Pacific had a direct connection to
the Belt Line; the other railroads had connections to Oakland via railcars
barged by ferry. Other port property was devoted to dry cargo, refriger-
ated warehouses, and miscellaneous goods-handling facilities, including
cold storage and the soon-to-be-decommissioned grain elevator and
copra terminal.

1.11 Aerial view of finger piers c. 1949. Board of State Harbor Commissioners, *The Progressive Port,* 1954.

While World War II generated a flurry of activity and the early postwar years were ones of general economic growth, by the 1950s, free-ways, aging docks, and other signs of change had begun to appear, and San Francisco and other Bay Area ports did not recover the levels of shipping they enjoyed during the height of the prewar years.[32] A new era was about to begin that would witness both a realignment in the hierarchy of ports in the Bay Area, and the reshaping of San Francisco's port morphology, even before containerization was to become an essential force of change at the end of the 1960s.

THE NORTHERN WATERFRONT

Originally, this area served as a beachhead for men seeking their fortunes in the goldfields and as the early center of commerce that grew to support the Gold Rush. The first permanent pier was constructed in 1847 at what is now the corner of Broadway and Battery streets. After years of filling the bay, this intersection is now a number of blocks inland, near the heart of the city's financial district. The area was the focus of shipping, fishing, and

1.12 State Belt Line engine moving cars near the Ferry Building. Board of State Harbor Commissioners, *The Progressive Port*, 1954.

industry, and in the 1930s, the bulkhead buildings became the backdrop for labor unrest and union struggles. By the 1950s, perhaps more than any other part of the waterfront, Fisherman's Wharf was an area in transition. Although still focused on commercial fishing and fish processing, the wharf also derived charm from being caught between two worlds and two times. The lagoon at Fisherman's Wharf itself berthed hundreds of vessels, and nearby businesses provided services for the fishing fleet.[33] By 1950, gasoline-powered boats were common, but a few remaining lateen-rigged sailboats recalled a not quite bygone era. In the late 1940s and early 1950s, while Fisherman's Wharf was already world famous, it had not yet been given over to tourist attractions, as can be easily gleaned from descriptions of "walks and plankings . . . often plastered with nets drying in the sun" and "oldsters of the crab fleet (who) still sit cross-legged, mending their nets by hand with long wooden needles.[34] In 1959, the ILWU union moved its hiring hall to nearby quarters. A longshoreman later said of the area, "I guess you really could say it was a 'fisherman's wharf.' And because we respected and enjoyed their community, we were always made welcome by our neighbors."[35] The wharf was still a working, industrial, and commercial place even as spreading restaurants and shops signaled its status as a destination for tourists from around the world (Fig.1.13).

In fact, the port provided berths here for foreign-flagged vessels that wished to make use of the Foreign Trade Zone (FTZ) at Pier 45.[36] Then, Pier 45 was only one of four such zones in the United States; now, there are many. Much of the remainder of port property in the area was devoted either to rail spurs and railcar storage for the State Belt Line or to commercial space primarily in what was referred to as Fisherman's Basin, later Fish Alley. But the wharf was for more than just commercial fishing. Until they were entirely replaced by trucks, riverboats carrying agricultural products such as rice, flour, barley, and fresh and prepared fruits from inland areas also used the wharf, and passenger ships and ferries made regular stops.

Beyond port jurisdiction, land use around the wharf was not dominated by hotels and shops, as it is today, but by a mix of warehouses, machine shops, iron works, chandlers, fueling stations, marine and shipping suppliers, and marine engineering and boat maintenance services. Some of the restaurants that would become part of the of the wharf's tourism engine were scattered among these businesses, especially along Jefferson Street. But as the 1950s moved on, maritime-related businesses at and near Fisherman's Wharf gave way to more general commercial activity, and by the 1960s, to tourist activities; its industrial days were soon to be over. A watershed moment in this transition, the conversion of Ghirardelli Square, would not happen until 1964.

Just below Fisherman's Wharf, the northeastern section of the waterfront bristled with piers. Across the Embarcadero, warehouses, mills, and other light industry choked the base of Telegraph Hill (Figs. 1.14 and 1.15). Only the incline of the hill itself separated the residences perched on it from the commercial and industrial activity below. A bit farther south, near the Ferry Building area but not within the port's jurisdiction, was the Produce Commission District, or simply the Produce Market. The market

1.13 Looking southeast across Pier 45 and the fishing fleet. San Francisco Port Authority, *Ocean Shipping Handbook*, 1958.

was a lively place of crammed streets, roofed sidewalks, and low build-ings that housed fruit and vegetable wholesalers; most of what was sold here arrived by riverboat. Across the Embarcadero, the piers, bulkhead buildings, and pier sheds in this section of the waterfront were used for general, break-bulk, and cargo-related activities, and the Belt Line Railroad spurs occupied a good bit of space. The Roundhouse, located at the foot of Lombard Street at the Embarcadero was used for turning and maintaining trains and was an area landmark, but a functional one rather than just historic, as it is now. Preparations for construction of the Embarcadero Freeway would clutter the Embarcadero from the Roundhouse to the Ferry Building before the end of the decade (Fig.1.16).

In the area around the Ferry Building, the finger piers were old and a number of them were in poor condition or condemned. The Bay Bridge, completed in 1936, severely reduced ferry traffic, so much so that by 1958 most of the Ferry Building had been converted to office use. Across from the Ferry Building area, between the Produce Market and Market Street was "the front." a rough-and-tumble area of hotels, bars, and seamen's hangouts named for Front Street. The ILWU hiring hall was there until its move to Fisherman's Wharf, as were salvage companies and Hills Brothers

I.14 View of finger piers near Telegraph Hill in 1956. Courtesy of the San Francisco Planning Department.

1.15 Bulkhead buildings along the Embarcadero in the northeastern waterfront, 1953. Courtesy of the San Francisco History Center, San Francisco Public Library.

1.16 Looking south over the Front c. 1954. Courtesy San Francisco Planning Department.

Coffee. Nearby portions of important commercial streets such as California, Sacramento, and Clay were home to freight and drayage firms, steamboat associations, chandlers, and export companies. The Ferry Building area's remaining maritime businesses and working character helped created an unsettled mix of waterfront-related uses and downtown offices.

THE CENTRAL WATERFRONT (SOUTH BEACH/CHINA BASIN)

In the central waterfront, maritime and related industrial activities were able to break free of the constraints of topography and the growing down-town—there were no hills or dense collections of buildings to hamper the spread of industrial activity, and warehouses, marshaling yards, and storage facilities were no longer restricted to a narrow ribbon of land. Between the Bay Bridge and China Basin Channel, piers were used for general cargo shipment; south of the basin, port land was used for mar-shaling and loading trucks, shipping petroleum products, ship repair, and berthing (Fig. 1.17).

Two of the most important of the port's specialized facilities were also here: the Refrigeration Terminal, which occupied a large two-story, con-crete building adjacent to China Basin Channel, and the Banana Terminal on the south side of the channel at Pier 60. Most of the port's seawall lots in the central waterfront were leased to Southern Pacific and the Atchison, Topeka, and Santa Fe railroad companies. During the late 1940s and early 1950s, the central waterfront was also the focus of many of the port's pier improvement and development projects, the largest of which was the new Mission Rock Terminal at Pier 50, completed in 1950. At twenty-nine acres, it housed two (later four) large, and for the time modern, concrete and steel sheds, and it was the centerpiece of shipping on the waterfront: "the facilities for receiving trucks were designed to be one of the most effi-cient and modern facilities for receiving and delivering cargo by truck."[37] Generally this part of the waterfront messy, busy, and industrial.

THE SOUTHERN WATERFRONT

Between the Central Basin and Islais Creek, much of the waterfront, both port and non-port property, was devoted to fields of warehouses and open

1.17 1956 aerial view of a portion of the Central Waterfront. Pier 50 is on the left and the China Basin Channel is the center. Courtesy San Francisco Planning Department.

storage, massive rail yards, and swaths of undeveloped vacant land. A number of piers and docks down on this end of the waterfront were privately owned and run. Union Oil, for instance, owned and operated Pier 66 and Pacific Gas and Electric maintained facilities at Pier 72. The dry dock was still privately owned and in full operation repairing and maintaining ships, and it had not yet taken its last commission for a new vessel.

The port's main facilities in the southern waterfront concentrated at Islais Creek, which was packed with heavy, maritime-industrial uses. Grain, copra, and cotton terminals loomed along the creek and were among the port's most important assets. Land alongside Islais Creek was also used for petroleum delivery, and as an automobile terminal and lumberyard. Other uses included fish processing, canning, and distribution; railroad car switching and storage; grain storage; gas and oil storage; and scrap-metal processing. A radio station reached its listeners from a tower rising above what was a disorderly but energetic place.

The fate that befell San Francisco's waterfront, as revealed in this now-and-then comparison, was not unusual; many older ports have suffered a decline in shipping, only to rise again some time later in a different form and with a new role to play in the life of their cities. But while the decline of industrial ports is a common, even global, theme, answering questions such as "What forces reshaped waterfronts, and to what purpose?" can reveal important particularities about how and why, and this is certainly the case with San Francisco. So, it is to these questions that the remainder of the book turns, starting in the next chapter with the most obvious: "What caused San Francisco's waterfront to fail as a center of shipping and maritime industry?" In answering this question, we will learn something of the port as an agency and the unusual circumstances affecting San Francisco's "gateway to the Pacific."

2

A Sea Change

What is a port? Fundamentally a port is a place where rail and ocean
meet, a seaboard center of economic distribution for vast regions.
The greater and richer the region, the more important the port.
—Board of State Harbor Commissioners, *Quarterly Report*, 1948[1]

PORTS THRIVE ON flows, especially the movement of goods and now-
adays, tourists and consumers. Shifts in flows can have severe consequences for a port, such as when shipping lanes are redirected
or when the flow of capital for infrastructure improvements is
restricted. For the Port of San Francisco, the 1950s were defined
by fundamental shifts in the nature of flows that affected its operations. On the one hand, the restructuring of the city's economy
brought with it a flow of investment into buildings and infrastructure around the port that indirectly hindered its ability to handle
cargo. On the other hand, the port was directly affected by changes
in technology that redirected shipping to the Port of Oakland. In
the end, the port could do little about such top-down forces, and
was already being affected by several issues that hampered the port's
ability to thrive, not the least of which was its own approach to
solving problems. When, that is, port managers eventually recognized problems were arising.

The Port in Muddy Waters

Even though the port brimmed with activity during the 1950s, the decade in fact marked the beginning of an end of an era for San Francisco's waterfront. The port was struggling to rid itself of the specter of past labor troubles and its harbor had become the worse for wear. Indeed, the 1950s and 1960s were the last decades that the Port of San Francisco was a state agency controlled by the BSHC, an arrangement then viewed with growing concern.[2]

Chief among the port's problems was the postwar drop in cargo moving across its docks, the result of several large-scale factors. In 1949, 5,090,000 short tons of dry cargo moved through the Golden Gate, 2,600,000 short tons fewer than in any year between 1925 and 1940, when the average was about 7,690,000 tons (Fig. 2.1).[3] Most of the decline in shipping could be attributed to the drop in coastwise and inland waterway cargo, as opposed to a drop in international trade. Highways replaced shipping lanes as trucking firms proliferated and offered cheaper and more flexible services for moving goods along the coast and into the interior.[4] However,

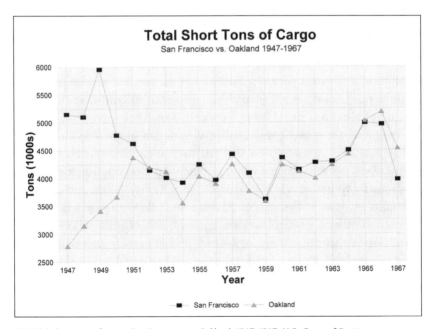

2.1 Total short tons of cargo, San Francisco vs. Oakland, 1947–1967. U.S. Corps of Engineers, *Waterborne Commerce.*

most Pacific coast ports shared in this decline; what affected San Francisco directly and particularly was increased competition. Although the whole Bay Area port network was challenged by other West Coast ports, especially Los Angeles/Long Beach, San Francisco faced stiffening competition from nearby Oakland and Stockton. Their ports, for instance, captured much of the canned goods and dried fruit cargo, partly because food-processing plants opened or relocated nearby, placing them near the expanding highway system. Even though broad in nature, the impacts of the production and transportation revolutions were not evenly spread.

Voices of concern were raised quickly as it became clear that the port's position was being challenged. In testimony at a state senate hearing, representatives of the Ship's Clerk Union and the ILWU criticized the port's loss of competitive edge and attributed it to a "smugness in the 'city that knows how.'" Critics asserted that there was a general "lack of go-getting" on the part of the port, and that groups such as the San Francisco Chamber of Commerce (the Chamber) were just not active enough in seeking out new business.[5] In a similar vein, one observer noted that since the end of World War II, "San Francisco, long dominant as a port, has found it difficult to overcome the lethargy which gradually settled upon her as a successful 'old port.'" Realization that other ports could take cargo from her was slow to bring about a counterreaction.[6] But despite the warnings visible in sailing schedules and cargo manifests, the port's officials, analysts and boosters generally held fast to the general sense that, with a little work, the port could be busy and prosperous for years to come. After all, it had also been noted that "few ports attract more diversified cargo or have a better general traffic balance than San Francisco. This factor alone puts the port into a favored position to continue to attract such commerce."[7] Another source of reassurance was that even with the drop in cargo moving through San Francisco in the early 1950s, and the concomitant increase at the Port of Oakland, the value of the goods moving across San Francisco's piers was among the highest in the nation.[8] It was also believed that the port would benefit from projected regional increases in manufacturing, trade patterns that would favor the Bay Area, and San Francisco's location at the crossroads of world commerce.

According to the Chamber, the port had only to do a few key things in order to tap into this potential: maintain a competitive and balanced rate structure (for things such as wharfage and demurrage fees and truck and rail subsidies), handle labor issues properly, and modernize piers, for instance by providing better truck access.[9] Primarily, however, the port had to promote itself. As noted in one report, because recent labor problems had been dealt with and rate structures were being made more competitive, the most important remaining issues were the "formulation and execution of coordinated solicitation, publicity, advertising and other promotion activities" (Fig. 2.2).[10] The Chamber was not the only organization that believed promotion was a key to success. In an analysis of the port's financial and organizational structure, the California Department of Finance suggested that the port establish an office with the purpose of educating the public and selling the port abroad.[11] Publicity, though, was not the only strategy offered. A state senate committee report released in 1951 concluded that certain rather pedestrian issues, such as operations, were the source of the port's main difficulties.[12] So, with problems identified and solutions at hand, the Port of San Francisco could relatively easily cement its role as *the* "general cargo port of the west" and "fulfill its destiny as one of the world's great ports," a sentiment that lasted throughout the decade.[13]

In keeping with this role, the BSHC ballyhooed the completion in 1950 of its then-modern Mission Rock Terminal at Pier 50 and proudly announced the expansion of Piers 15-17, which had been reconfigured into one large pier that housed a new ship-rail-truck terminal, similar to work done on Piers 30–32.[14] The BSHC also spent considerable effort to promote two other endeavors, their successful pursuit of a foreign trade zone after a twelve-year campaign, and their partnership with the new World Trade Center organization.[15] The former was only the fifth such zone in the country and the latter was an important symbol of the port's role in making San Francisco a center of global commerce. With such projects the port styled itself as "The Progressive Port of San Francisco" and the "Port of Prestige."[16] The BSHC undertook two other "improvements" as part of its public relations efforts in the 1950s: the BSHC changed its name to the San Francisco Port Authority, a title suggested to be more "user-friendly"; and it expanded the commission by adding two ex officio members, the governor and the mayor of San Francisco, the latter to add more local input.[17] These changes were intended partly to ease the public's concerns about state involvement in local affairs, which, with unpopular proposals to build freeways through San Francisco on the minds of many residents, was increasingly viewed as problematic.

The port was rewarded for its efforts in 1957, a year that brought more

2.2 The working waterfront as the Port advertised it. Board of State Harbor Commissioners, *The Progressive Port,* 1954.

cargo across its docks than had been handled in six years. By 1958, the outlook was so positive that the port boldly asserted that its "plan for future development is based on its conviction that world trade through the Golden Gate will continue its already spectacular growth that overshadows even the gold rush era which first gave the Port of San Francisco its place among the world's greatest harbors."[18] This statement was not entirely manufactured from the will to succeed. In 1959, Ebasco Services, Inc., a well-known New York-based engineering and business consulting firm, projected substantial growth in the amount of bulk and general cargo that would move through San Francisco between 1962 and 1980, both in absolute tons and in revenue.[19] The forecast was based on "the influence of new facilities which are projected to be in operation at that time" and the recapture of "the coastwise and intercoastal traffic as a result of the institution of some form of roll-on roll-off technique."[20] Ironically, their report was published in the same year that there was a marked decrease in shipping. It would take a few years of hindsight to see that their projection was generally accurate only until the mid-1960s.

Ebasco's analysis and the generally positive attitude about the future led the port to adopt a "build it and they will come" stance, based on the belief that modernization was a tide that lifted all boats, and technological change in shipping and goods movement was seen as incremental rather than revolutionary in nature. It was something that could be harnessed to the port's advantage, rather than being a force with which to contend. Neither the BSHC nor their consultants and supporters envisioned that world trade routes and shipping lanes could be redirected rather easily in response to technological shifts, working to the advantage of some ports and not others.

The unfortunate and understated reality, however, was that despite strong revenues and a valuable cargo stream, the port's financial condition was weak. As early as 1951, it was suggested that without the boost provided by World War II, the port, which had been operating at about a break-even level, would have been in worse shape.[21] Cargo operations were still going strong but they were not generating as much net income as they once had, due largely to fee structures and labor costs. The port was also encumbered by debt incurred to fund various improvements. Even the Belt Line Railroad had been losing money for years. At the end of the decade, although its income was increasing, the port was only healthy on paper because it was leasing out land for non-shipping functions, including restaurants, parking, and miscellaneous commercial activities—foreshadowing its future. Even as 1960 brought the port its greatest profit in five years, whispers of a dying port grew into steadily voiced assertions.[22]

Such contradictions only made the port's future more murky, causing port authority president Cyril Magnin himself (of the famed family of retail magnates) to send conflicting messages. Quoted in *Portside News* in 1963, he both warned of "major fiscal problems" that lay ahead and maintained the previous decade's optimism in stating, "I am confident we can keep the port solvent, modern and progressive in the years ahead."[23] Magnin's latter comment did not jibe with the port's actions, the essence of which had been to work within the margins of what was standard practice: tinker with rates and fees, build bigger piers to handle break-bulk cargo, and advertise the same merits that the Port of San Francisco had always relied on, even at a time when officials and maritime professionals knew that ships were being fitted for containers.

Causes of Decline Before Containerization

Accounts of port decline have focused almost entirely on containerization as the prime agent of change. Typically, a port's decline is associated with its inability to develop container terminals, commonly for reasons of site and situation or land-use issues. True, containerization has been the single most dramatic influence on shipping activity in many, especially older, ports, but important influences on the timing and character of a port's decline can precede it. This was the case for San Francisco, whose demise as a cargo-shipping port was set in motion before containerization. In addition to the large-scale, mainly external problems associated with world trade patterns and new competition, three main sets of problems precipitated San Francisco's decline: infrastructure and operational issues; stewardship by the state characterized by lack of interest and compromised politics; and downtown land-use changes generated by a new urban economy. The last of these held the most significant implications for the future of the port's northern waterfront.

INFRASTRUCTURE AND OPERATIONS PROBLEMS

> Worn out facilities? Yes, we have to modernize our port—but let's remember that many very busy ports today are doing well with facilities just as old and overcrowded as San Francisco's.[24]
> —Cyril Magnin

The drop in cargo handled after World War II did not immediately diminish the importance of the port to the city's general economic base. Even in later, harder times, it was estimated that one in ten jobs in San Francisco could be traced to port or port-related activity.[25] This made the port's condition a continuing concern not just to the agency itself but also to city leadership, labor, and commercial interests in general. That

1950 was not a good year for business at the port, but was for Oakland, did raise some flags—the port and its boosters were not entirely quixotic. And because a bad year for the port could mean a bad year for the city, Mayor Elmer E. Robinson and the board of supervisors together requested that the state legislature establish a fact-finding committee to evaluate the port's operations. Their request was joined by similar ones from the Commonwealth Club of San Francisco, the San Francisco Junior Chamber of Commerce, and the San Francisco Bay Area Council (BAC), an influential business organization founded in 1945. The state senate assented and quickly established a committee charged with evaluating not just San Francisco but the conditions of all Bay Area harbors. The inquiry produced in 1951 one of the earliest and most comprehensive examinations of the status of shipping in the Bay Area. Perhaps the committee's most basic finding for the region was that the decrease in shipping was related to infrastructure and operational problems that caused "the harbor, as composed of the various ports located along its shores, not [to be] fully competitive with other major United States harbor regions."[26]

Operational problems included those resulting from labor disputes. The report asserted that "a long record of [labor-related] tie-ups has done much to shake the confidence of shippers in the harbor's ability to move cargoes without interruption of services."[27] Strikes had a definite impact on the levels of San Francisco's tonnage in the late 1940s. Sailors struck in 1946, longshoremen in 1948, and there were two major strikes by warehousemen in 1949. The port tried hard to live down its past by pointing out willing, productive, and apparently contented workers to prospective shippers (Fig. 2.3). This positive spin was echoed by the San Francisco Chamber of Commerce, which asserted that labor issues were truly problems of the past. Of course, labor unrest continued to affect port activities throughout the 1950s, and would again become prominent as mechanization wreaked havoc on the waterfront workforce after the introduction of containerization.

Although the port implemented a few projects to modernize and maintain some of its facilities, such sporadic improvements could not deal comprehensively with the generally poor state of its infrastructure. The 1951 report found that after World War II, trucks accounted for 75–80 percent of the movement of goods once they were off the ship, and this in addition to the impact trucks had on coastwise and inland waterways shipping.[28] That trucking had eclipsed rail as the primary way to move goods presented physical and logistical problems for the Port of San Francisco. A 1959 survey of the port's facilities noted that twenty-nine of its

2.3 The inset says "Getting the job done." San Francisco Port Authority, *Ocean Shipping Handbook*, 1958.

thirty-seven finger piers were, at the time of the report, forty years old, and that the newest was twenty-two years old.[29] Such old piers were not designed to accommodate modern equipment. For instance, sheds had internal support columns that hindered the movement of goods. Many piers also had narrow aprons designed for rail access, which made it hard to maneuver trucks.

Still another difficulty was that, even before the arrival of giant containerships, general cargo ships were themselves getting bigger. While evolutionary and not revolutionary, this broad-based change in cargo transportation created many difficulties for San Francisco's aging facilities. Many of the port's piers were not large enough to accommodate the newest ships, their sheds had insufficient floor space to handle the larger shipments that came with bigger vessels, and they could not be easily adapted to handle large mobile cranes and heavier forklifts. Moreover, larger ships required more dredging, an expensive task that some years later was recognized as environmentally undesirable. Other problems that hindered the port's ability to compete for trade included: longer waiting time at docks; loss of the pallets used to convey goods between ship and shore; and the hesitation of drivers to incur additional wear on their trucks from driving over the hills in and south of San Francisco, as opposed to more direct or flatter routes in the East Bay. Pilferage of cargo was also of much concern to shippers.[30]

In a conclusion aimed especially at San Francisco, the senate committee concluded that "other factors being equal, the human elements of port organization, management, and promotion appear somewhat more significant in the modern picture of maritime commerce and world trade than modern facilities."[31] Such conclusions seemed oddly out of tune in an age when much of society was taken with grand designs and visions of futuristic efficiency and simplicity based on technology and new economies.

THE STATE-OWNED PORT

While the benefits and problems of state ownership of the port had been debated over the years, not everyone was convinced that such an arrangement was a main source of the port's trouble. For instance, in 1950 the San Francisco Chamber of Commerce stated that "the Committee believes questions of legal control in the operation of the Port are of secondary importance and that the primary concern is the active development of the Port through improvement, promotion, expansion of service, and the like, regardless of what the controlling entity may be."[32] But as the decade progressed, state ownership became increasingly controversial, and the state was criticized for a lackadaisical approach to its role in port affairs. Questions about the efficacy of state control of the port led Cyril Magnin to speak out on the issue in a 1958 editorial for *Portside News*: "I have talked to few shippers over the country who know—and fewer yet who care— who owns the port facilities, as long as they can expect efficient and economical service from the port and its related maritime industries in San Francisco. And I think that it is safe to say that in the recent past, relationships between the city and port administrations have been harmonious and productive."[33]

Indeed, not all the blame for the port's physical deterioration and waning status could be placed on the BSHC control because as a state agency it operated under certain restrictions. In particular, the budgeting system imposed by state ownership effectively hindered upkeep.[34] When the port decided that some function should be developed, it usually had to be approved by the California State Legislature, which also approved the port's budget. Until 1951, the BSHC had no authority to tax or issue bonds. When the BSHC was finally given the ability to float bonds they were limited to general obligation bonds, which are issued through the state legislature and are subject to voter approval at a general election. State ownership thus put the Port of San Francisco in a position quite different from any other California port. In particular, there was a disincentive for voters in other cities to approve bonds for a port that might be competing with their own. This made it difficult for the BSHC to raise money, without raising fees, to pay for repairs to piers, make improvements, such as widening aprons, or perform general maintenance. It is also an example of the localized differences that have significant impacts on the ability of places to adapt to changing circumstances.

Proposition 4, passed in 1958 as the State Harbor Bond Issue, is a testament to the perceived difficulties of getting such bonds passed. The port was so concerned with this proposition that it released what amounted to campaign literature—a document that took pains to explain its untarnished financial record and that the bond would be paid for by revenue from the harbor, not costing the public a cent. The document also included a section of quotes from "leading Californians" like Governor Knight and Attorney General Edmund G. Brown, and comments from newspapers including the *Los Angeles Examiner* and the *San Francisco Examiner* that all expressed support for the proposition. In an attempt at ballot-box legerdemain, it was subtitled the *state* harbor bond issue, even though $50 million of the $63 million requested by the legislature was earmarked for San Francisco.

Getting a bond passed was not the only problem. Further difficulties derived from the fact that the BSHC had to service those bonds through rates and fees it charged for the use of its facilities. This created a catch-22 for the port. As the cost of moving freight was considered one of the most significant factors in routing goods, there was pressure to maintain, if not reduce, rates charged by the port for wharfage, handling, and so on, so as not to create further incentives for shipping lines to avoid San Francisco. Yet the port had to rely on these fees to pay its debt. Any other funds had to be obtained directly from state coffers, money often hard to come by. When revenues were low, port management had to defer maintenance. Additionally, employees of the BSHC were hand-icapped by state legislation in their ability to solicit traffic—a rather conflicted situation as the board was charged with promoting the port.[35] Such was the legacy of state ownership that even in 1978, by which time the port had become a city agency, city officials sought to deflect blame for continued decline onto the previous stewardship, arguing that "the decrease of useful maritime uses has been caused by obsolescence since there was a lack of capital reinvestment in the maritime piers on the part of the State of California."[36]

The port, then, was in an unusual institutional position. As a state agency, it was affected by and responded to statewide politics and gov-ernmental tussles, which often became external or top-down sources of constraints for how the port functioned. At the same time, the port was an intimately local agency in that it was fixed in space and linked physically and economically to San Francisco. Local officials and boosters identified with the port as if it was theirs, and it was an essentially local entity because what happened to and at the port was directly connected to the city. And during the last fourteen years or so of state control, the board included San Francisco's mayor as an ex officio member, providing an official channel for the expression of local concerns. As a gubernatorial appointee, however, Magnin's political and administrative allegiances were clearly tied to Sacramento. As more state funding was needed for main-tenance and to keep pace with modernization, and as other ports in Cali-fornia expanded their operations and vied for business with San Francisco, local officials, and eventually San Franciscans in general, found themselves more and more at odds with Sacramento. The issue of state ownership would come to a head at the end of the 1960s, when even the state itself was becoming more ill at ease in its role as owner of a business concern that was losing money and on whose fallow land it seemed too difficult to develop new productive uses.

LAND-USE CHANGES IN THE NORTHERN WATERFRONT

It is not, however, the docks, wharves, and terminals that make a harbor but what is behind those facilities. A port must have a hinterland to

produce and move to dockside the goods and commodities shipped out-
bound, and it must have a market for incoming shipments.[37]
—State of California, *Port of San Francisco Bay*

Beginning in the 1950s, two important developments led to dramatic changes in land uses near port property along its northern waterfront: first, new methods of production, fabrication, and goods distribution became predominant; and second, the city's economic structure was radically altered by the rise of the service sector and the related birth of San Francisco as a postindustrial city. These broad transformations affected San Francisco's waterfront in very specific ways, not by affecting shipping directly but rather by making it difficult to run the port in an efficient and competitive fashion.

The postwar increase in Bay Area manufacturing and industry was seen as a good sign for Bay Area ports. However, as industrial activity grew it shifted location within the region. Businesses, particularly heavy industry and those that relied on material brought through the port, began to abandon San Francisco. This had the effect, slowly at first then more rapidly by 1960, of eroding the port's connection to nearby inland areas. Traditionally, production plants were multistoried and located near inputs—that is, raw materials or foodstuffs requiring processing and or packing. But changes in production and warehousing made such facilities obsolete. Efficiency was found in horizontally configured structures, and so businesses abandoned their waterfront locations in order to move to more suburban locations, where splayed-out, single-story buildings began an inexorable creep across seemingly endless tracts of cheap land.[38]

To a large degree, industrial relocation was enabled by the explosion in trucking, which was in turn tied to the expansion of the nation's highway system. Trucks eradicated the cost advantage of being located near inputs, which was in any case minimal compared to the savings in efficiency from new facilities in suburban sites. Additionally, raw, unrefined, or pre-production cargo was beginning to be replaced by manufactured items; for example, electronics and machinery began to displace fruits, spices, coffee, and sugar. The result was that few, if any, processing plants were needed near the waterfront and fewer manufactured or processed goods were being exported through the Port of San Francisco. Naturally, as the usefulness of a waterfront area location waned, many warehousing and distribution firms also abandoned the city as they too found efficiency elsewhere.

As industrial activities relocated, they were replaced by new uses. This trend was plainly visible in the Fisherman's Wharf area, where tourist-related retail and general commercial uses moved in to replace food processors and warehousing as well as other maritime-related businesses such as boat-repair shops and chandlers. In particular, the spread of motels along the wharf signaled its transformation from a place of production to one of consumption. The first motel did not appear in the wharf area until 1954, a second was built in 1959, and two more by 1963.[39] The most significant and symbolic of these changes were the adaptive reuses of the Ghirardelli mustard and chocolate factory and the Del Monte cannery. By the end of the 1960s, manufacturing, warehousing, and maritime-related uses in areas inland from the port ceased to dominate the built environment not just of the wharf but of much of the waterfront down to the Bay Bridge.

More than just the availability of land was involved. Reconfiguration of industrial plants occurred at a time when land values in central cities were on the rise. Business owners could not afford the rents or pay the market rate for land necessary to accommodate new horizontal industrial structures whose footprints could span city blocks. In particular, the flight of industry from San Francisco's northern waterfront, and from the city generally, was driven by the expansion of the city's Financial District and its hunger for office space—one of the key components of the realignment of many urban economies as they became postindustrial. By the mid-1950s, the downtown's Financial District needed to expand beyond its traditional boundaries, and changed the "highest and best use" of adjacent land from warehousing, distribution, and industry to high-density office buildings. Between 1946 and 1950, the city issued five permits to construct new downtown buildings. Eleven were issued between 1951 and 1955, and twelve between 1956 and 1961. Of the total office space constructed in San Francisco between 1929 and 1962, 22 percent (about 2.5 million square feet) was built between 1960 and 1962.[40] The rapid shift in San Francisco's economy that would generate such dramatic change is outlined in Figures 2.4 and 2.5.[41]

The decrease in manufacturing and warehousing activities and the increase in the service, finance, insurance, and real estate sectors over such relatively short periods of time reveals, in a basic way, the depth of San Francisco's economic transformation, both downtown and for the city as a whole. But these changes were not just in the formation of new firms and the creation of different kinds of jobs, they translated directly into a broad transformation of the built environment. Changes in the type and number

NUMBER OF DOWNTOWN ESTABLISHMENTS IN SELECTED SECTORS, 1953–1961

	1953	1961	% Change
Manufacturing	310	215	-30.3
Wholesaling	2363	1961	-16.6
Eating and Drinking	843	904	+7.2
Financial Services	1641	1853	+12.9

2.4 Number of downtown establishments in selected sectors, 1953 and 1961. San Francisco Planning Department, *Downtown San Francisco—General Plan Proposals*, 1963.

SAN FRANCISCO EMPLOYMENT AND ESTABLISHMENTS FOR SELECTED 2-DIGIT SICS, 1953 AND 1968

		1953	1968	Difference	% Change
Manufacturing	Employment	69479	57592	-11887	-21%
	Establishments	2141	1667	-474	-28%
Transportation	Employment	44955	54236	9,281	21%
and Utilities	Establishments	662	552	-110	-20%
Wholesale	Employment	49249	43573	-5676	-13%
	Establishments	3028	2694	-334	-12%
Retail	Employment	60269	58152	-2117	-4%
	Establishments	6110	4884	-1226	-25%
Services	Employment	48299	89448	41149	46%
	Establishments	6602	7286	684	9%
FIRE*	Employment	40522	59864	19342	32%
	Establishments	2433	2848	415	15%

2.5 San Francisco employment and establishments for selected 2-digit SICs, 1953 and 1968.
* FIRE = Finance, Insurance, Real Estate. U.S. Census, *County Business Patterns*.

of businesses and, thus, the labor force, customers, and the infrastructure necessary to support them, resulted in real changes to the cityscape. Where once there were warehouses, high rises offices spurted up, and restaurants and parking garages speckled the landscape, serving the new white-collar commuter population, and, increasingly, tourists.

San Francisco's shift away from industrial activities to a more service sector-oriented economy affected the port by changing the adjacent built environment. With the new physical landscape came increased employment density, which brought concomitant increases in both automobile traffic and the need for mass transit. This also created demand for retail and commercial businesses to serve a growing and changing downtown population, which generated the classic conditions for what planners refer to as "land-use conflict." In general, older maritime and industrial uses did not mix well with new commercial and tourist-related activities; it became operationally and economically difficult for the former to compete with the latter. For instance, trucks maneuvering from northern waterfront piers onto nearby roadways were faced with traffic congestion and ever-growing masses of pedestrians. Maritime-related businesses such as supply companies could not afford to pay increased rents. As logistics became harder to manage, and the commercial businesses that served maritime activity and industry relocated or closed, it became more difficult for shipping lines to justify using the facilities at the Port of San Francisco. Such problems contributed significantly to the reduction or elimination of calls made by shipping lines to the city's port.

This did not go unnoticed. For example, one reason that a raised freeway was built along the Embarcadero was to try to separate through traffic from the remaining working piers. It was believed that this would ease the stressful conditions along a section of the waterfront being strangled by the growing downtown, and provide better access to freeways for trucks. Construction of the Embarcadero Freeway was halted at Broadway Street by a citizen's revolt in 1958, but not before it made a tremendous impact on the morphology of the port's northern waterfront. Streets had originally been laid out to end in the piers, and this historical aspect of the city's grid design was disturbed, if not destroyed, by construction of the freeway. Most egregiously, its double decks hid the Ferry Building from view and became a harbinger of the port's changing role in the decades to come (Fig. 2.6). In the end, instead of helping port busi-

2.6 The Embarcadero freeway at the Ferry Building, c. 1960. Courtesy of the San Francisco History Center, San Francisco Public Library.

nesses, the freeway severed downtown from the waterfront, emphasizing the city's shift away from its historical maritime origins as it moved into its service sector future.

THE PRODUCE MARKET CONSUMED

One of the most dramatic changes to the land side of the northern waterfront was the remaking of the Front. The area derived its old maritime waterfront character from a variety businesses, including ship chandlers, import-export firms, union halls, storage facilities, and hotels (often serving ship's crews). At the edge of the city, it was a vibrant sailor's town of sorts. But the Front could not avoid the death stroke that came with the relocation of the Produce Market during the 1950s. While the market was nearly entirely outside of the port's jurisdiction, it was nevertheless intimately linked to it, physically and functionally. Spread over a number of blocks, the humble Produce Market was a somewhat worn and jumbled collection of warehouses and rolling door storefronts that were home to scores of fruit and vegetable wholesalers who distributed their wares to restaurants and grocers throughout San Francisco and the Bay Area (Fig. 2.7).

2.7 The Produce Market c. 1952. Courtesy of the San Francisco History Center, San Francisco Public Library.

The Produce Market occupied land made increasingly valuable by a downtown straining to support its nascent economy of white-collar jobs. It, and most of the Front with it, was doomed to be replaced by the Golden Gateway housing enclave and the Embarcadero Center office and shops complex, the two largest components of what was to be the Golden Gateway Redevelopment Area. The Golden Gateway was one of San Francisco's first urban renewal projects, and an early "success." Launched in the mid-1950s and built over a twenty-five year period, it resulted in a mini-city within San Francisco, its presence unmistakable in the skyline. It remains a monument to the ability of the local power elite to shape the city. Redevelopment of the Produce Market is an example both of local actors working to satisfy their own local development interests, and of top-down forces, such as secular trends in the economy, that are inevitably channeled into the locale through the focusing effect of local agents who ultimately affect the landscape.

In the first part of the 1950s, a mix of powerful local executives and urban elites decided that the 'best' use of the land occupied by the Produce Market was to accommodate expansion demanded by the newly energetic downtown; their efforts helped galvanize the Golden Gateway redevelopment project. Millions of dollars of federal urban renewal subsidies were available and San Francisco had a redevelopment agency in place a year before the federal enabling legislation, the 1949 Housing Act, was passed. It made perfect sense to corporate interests and city officials to take advantage of federal funding and to use the financial, legal, and planning powers of the newly minted agency to create a place that would signify San Francisco's important role not just in the region, or California, but also in the Pacific rim. It was, after all, a time of exuberant growth and endless possibilities.

Private business was fastest to the mark, with San Francisco mayor George Christopher not far behind. The campaign to relocate the Produce Market and construct a huge mixed-use project was launched by the (BAC), whose membership at the time included some of the West Coast's most powerful corporations, including U.S. Steel, Standard Oil, Bechtel, and the Bank of America, making it probably the most influential business group in the region, and something of a strong arm for global capital. To push the urban renewal agenda more effectively, the BAC decided it needed a San Francisco-specific group and thus formed the Blyth-Zellerbach Committee (BZC) sometime around 1952. The committee consisted of local business magnates who described themselves as "just a group of fellows devoted to San Francisco."[42] In fact, nearly every one of the members was on the executive board of the Bay Area Council. James Zellerbach was son of the founder of the Crown-Zellerbach Company, which dealt in lumber and paper. He was also a member Wells Fargo's board of directors and a U.S. ambassador to Italy. Blyth was an established financier.

The BZC was instrumental in pushing the city to initiate and move forward the urban renewal process. They influenced mayoral appointments, paid for consultants managed by the planning department and the San Francisco Redevelopment Agency (SFRA), and were strongly linked to the official citizen's group required by law to be formed for redevelopment projects. The BZC did most of its maneuvering in committee meetings and behind closed doors. But to be able to act with fewer restraints, and to participate more openly in the quasi-public process associated with urban renewal, an 'independent' report suggested that the BZC committee should have more visibility. They responded to the advice by joining up with the relatively ineffectual San Francisco Housing and Planning Association, an advocacy group, to form the San Francisco Planning and Urban Renewal

Association (SPUR) in 1959. As Chester Hartman observed "SPUR was devised to openly generate more 'citizen' (meaning business) support for urban renewal in San Francisco."[43] SPUR fostered a close but informal working relationship with the SFRA, and it was not long before Mayor George Christopher appointed the group to be the official citizen's advisory committee for the Golden Gateway redevelopment project.[44]

At the start of the Golden Gateway project in the early 1950s, the SFRA was felt to be weak and under-staffed, which slowed the process down and frustrated members of the BZC. To galvanize the project, the BZC supplied the planning department with the cash it needed to produce a quick proposal for relocating the Produce Market. A report was published in 1953 and was followed a year later with the recommendation that a redevelopment area be designated (Fig. 2.8). But even with a quick start the efforts of the BZC, the planning department, and the SFRA would not be fruitful until the end of the decade, when the influence of the visionary Justin Herman would help assure success for the first redevelopment project in the downtown area.

Redevelopment agencies are quasi-independent government agencies that have several important powers: they can use eminent domain to acquire property, they are not subject to local zoning ordinances, and they can establish tax increment financing. Tax increment financing is in a sense state sponsored speculation. Essentially, a redevelopment agency can float bonds secured against future tax revenue that, it is presumed, will increase substantially after development has occurred. This is a particularly important ability; in fact, redevelopment is considered by many of its practitioners and the jurisdictions that use it to be primarily a financial tool.[45]

In the California redevelopment process, a redevelopment agency must first establish a geographical survey area, the boundaries of which require approval by the local legislative body. In San Francisco's case, this is the board of supervisors. The survey is primarily a collection of land-use and related data that become the basis for identifying specific "project areas" located within the larger survey boundary. The redevelopment agency can only operate in legally established project areas. Once a project area is chosen, a redevelopment agency must demonstrate the presence of economic and physical blight, a critical and often controversial step. It should be understood that to exercise eminent domain, an agency must be able declare the subject area to be 'blighted.' Depending on circumstances, some

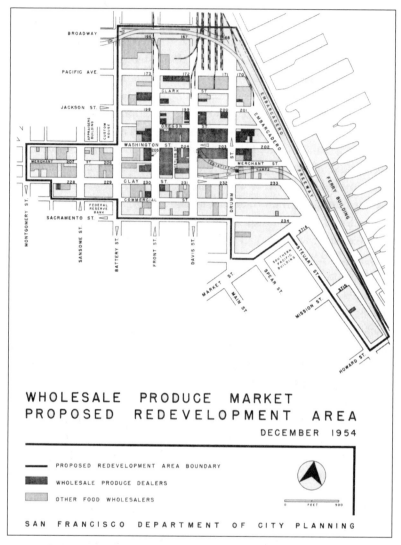

**WHOLESALE PRODUCE MARKET
PROPOSED REDEVELOPMENT AREA**

DECEMBER 1954

2.8 Map of the Produce Market. San Francisco Planning Department, *A report recommending designation of two redevelopment Areas under provisions of the California Redevelopment Act,* 1954.

time around this point a redevelopment plan is written. It is often accompanied by a "design for development" document that provides specific criteria that address elements of zoning or urban design, including building envelopes, setbacks, ground-floor use requirements, dwelling-unit mix, and so on. Together these documents are similar to what is known as an "area plan" and related zoning regulations.

The redevelopment process is one that includes many requirements and usually involves the planning department, and in some cases the port; final approval rests with the board of supervisors.[46] Once the plan is approved, the redevelopment agency can begin to use its powers to initiate development, which may involve disposing of public land, acquiring private land through eminent domain, and issuing requests for development proposals. In the case of Golden Gateway, the planning department delineated the new redevelopment area and provided arguments for declaring it to be blighted: the area in and around the Produce Market was described as run down, a fire hazard, unhealthy, and inefficient. To support these contentions, reports were conjured from the department of public health and the fire department. The former stated that there were "many potential dangers to the public health" (but also said no acute problems existed), and the latter noted 119 fire code violations and commented that the alleys and congested streets were "a deterrent to the efficient operation of this department."[47] The pressure was intensified when the planning department, again funded by the BZC, retained the nationally known architecture firm Skidmore, Owings and Merrill (SOM) to work up the first design concepts for the area in 1957.

The concept plan for Golden Gateway, referred to as Area E, was embraced by the planning department and the SFRA. Mayor Christopher praised the involvement of the BZC and thanked the planning department for its help. Of the former he said "you couldn't hire them to do it but they'll do it free."[48] Downtown businesses and interests groups worked hard to promote the project. It was, after all, in the national spotlight as an exemplar of early federally funded urban renewal projects. And Mayor George Christopher believed that it would be "one of the greatest things that has ever happened to the City."[49] Aside from the Produce Market businesses themselves, there were few, if any, voices raised in opposition until much later.[50] Perhaps the public was swayed by the "eminently practical plan," as Roger D. Lapham, Jr., president of the planning commission, described it.[51] In a similarly understated tone, perhaps not wanting to stir up a hornet's nest, Joseph Alioto, chairman of the redevelopment agency commission and mayor-to-be, soft-pedaled that "Nat Owings has come up with something that can be worked out."[52] In fact, the project met with no faint praise from parts of the public, at least as represented by Lloyd D. Hanford, the Chairman of the Citizen's Participation Committee for Urban Renewal (another predecessor to SPUR), who saw in it "the promise of a thrilling new city in the sky."[53] The *Chronicle* added to the potent mix of downtown elite and public agencies pushing the project by making sure whenever possible to describe the Produce Market area as "shabby," "ramshackle," "tumbled-down" or otherwise beyond its useful life. Clearing it away, it was intimated, was a reasonable endeavor, and would create a "Golden Gateway into downtown San Francisco."[54] This was not the first time, and would be far from the last, that a discourse around development would be placed in a framework opposing "old and run-down" versus "new and modern," the former being bad for the city, the latter good without question.

SOM's preliminary plans were approved by the board of supervisors in October 1958.[55] In an unusual move, Mayor George Christopher attended the hearing to impress upon the board the urgency of approving the plan, which had to meet a tight deadline or lose federal grant money. The final version was approved in May 1959. Once the BZC, SPUR, and the SFRA were able to establish a legal redevelopment area and declare it blighted, not much could stand in the way. The affected business owners initially fought very hard against the proposal but were in the end powerless. On the defensive, they shifted their strategy to getting the best possible facilities at their new site, which was several miles away near Islais Creek in the southern waterfront, where it remains today. They were also able to broker guarantees that produce firms would not be moved out one by one, which was a fortuitous parallel to Justin Herman's insistence that the parcels comprising the redevelopment project not be sold piecemeal, thus allowing it to be developed as a whole.

The concept plan for Area E became the framework for a design competition that called for specific proposals for each of the phases of the enormous endeavor. The request for proposals was released in 1959 and in 1960, Perini-San Francisco Associates was declared winner of the Golden Gateway housing piece. Of their proposal, contest judge Mario Ciampi said, "This will be one of the great projects of the West, and give a new and enriched way of life to our city."[56] The team that won the bid for what would become the Embarcadero Center was Crow-Box-Portman, a hodgepodge of out-of-towners who partnered with David Rockefeller.[57] The land was cleared during the competition and construction started on the 44 acre site in 1961. The project was not completed until 1986, with the opening of the Embarcadero Four office tower.[58]

One hiccup in the otherwise smooth process involved the port. A small parcel of land, along with sections of several streets, were within the port authority's jurisdiction. Without them, the sponsors would have been forced to redesign the project, subjecting it to costly delays. Staff at the port requested legal advice with regard to the sale of its property. The issue made its way to the office of the California Attorney General, who ruled in 1958 that the land was sovereign property of the state and could be used only for public commerce or navigation. However, it was also determined that the state legislature could free the land from the conditions of the public trust, thus enabling the SFRA to sell the land for private development.[59] The ruling, signed by Governor Edmund Brown, was prepared by Deputy Attorney General Miriam Wolff, who would, for a troubled while, become director of the Port of San Francisco. This decision would become something of a precedent for dealing with the burden of the public trust on several other occasions, some years later.

With public agencies and many downtown elite vested in the success of the project, the local Democratic Party machinery whirred into action. State senator Eugene McAteer sponsored the bill to authorize the sale of port land. It was passed by the legislature in 1959. The issue was not settled until 1962, however, when a squabble over the land's appraisal was resolved by Governor Brown. Cyril Magnin had been resisting pressure by the SFRA to sell the land for a dollar; a port appraisal valued the property at half a million.[60] An editorial by the *Chronicle* unctuously attempted to placate the parties involved—it referred to Governor Brown as wise, and said that Magnin and the other port commissioners "have given every indication of an equally intelligent approach to the problem," and that "San Franciscans can be particularly thankful that their port authority commissioners are not apt to be sidetracked by dubious technicalities when community betterment is clearly at stake."[61] Still, Justin Herman's redevelopment agency won out over Magnin, and the port sold off its parcels and street right-of-ways for $24 plus the appraisal fee.[62] The ease with which the public trust burden was lifted from these parcels of land would not be soon repeated.

Magnin was not particularly interested in opposing the Golden Gateway project, he was merely holding out for money, something his port needed. In fact, Magnin's interest in the northern waterfront was not necessarily as a working waterfront; rather, relocating the Produce Market advanced his vision of a new "Embarcadero City." As cargo operations declined, he and other officials began to think hard about alternative uses for port property in the northern waterfront, and mammoth transformations of the built environment on the land side of the Embarcadero suggested possibilities for new urban forms out over the water.

In the mid-1960s, the office, retail, and hotel parts of the project were for a while given the sobriquet of Rockefeller Center West, reflecting its scale, its aspirations, and part of its financial underpinnings. Ultimately, local boosters prevailed in the tussle to claim and in essence brand the project and it was named the Embarcadero Center. The discourse around naming the project hints at the slickness with which this development was promoted. Declaring that "San Francisco is one of the most exciting and vital cities in the country," Warren Lindquist, project manager for the Embarcadero Center allowed that "anything to do with San Francisco should be related to the community rather than lifting something from someplace else and imposing it in San Francisco."[63] This was quite a biased statement given that "the community" most intimately interested in the area, the wholesalers and other small business, were pushed out, and at the time no neighborhood groups had come forward to have their say. Furthermore, it is not unreasonable to suggest that vitality and excitement were actually diminished as a result of the new development.

Not until the early 1970s did the Telegraph Hill Dwellers (THD) neighborhood association take aim at the project, but as they represented a class very different from the workers below, they only became agitated at the physical form of the development and not by the displacement. Nevertheless, their concerns were not illegitimate, and they jumped into the fray by criticizing the accuracy of the environmental review document for the project, and complained that high rises would destroy views, block the sun, increase traffic, and "wall off the Bay"—something that would become a theme in future fights over the waterfront.[64] In this case, though, their often-formidable influence was ineffectual.

Golden Gateway was a slowly constructed example of Le Corbusier-inspired urbanism. Its International Style design included a collection of mid-rise apartment buildings and townhouses, and four slab high-rise office buildings perched above four levels of pedestrian walkways con-. nected to and by shops and plazas. In all, it includes 1,400 housing units, 3.5 million square feet of office (the equivalent of about seven Transamerica Pyramids), 270,000 square feet of shopping, two acres of parks and open spaces, a signature John Portman-designed Hyatt Hotel, and garages with about 5,000 parking spaces. With regard to its design, *Chronicle* architecture critic Alan Temko deftly summed up his otherwise laborious appraisal by titling his piece "The Long Shadow of Folly."[65] The project had many implications for class relations in San Francisco. Apartments were

2.9 Model of the Golden Gateway redevelopment project c. 1960. Perini-San Francisco Associates.
Courtesy of the San Francisco Redevelopment Agency.

mostly of the luxury kind, and many blue-collar jobs were replaced with
white-collar office employment (Figs. 2.9 and 2.10).

But for our purposes, the main point is that apartments, shops (and
not of the corner-store variety), a hotel, and eventually offices replaced
land-side uses that once interacted with and were of a similar nature to
port uses. Because the Golden Gateway completely recreated the area, its
impact on the port was not simply a matter of supplanting commercial
activity that supported the maritime waterfront. The project created land-
use conflicts that exacerbated operational problems affecting the port's
activities. Private automobiles and pedestrians created a crowd that further interfered with trucks and the flow of goods, as opposed to melding
in with them. After the removal of the Produce Market, what maritime

2.10 Golden Gateway as seen today. Photograph by author.

activity remained in this part of the northern waterfront was rendered little more than a suggestion that this was once a thriving part of a working port. It became a physically disjointed and not very welcoming environment for visitors, new residents, and office workers, made worse by the lumbering presence of the double-decked Embarcadero Freeway. Although not all as abrupt and sweeping as the Golden Gateway projects, land-use changes in areas adjacent to the port's northern waterfront would accelerate during the 1960s and beyond, indicating quite unmistakably that it was a changed place.

Urban economic transformations characterized by new methods of production and distribution, new kinds of work, and changes in the nature of labor constitute what are sometimes conceived of as broad-level or top-down forces that wreak changes in the local built environment. Or, put a little differently, urban development is seen to reflect the power of larger forces to transform the landscape. However, the Golden Gateway development is important to our story not just as an example of the impact of land-use change on the port but more generally as a reminder that dramatic urban transformation and related land-use changes do not result necessarily from outside influences or top-down forces. Indeed, the term *forces* in this context suggests something placeless, a power generated or issuing from somewhere other than the site in question. Delving into the Golden Gateway redevelopment project provides evidence that there are strong local forces that themselves effect the transformation of place. Capitalism, for instance, is not faceless and abstract, but is carried out by actors and agencies manipulating the world around them, and they are often local government agencies and gatekeepers not just corporations, shadowy executive boards, and international financial networks.

In some ways, production of the Golden Gateway and the Embarcadero Center was an act of creative destruction that attends economic restructuring and, concomitantly, is an example of the ability of capital to re-form a place. In order to sell or rent luxury apartments and to lease hundreds of thousands of square feet of Class A office space, there has to be a market for them. The demand for such things came as part of the wider transformation of San Francisco's urban economy, in turn part of a globally scaled transformation affecting many cities. However, the successful creation of the Golden Gateway and the Embarcadero Center came largely from the ambition of local actors who used the powers of the redevelopment agency and implemented them in a local setting and under local conditions. And the urban stage was set by many hands at several levels: federal urban renewal muscle and money, state and local agencies and their directors, mayors, local businessmen, and outside development teams. Boosterism, often imbued with the egos of local elites, was a critical motivating factor in the development of the Golden Gateway and the Embarcadero Center. The desire to rework the urban fabric sprouted not just from a localized profit motive; the financial risk and potential rewards, in terms of investment and capital accumulation went to firms outside San Francisco.[66] Temko's claim that the project was the "most ambitious construction project in the history of the city" is telling in this context. Such ambition written into the built environment comes not from faceless and abstract power, but from the egos of real people—powerful locals who got together to help put San Francisco on the global map as a "progressive" modern city. They were striving to build something that reflected a way of life, something clean, sleek, and dramatic, and something that might make them, and outside investors, a profit. The Golden Gateway redevelopment program reflected pride of place, and a willingness to destroy what did not fit into the dominant vision in order to create something new. More than a financial endeavor, it was an exercise of power to produce something of interest to the powerful—an act of imagination made material.

One cannot help but see it at least partly as an act of cleansing, washing away the dirty bits of urban society and replacing them with towers of prosperity. That the development did not require displacement of numbers of residents perhaps explains why it was subject to so little criticism. The only notable exceptions were late-in-the-game concerns over height, and Alan Temko's exhaustive critiques of its ultimate design. He did not find fault with the general concept of something grand and modern replacing the Produce Market, just the specifics of its implementation.

The nature of this development scheme also points to the difficulty in relying on one approach or direction, for instance top down or bottom up, to explain how a landscape evolves. An agency or executive, such as Justin Herman, can also embody a dual function, as both a source of local power and as a channel for larger, exogenous forces. So, the changes to the northern waterfront described here result from forces, or "power lines" to borrow loosely from Mike Davis, working from both "directions."[67] And the bottom-up forces exerted by local government and various actors were not simply reactive, they were proactive and even anticipatory.[68]

For the port proper, however, change was not brought about by an act of destruction and subsequent rebirth, instead it came in the more passive form of abandonment and disuse. While the city, especially downtown, was willy-nilly replacing its built environment, altering its class structure, and generally producing new sets of social relations and cultural norms, the port tried to manage the potential for change. While the steady decline in shipping was not soon replaced by new development, modernization and economic transformation, among other things, *were* the port's event horizon; there would be no escaping the problems they would engender in the 1950s. In fact, difficulties would increase during the 1960s, when technological advances in shipping proved to be a revolutionary force, and not the incremental improvement that the port, its consultants and boosters assumed it to be. So, on the one hand, the port spent considerable energy in attempts to retain its old functions; on the other hand, the port identified what it felt were appropriate places to become a vanguard of modern urbanism, as we shall see.

The problems faced by the port outlined here meant that it was even less able to compete with Oakland, which could more easily vie for business even before containerization became the standard, and it did so successfully. After 1952, Oakland's harbor ran neck and neck with San Francisco for several years until ten years later, in 1962, the Port of Oakland opened its first terminal dedicated to serving containerships. Soon thereafter, the top-down impact of 20-foot equivalent unit (TEU) metal boxes, about 20' x 8' x 8' 6" in size, hit San Francisco hard.

The Container Revolution

The final, insurmountable problem, one that generated a massive and permanent reduction in the Port of San Francisco's shipping activity, began in 1958, when Matson Line's containership *Hawaiian Merchant* left San Francisco Bay.[69] It was not until 1966 that the first regularly scheduled containership was employed in international trade by Sea-Land Services, a New Jersey-based firm, but Bay Area ports experienced a steady increase in containership traffic soon after the *Hawaiian Merchant's* departure. By the mid-1960s, American President Lines, a major New York shipper with a substantial Bay Area presence, had developed plans for full containership services to the Far East.[70] San Francisco probably did not feel the full impact of containerization until 1969, the year that the Port of Oakland soared ahead of San Francisco in total short tons handled (Fig. 2.11).

The rush to containerization was fueled primarily by two factors. First, expanding levels of trade worldwide and increased ship size necessitated greater efficiency in the movement of goods. Second, time at dock as a percentage of total costs for shipping goods via standard general cargo ships increased from 30 percent in the 1930s to about 75 percent in the 1960s—an increase attributed to steadily rising labor costs.[71] Goods shipped in break-bulk fashion have to be hand sorted and are generally handled four times: from their point of origin to shipside, loaded on the ship, unloaded, and then moved to their destination (Fig. 2.12). Containers allowed the

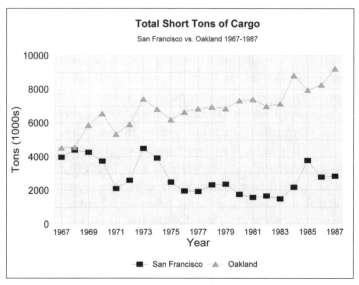

2.11 Total short tons of cargo, San Francisco vs. Oakland, 1967–1987. U.S. Corps of Engineers, *Waterborne Commerce.*

entire process to be mechanized, and in so doing, increased loading and unloading rates from twenty-five tons per hour per gang to up to six hundred tons per hour. This had the commensurate effect of dramatically reducing the amount of time spent at port, which in turn reduced dockage and wharfage fees substantially. Containerization also solved other problems associated with break-bulk: "pilferage, loss and damage, and . . . exposure to the elements."[72] Of course, reducing labor costs in this context translated into a substantial loss of stevedoring and longshoreman's jobs. For San Francisco, this meant thousands fewer blue-collar workers along the waterfront at the same time that office workers and white-collar employees in general were filling the sidewalks. This kind of change in the sociocultural character of the waterfront, while clearly represented in the built environment, is not plainly visible as such in the landscape.

The switch to containerized freight created difficulties for many ports because the economies of scale and efficiency realized by the new transportation technology had two major requirements. First, to develop facilities for handling containers meant a significant capital expenditure for cranes and other marshaling equipment (Fig. 2.13). Second, because containerships carry a tremendous amount of freight that can be unloaded very quickly, substantial areas of "backland" are need to sort and stack containers—space that many ports, especially older ones, did not have.

2.12 Break-bulk cargo c. 1958. San Francisco Port Authority. *Ocean Shipping Handbook*, 1958.

Containerization, then, presented major problems for San Francisco. Extensive shipping-related infrastructure was already in place. The cost of containerization comes not just with purchasing new equipment but also in altering or replacing existing facilities. Finger piers are useless to containerships, and must be removed or substantially altered. Channels must be dredged to accommodate containerships' deep draws. Rail lines and truck access often need to be reconfigured and improved. Surrounding land, which may have been devoted to other uses, may need to be acquired to provide space for the appropriate infrastructure and to store, sort, stack, and prepare goods to be moved to their final destinations. San Francisco had few places with sufficient amounts of flat, backland areas close to the waterfront. Finally, San Francisco was especially vulnerable to

2.13 Container cargo. San Francisco Port Authority, *Ocean Shipping Handbook*, 1966.

loss of business to ports that developed container facilities before it did because 70 percent of the cargo it handled from foreign trade was "suitable for containerization."[73]

The challenge of maintaining shipping activity was complicated for San Francisco by several other factors. First was the transformation of the Port of Oakland from a minor port of call to what would by the 1980s become one of the busiest harbors in the country. The Port of Oakland's metamorphosis was due initially to improvements made as part of the war effort in the 1940s.[74] Later, though, it was the ability of its director and the mayor of Oakland to secure federal economic development grants. The money would have done little were it not for important advantages that the Port of Oakland had when compared to San Francisco in the container age. Its old facilities were not as extensive as San Francisco's and there were plenty of potential backlands suitable for marshaling and other logistics. Thus with a significant source of capital, plentiful space unburdened by extensive facilities, no pressure from a nearby downtown, and management eager to adopt new technology, Oakland could build container terminals comparatively rapidly. In 1962, Sea-Land Service's *Elizabethport* arrived at Oakland's first container terminal. It was five long years after that before San Francisco completed its first container facility, but even then, it did so in only a limited fashion. Between 1968 and 1973, the Port of San Francisco lost at least five major steamship lines to the Port of Oakland.[75] The loss was so significant that in a report to the Economic Development Administration in the U.S. Department of Commerce, the city of San Francisco suggested that the decline in shipping from 5.3 million tons in 1964 to 1.7 million in 1977 could be "directly attributable to federal subsidies to the Port of Oakland."[76] Furthermore, the report stated that "the Port of Oakland's rapid rise to dominance in oceanborne shipping" resulted in a decline in the number of jobs in San Francisco related to waterborne commerce from 23,000 in 1964 to 11,000 in 1978.[77] The federal subsidies, the report argued, were also responsible for generally increasing the attractiveness of the Port of Oakland, encouraging steamship lines to move from San Francisco to their other facilities, ones not built directly with those federal funds.

The Port of Oakland had another advantage when compared to San Francisco—its geographical situation. Not only was San Francisco's once enviable site no longer a boon, but its location relative to the rest of the Bay Area, and to the whole country, became a disadvantage. Even though by the 1950s trucking supplanted rail as the primary way to move goods to the interior, rail access was, and still is, an important consideration for steamship lines. At its height, the Port of San Francisco boasted three major rail lines and itself operated the Belt Line Railway.[78] Compared to Oakland, though, San Francisco's location at the head of a peninsula added distance and time to distribution routes, making them more costly. Moreover, private rail lines had been experiencing difficulties due to competition from trucking, and demand for services in San Francisco had been decreasing since the early 1960s as a result of industrial relocation.[79] To make matters worse, even truck access to San Francisco was more difficult because of traffic and limited access to highway.

SUNK BY IN/DECISIONS

Even though San Francisco found, as did many ports across the country, that its site and situation were not advantageous with regard to the new technology, the southern section of the port's property could support a modest amount of container activity. So, what prevented San Francisco from succeeding in the age of containers? There are two parts to the answer. First, as we have seen, the port took an institutionally conservative approach to its business, and so, in character, it reacted slowly to the trend toward containerization when in fact it did have some choices. The port's hesitancy led to a missed opportunity when it came to the design and build of its much-extolled Army Street Terminal at Pier 80. Second, when officials did decide to adapt to changing circumstances, the unfortunate decision was to support an alternative, ultimately failed, technology called "lighter aboard ship" or LASH.

In its defense, the port received conflicting signals during the early days of the container. For instance, consulting firm Ebasco reported two opposite reactions to containerization in the same report. On the one hand, they acknowledged that shipping executives were of the opinion that container ships offered the best way to counter the increasing expense of handling break-bulk cargo. On the other hand, in response to a questionnaire administered by the consultants, it turned out that steamship company executives were not quickly abandoning older methods and switching to containers. The consultants concluded that "finally, even though significant amounts of cargo may be diverted to container ships . . . the great majority of vessels calling at San Francisco for a number of years will be conventional general cargo ships, which will likewise require more effective facilities."[80] Such findings help explain the apparent lack of urgency about the new technology, and why the port continued to pursue modern break-bulk projects, such as the Army Street Terminal. In 1960, a year after Ebasco's report was released, director Rae Watts announced that a container terminal at Pier 80 (the Army Street Terminal), the best site for such a facility at the time, was not likely, and that no shipping line had come forward to commit to such a terminal.[81] In 1966, the port was advised by its new analysts, Arthur D. Little (ADL), that "while we do not know the rate at which port foreign trade will become containerized, recent trends indicate that a new facility will be needed in the early 1970s." Eight years after the first containerships appeared, the port's consultants still did not suggest that a program for containerization was an urgent need.[82]

In this atmosphere, most major investments made by the port in its facilities during the 1950s and 1960s were not in constructing cutting-edge terminals, even though the port liked to think that they were. During the mid-1960s, the expansion of Pier 27 in the northern waterfront was described as being "designed and constructed as a vital part of the Port of San Francisco's long-range improvement program."[83] It was equipped with a deck that could support "the largest containers." Piers 27 and 50 were both included in a section on containerization in the port's 1966 *Shipping Handbook*, and were described as "excellent facilities for container cargoes," apparently because they both contained sizeable storage and marshaling areas. As neither pier could realistically handle containers, the port's description of these facilities now seems somewhat delusional.

That the port seemed overly conservative, perhaps even recalcitrant, was not unheeded. Board of supervisors member William Blake, a vocal critic, called attention to the lack of modernization by wryly commenting that "some of the piers there . . . still say 'walk your horses.'"[84] Long-time *Chronicle* columnist Herb Caen also took shots at the port. "What's going on down at the Port? Zzzzzzzzz."[85] Looking back at those early years, former director of public relations at the port, Don DeLone, points out that "everybody was talking about containerization in those days, and the industry publications were full of reports about the design and construction of container ships, so people were fully aware that the new vessels were coming on line."[86] Later, a new port consultant tried to explain the early lack of perspective: "Since [San Francisco] had a large existing base there was no need to attempt to introduce innovation in order to take cargo away from somebody else."[87] In fact, the port did try to introduce innovation twice and to strike while the containerization iron was still hot, or moderately so anyway, but it missed both times.

THE ARMY STREET TERMINAL AND LASH

Relying largely on Ebasco's recommendation, the port decided to construct a large new terminal in the southern waterfront at Army Street. This reflected the nascent strategy to abandon much of the northern waterfront to non-industrial maritime activities and to focus shipping and heavy maritime industry in areas deemed more appropriate because of space availability and relative seclusion. Dedicated in August 1967, the terminal was, in effect, a modern break-bulk facility (Fig. 2.14). Even

2.14 Drawing of Army Street terminal after its upgrade to containerization. San Francisco Port Authority, *Ocean Shipping Handbook*, 1966.

though consultants suggested that it be designed to accommodate containerships, the terminal was built with only a limited ability to handle containers. Nevertheless, it was described as the most advanced ocean shipping facility on San Francisco Bay.[88] In his account of the history of containerization in San Francisco, Donald Fitzgerald pointed out that at the time the Army Street Terminal was in the design phase, the Port of Oakland already had a container facility and a major shipping line, Matson, using it for container ships on the Hawaii route.[89] This suggests that the port and its consultants indeed suffered from a certain lack of vision.

In the same year that the Army Street Terminal was inaugurated, ADL shifted gears. In a second study commissioned by the port authority, this one entitled *San Francisco's Maritime Future, Revolution and Response*, the consultants expressed the urgent need to meet the challenge of containeriza-tion. They opened the report by stating that "it will not be possible for the port to maintain the allegiance of container-carrying steamship com-panies without providing special container facilities."[90] On the one hand, ADL argued, if the port did not respond to the challenge, its "failure to build a new, advanced cargo-handling terminal would mean the eventual loss of one-half or more of the Port's future revenues from trade" and that this could affect the growth of the entire Bay Area.[91] On the other hand, if the port acted quickly and surely, it could maintain its traditional posi-tion as nothing less than a "prime mover in the successful development of the West."[92] In justifying the investment in a new facility so soon after the dedication of the Army Street Terminal, ADL argued that the port was not dying and that such assertions were contrived. They pointed out, for instance, that the port authority derived more than four times the direct revenue from its trade operations than did the Port of Oakland, and that for two years cargo volumes had increased. They also dismissed many of the issues typically raised regarding the disadvantages that San Francisco faced in developing container facilities and competing with other ports. For instance, ADL did not consider San Francisco's site and situation as a hin-drance, noting that "concern about San Francisco's future as a major port does not stem from a basic flaw in location, but rather whether the Port can and will build facilities demanded by the new containership technology."[93]

The consultants also refuted the idea that traffic congestion would hinder the port's growth because the I-280 freeway was about to open, and would directly serve the southern waterfront. Finally, they pointed out that the port offered the advantages of a plethora of shipping-related services—an FTZ, banking and insurance firms, customs brokers, fueling, and so on—all at its doorstep. So, ADL argued that the port could con-tinue to be competitive if it were to build the right facilities before the competition could lure away shipping lines. Thus the consultants recom-mended that a new "100% container" facility be built as quickly as possible at India Basin, south across Islais Creek from the Army Street Terminal. They admitted, however, that exactly what kind of facility to build was difficult to determine because maritime technology was still in a state of flux. For instance, a standard for container size had not yet been adopted and other new shipping methods were still competing with containers, for instance LASH. In fact, the port's second new facility would be devoted to that abortive technology.

Lighter aboard ship technology was developed from military systems and was emerging around the same time as container ships. LASH was intended to allow ships with deep draws to anchor offshore and thus serve shallow water ports, or ports with limited facilities. Lighters loaded with containers would be floated by tugs from ship to port facility. Despite widespread support, including from the Maritime Administration (a division of the U.S. Department of Transportation), the LASH system proved clumsy and met with various operational difficulties both at home and abroad. It quite quickly failed, out-competed by the more flexible and efficient standard container system.[94] When finally it decided to embrace new technology, why did the port take a risk with an unproven shipping method? Much of the answer lies in the fact that the port had thrown in its lot with Pacific Far East Lines (PFEL), an up-and-coming shipping firm that made the fateful decision to adopt LASH technology. The port had a tenant ready and waiting to move in and could thus justify the construction cost of a new LASH terminal. In that context, the decision made some sense; with hindsight, though, it seems precipitous.

San Francisco opened its LASH terminal at India Basin in 1972, the first of its kind. Fate, however, was not kind to PFEL. The company's passenger line was losing money, and would ultimately fail. Moreover, PFEL had invested substantial funds to purchase ships designed for LASH, and the new technology was not fulfilling its promise. Then in 1974, PFEL was acquired by Freighters Incorporated, a firm headed by John Alioto, Mayor Joe Alioto's son.[95] His stewardship did not save the shipping line, which had incurred massive debt and owed back rent to the port. The firm was forced into bankruptcy and ultimately dissolved in 1978. Essentially, LASH went down with it and the port was left with a sizeable investment in an unusable terminal. The decision to pursue LASH technology instead of constructing a standard container facility was a particularly important decision that took the port in the wrong direction. In the port's defense, Historian Donald Fitzgerald has argued that while the port had one foot stuck in the past as it looked to the future, its conservative approach was understandable given the industry's general state of flux.[96]

Containerization is an example of technological innovation that acted as a top-down force that evinced itself in ways reflecting local conditions, such as the difference between San Francisco's and Oakland's sites and situations, and the varying approaches to port management by their respective administrations. With respect to the latter, decisions made regarding the Army Street terminal and LASH served to hasten the port's maritime demise.

Although the port responded to its challenges with some capital projects and improvements to its piers and cargo facilities, its efforts were not enough to stem the rising tide. In the northern waterfront, the difficulties the port had in retaining shipping activity and maintaining its infrastructure were apparent in the physical landscape: a number of piers were condemned or in poor shape; some of the Belt Line tracks were removed from service; and in the early 1950s, Piers 43 and 45 were converted by the port into moorings for the sailing ship *Balclutha* and the WWII submarine *Pampanito*. Recognizing the state of the northern waterfront, the fundamental question on the minds of the port's administrators, and of politicians, developers and their capitalist brethren, as well as neighborhood groups and activist organizations was "What should be done with the waterfront?"

It is difficult, however, to make informed—even directed—decisions regarding the future of an agency and its functions without reference to a long-term strategy, as expressed either in a facilities plan or in a policy document. The port had neither, relying instead on consultant advice and the aspirations of its most visionary representative, Cyril Magnin.[97] Years would pass before the port would put on paper a formal articulation of its own vision for the future and the policy road map to get there, a situation for which it would pay a steep political price. However, it is safe to say that most agreed that because modern cargo-handling facilities really could be accommodated only in the southern waterfront, then that was where the port should establish a redoubt for its cargo and heavier maritime operations.[98] Concomitantly, the port and its administrators started to think about the future of the northern waterfront in a different light. There, disused land and decaying piers beckoned with a different, non-maritime potential.

3

In the Absence of Plans

Grand Schemes of the 1950s and 1960s

THE PORT OF the 1950s was on the verge of becoming a cargo back-water. Yet Magnin and the port authority were in control of one of the most famous and evocative waterfronts in the world.[1] So, even while the port wrestled with how to maintain cargo operations, it began to reimagine itself. One might guess that Cyril Magnin took up the task cleaving to the famous aphorism ascribed to Daniel Burnham, "make no little plans, for they have no magic to stir men's hearts," because he cast his eager eye along the waterfront's northern stretches in search of its grandest potential. The port's desire was to harness the larger forces at work to realize a vision of the waterfront as a paragon of modern urban living and corporate success, built on the efficient movement of automobiles and new methods of air transportation. It was to be a place of office towers and high-rise apartment complexes, heliports, and STOL pads.[2] The new value of the northern waterfront was as the front door to an evolving city, opened onto the future. Getting across the threshold, however, would prove to be difficult.

When the port first began to pursue this course, it did so essentially as a top-down force. A state agency, it functioned outside local control as it sought to exploit the processes of economic restructuring and to attract investment to the waterfront via the so-called second circuit of capital. However, that the port decided to take advantage of its position by attempting to summon mammoth projects out of the murky bay water only served to draw the attention of local power bases. Most significant, the planning process, made stronger by citizen activists and idealistic planners, was taking on a more critical role in debates over urban development, and would begin to have an influence over the port's activities.

The Absence of Plans

At the midpoint of the twentieth century, planning in San Francisco was only just becoming an established and influential activity of local government. A professional planner was hired as the first full-time director of planning in 1942, and the newly created agency had a staff of sixteen.[3] The city's first master plan was adopted in 1945.[4] The plan consisted of just three sections—land use, transportation, and public facilities—and there was a definite modernist tinge to its purpose. Planners scaled-up Le Corbusier's description of "houses as machines for living" to the more grandiose "a city is like a gigantic machine. It should run smoothly, like a ball bearing."[5] By the mid-1950s, local forces were starting to coalesce around a number of issues relating to urban development: freeway construction, the spread of high rises, and environmental degradation associated with unmanaged growth. The intensity and character of debate over changes to San Francisco's physical form and its relation to the environment helped planning mature quickly. And as politics in the city focused more on development issues, the planning department's position strengthened and it became enmeshed in the city's power structure. Planning staff grew to twenty or so professional planners and their goals became more progressive. Some revisions and additions were made to the master plan and work on a new zoning code was initiated. The idea that planning was not just about setbacks, apartment blocks, and one-way streets but about establishing a policy framework for the vision of the city's future in a more considered fashion had taken root.

At the time, the port turned a blind eye to planning; it considered itself to be beyond such interference and did not seem to consider itself an agency that should engage in such an endeavor. Nevertheless, the port had begun to formulate ideas for reshaping parts of the northern waterfront around 1950, before urban changes in San Francisco had begun to stir up significant anti-growth activism and the city, through its planning department, had acquired any significant influence over its activities. Not surprisingly, then, the port did not have a comprehensive policy document of its own, and the regulatory structure now associated with the use of its land had yet to be formulated.[6] For all intents and purposes, even public trust limitations on development were not yet an onus. What the port did have were reports from committees and consultants that offered advice on everything from administration and management to infrastructure analyses. While the documents did have some strategic components, primarily related to operations, and offered development programs for physical improvements, they were neither expressions of nor responses to established policy, nor had they been worked out in reference to a larger framework or context. Without this basis, the port began to function (without outwardly acknowledging it) partly as a real-estate agency.

What this situation led to, at least in the 1950s, was essentially a somewhat sporadically implemented capital improvement program. Its endeavors were not infrequently couched in more grandiloquent terms. According to the state's 1951 analysis, the BSHC was moving "toward establishing a *master plan* for development and modernization of the Port of San Francisco."[7] By "master plan" the authors really meant a set of projects with some promise of implementation. It was a facilities plan, or an act of capital project planning, and not a policy plan. As such, the "master plan" initiated projects to repair and upgrade piers, construct sheds and other buildings, and expand facilities. It was a program of limited scope geared to respond to a limited set of forces and was hardly a real "master plan for development." As William Alonso has pointed out, what is of particular importance is not just a plan but also a planning process, of which there had been none.[8]

As planning in the city evolved, the differences between the two sides of the Embarcadero became starker. On the water side was an area outside city jurisdiction that had no land-use plan or policy document addressing its future. On the other side was an agency with increasing power to manage the city's growth and change. As the port added real estate development to its business portfolio, the planning department viewed the waterfront as territory that should be subject to the same set of rules that applied to the rest of the city. The playing field needed to be equal, but it was not. Planning Director James McCarthy openly lamented the inability of his department to respond to port proposals: "In effect, the

Port Authority may allow anything on its property while city property is governed by the overall provisions of a zoning code and often more restrictive provisions that apply to specific redevelopment projects."[9] This invisible but effective form of spatio-political divide emphasized the port's role as an outsider, a state agency attempting to impose its will on the locale in which it operated. Even state analysts, fairly removed from the everyday workings of local agencies, recognized that this stance was "unwise and does a disservice to the Port of San Francisco. The future development of the Port depends not upon the efforts of the Board alone but upon mutual cooperation among several organizations."[10] A few years later, Ebasco would comment that

> the absence of a well-coordinated plan for the water front leads to the dan-ger of conflicts of interests and opposing objectives. Any carefully prepared long-range development plan for an area inures to the benefit of the entire community and should not subordinate the interests of one group in favor of another group. There is a record of misunderstanding among the officials of the City and County of San Francisco and the San Francisco Port Authority.[11]

This kind of bureaucratic disquietude had particularly important implications in the northern waterfront area where the once-strong con-nection between the form and function of port land and the adjoining city land was weakening. While the city's *Zoning Code* could not influence the port directly until 1964, it, and the *Master Plan*, could and did influ-ence what happened adjacent to port property. Determinations regarding height limits and zoning could have an indirect impact on the port by encouraging land uses that might conflict with the maritime and related industrial uses of port land. And insofar as they encouraged businesses with no connection to the port to locate nearby, they helped create a func-tional disconnection between city and waterfront, as happened with the Golden Gateway.[12] In any case, while the jurisdictional separation was real at an administrative level, in practical reality what happened on one side of the line affected the other, in a way mirroring the overall history of the relationship between the city and its port. This situation raised the hackles of port officials, especially Magnin, who felt that the port's inde-pendence was critical and needed to be maintained at all costs.[13]

It was in this environment of contentious interactions that Cyril Magnin honed in on the bottom line; he knew the port needed to make money for its owners in Sacramento. Thus with no little abandon Magnin led the port into the real estate business. But the port's nature as a state agency embedded in the local context complicated its position. When and where the port's attention was focused on supporting maritime activity, its goals and the city's jibed and it could function as an insider of the San Francisco socioeconomic scene. But when it pursued its real estate agenda, especially during the 1950s and 1960s, it demonstrated itself to be something of an outsider with little concern for local values. This was readily apparent in a proliferation of "grand plans"—ill-considered schemes for development of incautious proportions, based on ideas for radical changes to port land uses. The remainder of the chapter will examine some of these proposals, as well as a battle over height limits that had important implications for the port. By the end of the 1960s, the port was faced with a stark lack of success, and began to accept that perhaps engaging in some kind of planning effort could be worthwhile. The chapter concludes with a consultant-led effort to do so, something that involved the port's first effort to coordinate with the planning department.

FROM THE FERRY BUILDING TO THE FUTURE: THE WORLD TRADE CENTER PROPOSAL

Despite real and potential woes, the port in 1950 had not yet reached the point of determining what facilities it should give up to other uses. The idea of pursuing commercial development of northern waterfront property as a way to generate funds to maintain or modernize its maritime facilities was not yet fully formed—with one major exception. In 1946, the 56th Session of the California legislature responded to a proposal "made by a group of public spirited citizens that a group of buildings, to be known as the World Trade Center, be established in San Francisco, for the purposes of fostering and developing world trade."[14] The assembly passed a resolution requesting that the BSHC, because of its inherent interest in commerce, determine whether the World Trade Center (WTC) could be appropriately located on property within its jurisdiction. Thomas Coakly, president of the BSHC at the time, hired Dr. Tadeusz B. Spitzer to analyze the possibility. It nearly goes without saying that Spitzer was most enthusiastic in his conclusion that a WTC on or near the port would help San Francisco become a center of world business. The report was graced with a drawing by famed local architect William Gladstone Merchant that would make any modernist proud.

The California State Assembly was encouraged by the report and by the BSHC's eagerness to provide a home for this beacon of nascent contemporary global commerce. In 1947, it created the WTC as a state agency, the first of its kind in the country. Subsequently, the newly minted agency located its offices in the Ferry Building. The port's new sister agency was eager to leap dramatically into the second half of the century, and the BSHC was there to push them forward, believing that the project would "materially facilitate and stimulate trade between the United States and other nations of the world."[15] It was after all the goal of the BSHC and its boosters to make the Port of San Francisco into the western gateway to a new age of commerce.[16]

The first location suggested for the WTC may have been a shot across the bow for Produce Market businesses, as that is where Merchant laid out his nine-block concept plan, the same location at which the Embarcadero Center and Golden Gateway would later be constructed. But the potential difficulties of acquiring the site and the lengthy condemnation procedures seemed troublesome when compared to the benefits of placing the WTC at San Francisco's front door.[17] So, after further deliberation, the port and the WTC agreed that the best site for the new edifice to market capitalism was right on top of the Ferry Building. By 1950, commuters passing through the Ferry Building constituted a mere trickle. Its main use was for offices. In the calculus of business, this must have meant that a public building held little value, and so it was that a massive new development was proposed to replace the Ferry Building and several other nearby structures and piers (see Figure 3.1).

Blinded by the light of progress, some observers in the late 1940s and early 1950s perceived that the Ferry Building was of the past and could be sacrificed to the future. Always ready to grease the gears of commerce, the *San Francisco Chronicle* editorial board allowed that there would be "sentimental objections raised to the WTC Authority's bold proposal," but that all San Franciscans should give "careful and favorable consideration to the new kind of monument the Authority has proposed."[18] It was the *Chronicle*'s feeling that the project should begin as soon as possible, and that the Embarcadero Freeway, then still just in the planning phase, should be integrated into the project.

Plans for the WTC were lauded in a lecture at the Commonwealth Club

Tinted areas show how the World Trade Center will   ultimately bring a new look to the waterfront.

3.1 Drawing of the World Trade Center Proposal. San Francisco World Trade Center Authority, *Prospectus: San Francisco World Trade Center,* 1951.

of California given by a U.S. Department of Commerce official, who noted, "I can only say that they are imaginative and wonderful, yet thoroughly practical. I am sure the plans will go through completion and that this will be one of the finest monuments in the world to faith in the future of free-flowing world trade—and a monument will be alive and teeming with activity directed toward making San Francisco a truly important center in world trade."[19] Chairman of the WTC Authority Leland Cutler hired Merchant to flesh out the design of the landmark project and by 1951, had started to seek tenants.[20] The 1951 World Trade Center project prospectus offered a "preview to wonderland." It is not a wonder, however, that the proposed 3,000,000-square-foot development centered on a thirty-story tower was never completed. Proclamations of greatness gushed from many officials, including Governor Earl Warren, San Francisco mayor Elmer E. Robinson, the U.S. Secretary of Commerce, and even Nelson Rockefeller.[21] The WTC was intended to provide technical and transaction services, translators and interpreters, and a "pleasant and convenient" surrounding in which foreign and American businessman could meet and dispatch the world's business. Yet the high modern design, which incorporated "international" restaurants, a reference library, shops, offices, and "sheltered plazas," was not to be. Public outcry was fierce, and early on in the process, board of supervisors member Marvin Lewis exclaimed that "they might as well tear down the Eiffel Tower in Paris or the Statue of Liberty in New York."[22]

Not one to give up easily, B. J. Feigenbaum, president of the World Trade Center Authority, insisted that "we have not lost sight of the long-range plan for a group of center buildings in the Ferry Building area."[23] But by 1955, support for the revenue bonds that were required to fund the project had evaporated and attention was directed to the plans for the Embarcadero Freeway, which were close to implementation.[24] A double-decker freeway structure running through the site would certainly have made Merchant's design impossible. Thus he was ultimately limited to renovation work that provided the WTC with permanent offices in the north wing of Ferry Building.[25] The landmark could now add state-sponsored speculation to the list of things it had survived.

DREAMING UP THE WATERFRONT OF THE FUTURE: EMBARCADERO CITY

About the same time that the WTC project was being drawn up and then scaled back, the California Department of Finance, at the request of Magnin and the BSHC, was performing a management survey of the port, published in 1955. Buried among 109 suggestions for improving port operations was the suggestion that "facilities not needed and not economical to maintain should be eliminated unless other revenue-producing uses can be found."[26] The report also included a section entitled "Property Management," which stated that "there is a need for broader and more complete *long-range planning* of physical improvements and land use, for development of written policies and procedures."[27] The authors pointed out that it was impossible to create a clear picture of how the port made decisions about projects or how those projects were prioritized. They also recognized that the "complexity of economic factors affecting (the port's) operation make the existence of a sound master plan essential to good management."[28] This master plan should contain an analysis of the port's economic and shipping status, a system of maps, project folders, and a description of capital outlay. It would be fifteen years, however, before planning would become a major and effective tool to be used by local actors and agents in adjusting to external, economic pressures on the landscape.

The Department of Finance report was not the kind of long-range policy and decision-guiding document that is the foundation for true planning, but it was the first official utterance regarding the port's need to develop some kind of land-use and development policy. The Department of Finance placed responsibility for developing such a plan directly in the lap of the director and his staff; there was no mention of establishing a planning section. The analysis also suggested "that when the Board is considering large capital outlay expenditures for projects which depend for their success upon complex economic factors, it should at the same time examine the advisability of obtaining expert advice and consultation. . . . The Port of San Francisco should have the benefit of such analysis before committing itself to large expenditures for capital improvements."[29] So, while the Department of Finance study did not outline policy plans or generate potential project schema, it did suggest obliquely a path to take: identify old and uneconomical facilities, determine other revenue-generating uses for them, prepare a "master plan for development," and, when capital is available to fund projects, engage consultants to advise the port on a course of action. All of these steps would be taken in just a few years, in the process of trying to conjure an "Embarcadero City" out of the planks of old piers.

The decline that began to creep through the port in the 1950s, especially in the northern waterfront, was fully apparent by the mid-1960s, and it created a potentially fertile place to sprout new urban functions. Decrepit piers, vacant sheds, and seldom-used Belt Line Railroad spurs all presented opportunities for development on a huge scale. So, in February 1959, just a few months after voters approved the $50 million State Harbor Bond, the port authority unveiled another audacious concept—Embarcadero City, which was a proposal for "sweeping changes in the direction of San Francisco's future waterfront development."[30] Cyril Magnin was not a successful businessman and administrator for nothing; he saw opportunity all along "his" northern waterfront. He and his architects were given to thinking big, and Embarcadero City was a monumental vision, a grand concept plan sketched into the realm of the possible by John S. Bolles and Ernst Born (Fig. 3.2).[31]

The Embarcadero City scheme was the fabrication of unrestrained modernist dreams—a panorama of apartment buildings, hotels, shopping plazas, offices, large restaurants, theaters, hotels, arenas, boat harbors, and convention halls stretching from Aquatic Park to the Ferry Building, that would "make San Francisco the most beautiful city in the world."[32] At its unveiling in early 1959, Magnin raved that it would be "a new frontier within the city that can help San Francisco grow into the greatest metropolis in the world."[33] The plan elicited gushing praise and Governor Brown, also present at the unveiling, described it as "bold and imaginative, the type of thinking we need in California" (Fig. 3.3).[34] State senator Eugene McAteer called it "the greatest forward step in San Francisco's history since the rebuilding of the city after the 1906 earthquake-fire."[35] Reaction to the project from the *Chronicle*'s editorial board revealed a feeling of trust in the port and lent to the project perhaps more credence than it deserved: "Here is a waterfront project which derives not from some dream-center, but one which is brought forward by the San Francisco Port Authority itself."[36] The tomorrow-land project, also supported by Mayor Christopher, was to commence in two years.

Magnin was careful to stress that Embarcadero City would be realized by private investors and developers and that it would not be implemented as one giant construction project. In fact, he stated publicly that the port's 1958 bond money was to be spent on southern waterfront projects, disassociating those funds from Embarcadero City. The resulting development he argued further, would guarantee that the port would always be self-sustaining.[37] But ultimately, despite the stance taken by the *Chronicle*'s editorial board that the city should do everything possible to bring it to fruition, Embarcadero City would fade away. The failure of two projects at the end of the 1960s, discussed later, ensured its demise. The plan was too general, too

3.2 What the future could look like—Embarcadero City compared to the waterftront c. 1960. Courtesy of the San Francisco History Center, San Francisco Public Library.

3.3 Cyril Magnin (left) and Governor Brown pointing the way to the future. Courtesy of the San Francisco History Center, San Francisco Public Library.

unformed, and relied entirely on private impetus to invest capital without a structure or project prospectus, or any real development program. That the port's own consultants did not consider it as part of a plan for action probably helped stymie it.

Nevertheless, two pieces of legislation important not only to the project but also to the port's future came out of the bid for Embarcadero City. In June 1959, Governor Brown signed two bills brought to him by state senator McAteer. The first remedied restrictions on the port's commercial leasing abilities by allowing the port to enter into ninety-nine-year leases with developers and future tenants, extended from the forty years then permitted. Because the State of California does not allow the sale of land held in the public trust, the ability to offer long-term leases was especially important for attracting development.[38] This change was considered critical for launching the Embarcadero City concept. The second measure was labeled "Waterfront City" by *Portside News* and described as the creation of an eighty-block area wherein the port would be able to combine existing commercial and navigational uses with privately financed retail, restaurants, apartments, marinas, and myriad other activities.[39] This was achieved through an amendment to the *California Harbors and Navigation Code*, which added Section 3000(d) in 1959, just as Embarcadero City started to glimmer brightly on the horizon. The amendment gave the port authority the power to "devote as much of its property as it finds not required for . . . [maritime use] . . . to such development and use as will, in the finding of the authority, yield maximum profits, when leased to private persons or agencies, to be used in the furtherance of commerce and navigation."[40] While these bills did little to turn the Embarcadero City idea into reality, they provided the port with the authority to pursue development of non-maritime uses with little outside interference.

Even though Embarcadero City never achieved any real footing, the port held to the general concept for a number of years. One consequence was that it brought to light in undeniable fashion the port authority's thinking about their waterfront, if only as sketches and models.[41] Magnin asserted repeatedly that one of the port's priorities was to support, if not expand, its shipping business. But in describing the vision for Embarcadero City, he recognized that much of the northern waterfront was not capable of accommodating new methods of cargo handling. Thus the Embarcadero City proposal made clear for the first time that the port's intent was to devote the southern waterfront to maritime activities, while north of the Bay Bridge it advertised the possibilities of a new, ultra modern, waterfront and gave the public a first sample of (unwritten) port land-use policy for areas abandoned by maritime businesses. The result was a financial scheme reflected in a spatial pattern; rents and leases from commercial development of the northern waterfront would be used to support further enhancement and modernization of shipping facilities in the southern waterfront. The financial linkage between commercial development and maritime activity would become particularly critical after the port was returned to the city.

The Embarcadero City scheme helped establish an important, long-running discourse—that shipping must be preserved, but to do so required leveraging the possibilities of real estate development. Moreover, the goal of such development was to produce a sort of triumphal architecture and design that would help San Francisco lay claim to a new place in the global urban hierarchy. Embarcadero City signaled to the world that the city was ready to embrace new modes of capital accumulation and investment associated with the postindustrial economy. It was made a highly symbolic vision, and perhaps more meaningful, because Embarcadero City was to spring as new life from the spaces of the old modes of production and distribution—an urban-organic cycle of death and resurrection. Nevertheless, as with the World Trade Center before it, a vision it would remain.

Undaunted by the inability to make Embarcadero City an immediate reality, and with bond money in one hand and architectural sketches in the other, the port authority took the Department of Finance's advice and engaged Ebasco to perform a thorough analysis of the port, "to see if future pier construction and the Embarcadero development was [sic] 'pointing in the right direction.'"[42] The 1959 study was entitled *Facilities Improvement Survey for the San Francisco Port Authority*. The heart of the report was a pier-by-pier, lot-by-lot survey of the port's facilities and an evaluation of their condition, general usefulness, and contribution to the port's income. But while the report was primarily a technical document, along with several specific recommendations pertaining to operations and facilities, it made one very important general recommendation: that the port concentrate its cargo-handling facilities south of the Bay Bridge and promote commercial development north of the Bay Bridge.[43] Ebasco argued that the port could remain an important cargo port, but that over time, cargo operations would abandon the northern waterfront, either because the facilities were or would be outmoded and were not worth upgrading, or because land-use changes and congestion would impair the efficient movement of goods.

The report suggested configurations for potential new facilities in the southern waterfront and evaluated possible commercial developments on port property in the northern waterfront. The latter was considered with a twenty-year horizon in mind for phasing out most cargo operations, the typical time span covered by contemporary planning policy documents. Figure 3.4 is a map showing the consultant's take on what parts of the northern waterfront could be used for various commercial developments. The report averred that:

> the solution to the Port's need to (a) provide more effective facilities for ship-ping and (b) improve its operating profit rests in constructing new facilities, and in eliminating all of the expenses associated with over-aged, ineffective properties, including elimination of certain operations, such as, possibly, the Belt Line Railroad. It is also clear that some of the properties which may be no longer needed by the Port Authority for shipping activities can be used for other purposes on a profitable basis.[44]

Ebasco recognized some of the constraints that accrued to development on port property, for instance the cost of having to drive deep piles and provide other expensive substructure associated with new construction, whether on piers or on land. Thus the report observed that the value of the land would be best taken advantage of if developed intensively.[45] Some of the possibilities the report outlined included constructing 400,000 square feet of office space near the Ferry Building; providing substantial amounts of parking; and building apartments in the area between Fisher-man's Wharf and what would become the Golden Gateway. Ebasco's sug-gestions for developing cargo facilities were more serious and detailed, and included guidelines and actual design proposals for new facilities.

Clearly, their analysis paralleled Magnin's vision for the northern water-front, hinting at some level that the consultants may have been ghost-writing for him, as evidenced in these expressions of enthusiasm for the general idea:

> There can be no doubt that if water-front properties not needed for shipping activities can be consolidated in one or more contiguous areas or strips, an opportunity is afforded to San Francisco to create one of the finest water-front developments in the world. The natural harbor, the international status of San Francisco, the ethnic mixtures of the City's peoples, and San Fran-

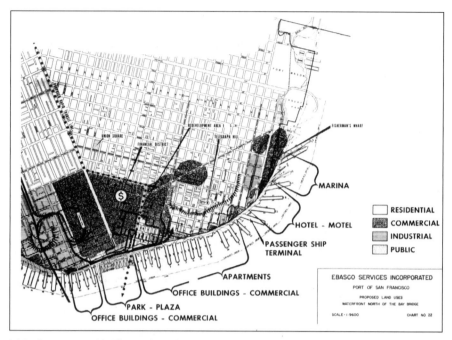

RESIDENTIAL
COMMERCIAL
INDUSTRIAL
PUBLIC

EBASCO SERVICES INCORPORATED
PORT OF SAN FRANCISCO
PROPOSED LAND USES
WATERFRONT NORTH OF THE BAY BRIDGE
SCALE - 1:9600   CHART NO. 22

3.4 Land uses proposed by Ebasco. Ebasco Services Incorporated, *Port of San Francisco Facilities Improvement Survey for the San Francisco Port Authority.* San Francisco Port Authority, 1959.

cisco's position as the "gateway" to the Far East all compound to provide a rare opportunity to make San Francisco a truly famous city among the great cities of the world.[46]

Furthermore, "with the possible exception of the appearance of the Embarcadero Freeway structure itself, no significant barrier exists to limit the most effective development for the water-front area *after* provision has been made for shipping activities."[47]

The press accepted as perfectly reasonable that the port should support activities other than strictly industrial/maritime ones. But Ebasco never evaluated the Embarcadero City concept or even referred directly to "Embarcadero City." In fact, the only direct reference to plans for the northern waterfront was in the 1959 Summary Report of their analysis, wherein Ebasco described the Bolles Plan for Embarcadero City as "the seed upon which private capital will come forward with interesting approaches to the utilization of the area."[48] Furthermore, their support for rebuilding the northern waterfront was not unqualified; Ebasco noted that some facilities in the northern waterfront were still productive and should be maintained to serve the shipping needs of the port. While they suggested that commercial development of the northern waterfront was appropriate, they also stated quite plainly that "the absence of an up-to-date development plan for the San Francisco waterfront area makes it difficult to establish the most effective base which the San Francisco Port Authority should use to develop long-range plans of its own, particularly plans concerned with alternate uses of existing properties."[49] This statement also helps put their comments regarding the Bolles Plan in context: Embarcadero City was not itself taken seriously as a plan for development. Ebasco also noted that it was impossible to come up with a final plan for the port's unused land because such a plan would depend on the unpredictable interests of private capital.[50] Their assertion also pointed to one of the main weaknesses of the Embarcadero City concept, that it did not sketch out the financial picture by, for instance, identifying likely investors or prospective tenants.

The report was important primarily because, for the first time, a port document included suggestions that amounted to land-use policy—a long-term vision of the form, function, and spatial arrangement of the port. Of course, there are crucial differences between Ebasco's suggestions and actual policy. Consultant reports are advisory documents and do not carry the weight of policy or a plan. Planning policy is generally broader in scope (even while it may be geographically focused), undergoes staff evaluation and modification, is subject to some form of public and interagency review, and is adopted by an official public body, giving it legal standing. The process of developing policy also involves vetting it with existing legislation, ordinances, or resolutions under development, and complying with directions from executive offices, administrative requirements, the city's charter, and findings by the city attorney. Ebasco's report did not deeply investigate commercial development, include real land-use policies to help guide decisions, describe implementation strategies, or even develop pro forma programs for commercial development. Nor was it vetted in public in any meaningful way.

OUT OF SCALE IN FISHERMAN'S WHARF

Concerned that none of the money from the port's 1958 bond had been targeted for their corner of the waterfront, Fisherman's Wharf merchants

3.5 Sketch for a new Fisherman's Wharf by Bolles and Born. San Francisco Port Authority, *A Plan for Fisherman's Wharf*, 1961.

pushed for a study of their own. To their eventual chagrin, they got what they wanted. Hot on the heels of Embarcadero City, the port authority once again called on John S. Bolles and Ernest Born to conceive a master plan for Fisherman's Wharf. This was a chance to use a cornerstone piece of the waterfront to bring Embarcadero City one step closer to reality. Published in 1961, it was entitled simply *A Plan for Fisherman's Wharf*, and was indeed much more of a plan than Embarcadero City (which did not get much beyond that most seductive of architects' carrots—the scale model) (Fig. 3.5). But while it was a more geographically focused endeavor than Embarcadero City, it still fitted the modernist mold of "bigger and bolder is better," and it emanated an eagerness, a feeling that something grand was at hand: "The Embarcadero is always changing. What is the future of this legendary water site in the next score of years? The clue lies in Fisherman's Wharf, the first of the Port Authority properties to be planned for redevelopment and for new uses under the guidance of the San Francisco Port Authority."[51]

The plan (which was really a development prospectus in policy plan clothing) called for relocating the fishing fleet and fish-processing and fish-packing facilities to a new pier and constructing a "Palazzo Del Pesce" that would serve wholesale dealers and shippers and contain a retail fish market that would host cooking demonstrations and exhibitions related to fish and fishing. The plan, ever grandiloquent, stated that "through brilliant and imaginative design, the fish market could be the most spectacular and popular feature at the wharf—except for the fishing boats . . . (and it would be) a fusion of carousel and palace."[52] To complete the vision "a great convention hall to serve the entire Bay area and northern California" was proposed.[53] The plan included city property as well, for which it proposed a mix of commercial uses, parking garages, lecture halls, museums, and pedestrian malls. Pedestrian malls, of course, would soon be all the rage in downtown revitalization across America. While quite mesmerizing, this kind of fantastical plan threatened the existing character of the waterfront in the most direct way possible—with complete evisceration—and put some policy makers in an awkward position. On the one hand, state senator Eugene McAteer was determinedly pushing legislation that would advance Embarcadero City, on the other hand, as president of the Fisherman's Wharf Merchants Association, he expressed strong reservations about the encroachment of business not related to the fishing industry and mused that "when you . . . wash away the charm and dignity of the area, you are ruining San Francisco."[54]

The plan was never implemented. Local fishermen, understandably concerned, barraged Magnin with angry phone calls, forcing him to distance himself from the plan. He did so by saying that some of its elements would not be undertaken for years, and that others were probably inappropriate.[55] Another issue helped keep *A Plan for Fisherman's Wharf* on the shelf. Trustees of the Maritime Museum were about to commence work on a state park, referred to as Project X, which included restoration of the historic Haslett Warehouse (proposed for demolition in the Bolles and Born plan), and creation of open space and a historic schooner display. The project would end up creating part of what is now Aquatic Park and the Aquatic Park Historic District, later contained within the San Francisco Maritime National Historic Park.[56] The emphasis on public space and the absence of a development footprint did not jibe with the proposed concept for Fisherman's Wharf.

The plan also ran afoul of Mayor George Christopher, who was frustrated by the lack of coordination between the port authority and the city. Mayor Christopher scolded Magnin and the port authority, telling them that the plan was in violation of city policy and that it was imperative that they consult the planning department before pursuing any part of the plan.[57] This was another skirmish in what would become a protracted, if sporadic, inter-jurisdictional turf battle. Government agencies were not the only ones at cross-purposes. Local actors were also divided over what to do in Fisherman's Wharf. Merchants were in favor of the plan, at least initially, while those involved in fishing and related businesses were adamantly against it. One set of advocates sought to tap into money and a process that originated from the top-down sphere of the state and its potential development partners, others rallied against it. The failure of *A Plan for Fisherman's Wharf* attests both to the need for an established planning process that leads to publicly informed and formally adopted plans and to the problem of creating them when groups are at odds.[58] Unfortunately, intractability has characterized many parties involved in Fisherman's Wharf. In the half century since the plan was released, it has proved to be very difficult to create enough consensus to support successful planning for the wharf.[59]

This account also provides us with an example of competition over the use value of a place. The plan proposed dramatic change for an area that was functioning well for its main users, fishermen and local businesses. The proponents for change attempted to leverage a discourse built on an image of modern commerce and spectacle, even commerce *as* spectacle, in order to capitalize on potential exchange (and symbolic) value. This was quite different from the characterization of the Produce Market as decaying and in need of new life. Such an "organic trope," as Timothy Gibson might describe it, can be a powerful part of the rhetoric employed in support of urban redevelopment.[60] In the case of the wharf, political power favored the current users of the space, in part perhaps because it could not be characterized as dead or dying and in need of resuscitation.

Fear of Heights

Modernist urban visions began to blur in the 1960s as San Franciscans aligned themselves against pressures that threatened to alter the landscape. Activists fought proposals to extend the freeway system to Golden Gate Park, others organized to face the SFRA, whose powers Justin Herman used to chilling effect, and lances were lowered at a spate of new office buildings.[61] One especially important aspect of the rising tide of grassroots activism was concern for public open space and access to the bay.[62]

In the face of an increasingly extensive and massive built environment, the bay as a natural place, a respite from the urban fabric, was becoming increasingly important to a growing spectrum of people (as was the amount and quality of the water itself). While some rather zealous views were formulated—at one point, there was a push to replace the Ferry Building with an open plaza—there were legitimate fears that San Francisco was on the verge of privatizing its waterfront. The Embarcadero was a public right-of-way, which, at the very least, brought people in direct proximity to the bay and to whatever hustle-bustle adjoined it. Transit sheds and bulkhead buildings served as physical reminders of what the waterfront was, or used to be, and their modest profiles where not overwhelming. One could walk up any of the many vertically oriented streets that run into the Embarcadero and, from up high, look back over low-slung waterfront structures to uninterrupted vistas of the Golden Gate.[63]

Embarcadero City and the other proposals described above threatened to destroy the physical characteristics that made the waterfront approachable and recognizably related to the natural environment, at least in practical ways. They also heralded a different kind of separation from the waterfront. San Francisco grew out of its waterfront, something that has figured prominently in its citizens' collective awareness of its history. This commonly held view of urban historical origins created a strong public connection between San Franciscans and their waterfront, one that persists today. If the maritime activities that helped establish San Francisco were to disappear and their physical and symbolic markers were to be replaced by commercial and office developments, not only would a large and essential part of the city's built environment be destroyed but some history would be as well. Thus both economically driven "grand schemes" and individual proposals, especially when considered cumulatively, were forces of privatization *and* nullification, a part of the modernist vision that, with little respect for natural setting or collective memory, would wash away the flotsam and jetsam of leftover (yet still important in the public mind) urban places and replace them with the clean lines and bold geometry of the socially controlling and infertile future city.

But the modernist recasting of the waterfront that Magnin and his consultants envisaged could only have been pursued in the absence of local control over its property, and this was about to change. And so it was that a particularly significant skirmish over building heights started on the hills at the northern edge of San Francisco that would envelope the waterfront below. More than a clash over building form and topography, the fight was over private and public values in the experience of the city.

As an urban place, San Francisco has always been in the shadow of New York, the only city in the United States with a higher population density. San Francisco aspires to many New York qualities, but the height and intensity of its built environment are not among them. Indeed, San Franciscans know well the cries to prevent the city from being "Manhattanized." They have echoed through many of the city's development battles and political disputes.[64] An early, if not the earliest, invocation of New York as a warning was made in 1960 by planning director James R. McCarthy. What moved him to speak out was not concern for the loss of industry to new residential construction in the northern waterfront, but that proposed new development was too dense, the new buildings too tall. The circumstances prompted McCarthy to suggest that "San Francisco's zoning laws will have to be changed to prevent construction of a 'China Wall' of skyscrapers along its waterfront. . . . 'We want to avoid what has happened in lower Manhattan in New York, where views of the bay are blocked by high rising buildings.'"[65] His comments likely encouraged certain citizens' groups, especially members of the Russian Hill Improvement Association (RHIA), who were at the center of one of the city's early battles over high-rise development.

The contention over height limits in the northern part of San Francisco ensued from a proposal to construct twin apartment towers on the site of the Souther Warehouse (once the old Fontana spaghetti factory), just above Ghirardelli Square and Fisherman's Wharf. The plan for two seventeen-story (about 170 feet), slightly curved buildings became the target of residents living on the hill, whose views, and sense of propriety, were being challenged by the new, modernist structures. With membership consisting of many upper-class San Franciscans, the improvement association had unusually deep pockets, enabling it to hire a law firm to take on the developers.[66] The firm, an outfit with offices on Montgomery Street in the heart of downtown, was instructed to "take any legal action necessary to prevent the apartments from being built," according to their representative, none other than Caspar W. Weinberger.[67] Despite being among the wealthiest and most influential in the city, Russian Hill residents were unable to halt the Fontana project; their mobilization came too late. The apartments were built and, even today, are oft-cited by locals as an example of heinous, topography-flattening, view blocking, un-San Francisco design (Fig. 3.6).[68]

3.6 Fontana Apartments today. Photograph by author.

The fight did not stop with the failure at Fontana Apartments. Instead, Russian Hill residents and their attorney were galvanized to support the idea of a 40-foot height limit in a larger geographic area so as to prevent future development fiascos. Director McCarthy had pointed out early on that opposition to Fontana Apartments was likely to touch off a larger fight over zoning, and he was right. Initially, McCarthy himself hesitated at the idea of forty feet, which restricts buildings to three or four stories, and wondered aloud if fifty or fifty-five feet would be better. Nevertheless, in June 1961, his bosses on the planning commission, pressured by RHIA and a growing group of supporters, voted to impose a blanket 40-foot height limit on a 100-block area of the northern waterfront and gave department staff two years to come up with a more refined solution.[69] The resolution was forwarded to the board of supervisors and sent to the Public Buildings, Lands, and City Planning Committee, where it languished for a number of months.

Meanwhile, Weinberger cleverly established a discourse that made Russian Hill residents' problem a larger, more public issue. Russian Hill residents should not be thought of as engaged in a "selfish move to save our own views." Rather, he argued, their crusade was to prevent a "Chinese Wall" and establish a "flexible height limit that will allow progress but not destroy views or the sense of being near the bay." Their fight was "the start of a city-wide campaign to preserve San Francisco's waterfront beauty."[70] Perhaps feeling vulnerable to criticism that their motives were selfish, they worked hard over the course of a year to demonstrate broad public support by forging a large coalition that included twenty-two improvement groups and neighborhood associations from around the city and even beyond it. One result of their effort was to be able to present to officials a roll of eight thousand signatures in support of the 40-foot height limit.[71]

Of course, the attempt to restrict height limits in a large area raised the stakes substantially and thus drew the attention and ire of the wider development community. A coalition was formed that included the San Francisco Real Estate Board, the influential Building Owners and Managers Association, the Associated General Contractors, and the San Francisco Building and Trades Council (an AFL-CIO affiliate), among others. This group attempted to establish its own discursive framework by naming themselves the Citizens' Progress Committee and retaining another Montgomery Street law firm to provide them the necessary rhetorical punch. However, they were not served well by their counsel, Joseph Martin, Jr. He argued brashly that people who wanted to restrict height limits were interested in beauty, not economics, a real misread of the temperaments coloring the debate. The same point was made later by the executive secretary of the San Francisco Real Estate Board, who, by complaining that the Planning Department's analysis "is concerned with beauty, with overcrowding, even with sunshine and shadows, but not with economics" unabashedly gave voice to the narrow prerogatives of capital.[72]

Insistence that the logic of real estate economics provided the most rational and objective foundation for decisions regarding building height left most board members unmoved. In fact, they were quick to point out that the Citizens' Progress Committee was advocating on behalf of *their* own self-interest. The RHIA could have been accused of the same thing, but linking their argument to the wider concerns of the community created an effective shield. In a different time, the idea of development as progress for the whole community might have been a persuasive counter, but such was not the case here.

Martin was forced to maneuver behind the scenes. The result of his machinations was to convince board member Clarissa McMahon to pull the height-limit proposal out of committee and schedule it for a full board meeting, before public hearings could be scheduled. Martin reasoned that expediency was required for such an urgent issue. His real concern, though, was that the members of the San Francisco Public Buildings, Lands, and City Planning Committee supported the temporary 40-foot height limit, and he thought it would be advantageous to get the issue to the full board before it was endorsed by the committee and before the planning department could complete its study. Supervisor McMahon was quickly and fiercely lambasted for what was to many an inexplicable action. Even Mayor Christopher commented on the move, and, just six months after registering his indignation at their original vote, sided with his commission: "I think it is absolutely imperative that nothing be done without finding out the considered opinions of the planning department and the experts who are working on the job."[73]

The mayor's intervention was a boon to the cause of height limits, and a setback to Citizens' Progress Committee. Supervisor McMahon soon recanted her decision and the proposal went back to committee. When the measure was forwarded again to the full board in May 1962, the vote was 9-0 (with two members absent) to impose 40-foot height limits across the northern waterfront in accordance with the planning department's recommendation, pending completion of its study. Predictably, the *San Francisco Chronicle* published a brief editorial characterizing the 40-foot height limits as a straightjacket, and the board as being wise to make them temporary. The *Chronicle* was perhaps the last holdout, though, as even SPUR broke ranks and sided with the planning department's height-limit proposal (though, to be fair, that decision presaged SPUR's evolution into a more complexly motivated organization).

In October 1963, the planning department released its report and recommended that the 40-foot height limit be made permanent for much of the northern waterfront, with higher limits allowed in other areas. The role of the Fontana Apartments in fueling the contention over heights was underscored by Planning Commissioner James Kearney when he commented on the report: "In the Fontana Apartments land has been exploited by builders for the benefit of a few, with complete disregard for the welfare of the rest of the community."[74] Despite complaints that the uniform height limits were crude and would lead to unimaginative development, the planning commission approved the proposal and sent its resolution to the board of supervisors.

Importantly, this found the planning department, an agent of the local state, giving official voice to and therefore promoting to a wide audience, ideas based on aspects of the public interest—that certain things, especially enjoyment of nature, including views, are the rights of the whole citizenry, not something to be given over to private real estate interests and the locally situated machinery of capitalistic urban development. This should not be a surprise to those familiar with the urban planning field at the time, especially in the Bay Area, given the influence of the Department of City and Regional Planning at the University of California, Berkeley. Even as early as 1939, the goal of Telesis, a group of local architects and city planners that included a founder of the Berkeley's planning school, had as their purpose "the betterment of the physical environment and its social purposes."[75]

About the time that the planning department was working on its report, a softening of the "hard line" between the port and the city occurred when port commissioner Cyril Magnin and Mayor Christopher cooperated to persuade the state legislature to increase the city's influence over the port. This was done through an amendment to the *California Harbors and Navigation Code*. In 1963, the state legislature added Section 3000.7, which stated that "the [Port] authority shall request the City and County of San Francisco to provide zoning ordinances for property the authority intends to lease . . . and the city and county is hereby authorized to prepare and adopt precise plans and zoning plans for such property."[76] Of course, zoning determines land uses and building heights, among other things. There were three important caveats. First, this applied only to land that the port declared surplus to its maritime needs and that it intended to lease. Second, the zoning had to allow the port to use the property to generate maximum profits consistent with surrounding land-use pattern. That is, if the port land in question was near city land zoned for office development, then it too should be zoned to allow office. Third, if the port authority did not like how it was zoned, it could appeal the ordinance to the state's planning advisory committee. Even with these exceptions, the clash over heights in the northern waterfront quickly took on new importance for the port because there was now the potential to limit its own property development.[77] The debate over heights was a city issue, however, and the port had to stay on the sidelines even though it would be affected by the outcome.

The final board hearing was held on February 3, 1964; attendees, including newly elected mayor John Shelley, packed the space. The mayor's presence was an unusual indication of the importance of the subject. No public comment was allowed. Letters from the two opposing attorneys, now just figureheads because the debate had been elevated to such a large scale, were read into the record. Weinberger finalized his argument with a little exaggeration, urging support for the measure because "it will preserve for future generations one of the priceless assets of San Francisco, the *whole relationship of the city to the Bay* . . . and particularly, the views enjoyed by the public from publicly owned lands, such as Coit Tower and other city-owned recreational spaces."[78] He also invoked basic planning principles and the city's *Master Plan*:

> Much more than that, it is a proposal designed to prevent serious overcrowding, heavy additional traffic, police and fire protection problems, all of which go with the unplanned and uncontrolled building of high rise apartments in areas where the City's Master Plan specifically declares they should not be built. The Master Plan has for years provided that the height of buildings should generally follow the contour of the land, and that low rise buildings should be built on the low lands, such as the northern waterfront, and high rise at the tops of hills so that the loss of views, etc., will be minimized.[79]

Similarly, lower heights would "preserve to the general public the depth and breadth of view, the clear delineation of land forms and the sweeping panoramas that are the present heritage and greatest asset of San Francisco."[80]

For his part, Martin's counter-argument was mainly a reiteration of comments made by Livingston and Blayney, the planning firm he and the Citizens' Progress Committee hired to support their position. Essentially, their role was to suggest to the planning department how the agency might undertake its analysis. After complaining that the planning department ignored all advice, guaranteeing a single outcome, they proposed allowing Planned Unit Developments (PUDs) as exceptions to the height limits. PUDs were at the time a new tool intended to relax code requirements to allow "imaginative development of large parcels of land without the necessity of rigid adherence to the existing zoning classifications."[81] Typically, PUDs require approval by planning commissions or similar governing bodies. Their suggestion did not make an impression, but the allowance was made, although probably unnecessarily because the port could appeal imposition of height limits to the state Planning Advisory Committee.

In the end, it was not much of a contest. Supervisor Roger Boas explained his support for the measure in a blunt characterization of the Citizens' Progress Committee: "Their concern is, and must be, with personal economics. Ours is the broader view. They're eying the waterfront property as children do a piece of candy. . . . I don't blame them. It's one of the choicest pieces of real estate in the United States. . . . We're putting a sign on our hills and waterfront that says 'not for sale.'"[82] And according to Supervisor Jack Morrison, "No proposal before this Board ever had more public support."[83] Height limits were adopted in February 1964 in a 9–1 vote, with one absentee. The momentous decision reflected the ability of a coalition of local interest groups, with support from the planning department, to preserve the character of a place, and at least some of its public value, in opposition to lobbying from powerful real estate interests and other local representatives of capitalist development, as well as organized labor. Labor was, and often is now, in the somewhat conflicted position of supporting capital investment to create jobs for union workers. It is beyond the scope of this work to address satisfactorily the role of labor in development, but we will see another example in the next chapter.

So, initially sparked by the concerns of a few for their private views, the threat of building along the waterfront stimulated opposition from a confluence of interests that were mutually supportive. After all, if the private view from a house on Russian Hill were blocked, then public views from streets would also be casualties of development. The public outcry was also part of a wider concern with open space, and the presence of nature in the city and around the bay. Indeed, struggles such as this can be placed in the larger context both of the development of the environmental movement that produced groups such as Save the Bay, and of anti-growth coalitions from which sprang San Francisco Tomorrow (SFT).[84] That these powerful movements loomed large in the background helps explain the board's unusually lopsided vote. For our purposes, what is most important about this event is that the 40-foot height limit would severely limit the port's prospects for recreating its northern waterfront, especially once it became a city agency and would not have recourse to appeals. As many developers will argue, forty feet of development potential will just not produce enough profit to subsidize uses like container terminals or nonprofitable things such as parks.

TOPPLING A TOWER

In 1964, the same year new height limits were established for most of the northern waterfront, Northern Waterfront Associates (NWA), a consortium of influential San Franciscans led by ex-planning commission president Roger D. Lapham, Jr., came forward with ideas for an enormous development called International Market Square, located at the base of another hill full of activists. Their project, however, was in an area newly designated for 84-foot heights. NWA had quietly purchased about twenty acres of land between the Embarcadero and the base of Telegraph Hill, stretching from Pier 35 south to Pier 17. At one time, this area was the heart of the city's first warehousing district. In the mid-1960s, it was home to a number of historic structures, including the gold rush-era Sea Wall Warehouse that once served clipper ships. NWA asserted that the structure was too deteriorated for reuse, and despite intervention by the Junior League and a bevy of activists, preservationists, and historians, eventually bulldozed it in 1969.[85] However, as the first phase of their project (the only part to be completed), they did in fact rehabilitate the two historic National Ice and Cold Storage Company's warehouses, together known as the Ice House.

International Market Square, was to be a collection of halls, markets, showrooms, shops, restaurants, exhibition space, and a hotel that would tower 184 feet high. Despite being more than twice the existing height limit, politicos and boosters greeted the idea with enthusiasm. "Mayor Alioto, like his Port Commission, reportedly was delighted with the International Market Square. 'The Northern Waterfront Associates' plan is very important to us,' he said. It is going to be complimentary [sic] to some larger plans we have for the whole waterfront.'"[86] Sponsors and supporters of this eight-block, 15.4-acre leap into urban destiny characterized the area it was to be built in as a collection of dilapidated "ancient brick buildings and ill-lit alleys," ignoring their historical importance.[87] In fact, Lapham claimed that property owners in the area were actually grateful that someone was willing to take the property off their hands.[88] Roger Kent, vice president of the Telegraph Hill Dwellers Association (THD) and the main spokesman for a group called POW (Preserve Our Waterfront), was concerned not just with the view from Telegraph hill but that of Telegraph Hill itself, and he called for drastic changes to the project. THD was becoming a powerful voice in the affairs of its neighborhood. Founded in 1954, it helped establish the 40-foot height limit along the waterfront and played a critical role in halting the construction of the Embarcadero Freeway.[89]

Allan B. Jacobs, who succeeded James McCarthy as planning director, also voiced many criticisms of the project and insisted that its scale and design be rethought.[90] Typical of his tenure, Jacobs stood his ground in negotiations with the sponsor's architectural "dream team" (which included famed landscape architect Lawrence Halprin). The result included a reduction of height to the existing 84-four-foot height limit and design changes that would break up the structure's monolithic bulk. A shorter building at the base of the hill would also respect the natural, physical form of the landscape, planners argued.[91] Jacobs ended up supporting the project because the sponsors made all of the alterations he requested, and because NWA was required to enter into a set of special concessions in return for which the city would vacate the sections of street needed by the project.

While the sponsors made significant changes, including the addition of retail shops along the Embarcadero and roof gardens, the original design apparently was burned into the minds of its opponents. Karl Kortum, president of the San Francisco Maritime Museum, maritime historian, and waterfront activist, called the changes "frosting" and pointed out that it was still a "wholesale project, dedicated to the secrecy that has to prevail between wholesaler and the merchant buying from him. The exclusion of the public is a necessary evil."[92] POW and Kent also accused Jacobs of sabotaging his own planning process, because the project had started the approval process while planning studies for the northern waterfront were still underway (see below). The Telegraph Hill Dwellers decided to request a height reduction in the area to forty feet, which was rejected.[93]

Not easily dissuaded, THD sued the city, claiming that the city could not sell public streets without going to bid. The actions of the THD frustrated Mayor Alioto, who asserted that "forty people can't stop a $100 million project."[94] This would not be the first time he was wrong about such things. Ultimately, the project was delayed for several more years, its permits expired before it could secure funding, and the project's interim financier, Traveler's Insurance, pulled out of the deal.[95] As project director James O. Goldsmith put it, "you can [only] hold something together so long."[96]

The fight over the International Market Square and the battle over height limits on Russian Hill demonstrate how local actors and the local conditions they create can make it difficult for finance and investment, as part of the larger flow of capital, to seep into and reshape the built environment. More specifically, these contestations underscore issues that development proposals on port property now face. First, San Franciscans were willing to fight hard to protect their hills, their views, and their history—especially as they related to the waterfront. As concerns for the health of the bay and the need for open space gained momentum, ultimately to be formalized in policy and regulation, they established a countervailing discourse to the one being promulgated by the port and its consultants: that the waterfront could help make San Francisco a world-class city not just through maritime commerce but with postindustrial development of corporate headquarters, entertainment, and recreation. Many of the activists and neighborhood organizations were well-heeled, well connected, and well organized. The political battles they fought reflected the desire to retain a visual, physical, and functional connection to the waterfront even as its use and purpose changed.

Second, height limits are very important. They directly affect the financial potential of a project and the design of its various elements, and thus the character of the built environment. The successful imposition of height limits can also be seen as an example of use value winning the day over exchange value. Lowered height limits helped preserve physical beauty, topographical character, and the unique relationship between the built environment and the natural setting, thus preserving views from public streets and protecting the public's experience of place. This trumped exploitation of the area for the primary purpose of increasing economic value, for increasing profit. However, it is important to be cognizant of the fact that it was generally an elite, wealthy public that supported lower height limits at the cost, ultimately, of construction jobs for blue-collar workers. Russian Hill and Telegraph Hill residents were able, after a fashion, to "make the city after their own hearts," but only by preventing another group from participating in its creation.[97] Lowered height limits effect an increase in the exchange value of private property just as they decrease the exchange value of commercial property where development potential was lessened. Guaranteed views increase property values and lower heights mean lower density, which in turn limits the supply of housing, thereby raising property values.

Third, San Francisco's planning function was becoming more powerful and bureaucrats and citizens were becoming more skillful at taking advantage of the tools it provided. Jacob's relationship with Mayors Shelley and Alioto and the respect that the planning department was earning under his stewardship was a critical part of the politics of development in the city. In fact, the role of the planning department should be highlighted here. The work of its staff and the professional opinions of its director were necessary to the success of height-limit advocates.[98] That the planning department was vocally concerned with the public good, or at least one aspect of it, and was able to articulate a certain sensitivity to the character of the urban landscape, influenced its commission and the board of supervisors. The agency's increasing involvement in waterfront development did not make for a beautiful relationship with the port, however, even with consultant matchmakers brought in.

Consultants on the Waterfront

In the context of new height limits for port property and with the example of International Market Square to underscore the reality of such restrictions, and in light of the shift in jurisdictional power triggered by the *Harbors and Navigation Code* amendments, Magnin softened his typically tough stance. The emerging possibility that the port could be transferred to the city also probably helped Magnin and his commission take a somewhat more conciliatory approach to revitalization. Thus, in 1963, the port began to work with the city in its attempt to plan for a new northern waterfront.

After six months of negotiations, the port authority agreed to work jointly with the city planning department to hire consulting firms Arthur D. Little (ADL) and John S. Bolles Associates to perform a comprehensive land-use and economic analysis of the port's activities. The announcement was greeted with enthusiasm.[99] Mayor Shelley indicated that he would form a citizen's advisory committee to follow the process, a decision that lent legitimacy to the hope that there would be a new spirit of cooperation between the two agencies and signaled the growing influence of citizen participation in the planning process.

Nevertheless, the unprecedented effort at interagency collaboration stuttered, delayed by bureaucratic feuding and a case of mayoral impotence. That it took nearly two years for the mayor to appoint members to the waterfront advisory group was an obvious sign that fostering coordination was a frustrating endeavor and that the mayor had a hard time mending fences.[100] The maxim "you can bring a horse to water but you can't make him drink" is apt. Mayor Shelley turned to the guardians of downtown for help; the Blyth-Zellerbach Committee was always willing. It was accepted that the BZC would act as liaison between the city and the port. In an arrangement similar to that made for the Golden Gateway project, the BZC also paid for the city's share of the planning effort. Finally, in 1966, ADL published the first of two commissioned reports.

The Port of San Francisco: An In-Depth Study of Its Impact on the City, Its Economic Future, the Potential of Its Northern Waterfront was greeted with fanfare. A *Chronicle* headline enthused that it was a "Breathtaking Plan for the San Francisco Waterfront."[101] Its purpose was to analyze the port's present and future cargo operations, to determine if maritime activity in the northern waterfront could be relocated to the southern waterfront, and then to propose how much and what development would be feasible for the northern waterfront. To some degree, they covered ground Ebasco had trod seven years earlier. The report also served as the background study for the plan to be prepared by John S. Bolles, go-to man for the planning department and the port, that would cover both the water and land sides of the northern waterfront.

The ADL report came to several important conclusions, although, as Cyril Magnin pointed out, it "contained no major surprises."[102] First, the report asserted that the port's decline was a "myth." At the time of writing, the amount of cargo coming through the port had not declined in absolute terms and was in fact predicted to continue to grow at 1.5 percent annually through 1990.[103] ADL also drew connections between the value of each ton of cargo, which was considered very high, and the creation of employment and income, demonstrating that the port was still one of the largest contributors, directly and indirectly, to San Francisco's economy. The report estimated that between 11 and 14 percent of the city's employment was attributable to the port: 23,000 jobs directly, 52,000 to 67,000 jobs total.[104] They also connected the traditional economic function of the port with the economy of the city, noting that "numbers alone cannot fully indicate how the Port's valuable cargo has helped the city attract offices and headquarters, nor the role the Port is playing, today as in the past, as an integral part of the city's present character and future development."[105] This formed part of ADL's argument that it was important to maintain and upgrade the port's facilities. And, as Ebasco had thought seven years earlier, ADL concluded that the port could shift much of its shipping activities to the southern waterfront. Maritime commerce was, after all, still the port's main mission and ADL's proposal made economic sense at the time. By the end of the 1960s, this "policy" would become a generally recognized strategy. The *Chronicle* referred to it absently as a "trend."[106]

ADL also made a number of specific recommendations concerning the redevelopment of the northern waterfront. While no mention was made of Embarcadero City, its essence was apparent in some of their proposals. Above Pier 35, consultants suggested that the State Belt Line be reduced and viable shipping activities be relocated to the southern waterfront. This would make other piers available for an "expanded development program" to include commercial and tourist activities, restaurants, shops, and hotels, while maintaining and enhancing the fishing activities in that area, especially at Piers 43 and 43½.

The area from south of Pier 35 to the Ferry Building was proposed to be reserved for maritime activity, not just because the area accommodated some foreign trade but because maritime activities would "continue to enhance the attraction of the area by the authentic maritime atmosphere that they bring to the Waterfront."[107] Not many years earlier, "authentic" maritime activity was separated as a place of work from places of leisure. With their comment, the consultants underscored a significant transition—that some maritime activity was valued not just for the perpetuation of commerce and industry but as something to be put on display and consumed visually, thus increasing the value of nearby areas as part of the new waterfront spectacle. In the Ferry Building area, which included Piers 1 through 24, ADL foresaw the provision of "a dramatic site for an urban office and commercial complex."[108] A mix of open space and commercial development was proposed for a platform being constructed over the Bay Area Rapid Transit's (BART) underwater rail tube, just behind the Ferry Building. The platform was also identified as a site for the "city's long-awaited permanent heliport."[109] Several development schemes, including U.S. Steel's, would in fact be pursued for this area just a few years later.[110]

Overall, "the optimum use of the port's property would involve the expansion of commercial, recreational, and, perhaps, residential uses within the area controlled by the port authority."[111] As Ebasco had suggested, new commercial development would be undertaken using money from private sources with the port maintaining ground leases. In a way that Ebasco's proposal had not, the ADL report brought front and center the idea that revenues from development projects targeted for areas no longer needed for shipping activities could support development of modern marine terminals and other cargo-related operations in the southern waterfront. This financial/development arrangement, sometimes referred to as "piggy-backing," was thought to be critical to helping the port maintain its financial independence. Clearly, being able to avoid cash infusions from the city and state meant that it would be easier for the port to retain more control over its own management, which was quite important to Magnin.

The ADL report did not present a policy framework or provide much specific, long-range advice. Though it sketched a four-phase implementation of its suggested program, the report paid most attention to the future of the southern part of the port's property, for which "all planning should consider the longer range potential portions of this area have for mixed wharfage and other commercial development."[112] One exception stood out. ADL's program for the area from the Hyde Street Pier to Pier 35 (at the time the extent of Fisherman's Wharf), included "development criteria," which were phrased much like typical planning language. Of course, these were just advisory statements. Examples included:

- Each area, and the entire Waterfront, should maintain a consistently authentic atmosphere.
- Each development should complement other development.
- All construction and physical facilities in the area should be designed so as to enhance the overall atmosphere of the area.
- All specific developments must be designed to permit an integrated flow of vehicular and pedestrian traffic throughout the entire area.[113]

Other statements sounded like the kind of advice given to business enterprises and would not be part of a public policy document:

- Each programming area should be developed so as to be marketable to private operators.
- Individual operators should be required to conform to business practices that will add to the value of the entire area.[114]

The non-maritime development program ADL suggested was ambitious enough to make some officials nervous. An argument between city supervisor William Blake and port director Rae Watts grew out of the idea that the port could develop its waterfront without much input from the city—even though analysis then underway was supposedly a joint effort with the planning department, and the port had ceded some control over its land to the city, after a fashion. The planning department had similar fears and was concerned that the port would ignore the consultants' proposal for

40-foot height limits along much of the waterfront. Magnin responded to the skepticism in a reminder that "in order to convince the city we [the port] would not do anything questionable, I agreed to join with Mayor George Christopher in asking the Legislature to pass a bill covering the situation."[115] Objections were raised that the port was able to avoid zoning controls, including height limits, with its power to appeal them to another state agency. In a rather crafty response, Magnin offered that the port would be happy to refer matters to the city's board of permit appeals, if the legislature approved. The board of permit appeals was described at the time as being the "most lenient agency in California."[116]

Another thorny issue was raised by Supervisor Blake, who asserted that the port would be given an unfair advantage if it could offer its property for development free of taxation and that the city should be able to benefit from non-maritime development by assessing property taxes. This would later become part of his argument for supporting the port's transfer back to the city. That restaurateurs on Fisherman's Wharf were exempt from possessory tax particularly irked the supervisor. Magnin's response was that "the people of San Francisco and California should know, once and for all, that the port authority is not a tax collecting agency for the City and County of San Francisco" and that it was the board that had years ago forgiven the taxes.[117] Further debate elicited a few heated exchanges between Blake and Magnin over which public entity should benefit from development of the northern waterfront. Blake fumed that the port should be ceded to the city because "they've done nothing since the State has run it. It hasn't changed a bit since 1902."[118] He was not the only supervisor on the board who resented the port. Supervisor Jack Morrison testified that "San Francisco should have full and complete control over zoning and development of the Port."[119] Blake would soon get his wish, but it would not satisfy Morrison's desire for control.

Bolles Associates released their report in spring 1968, but reception was initially cool, to say the least. It called for cooperation between the city and the port authority, which had a predictable lack of impact, and the report's vision for the northern waterfront drew the ire of port authority nemesis Supervisor Blake, who exclaimed "this plan is too far out. . . . You social planners couldn't even build an outhouse in San Francisco."[120] Supervisor Leo T. McCarthy (later speaker of the house in the California State Legislature) added his voice to the chorus of criticism leveled at Bolles and the planning department, who were taking heat for not sufficiently including property owners in the process. Defending his agency, planning director Allan B. Jacobs pointed out that many groups and city agencies had in fact been involved.[121]

Development, especially when it occurs rapidly, is thick with politics, and sensitivities regarding any proposals for the northern waterfront were especially heightened. On the city side, construction of the view-blocking Fontana Apartments, the proposal for International Market Square, rehabilitation of Ghirardelli Square and the Cannery, and the construction of Golden Gateway and the Embarcadero Center, were combining to make the area "one of the most attractive and fastest-growing areas of private development in San Francisco."[122] Redevelopment agency director Justin Herman, responsible for much of the change rippling along the waterfront, described it as "the most valuable asset we have in San Francisco."[123] In the same breath, he helped prepare the ground, as it were, by describing the northern waterfront as "virtually defunct because of the low intensity of uses," underscoring, as an alchemist might have, that there is money to be made from converting underused piers into glass, steel, and concrete.[124] Such discourse raised alarms with the increasingly vigilant guardians of the waterfront.

Elements of Bolles' early proposal paralleled some of the suggestions of partner firm ADL, but the scale models and drawings employed by architects and designers lend more reality to their concepts than tables and charts, perhaps helping raise collective hackles. The initial plan appeared to be another blueprint for a futuristic panorama of waterfront development, with the subtly expressed but important difference that it showed concern for public open space and access to the bay (Fig. 3.7). Among other things, the plan called for putting the Embarcadero Freeway underground, constructing a low-speed monorail from the foot of Market Street to Aquatic Park, and constructing residential buildings just north of the Ferry Building and office facilities to the south to the Bay Bridge (Fig. 3.8).[125]

Seven months after its initial release, Bolles presented the final document to the port authority and planning department in a joint hearing in November 1968. In the two years it took Bolles and the Citizen's Advisory Committee (not to be confused with the Citizens' Progress Committee) to complete the document, most people's attitudes toward it had changed. Support even became enthusiastic for what was the most formal and complete expression of a plan yet produced for any part of the waterfront. Although somewhat more restrained than the initial version, a

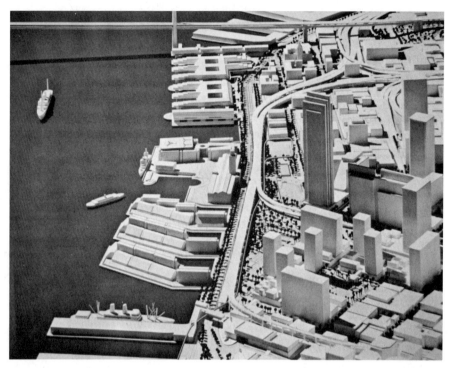

3.7 Model reflecting development ideas for the Ferry Building area. John S. Bolles Associates, *Northern Water-front Plan*, Port of San Francisco, 1968.

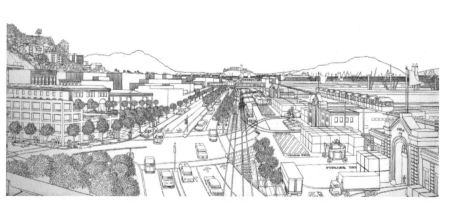

3.8 Sketch of proposed changes to the Embarcadero. Note the elevated tram above the bulk head buildings. Telegraph Hill rises to the left. John S. Bolles Associates, *Northern Waterfront Plan*, Port of San Francisco, 1968.

result of public pressure, it was still described idealistically as "an ambitious 20-year plan to develop the city's northern waterfront with new industry, homes, transportation systems, landscaping, promenades and underground streets."[126] Indeed, it was a true draft plan, and formed the basis for the first real policy document for the waterfront, the planning department's more modestly toned *Northern Waterfront Plan*, adopted as an amendment to the city's *Master Plan* in summer 1969.

Even as external forces contributed extensively to the demise of the port as a traditional maritime operation, they were helping transform the city across the Embarcadero from the waterfront. And so, as the movement of cargo over the city's docks ebbed, the port attempted to tap into new flows of capital, to ride the tide of postindustrialization. But the manner in which it pursued its goals incited already edgy representatives of local forces. Its grand plans were an assault on the waterfront, an audacity that triggered local actors and agents to be at the ready for the next round of proposals. The main bottom-up response to the changes being witnessed by neighborhood activists and organizations, bureaucrats, and advocacy groups was to promote a robust planning function.

Planning is not a passive defensive mechanism, but an active method of asserting local will, of tempering the top-down pressures brought by state policy, the interrelation of technological change and economic restructuring, and their effect on the built and natural environments. Initially, in our case, the primary tool was zoning, especially as expressed in height restrictions. But zoning is a blunt instrument, as planners say, and it is only part of the kit used to guide change. Local actors recognized the need for a more comprehensive and nuanced approach to waterfront revitalization, one based in planning policy and a solid regulatory framework. And the best way to effect this, it was increasingly recognized, was to take back the port from the state.

4

Don't Fill Me In

The Rise of Regulation and the Decline of Modernist Visions

THE TRANSAMERICA PYRAMID is probably San Francisco's most iconic building. While now it is a symbol of the city's cultural and economic place on the world stage, its construction in 1969 represented something more immediate—a victory for downtown development machinery and a defeat for emergent anti-growth forces. Perhaps the pyramid's success, just one of a crop of new office towers rising up, encouraged the port in its continued quest for an Embarcadero City. But while corporate expansion was succeeding downtown, at least until the mid-1980s, frustrating the likes of the Telegraph Hill Dwellers, they and other local forces proved more successful at stopping development along the waterfront.[1]

Just as Magnin teamed up with Mayor Alioto to seek out investors for port projects, three crucial events occurred at the end of the 1960s that created an entirely new functional environment for the port that drastically limited the possibilities for revitalizing the waterfront. These events were: the adoption by the planning department and board of supervisors of the first *Northern Waterfront Plan*, with attendant changes in building height limits and zoning controls; the transfer of the port from the state to the city in 1969; and passage of the 1965 McAteer-Petris Act creating the Bay Conservation and Development Commission (BCDC), which subsequently published the 1969 *San Francisco Bay Plan*. Together they combined into a complex policy framework that altered the playing field into one marked out by concern for both the public use of the waterfront and the preservation of maritime activities. If an absence of land-use and policy plans characterized the 1950s and 1960s, then the end of the 1960s can be seen as the initiation of the next stage in the evolution of waterfront planning policy and regulation, one identifiable by a clash between development pressures and the manifestations of increasingly bureaucratized local power.

The new policy and regulation rampart was erected just in time to break apart the last wave of proposals for "grand schemes" of mixed-use commercial development projects that would surge as the decade ended. In this round, however, the port itself actively played the role of capitalist entrepreneur. These proposals all centered around the Ferry Building, with a view to appropriating the area as a favored location for the extension of the city's burgeoning postindustrial economy. Not only did these projects underscore the reduced importance of maritime activity in the city but they even threatened the city's ability to maintain symbolic and historic reminders of such functions, as represented by the landmark Ferry Building and its place on the Embarcadero at the foot of Market Street.

The Northern Waterfront Plan

The work performed by ADL and Bolles served two purposes. First, it coordinated port and planning department activities, even if it did not foster complete cooperation; second, it provided the background information and analysis that would enable planning department staff to work quickly toward producing a formal public planning document. The draft plan, which the consultants presented to the planning department in November 1968, was received enthusiastically. Its release was followed by a period of public comment, several public meetings, and an evaluation by planning staff. The consensus was that the consultants' plan was a good one, so planning staff went about distilling from it the final *Northern Waterfront Plan*, which was adopted in 1969. The plan boundaries extended from Aquatic Park south to China Basin and included areas several blocks inland of port property. Intended to cover the sixteen-year period until 1985, the *Northern Waterfront Plan* was unusual in that it was more than just strictly a policy document. It also contained a set of proposals and a section on implementing them. The plan's basic purposes were to "guide future development in all areas on and contiguous to the harbor in a manner consistent with the interests of San Francisco. The Plan should provide guidelines whereby public and private interests can work together to fulfill the social, economic and physical objectives with maximum benefit for all,"[2] and to "develop living, working and leisure activities and supporting facilities in the northern waterfront which will serve all persons in the immediate area, the City and Bay region, and tourists, and which complement or supplement the maritime character of the area."[3] These goals were certainly more oriented to the public interest than the schemes thus far proposed, as emphasized by the fact that public comment was solicited and given some measure of real consideration in the plan. Clearly, such statements were intended to appeal to a broad spectrum of local actors, and represented an attempt to reconcile external pressures for change with locally defined needs.

One of the most important aspects of the plan was that it called for restraint in developing the northern waterfront. For instance, following the consultants' lead, the plan suggested that the area between Piers 9 and 35 should remain in maritime use and be supported as such for as long as economically feasible. In fact, the plan even suggested that "public subsidy should be considered, when required, in order to preserve for as long as possible some authentic port operations as an element of the waterfront."[4] Should shipping and related activities be replaced, the plan advocated open space and housing as priority uses, although the latter would be prohibited on much of port land by BCDC and the public trust. This had the potential to limit quite severely the area of commercial development available to the port, at least for the fifteen years of the plan's horizon. Furthermore, height limits proposed as part of the plan were more restrictive than the port would have liked, even in the area around the Ferry Building where the planning department concurred that commercial development was appropriate. This incensed port director Rae Watts, who chafed at the restrictions it represented and criticized planners as "being unrealistic in their schemes."[5] The port was going to have to live with these restrictions, however, because by the time the plan was adopted in early summer 1969, the port would, after about one hundred years, again be within the city's jurisdiction. Adoption of the plan completely turned the tables on the port. Despite the plan's support for commercial development in some places, Watts complained bitterly that it gave too much control to the planning department and was too restrictive to allow the port to undertake economically feasible projects in the northern waterfront. Without that commercial development, Watts vehemently argued, the port would be unable to "provide for the needs of the maritime industry."[6] But, as Planning Commissioner Mortimer Fleishhacker remarked to those present at the adoption hearing, the planning department was responsible for planning the city, including the port, whether the port liked it or not.

The *Northern Waterfront Plan* consisted of several sections, the first of which was composed of general objectives drawn from the *Master Plan* (now the *General Plan*) and policies to pursue them in the northern waterfront. These objectives and policies set the context for the main body of the plan itself, which consisted of a series of proposals for actions that would support the plan's policies. These proposals were divided into four subject areas: land use, transportation, open space, and urban design. Examples of land-use proposals, perhaps the most important of the four elements, included: developing open space and a pedestrian promenade along the water's edge between Piers 37 and 41; expanding water-oriented retail, restaurant, and commercial uses; developing a cluster of hotels and motels in and around Fisherman's Wharf; developing housing along the base of Telegraph Hill across from Piers 9 through 35; replacing Piers 1 through 7 with medium-density housing and office and commercial uses; and developing office space south of the Ferry Building "to complement the downtown office district."[7] No changes were proposed for China Basin, which was deemed important for shipping, with an exception for the possibility of a STOL port. The plan drew some criticism because it allowed for development over the water and permitted commercial development on a scale that some deemed inappropriate for the waterfront. According to detractors, these allowances rendered it insufficiently sensitive to the environment. Modern, jet-age thinking was not entirely superseded in the transition from Bolles' proposal to the public document that was based upon it.

While the concept of place had been utterly absent from consultants' analyses and developers' prospectuses, some of the most critical and meaningful policies in the *Northern Waterfront Plan* were place-related. Sections on urban design, for instance, expressed eloquently and romantically the relationship between the built environment and the natural setting:

> The northern waterfront presents to San Francisco an extraordinary opportunity to develop a dramatic and delightful physical environment. The potential for drama and beauty is created by the area's natural qualities of

the Bay's waterscape and the dominance of the surrounding hills and land forms. The interaction of natural environment of the Bay, land forms, and sky with the man-made urban environment and the vivid spectacle created by constantly changing patterns of light and color create a magnificent setting that provides rich and unforgettable images to both residents and visitors.[8]

Discussion of urban design also provided some of the basic reasoning for restricting the physical parameters of development in the plan area, and in doing so, echoed some of the arguments recently expressed by supporters of height limits in the northern waterfront. In this regard, a key statement in the plan was:

> The underlying design philosophy of this Plan is that urban forms should fully develop the outstanding natural beauty and qualities inherent in the character of the northern waterfront. The form and arrangement of the man-made urban elements should be determined by and subordinate to the great natural forms of the water and the land.[9]

The logic and sentiment in these statements were reflected in the height and bulk restrictions that the port would find so vexing (but which critics considered still too lax). For example, as we saw earlier, it was determined that buildings should respect the forms of hills. This was, and is, achieved by requiring buildings at the base of hills to be shorter and allowing taller buildings on the tops of hills, preventing a "leveling" of topography that could occur if taller buildings were built at the base of hills with shorter ones above. Buildings should also step down in height toward the water (also following the conclusions of the 1964 planning department height study). Forty-foot height limits along certain sections of the waterfront were intended to prevent new structures from dominating the existing low-slung transit sheds and bulkhead buildings. And of course, height limits would also help protect "one of San Francisco's most valuable assets"—its many views.[10] Important to note is that including this vision for the built environment in a planning policy document created a context, ex post facto, for the height limits adopted earlier. If anyone wanted to challenge such limits, they would now have to address the underlying city policy, and not just a section of the planning code and zoning maps. However, while such things complicate efforts to pursue development outside of regulatory parameters, they do not make it impossible.

In all, the plan presented quite a different vision for the waterfront than had come from the port authority, their consultants, or the calculations of financial analysts. Still, it recognized that the requirements of the port were essential to the plan, and that generating revenues was vital to the expansion and modernization of port maritime facilities. Thus commercial development was suggested for the areas immediately north and south of the Ferry Building. The plan also made clear the role that accommodating visitors and recreation was beginning to play in decisions that would shape the built environment of the northern waterfront. Modernist visions may have begun to give way to a more publicly informed planning process, but the *Northern Waterfront Plan* also reflected a change in San Francisco's economy to one increasingly reliant on services and tourism. Indeed, it helped officially to nudge the city into a role a little more attuned to those activities. With statements such as "the maritime atmosphere of Port and shipping activities adds genuine interest, variety, and amenity to the waterfront environment and is a part of San Francisco that cannot be easily replaced," the plan recognized a new value in traditional waterfront activities.[11] Probably taking a cue from ADL, the plan appropriated the remaining traditional maritime activities in the northern waterfront and assigned to them as much importance for their ability to attract visitors to the area as for their inherent economic function. Of course, similar thinking was expressed in *A Plan for Fisherman's Wharf* earlier in the decade, but that plan was never officially adopted.

After adoption of the *Northern Waterfront Plan* as an amendment to the *Master Plan*, the intention was to take the implementation section of the plan through its own legislative process. Referred to as the "Implementation Plan," it included changes to zoning districts, height and bulk controls, and proposed the creation of special use districts (SUDs).[12] It also addressed interagency coordination and identified what actions agencies would need to take to make aspects of the plan happen. In fact, the planning department felt that all of the major goals and proposals presented in the plan should be achieved for the most part within the plan's sixteen-year time frame. Almost two-thirds of the area covered by the plan was in public ownership, and almost half of that was in the port's jurisdiction. Perhaps somewhat quixotically, the plan's authors suggested that given this situation, public agencies were in the position of being able to follow through on ideas for land use and urban design established in the plan, of actually being able to make the plan happen.

But the main body of the plan was not drafted in a way that would really encourage change to occur. The plan established what options were available but could not include the political or financial mechanisms to carry out projects. The Implementation Plan was the document that outlined measures with "on-the-ground" impacts.[13] Some of the implementing actions were adopted soon after the plan was approved, for instance, the special use districts were established in 1970 (and have been amended several times since). But what to do with height limits, one of the most important planning tools, became locked up in the struggle over U.S. Steel's push for a 550-foot limit, as we shall see later.

By formally adopting the *Northern Waterfront Plan*'s vision for development, the planning department and the city created an impediment to investors and developers who would otherwise have used the waterfront with a view only to profit. However, what most helped make height limits, planning documents, policy statements, and new layers of approvals and restrictions a reality for the port was its return to the city. In this case, there was a successful combination of local boosters, who saw the possibility for profit in recapturing the port, together with a public that responded to the idea of a city reunited with its port. Returning the port to the city would sever the agency's direct ties with the state, thereby making it a more truly local agency. In turn, this would relocate the port within the set of power relationships affecting the waterfront. Had the transfer not occurred, it would have been difficult to impose policy decisions derived from the *Northern Waterfront Plan* on the port. Ironically, after the transfer, the port would view revitalization with an eye to profit partly as a result of public mandate.

The Impetus to Transfer

Governor Pat Brown came down to the Ferry Building for some international event in the World Trade Center and was standing with a few of us in the WTC lobby when Mayor George Christopher walked in with his retinue. He came up to Brown, extended his hand and said "Hello, Governor, welcome to my city." With no hesitation at all, Brown shot back, "Welcome to my port."[14]

—Don DeLone

The issue of whether the port should be a city rather than a state agency had been hanging in the background for a number of years. As early as 1951, only a year after the San Francisco Chamber of Commerce argued that port ownership was not the most crucial factor to the port's vitality, the board of supervisors had taken up the issue. Then president of the board of supervisors George Christopher (later mayor) even presented a resolution requesting that the state legislature take action to return the port to city jurisdiction, but nothing came of it or of any of the early debates.[15] By the 1960s, it was obvious that the port's northern waterfront was suffering from serious neglect. The port's cargo operations and financial status were seesawing, and it was clear that Oakland was becoming an extraordinarily successful port. Furthermore, tensions between the city and the port regarding development were becoming more of a problem as the city evolved. The planning department reported to its commission that "it seems pertinent to question whether the Port Authority should have sole control, as it does at present, over properties which it intends to lease to private developers for non-port uses. . . . In any conflict of interests between the City and the Port Authority arising over proposals for the development of Port Authority property by private interests, the Port Authority enjoys an enormously disproportionate advantage."[16]

City officials became convinced that state control of the port was not in San Francisco's interest, and Supervisor William C. Blake (who owned a ship-repair business) helped lead the charge to recapture it. Supporters of the transfer argued that the state was avoiding its fiduciary responsibilities to the port. San Francisco's port had always been a self-sustaining agency with no access to local tax monies and, as a state-owned entity, relied on financial aid that had to come directly from state coffers. Other California ports could receive money through their respective local agencies, making them more competitive. Furthermore, as a state agency the port was ineligible for federal development grants—grants that the Port of Oakland competed for successfully.

The Arthur D. Little report helped bring the issue to the boiling point, clearly outlining the next stage in the use of 527 acres of waterfront land. The idea that the state rather than the city would be behind such important changes disturbed many San Franciscans. Reacting to the future envisioned by the consultant, Supervisor Blake raised anew the transfer standard and argued that the land should be on the city's tax rolls when development took place. According to the *Chronicle*, he said that otherwise "a chance for new tax revenue would be passed up and an unfair advantage gained by developers located on state-held land."[17] Cyril Magnin responded quickly, saying that the city would in fact derive tax monies from development on or in place of old piers: "If the supervisor had done his homework before speaking out . . . he would realize our program can produce millions of dollars in new tax revenues."[18] By the time the debate became more widely public, arguments for transferring the port included not just the potential to increase tax revenues and eliminate financial favoritism, but that it would also put an end to the lackadaisical approach to facility maintenance and general mismanagement that were hallmarks of recent state steward-ship (this latter point is somewhat ironic, as it was mismanagement that caused the state to take over the port in 1863).

Magnin's rather overbearing and defiant stance proved ineffective, especially once the *Chronicle*'s editorial board made its feelings apparent. A few days after the exchange between Blake and Magnin, an editorial appeared in the *Chronicle* that supported Blake: "These are good points, worthy of earnest attention, but they do not reach far enough. The City of San Francisco has for too long been divorced from the management of its own port. It should move vigorously to regain ownership from the State."[19] In the short run, Supervisor Blake authored a resolution to order Mayor Shelley not to enter into any agreements with the port authority on land deemed surplus to shipping needs (as required per the 1963 amendment to the *Harbors and Navigation Code*). This only triggered more heated debates. The already testy relationship between Supervisor Blake and port director Rae Watts degenerated into open confrontation a month later when the board of supervisors was considering Supervisor Blake's resolution that San Francisco's official stance should be to return the port to the city. Watts called Blake a "cheap, tin-horn politician" and Blake labeled Watts "a man who would be on welfare if he weren't at the public trough."[20]

Support to transfer the port to the city grew rapidly as business leaders and labor unions realized that a flood of jobs and money could gush from extensive waterfront development, and that tax income to the city was potentially huge. With regard to the last point, the city's assessor, Joseph Tinney, claimed that the city had been losing "at least a million dollars a year" because it had no stake in port land.[21] SPUR was also eager to effect the transfer and issued a report in 1968 entitled "San Francisco Port . . . Asset or Liability?"

Based largely on the 1966 ADL report, SPUR argued that because the port was operating at a loss it would be forced to generate income by developing the extensive tracts of northern waterfront property no longer needed or suitable for cargo operations. The port authority would be "thrust . . . into the business of real estate development as its most practicable source of income necessary for the subsidization of the maritime operations."[22] SPUR concluded, in what was for them at the time an unusually populist position, that only under city jurisdiction would port land be developed in a fashion that would benefit all San Franciscans, not just commercial interests: "Optimal utilization of portions of this acreage may not be for public open spaces, housing or recreation. Thus a conflict of interests between the financial needs of the Port and the environmental, social and cultural needs of the City may develop under the present port ownership."[23] It should be pointed out, however, that SPUR did not shy away from more profit-oriented reasons for obtaining control of the port. After all, SPUR was still an organization with deep roots in business and the political machinery of development. Its board of directors in 1968, for instance, included Planning Commissioner Mortimer Fleishhacker, Jr., and business tycoon John L. Merrill.[24]

Supervisor Blake's efforts to convince his peers that the time had come to reclaim the port were helped immensely both by the election of Joseph Alioto as mayor in 1967 and by the completion in 1968 of Bolles' *Northern Waterfront Plan*, which contained the policies that could make some of ADL's development concepts possible. Alioto, who became notable as an anti-trust lawyer, was from a family of restaurateurs and fish wholesalers who had long been port tenants, so his interest in port-related issues was natural. Given his personal connection to the port and a study that suggested tantalizing futures for the waterfront, it is not surprising that Alioto staunchly supported the idea of the transfer. As discussions moved along, the city's efforts to retake the port found an unlikely ally in Commissioner Cyril Magnin himself. While he must have seen the writing on the wall, his decision to come out in favor of the transfer likely was influenced by Mayor Alioto's disposition, as the two men were generally on the same page regarding issues of urban development. At the same time, relations between the port and the state were becoming uncomfortable. A *Chronicle* piece even described the state of affairs as a "cold war," reporting that port director Watts was forced to cancel his attendance at a meeting because out-of-state travel was being restricted by Governor Reagan.[25] At a "Get the Port Back" luncheon held by SPUR at the elite St. Francis Hotel,

Magnin showed that he had changed his tune by stating that regaining the port "would be the greatest bargain the City ever bought."[26] He cautioned, though, that the port should remain independent, and not be shackled by the board of supervisors, a concern that he shared with Miriam Wolff, the port's attorney.

State assemblyman John Burton (a Democrat representing San Francisco and later one of the state's most powerful machine politicians) agreed to author the bill that would effect the transfer, and began to shepherd it through various state committees. Based on signals that the idea of a transfer was being received positively in the governor's office and in the legislature, Alioto appointed a sixteen-member committee to negotiate the details with the state.[27] However, the state's Department of Finance, headed by Caspar Weinberger (in one of several career moves) began by opposing the bill, insisting that the city would have to pay an adequate fee for the port, then estimated to be worth $350 million; later amendments that finalized the purchase price and related financial matters garnered that agency's support. The state assembly approved the transfer in May 1968, and the state senate approved it in August, with four conditions: first, the transfer had to be approved by San Francisco voters and thus be placed on the next ballot; second, the city had to assume $55 million of the state's bonded indebtedness; third, within ten years of the transfer, the city had to issue $50 million in bonds for improvements; and finally, an additional $100 million had to be invested in the port in a twenty-five-year period.[28] The transfer also resulted in reducing the amount of time the port could lease property, from 99 to 66 years.

Alioto, perhaps the state's leading Democrat at that time, had been accustomed to criticizing the governor, but on the occasion of the signing, had only praise for Reagan. According to a report by the *Chronicle*, the conservative Reagan supported the bill because it represented a step toward local control.[29] After the governor signed it, state senator George Moscone (later mayor of San Francisco) amended the bill to rename it the Burton Act. A few weeks later, in a 10-1 vote, the board of supervisors accepted the state's conditions, with one exception. The board voted to give the mayor the power to appoint the director of the port, instead of keeping that power with the port commission. Miriam Wolff opposed the move, which would have obvious repercussions for the political power relations between the port and the city. Next, it was up to the voting public of San Francisco.

The *Chronicle* editorialized that "the future welfare of San Francisco" was at stake, and that the state would not invest the $100-150 million needed to replace obsolete piers, maintain facilities, construct a new passenger terminal, and generally support shipping.[30] Seemingly every city official, socialite, union, and booster organization supported the transfer, which Thomas Mellon, the city's chief administrator, assured would not cost San Francisco tax payers a cent.[31] A full-page *Chronicle* ad boasted that the city would benefit from an increase in jobs, payrolls, and business revenue, and that port profits averaged $1 million per year (Fig. 4.1). The transfer effort was bolstered by a public relations firm that, as Richard Reinhardt sardonically put it, "began a campaign of enticement: 'The Port means money in our pockets. . . . Opportunity knocks. . . . The Greatest Bargain of the Century."[32] The transfer agreement was placed on the November 1968 ballot under propositions "B" and "C." Proposition B (the Burton Act) contained the legal transfer and associated requirements while Proposition C was the amendment to the city charter that set up the port commission. Both propositions were approved overwhelmingly by San Francisco voters, and the port was officially reunited with the city on February 7, 1969, signaled quietly by a changing of the flags flying from the Ferry Building. The agency also replaced its designation as the San Francisco Port Authority with the simpler Port of San Francisco. Despite favorable reaction by officials and the public to the return of the port to the city, the conditions attached thereto would only serve to inflame the battles over waterfront development and perpetuate the tensions between the planning and port commissions.

Friction between the SFPD and its new sister agency was exacerbated by the financial requirements associated with the port's transfer. This was the case even though the deal seemed a bargain at the time, partly because it was expected that commercial development in the northern waterfront would satisfy the financial obligations placed on the city-run port as part of the transfer. However, the Burton Act and the Transfer Agreement included the requirement that the port *maximize* the amount of rent derived from land declared no longer needed for maritime uses, a stipulation that was also written into the city's charter.[33] This condition was crucial, and the impact remains so today, because to satisfy the requirement to invest $100 million in development of shipping, shipping-related, and general navigational uses, the port would have to pursue development that would generate the most income possible from surplus land. And that was just the kind of development that has been, and is, the most controversial.[34] This condition only increased the pressure on the port's administration and real estate staff to

4.1 November 4, 1968 advertisement in the *Chronicle* promoting the transfer. Permission to reproduce kindly granted by the San Francisco *Chronicle*.

chase massive commercial projects, and placed the agency directly at odds with BCDC and the city's attempts to control the nature of its own port's development. In later decades, this situation would also pit the different divisions within the port against one another, in particular the maritime and real estate divisions. Real-estate, for example, would scrutinize the port's maritime activities at every opportunity and where they looked marginal, the potential for some form of development would loom up.

While more recently the obligation to maximize return from investment has been treated a bit more leniently, it created extreme pressure on
the port during its early years as a newly created city agency. The port
authority was placed in something of a bind—it had to chase income
through implementing commercial projects, but these projects were limited in scope because the port was under city jurisdiction and subject to
its zoning code controls and related approval processes and, practically
speaking, its policies, such as those in the newly adopted *Northern Waterfront Plan*. And it no longer had any way to circumvent zoning restrictions
on non-maritime development by any appeal to the state's planning advisory board. The ways in which the board of supervisors structured the
reintegration of the port with the city did, however, leave the port fairly
independent. According to Richard Reinhardt, the board gave up nearly all
opportunities to maintain any direct control over the port through Proposition C: "(the Board) had voted 10 to 1 to deny themselves any review
of Port Commission contracts, commercial agreements or development
plans. All members of the Board except Leo McCarthy apparently accepted
Magnin's view that 'the Port is a business and . . . can't be expected to run
to the Supervisors with every contract.'"[35]

Reinhardt argued that the port sought to divest itself of both state
and local control, to become a "free-swinging, independent operation, lib-
erated from the bureaucratic powers of government and (with) all the latitude of private enterprise."[36] While his interpretation is a little extreme
and not entirely accurate, it does point out an attitude that would contribute to difficulties with interagency cooperation, sometimes creating
tension. Furthermore, in 1978, an amendment was made to the city's
charter that required that lease of real property in excess of ten years or
that would generate $1 million or more in revenue had to be approved by
the board of supervisors. Over the years, this has allowed the board to exert
a fair amount of influence over the port.[37]

Regardless, the transfer was considered a victory by SPUR, the Chamber
of Commerce, unions, the development community (and thus Magnin), and
real estate businesses; to many, the port was a potential treasure chest.
As soon as the transfer went into effect, Magnin wasted no time sending
out the call for developers. Advertisements were placed in newspapers as
part of a nationwide campaign: "Prime waterfront property in San Francisco is now available for commercial development. The Port can now offer
downtown waterfront property from famed Fisherman's Wharf to the Bay
Bridge. Much of it is zoned for hotels, motels, restaurants, entertainment,

retail shopping, office buildings, and apartments. Sites are available on long term leases with flexible terms specifically designed to be attractive to private capital."[38] Seemingly, the door had been swung wide open. Proposals came from many quarters for many parts of the waterfront, but the forces of change and resistance swirled most turbulently around the Ferry Building, testing both the city's ability to establish appropriate height limits and the mettle of the young BCDC.

The Birth of the Bay Conservation and Development Commission

Incensed by the City of Berkeley's plan to expand its urban boundaries by filling San Francisco Bay, Kay Kerr, Sylvia McLaughlin, and Esther Gulick launched a landmark grassroots action to protect the bay's rapidly diminishing and polluted waters. Bay fill, which includes piers, had reduced the amount of open water in the bay by about a third and wetlands areas by more than 75 percent. Galvanized by a 1959 U.S. Army Corps of Engineers map showing the bay reduced to a deepwater shipping channel, the three women rallied thousands of supporters and in 1961, founded the Save San Francisco Bay Association, later shortened to Save the Bay.[39]

Save the Bay was extraordinarily successful at exerting pressure on local city councils and politicos in Sacramento, and was able to launch law suits and intervene in court proceedings related to major development proposals. This can be explained partly, as we saw in the battle over heights, by the elite status of the core group of actors. Kay Kerr, for instance, was married to Clark Kerr, president of the University of California, Berkeley.[40] Perhaps most important, the organization had strong support from Eugene McAteer, state senator from San Francisco, and assemblyman Nicholas Petris from Richmond, a town known for its oil refineries and thus as a destination for giant tankers.

Legislative attempts to restrict fill were not successful until 1964, when Senator McAteer worked to pass a bill that placed a moratorium on bay fill and required a study to be completed in four months. In early 1965, the commission responsible for managing the study, headed by McAteer himself, recommended the creation of the Bay Conservation and Development Commission (BCDC) as a temporary agency, and that it be given four years to prepare a plan that would set forth the policies to guide its decisions and actions as related to protecting the bay and its shoreline. The bill that established BCDC, the McAteer-Petris Act, was passed in 1965. Commissioners include both governor's appointees and representatives from city and county governments throughout the Bay Area. It is thus a kind of hybrid state-regional-local agency with emphasis on the regional.

The new commission's first executive director was Joseph Bodovitz, who left his position as SPUR's first deputy director to take the job. Public support for protecting the bay, and therefore for BCDC, was broad and vocal. When it came time to decide whether to make BCDC a permanent agency, enough influence was brought to bear, even by some of his appointees, including state finance director Caspar Weinberger, that Governor Reagan supported its continuation. In 1969, with the help of assemblyman John Knox (McAteer had since died), the McAteer-Petris Act was amended to make BCDC a permanent agency and to adopt its *Bay Plan* as law. Resistance from developers and the real estate industry was stiff; the act passed by a single vote.

The commission's jurisdiction includes bay water and tributaries up to the point of highest tidal action, all shoreline located within one hundred feet of the bay's mean high tide (referred to as the 100-foot shoreline band), and all wetlands. Commission authority thus extends to much but not all of the port's jurisdiction, particularly the piers, wharfs, and pile-supported structures. Generally, the shoreline band reaches only to the Embarcadero; the roadway itself and most of the port's seawall lots are beyond BCDC's jurisdiction. This boundary was significant for a while because it meant that, until the public trust was given stronger legal teeth in the early 1980s, the port's use of its property outside of BCDC jurisdiction was limited only by the city. Thus the planning department, its commission, and the board of supervisors were the main barriers to completing projects on areas beyond BCDC's jurisdiction, primarily seawall lots.

The commission's main task is to administer a comprehensive and enforceable plan that will protect San Francisco Bay and its shoreline. To accomplish this, the agency regulates dredging, fill, and to a certain degree the uses of land within its jurisdiction. Moreover, it does so as an agency now considered to be in and of itself an exercise of the public trust.[41] The uses of fill are limited by BCDC to water-related activities, which include port facilities, water-related industry, bridges, wildlife refuges, water-oriented commercial recreation, and public assembly. That offices and housing are not allowed on new or replacement fill is important. Within the 100-foot shoreline band, BCDC requires that development be designed to provide the maximum feasible public access to the bay.[42] The commission exercises its authority through its permitting process. For instance, as conditions of the approval of a permit, BCDC can require public improvements consistent with the project, like improving access to the water by building paths, or providing signs and benches.

The BCDC's *Bay Plan* did not restrict uses of existing fill, or of some parts of the shoreline. So, if an extant pier was physically capable of supporting housing without significant alterations, the residential development could be permitted.[43] These loopholes would be closed by the later solidification of the public trust doctrine. The commission's control of the design of public access, and later their influence over general project design gained by the threat of denying a permit, would become quite controversial, leading to years of very difficult relations with the port and planning department. As a result of the 1969 *Bay Plan*, BCDC evolved into the first agency in the United States to exercise control over physical development as a way to protect the environment. The creation of BCDC is an example of the ability of a local group to wield sufficient power to have their concerns formalized in policy and regulation. Furthermore, BCDC helped establish more generally the influence of the environmental movement on planning policy: the environment was (and is) considered to be not just the physical quality of the bay water but also its accessibility and thus the view corridors to and open space along the water. So, the bay's social and cultural value, and in turn its use value as publicly conceived, are largely protected from appropriation by the freewheeling forces of privatization by a public agency. The first significant development project on which BCDC would cut its teeth was a 1969 proposal to develop an area north of the Ferry Building.

BCDC vs. Ferry Port Plaza: Regulation 1, Development 0

As a new city agency strapped by the requirement to invest $100 million in itself, the port was moving hurriedly to pursue commercial development projects. Essentially, this was the only real way for the agency to generate the necessary capital. Thus while not recommended by the ADL plan, the port declared that Piers 1, 3, and 5 were no longer operational, and that Pier 7 would soon be available for development.[44] The port turned on its beacon and attracted a proposal from a team of outsiders: Oceanic Properties, Inc., a division of Honolulu-based developers Castle and Cooke and New York financiers Kidder-Peabody. In turn, Oceanic tapped attorney William Coblentz, a rising star in the local power structure, as their spokesman and go-between. Coblentz had a short stint in the state attorney general's office under Governor "Pat" Brown and would later sit on the board of regents of the University of California and serve on the San Francisco airport commission. His respected and powerful law firm, now called Coblentz, Patch, Duffy, and Bass LLP, has a long history in San Francisco with a strong practice in land-use and development law. In this case, the proposal they lobbied for was a mixed-use development called Ferry Port Plaza, designed by Skidmore, Owings, and Merrill (SOM) and which was intended to replace Piers 1 through 7 with a luxury hotel, offices, shops, and parking all crammed onto a single forty-acre pier (Fig. 4.2).

Mindful of new requirements for projects (both as regulation from BCDC and as a response to the Planning Department's *Northern Waterfront Plan*), the design presented to the port included public access to the water by "perimeter esplanades, parks, and open plazas" and it protected view corridors from streets leading to the project.[45] The buildings were designed to conform to height limits, although at the time those limits were still under review as part of the *Northern Waterfront Plan* adoption process. Nevertheless, it was expected at the time that eighty-four feet would be approved, which the Ferry Port Plaza project sponsors supported, even though they indicated that the project was planned to reach up to 125 feet in some places. Oceanic hoped that a project designed to be supported on pilings, not solid fill, and to cover only 40 percent of the site would cause BCDC to view it favorably. Fill, however, would eventually be defined to include just about anything that covered the water, including structures built on piles or cantilevered out over the water.

SO CLOSE, YET SO FAR

In September 1969, the port entered a lease agreement with Kipco, Inc., a firm created by Kidder-Peabody, for the forty-acre area, an arrangement that would bring a substantial sum into port coffers, and, once developed,

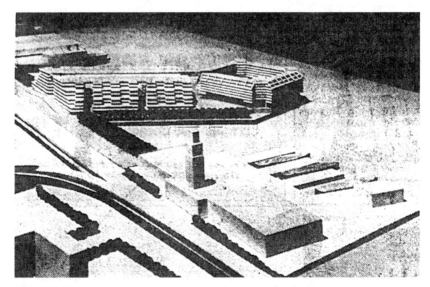

4.2 Model of Ferry Port Plaza proposal, shown above the Ferry Building. San Francisco *Chronicle*, July 18, 1970. Permission to reproduce kindly granted by the San Francisco *Chronicle*.

to the city's general fund through large tax payments. By February 1970, the development team had attracted another partner, the prestigious Ford Foundation. The project was moving forward so well that a spokesperson for the sponsors indicated that, given continued smooth sailing, construction would start by the end of the year.[46]

Design changes delayed submission of the project to the planning department until June 1970. The project had grown a bit, promising a 1,200-room hotel (instead of 800) to enclose a "'Grand Court sculpture garden' with trees and reflecting pools."[47] Somehow, under the hotel, parking would be provided for 2,400 hundred cars—a vision of modern accessibility quite in keeping with earlier grand schemes. It also incorporated a 500-foot glass galleria flanked by two levels of shops and six of offices. The "parks" and esplanades survived the redraw, but along with the rest of the project, would not survive the approval process.

Although the port had already entered into a development agreement with the sponsors, the project still needed approvals from the planning department, the board of supervisors (which it would get), BCDC, and the Corps of Engineers. Things began to take a turn for the worse during fall 1970, when environmentalists organized to protest Ferry Port Plaza's 16-football-fields-sized footprint over the bay. In a hearing before BCDC, port director Miriam Wolff, recent successor to Rae Watts, argued that the project was necessary to help generate the money required by the transfer agreement to be invested in port facilities—that or the city would have to dip into its own pocket.[48] However, the pivotal issue at the time was whether an opinion from the California Attorney General would support an administrative rule known as "the rule of equivalencies," proposed by BCDC's executive director, Joseph Bodovitz. The rule would allow new fill for development (including development on piles) if an equal surface area were opened up elsewhere, resulting in no net increase of bay fill. The Ferry Port Plaza proposal would have filled more of the bay than was to be freed by removing the old piers, so the port offered to demolish the crumbling Pier 41.

The stakes for the port associated with the "rule of equivalencies" were great enough to get the *Chronicle*'s buy-in, support from Mayor Alioto (almost a given), and accolades from the Northern California Chapter of the American Institute of Architects and the Chamber of Commerce. The *Chronicle*'s editorial board, this time voicing a "fair-is-fair" kind of argument, said that the rule was sound, as it would allow the replacement of "beaten up old piers." They stated, quite plainly, "We think it ought to be adopted."[49] In the same issue, the *Chronicle* printed a long letter from Director Wolff appealing to the citizenry, saying that the project would not shrink the bay, and that the port would be replacing "decrepit, uninteresting property with an exciting, esthetic and visually pleasing treatment."

For his part, the mayor perpetuated the discourse of decay and rebirth by stressing that "the very life and future of the port rests on getting a development of this kind" and that "this is not a get-rich quick scheme for a few, as some have charged. We sought the development; we invited it."[50] Of course, just because a public agency was attempting to act as a magnet for private capital did not mean that investors would not profit handsomely. This case is not uncommon, as we have seen, of local actors and gatekeepers reaching out in an attempt to attract capital, to tap the veins of an outside source of power. Their success, or lack thereof, contributes to the character of a place, helping differentiate it from others. It also helps crystallize what is often an abstractly described process of capital flow.

Even more than International Market Square, Ferry Port Plaza galvanized public reaction to grand schemes for a "world-class" waterfront (a dated concept, despite its use in current parlance). Hundreds of people from numerous groups packed BCDC hearings. Calls to "prevent the rape of the waterfront" issued from a growing list of protestors, including the League of Women Voters, Marin Conservation League, Friends of the

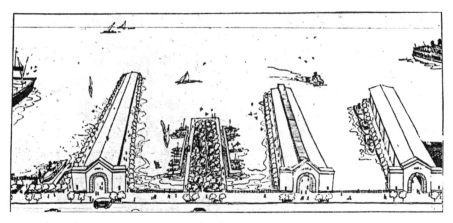

4.3 Pier designed as open space submitted as counter-proposal to Ferry Port Plaza. San Francisco *Chronicle*, October 12, 1970. Permission to reproduce kindly granted by the San Francisco *Chronicle*.

Earth, and two local advocacy groups, San Francisco Tomorrow (SFT) and San Francisco Beautiful, and echoed loudly throughout the meeting hall.[51] A collection of neighborhood groups and activists referred to as the "conservation coalition" even submitted a counterproposal (Fig. 4.3). One could expect no less from a city of so many freethinkers in a region that helped catalyze the environmental movement. In an odd, inscrutable twist, Ferry Port Plaza architects SOM likened the alternative to Ghirardelli Square, suggesting that such a thing at the city's doorstep was a bit cartoonish.[52]

A few days after SOM calmly dismissed the rival proposal, Attorney General Thomas C. Lynch handed down his opinion, all but killing the project. Essentially, he held that BCDC did not have the legal authority to adopt a rule that would enable such development, unless it could be proved that the proposed developments were water oriented. In such cases, fill is allowed. Lynch argued that the project as designed was in fact adding fill for non-water-related uses. Furthermore, BCDC regulations require disapproval of projects that could be just as easily constructed away from the water. BCDC director Bodovitz, although he asserted that ultimately it was BCDC's decision as to what constituted water-related uses, admitted that Ferry Port Plaza, with its big office building, was not particularly water oriented. Mayor Alioto tenaciously stuck by the project, arguing "there is nothing in . . . the ruling which precludes the BCDC from approving the application" and officials from Oceanic decided to view the delay as a "normal procedure of business."[53] The BCDC commission voted 22-1 against recommending the project.

Mayor Alioto railed against the decision, concluding that BCDC did not have the power to create "a condition that effectively embalms rotting piers."[54] While he was wrong about BCDC's power, he was probably right about the impact of the decision. Disallowing general offices and housing as part of commercial development, two of the least water-oriented uses, can cripple the ability of an agency or project sponsor to provide those non-revenue-generating features that are desired. That is, office and housing are often the "economic engine" of projects that pay for amenities that would otherwise not be provided (unless hard-to-get public money could be leveraged). Without the office development in Ferry Port Plaza, there was no way to provide esplanades next to the water and there might not be the money to remove old or rotting piers. More fundamental at the time, though, was the sobering notion that the port might not be able to generate $100 million to invest in its maritime facilities if its options for development were so severely limited.

Mayor Alioto tried to get BCDC to buy into the *Northern Waterfront Plan*, which, as adopted, incorporated the Ferry Port Plaza design. He seemed to hope, not entirely unreasonably, that because the project was in essence part of a comprehensive plan for the northern waterfront, it should be seen as a reasonable endeavor. Such logic did not impress BCDC. But the mayor carried the battle further, insisting that the city should not "be stymied by one man's opinion. . . . The law is not a permanent thing."[55] And with that, in March 1971, the port would file an ultimately unsuccessful suit against BCDC over Ferry Port Plaza, which was the first port development proposal to be scuttled by BCDC and its newly formalized regulatory power.

The City vs. Ford Motor Company and U.S. Steel: Regulation 2, Development 0

At about the same time that Ferry Port Plaza was being debated, the port was pursuing development just to the south on the site between the Ferry Building and the Bay Bridge, an area characterized by crumbling finger piers, many of which were more than fifty years old at the time. The 1,500-foot stretch extending from Pier 14 to Per 24 was removed from shipping use not long after the port's transfer. Consultants had recommended that the piers be removed and that the area be developed with commercial and office uses. As with the site of the Ferry Port Plaza proposal this became a nearly immediate priority for the city's newest agency. The concept was also supported by the *Northern Waterfront Plan*, which suggested that such uses were appropriate here because they would become an extension of the downtown. Eagerly, the port cast its net, fishing out two proposals for the site, one by Ford Motor Company and another by U.S. Steel.

Ford produced a nearly unbelievable scheme for a multipurpose "urban dealership" to be owned and operated by a real estate subsidiary of the automobile giant (Fig. 4.4). This project, designed by architect William Pereira (whose credits included the Transamerica Pyramid), would have resulted in an almost stereotypical dystopian suburban fantasy/nightmare—a mall, restaurants, and car dealership built over the water and connected to downtown via massive freeway-style ramps.[56] One particularly obtuse feature was the inclusion of fifteen acres of parking—enough for 4,500 cars—to help remedy congestion! While it adhered to the 84-foot height limit proposed as part of the *Northern Waterfront Plan*, the project was designed to be built on piles. This approach did not result in directly filling the bay, but it did involve building over the water. In all likelihood, BCDC would have interpreted this as tantamount to fill, dooming the project. But, despite representation by William Coblentz's law firm, Ford's proposal did not catch the eyes of the port commission, who were more distracted by the shiny, 550-foot object dangled by U.S. Steel; in May 1970, they voted 4-0 to consider it and not Ford's proposal (Fig. 4.5).

U.S. Steel's monumental proposal was steered to the port commission somewhat on the sly. The company was keeping a low profile by using local agents to "shop" the project. Their architects, however, were the high profile Skidmore, Owings, and Merrill, who were also designing Ferry Port Plaza.[57] The *Chronicle* put the proposal on its front page on December 13, 1969, a week after announcing Ford's plans, and included an artist's sketch that made clear the project's scope. The scheme was to replace the existing piers with a cruise terminal, shopping center, twenty-five-story hotel, and a forty-four-story office, which, at about 550 feet, would have been taller than the pylons of the Bay Bridge, dwarfing most nearby development. The battles lines were drawn quickly. Business interests, including the Chamber of Commerce, port officials, and labor favored the project, while community activists, architects, conservationists, and planning department staff did not.[58] SPUR supported the project initially, but changed its position toward the end of the debate.

4.4 The Ford proposal for development of the Ferry Building Area. William L. Pereira and Associates. *Planning Study: Ford Urban Dealership San Francisco.* 1969. Courtesy of Johnson Fainn.

4.5 Model of the U.S. Steel proposal for development between the Bay Bridge and the Ferry Building. San Francisco *Chronicle*. December 13, 1969. Permission to reproduce kindly granted by the San Francisco *Chronicle*.

The heart of the argument over the U.S. Steel proposal centered on height limits, an issue becoming a common flashpoint for debate in San Francisco. Just as the project was making the rounds, the planning department was reviewing changes to the *Planning Code* that would alter height limits. This was being done as part of the process of approving various actions that would implement polices established in the *Northern Waterfront Plan*. Essentially, a policy in a new plan may call for changes to the *Planning Code* but actually making the change to the code requires a separate administrative and approval process. A month after the U.S. Steel proposal was unveiled, the planning commission approved a motion to adopt 400-foot height limits in the area between the Ferry Building and the Bay Bridge, despite opposition from planning department director Allan B. Jacobs. Commission president Mortimer Fleishhacker, Jr., voted against it. The more modest height limits proposed for the remainder of the northern waterfront were approved as proposed in the department's plan, making clear the political intentions toward the site in question. Pushing hard, newly appointed port director Miriam Wolff appealed to the planning department and the board of supervisors, arguing that even four hundred feet would not allow a building large enough to keep the interest of developers.[59] The port argued that it desperately needed a new passenger terminal and that it could not afford to construct one, let alone demolish rotting piers, without a substantial moneymaking project.[60]

In fall 1970, the board of supervisors returned the height-limit issue to the planning department, strongly hinting that 550 feet was preferred. This was not the base of Telegraph Hill, after all; rather, it was an area generally thought to be appropriate for some form of commercial development. The planning commission duly took up the proposal and, over public protests against "Manhattanizing" San Francisco, approved 550 feet in a 4-2 vote. SFT's Norman Rolfe expressed the frustration of many, stating that "we've had the argument that there will be a great exodus from the city if we don't roll over and play dead to every developer who waves a wad of money."[61] Ex-planning commissioner Gardner Mein took the anti-high-rise rhetoric a step further, exclaiming that "high rises are like heroin. . . . Once you start, you can't stop, except by drastic means, and by then it's too late." Mein was supported by Supervisor Roger Boas, who pledged to fight the project, remarking that "the board of supervisors should stand on the side of San Franciscans."[62] Board president Diane Feinstein, one of the project's most vocal critics, suggested that the building should become part of the Yerba Buena redevelopment area, a revitalization project being undertaken in a nearby section of downtown.

The two sides were polarized; either the project was a gift to San Francisco that would create jobs, help provide important waterfront amenities, and mark San Francisco as a first-class city, or it would doom the city's heritage, destroy the relationship between the place and its setting and privatize the waterfront. Thus views were also part of the debate, with supporters arguing that the proposed single slender tower would block fewer views than a shorter but more massive structure. Mayor Alioto also chafed at the idea of lower heights, saying that he would rather see a high-rise building and open space than a 40-foot "Chinese wall" running the length of the waterfront.[63] Architect Ernest Born, who helped design Embarcadero City, had become a member of the art commission, and remained true to his modernist roots by piping up in favor of U.S. Steel, suggesting that the tower would be "one of the great things in the country . . . one of the finest of our times."[64] As the debate continued, some protestors placed the blame for the offending proposal on city officials instead of U.S. Steel. In fact, throughout all of this, U.S. Steel was fairly noncommittal, perhaps a calculated move. Representatives said that the project would require a year of study and engineering tests, which could not begin until the height-limit issue was settled.

The pressure against U.S. Steel's proposal mounted with the creation of a citizen-activist umbrella group called the Citizens' Waterfront Committee and the publication of a report financed privately by Supervisor Boas and Planning Commissioner Fleishhacker. The latter pointed out that the proposed project did not conform to *Master Plan* policies as set forth in the *Northern Waterfront Plan* and further suggested that the Burton Act requirement to invest $100 million in the port be rescinded (in fact, it was later reduced to $25 million). Responding to mounting pressure, the board of supervisors could no longer delay the vote and on February 16, 1971, voted 6-4 to impose the original 84-foot height limit for 90 percent of the area in question, and 175 feet for the remaining ten.

During the debate, several supervisors pointed out that the height-limit issue was actually moot, because BCDC would not allow the construction of office buildings in any case, as seen in the case of Ferry Port Plaza. Oddly, Director Wolff made the same observation, but persisted with her stance, perhaps hoping for a favorable result from the city's suit against BCDC. On the one hand, after the vote, board members Ronald Pelosi and Roger Boas said that the port ought to get out of the real estate business and stick to shipping, a curious statement given the clear impetus for development built into the port's transfer and the northern waterfront's increasingly rundown and outmoded facilities. On the other hand, Supervisor Mendelsohn, referring to the port's aging bulkhead buildings, said that a plan which included tearing down "those stucco portals to nowhere" should be adopted.[65] Clearly, the question of what to do with the northern waterfront was far from settled. But, with the defeat of the U.S. Steel proposal, there could be a collective sigh of relief for many and a renewed vigor in making sure that plans were put into place that reflected the public interest and supported a more vibrant public realm, rather than a heavily privatized piece of waterfront.

Again we see organized labor on the side of a land-use debate at odds with environmentalists and the larger public and on the same side of the table as the stewards of capital against whom it so often struggles. Geographer Andrew Herod has suggested that "particular groups of workers may, in fact, gain more in real terms (for example, continued employment opportunities) by organizing around spatial concerns than around class ones."[66] Labor's support for the U.S. Steel project substantiates this idea to some degree. Automation caused many union jobs to disappear from the waterfront, and development would have offered alternative work and the hope that new container facilities constructed from revenues generated by such development would help keep the port's shipping activities alive. The waterfront thus became a territory to defend, a place that could produce jobs for blue-collar workers.[67] Making this happen meant labor had to work across class lines to encourage development, in this case a huge construction project. However, unlike the garment manufacturers in Herod's example, who could protect a space in Lower Manhattan to perpetuate their industry, a development like that of U.S. Steel would have offered only temporary reprieve to some workers. Moreover, it would have created a space that emphasized white-collar employment and bourgeois consumption; workers would have had a hand in pulling the rug out from under the feet of their own class. As it was, a discourse of development supported by an appeal for blue-collar jobs lost out to a discourse anchored in aesthetics and environmentalism.

The Public Sphere Expanded

The transfer brought the port into a new environment by transforming it from an agency heavily influenced by external connections into one more a part of the local political, policy, and planning context. However, the conditions imposed on it as part of the agreement, especially the onus to maximize profit, forced the port to pursue commercial development not just to support maritime activities but also to reduce the financial burdens it acquired as part of the transfer. This placed the port in the position of pursing goals at odds with how much of the public thought about the waterfront, increasing the potential for conflict with other local actors as it sought to tap into, or become a magnet for, capital investment.

But because real estate development was integral to the survival of maritime operations, as the port doggedly argued, a main "public" objective for the port was to ease the way for private interests to pursue commercial enterprise. A main difference between the port and a typical developer, though, was that the port was not seeking profit as part of what might be called an accumulation strategy. In any case, as landowner and project sponsor, the port sought to partner with private developers to implement its ideas for the use of public land. The port actively involved outside parties—agents of top-down forces such as the state and out-of-town real estate investors with national and international portfolios tied to extensive financial networks—to transform the waterfront. The phrase "public-private partnership" that would come to be much in vogue during the 1990s has roots decades long. The port's development proposals presented a striking contrast to traditional uses of the waterfront, and were seen moreover as threats to the water itself, thus running headfirst into very different ideas about what uses of public land and water should be.

And so the port's new position in the hierarchy of government, combined with the defeat of U.S. Steel, signaled the end of the agency's flirtation with modernist ideals—grand schemes for massive structures, an ordered and clean-lined waterfront, a stronghold in a new age of commerce, that would sweep away a past unfit for contemporary conditions. Had they been realized, the proposals of the 1950s and 1960s would have greatly privatized the northern waterfront, creating a more exclusive realm for a select part of the population and even more of the surface of the bay would have been paved over by modern urban advancement. But the development process was not able to stamp itself onto the landscape willy-nilly. Because none of the port's development schemes came to fruition meant that the waterfront remained largely unchanged, except that it was left to become increasingly moribund. This in turn meant that the slate remained clean for future proposals, but in a very different planning and regulatory context and with a much different potential to change the physical landscape. Indeed, the port's concepts for a bold new urban waterfront for living, tourism, and office work, but not for making or moving goods, were very different from the much more modest projects that would be proposed later, once formal concerted planning efforts were established and comprehensive plans and regulations were set forth. The differences can be characterized in terms of scale, approach, appropriateness to context, level of public benefit, and influence on the role of the city—that is, to whom or what the proposal was geared: tourists, business, maritime activity, industry, residents, commuters, and so on.

Clearly, the question of whom the waterfront was for was at the heart of the debate over these proposals. The success of local power was to make the answer to this question more subject to local judgment, to the concerns of actors and agencies working from the bottom up. This was achieved by creating new regulatory bodies and strengthening the planning process. Once a city agency, the port and its managers could not ignore the situation, and San Franciscans were not about to let them.

5

In Local Hands

New Pressures of the 1970s

THAT THE PORT had become a new city agency was a relatively straightforward change that had no immediate impact on the life of the average San Franciscan, other than to elicit a sense of pride of place perhaps. The transfer represented a shift in bureaucratic domains of only limited meaningfulness to most, and certainly there were no outward changes. Of course, for the port and those concerned with waterfront goings-on the reality was quite different. The agency's new status was a shift in local conditions to which both bottom-up and top-down forces had to adjust. It altered the nature of interactions among local and outside actors and agents; newly empowered players led to a new dynamic in the politics of planning.

Local stakeholders, particularly the mayor, members of the board of supervisors, and citizens' groups were now in a position to influence the port's affairs much more directly. And, as the agency was faced with many troubles, they were keen to do so. Attention to waterfront issues quickly widened and intensified. Fueled by local criticism, emphasis was placed on the need for a formal, policy-based vision for the port's future—a future nearly entirely fleshed out by local actors. This new stage in the evolution of waterfront planning policy and regulation was characterized by its stultifying effects on attempts to develop underutilized land in the northern waterfront. But the port's cargo operations were not entirely gone, and some still maintained that maritime operations could be resuscitated and the flow of goods reopened, despite evidence to the contrary.

Agency on the Rocks

During the 1970s and 1980s, the Port of Oakland moved along a trajectory of growth that would eventually make it the fourth busiest container port in the United States. Although San Francisco retrofitted Pier 80 to handle containers in 1967, it was not converted into a major container terminal until 1976, and to little avail. San Francisco's inability to compete with Oakland was by now unmistakable; it lost shipping lines and faced a severe reduction in the amount of cargo it handled. For most of the 1970s, the port's finances danced precariously close to the red line.

The decade or so after the transfer was a difficult time for the port in other ways. Reintegrating a large landholding agency comprising myriad economic and social functions into the city's bureaucracy was messy. The details of the Burton Act had to be ironed out, rules and regulations institutionalized, and new administrative practices established. The process was made especially thorny because the port was not going to be a typical agency connected to the city through its general fund. Rather, it was refashioned as an enterprise agency, reliant entirely on its own sources of income to function.[1] Furthermore, newly adopted city laws regarding conflict of interest resulted in the resignation of a number important figures, including several port commissioners, and generated a number of investigations and inquiries, none of which helped the port's already bruised image.[2] Moreover, the port went through five directors in fewer than ten years. Many of these difficulties were made worse by—or themselves intensified—the port's often contentious struggle to develop its property, always, it argued, to support shipping and regain something of its former greatness.

NOT DEAD YET?

Despite the gloomy maritime situation, some port commissioners, union officials, businesses, and members of the public believed that new, modern facilities would reposition the port as a primary cargo handler and that shipping even in the northern waterfront should not be abandoned. Indeed, there were still many people at the time who felt it important to protect shipping activities because they believed them to be important to the city's general economic health.

Of this group, some felt that city control of the port would actually weaken its competitive position in shipping rather than improve it. This was not an unreasonable stance given that a main argument for the transfer was that it would be a boon to non-maritime development. The *San Francisco Bay Guardian* went so far as to argue that the port was trying to dupe the public into supporting redevelopment plans, and that it was ignoring its own consultants when it suggested that shipping in the northern waterfront was not sustainable. Its editors never seemed to believe that the port was pursing commercial projects in an effort to support shipping, and that decline in the northern waterfront was real, and that at least some port staff were working to keep cargo operations alive. In fact because there was still keen interest in bolstering shipping, a number of significant programs were initiated in the 1970s and 1980s to improve and develop container and other maritime-industrial facilities.

Differing views about what the port should concentrate on underscore the difficult political situation in which the agency found itself. A grand jury appointed to oversee the transfer noted that in its first three years as a city agency, the port "has found itself handcuffed in its efforts to regain the top position it formerly held among West Coast ports" because of local politics.[3] The fact that there was a constituency (and requirement imposed by the transfer) pushing the port to keep its maritime operations alive helped keep the agency between a rock and a hard place.

But even while the port had one eye on the central and southern waterfronts, it was the northern waterfront that attracted most of the attention of neighborhood organizations, advocacy groups, and officials desperate for new sources of income. Its worn fabric needed to be repaired and stitched back into the city. Moreover, as portions of the northern waterfront fell further into decay and disuse as shipping and maritime activities declined, what comprised the northern waterfront, functionally speaking, began to creep south, and it became more urgent to figure out what to do with the waterfront. The question was not new, but was now being asked in an entirely different context by many constituencies, each with different concerns and new ways to insert themselves into the process to alter the port's course.

New Local Influences on the Port

There are five particularly important ways in which the port's status as a city agency subjected it to new influences. All would affect the waterfront landscape either directly, for instance by restricting certain land uses, or indirectly, by introducing new political pressures to pursue certain goals, for instance to provide access to bay vistas and the water's edge. First, the port's budget and administration came under scrutiny. Second, the mayor became an important figure in the port's political life. Most important, the mayor was now responsible for appointing port commissioners and confirming the commission's nominations for port director.[4] The influence of the mayor's office was also felt through special committees. Third, neighborhood associations, activist organizations, and special interest groups were made more influential because they could now apply pressure on the port through government agencies directly involved with the port's activities, whether through hearings or ballot-box activism.

Indeed, the port was now faced with a charged-up and vigilant public. The port's transfer had the effect of empowering citizens, who were now dealing with a city agency that was responsible to the mayor and in some ways to the board of supervisors, and not to the state and its more removed, less accessible political mavens. Interested parties could also make use of a new set of tools in their attempts to alter or possibly halt projects. Made available through a rapidly changing planning context, these new tools included general plan policies; historic preservation standards; the ability to protest and appeal planning entitlements (for instance conditional use permits); and the requirements of the environmental review process established by the California Environmental Quality Act (CEQA).

Related to this, the fourth source of pressure came from the port's new "sister" agencies, in particular the planning department and the SFRA, which found themselves in a new position to try their hand at influencing the port directly, especially through policies pertaining to land use and urban design. For example planning department height limits became undeniably applicable to port property, directly imposing new restraints on the physical parameters of the development of port land. More broadly, the *General Plan*'s policy goals and objectives could also be related, if not applied directly, to the port. Fifth and finally, the port was now subject to local ballot-box initiatives. The first three of these new sources of influence will be discussed in this chapter. The role of city agencies will be addressed in chapter 6, and the final point, which has proved to be of particular importance, will be addressed in chapters 7 and 8.

FINANCIAL WOES

The port was able to maintain a positive balance in fiscal year 1971–1972, despite a major longshoremen's strike.[5] But in 1972, Mayor Alioto's Port Committee, established to evaluate shipping's potential in the future and to recommend possible development projects, testified that the port would need subsidies to stay afloat financially. The port needed to make up for the income it had hoped for but failed to generate from real estate ventures in the northern waterfront. That same year, the San Francisco County Grand Jury, assigned to monitor the port in the first years after the transfer, issued a statement warning of the port's severe financial difficulties and their repercussions: "Unless corrective measures are adopted and implemented very quickly the maritime business that is slipping away from the grasp of the port will slip even faster and result in severe economic difficulties."[6]

By the middle of the decade, the port's financial condition was nearly desperate. In 1974, Mayor Alioto called for a probe into the port's financial problems, something the board of supervisors had twice voted against.[7] Supervisors Quentin Kopp and John Barbagelata, concerned that the port had been handing out sweetheart leasing deals, were particularly vocal in opposing any official probe, claiming that another inquiry would interfere with the grand jury's own investigation. The board did eventually ask the state for an audit of port management. The state agreed, and state auditor Harvey Rose issued a report at the end of the year. According to the *Chronicle*, Rose "charged that the Port had consistently over-estimated its revenues and prepared 'unrealistic budgets' in a futile attempt to avoid city tax subsidies."[8] As then interim port director Bernard Orsi commented, the report's conclusion that the port was in serious financial difficulties was no surprise. And indeed, in 1975, the port commission passed a budget that was $1.52 million in the red. However, a way was found to shuffle money around, allowing the port to avoid dipping into the city's general fund.[9]

Earlier promises made by Mayor Alioto and port commissioner Cyril Magnin that the port would be able to support itself seemed likely to be broken a year later, when the 1976 budget was short $2 million.[10] Funds were again reallocated, but even after some financial legerdemain, the balance remained in the black only because of an insurance settlement for Pier 37, which had burned down. By 1977, recently elected Mayor George Moscone and the port decided it would be worth repeating Mayor Alioto's earlier requests to the state to cancel the bond debt that was part of the transfer agreement. Nearly half of the port's budget went to paying off the interest on $86 million in bonds that it acquired as part of the conditions of the transfer.[11] Moscone's appeal in August 1977 was unsuccessful. While the state did eventually agree to stop taking a share of returns greater than $250,000, it never released the city from its bond debt obligations, which have only recently been paid off.

The port's financial problems had other sources. Naturally, some of the blame for the port's poor financial position was placed on the port's inability to implement real estate development projects, but there were more direct causes. Not as much cargo was moving through the port. The loss of several major shipping lines meant a reduction in freight handled, and therefore, a reduction in income from rents, wharfage fees, and related charges. In 1974, the port suffered an especially big hit with the loss of American President Lines (APL), at the time the port's longest-standing tenant. APL had signed on as the primary tenant of the port's new terminal at Pier 94, but its departure meant that the port had no one to occupy its new facility. Instead of earning $3.5 million per year, the port was accumulating debt service on the $30 million city bond passed by voters to build the facility. The port attempted to get Pacific Far East Lines (PFEL) to lease the terminal, but they would not agree to the rent, which was just as well as the firm went out of business in 1978, sunk by the failed LASH concept.[12]

Budget problems were also blamed on the port's failure to collect overdue rent and to increase rents on some of its properties, including the Ferry Building, when the opportunities presented themselves.[13] This became something of a public embarrassment, and was observed in particular by the grand jury, which noted the apparent lack of supervision of commercial leases. It also criticized the imbalance between the amount of money being invested in shipping facilities and the income it was receiving from its shipping tenants. Pier 80, for instance, was getting an $8 million upgrade but was not fully used.[14] Poor rent-collection practices were still an issue several years later, causing port director Tom Soules to acknowledge them publicly, attributing the situation to bad management, which created backlogs in the accounting department. Soules, not one to miss an opportunity to comment on the way things worked at the port, explained that there was a lot of pressure for the port to use a "light touch" when big clients could just move across the bay.[15] At one point, PFEL owed the port nearly $2 million in back rent. It was a time of "dead beat tenants," as one *Chronicle* article referred to the various businesses that were in arrears.[16] But in 1979, the port director, Edward L. David, could finally announce a profitable year, saying that the failure of PFEL and States Steamship Company allowed the port to find new, healthy firms (Lykes Brothers, American Flag Line, and Taiwan-based Evergreen) to which they could lease their facilities, including Pier 94.[17]

Financial difficulties, accusations of mismanagement, conflicts of interest, the probes and investigations they generated, and the new involvement of the mayor in the port's activities created at best an unsettled atmosphere in the upper echelons of the port's administration. One result was an unusual instability in the office of the director. Several anecdotes reveal the particularly contentious air that surrounded the port during most of the decade, and into the mid-1980s.[18]

DIRECTORS ADRIFT

In 1972, Supervisor Kopp, later a state assemblyman, highlighted a conclusion made by the grand jury that bad management was a main cause for the port's decline and precarious financial situation. To him, this was an indication that Director Wolff should resign.[19] About a year later, Wolff would indeed find herself on the outs. A staunch supporter of LASH technology and someone generally more interested in the port's maritime functions than in real estate, Wolff was also known to be aggressive and vigorous in defense of the port's agenda, characteristics that made her vulnerable to scapegoating when city officials decided that it was time to replace her.[20] Her stance put her somewhat at odds with Mayor Alioto and Cyril Magnin, both of whom favored concerted efforts to pursue commercial ventures. That the port's position only worsened during her tenure, and that the few commercial proposals of consequence that came past her desk failed to go anywhere, in particular Ferry Port Plaza and U.S. Steel, did not help her cause. She "left under pressure from city officials disenchanted with her work," as the *Chronicle* put it.[21]

Wolff was replaced in the interim first by Edward L. David (who would later become director under Mayor George Moscone) and then by Bernard Orsi, a close political ally of Mayor Alioto. Orsi took over the position until his permanent replacement was found. This was Tom Soules, who in turn would find himself in political hot water. Soules, a port director from Boston, was nominated by the port commission and confirmed by Alioto in January 1975.[22] Soules was hired because, in his own words and referring to Orsi, "the people of San Francisco, through the press, rebelled at having a political toady run this port."[23] That Soules got the job made some of the more development-minded people happy because of his work in Boston, which was considered an example of successful waterfront development. The hope was that he would be able to do something similar in San Francisco.

Soules, whose interests were actually oriented toward improving traditional maritime activities, had a different view of his purpose. His anti-development stance, quite untenable given the political and practical realties facing the port, was based on a vision of the working waterfront, and he openly voiced his skepticism: "There are people that want the Port's real estate so they can get rid of the railroad tracks, the hustle-bustle of business on the piers, just so they can have clear views."[24] He also remarked that no port in the world could survive if it became a political football. Soules made things even more difficult for himself by contesting requests for leases made by politically connected prospects.[25] This and his rather gruff, impolitic approach put Soules on the wrong side of Moscone, who was elected during his third year as director.

Unfortunately for Soules, Moscone gained control of the port commission through several key appointments. The only appointee left from Alioto's administration was labor leader Harry Bridges. In 1977, Moscone and two of his main allies on the commission—Jack Morrison and James J. Rudden—asked Soules to step down. Soules fought to keep his post, but the commission fired him, claiming that he was "a poor administrator who was unable to revive the long-dormant waterfront and unwilling to take advice." The day he was given notice, Soules remarked that "the mayor and the commission think they can give the public the illusion that they are fighting for shipping. But that's what I've always done, not them."[26] With Soules out, Moscone and his port commission were free to select a director who would support their vision for the waterfront.[27] The mayor approved the commission's selection of Edward L. David, a longtime employee of the port. Sadly, the assassination of Mayor Moscone made their relationship a short one.

The primary observation to be made from the preceding discussion is that the port's new status as a city agency placed it in an entirely new political, administrative, and managerial realm because the port had become more directly important to local politicians. Mayors recognized that the fortunes of the port would have significant consequences for their administrations. This meant that the port directors would have to deal with the pressure to respond to mayoral imperatives. The port's budget problems were particularly unfortunate because it was expected that the transfer was going to line the city's collective pocket. Instead, financial problems placed the port under intense public scrutiny, particularly when it became known that it could not even collect the rent. Attention to the port's fiscal situation only served to charge further the political atmosphere around the port because politicians now had to deal with the possibility that this new agency might not be able to maintain its self-sufficiency. Alioto, Moscone, and their successors recognized the potential impacts of the port's success or failure on their administrations. Tapping into the city's general funds to bail out the port, although potentially necessary, would not have been attractive.

That the mayor, and to a lesser degree the board of supervisors, were now playing direct roles in how the port functioned made it harder for the port to establish policy regarding the use of its land and its future as an agency. The struggle to create consistency between the mayor's and director's vision for the port (and often the commission's) resulted in turnover at the director's level, which helped stymie the port's ability to establish firmly, let alone pursue consistently, a set of goals and priorities. One result was that the question of how to strike a balance between commercial development and maritime industry was a major point of contention, both within the agency and among those who would influence its course. This was both reflected in and perpetuated by the lack of a body of coherent policy for the port, particularly in the form of a planning policy document, that could provide general guidance and some structure for decision making. Other agencies, particularly the planning department and BCDC, did establish policy for the waterfront. But the lack of coordination among policy-making bodies, and the fact that the port was not one of them, was another source of delay in revitalizing the northern waterfront. Furthermore, this situation contributed to the decline that would begin to find

its way to the port's southern waterfront, despite several projects undertaken to modernize its facilities. Lacking its own plan also meant that the
port really did not have a formalized, public voice, making it susceptible to
being the political football about which Director Soules openly worried.

A PIECE OF THE ACTION: CITIZENS' GROUPS
AND OFFICIAL COMMITTEES

Public concern over the issues generated by the U.S. Steel project did not
die with its defeat in 1971. On the contrary, the whole affair was so unset-
tling to those concerned about the port and the waterfront that it helped
galvanize activists to create at least two citizen's committees and drew the
attention of the fairly young SFT. Encouraged by their role in the creation
of the BCDC and the subsequent defeat of U.S. Steel, groups such as SFT, the
Bay Chapter of the Sierra Club and neighborhood organizations including
the Telegraph Hill Dwellers Association and the Potrero Hill Residents and
Homeowners Association began to advocate more broadly for public access
to the waterfront and for more publicly minded development.

Indeed, everyone who had a stake or interest in the port seemed to
form special port-related committees or put waterfront issues on their
agendas. Each group had somewhat different concerns and purposes, but
all saw advantage in the city's new stewardship of the port, which made
the new agency responsible not just to other city agencies and the mayor
but to these committees and advisory groups as well. In particular, savvy
neighborhood and advocacy groups could influence the tenor and often
the nature of the debate over what to do with the waterfront through
their involvement in the local political process, something they had been
a part of for a long time and knew intimately. Now, however, there were
political, administrative, and legislative means to influence both waterfront-related policy and specific decisions about development. They could
become engaged in the growing role of planning and policy formulation,
and participate with realistic hopes of affecting the process and ultimately
the physical form of the waterfront.

Not only did the public influence the content of planning documents
but it could also then use the policies to evaluate and even contest development they considered inappropriate.[28] The struggle over the future
of the waterfront had finally been brought to familiar turf. San Fran-

cisco had cut its activist teeth in the 1950s during the freeway revolt and sharpened them in fights over redevelopment and the "mad rush to the sky," albeit a number of battles were unsuccessful.[29] So, as the port was brought into the sphere of influence of a city reeling toward visions of shining urban renewal and a downtown of corporate glory reaching skyward, it was also facing an experienced public. The subsequent discussion will touch on the interests of a few of the most influential of these citizens advisory committees.

Unhappy with the U.S. Steel proposal and the actions of the port commission, board of supervisors member Roger Boas and planning commissioner Mortimer Fleishhacker, Jr., formed a small private committee sometime around 1970 and commissioned a study of the port. The report concluded that revenue generated by commercial development would not be sufficient to pay for needed modernization. So, in addition to coming out against both the U.S. Steel project and a proposal for a new passenger terminal, the "citizens' group" (as *Chronicle* referred to the Fleishhacker-Boas committee) advised Mayor Alioto that the port had better build a new container terminal at Islais Creek if it was to have any hope of staving off San Francisco's demise as a major shipping port. In a letter to Mayor Alioto, Boas and Fleishhacker wrote, "instead of turning to real estate development, the port should turn to the city for financial support," something that the port was loath to do.[30] Responding to the advice to modernize, which fairly closely followed their own evaluation, the port commission did in fact pursue projects to upgrade their cargo operations. With successful passage of a 1971 $34 million bond measure, secured by prearranged leasing agreements to fund the project, the port was able to avoid financial dependence on the city and initiate construction of a new terminal at Pier 94 on Islais Creek, although even that project would not significantly staunch the loss of cargo.

The goals of the Boas and Fleishhacker committee were different from those of the more truly citizen-based group of the 1970s, the very active Citizens' Waterfront Committee (CWC). The Fleishhacker-Boas committee was interested in supporting and continuing the port's maritime functions while the CWC's interest was in saving the bay from further fill, and getting the port to come up with a long-range plan that would ensure public benefit from shoreline uses. The CWC was an umbrella group formed late in 1970 largely in response to the U.S. Steel and Ferry Port Plaza projects.

Richard N. Goldman, the CWC's chairman, heavily criticized the port, saying, "we look forward to an orderly development of the waterfront to which the community can point with pride rather than disdain."[31] The CWC maintained a deep suspicion of the port's claim that it needed commercial development to support cargo and other maritime operations. The committee thus unveiled its own plan for the northern waterfront, one that concentrated on providing open space and commercial recreation (shopping and entertainment, for instance). The CWC also claimed that their plan could be implemented at no cost to taxpayers. Lawrence Livingston, Jr., primary author of the CWC plan, also argued that the third of the port's land not needed for maritime operations could be leased for private development that could then pay for public access for the other the two- thirds, most of which was in the northern waterfront.[32] Their proposals included building an elevator and funicular system at Telegraph Hill and turning Pier 33 into a "maritime park" and restaurant (Fig. 5.1). Their vision for the Ferry Building area would have pulled the shoreline back away from the terminal itself, making it an island that, theoretically, would have provided access to the bay for hundreds of thousands of people.[33] Not surprisingly, the CWC's particular proposals were not implemented, though their general call for open space and public recreation did indeed resonate. And while not necessarily realistic, some of their suggestions for funding more modest projects (HUD grants, for instance) were pursued.

Goldman and the CWC, working with SFT and a group of planners and architects, spearheaded another plan for the Ferry Building area, this time with a grant from the National Endowment for the Arts. Called Embarcadero Gardens (or sometimes Tivoli Gardens), the 1973 proposal called for converting the area between Piers 7 and 24 into a place of "floating restaurants, a carousel, a show boat, an esplanade for strolling lovers . . . fountains, boutiques, and picnic facilities 'all with a maritime flavor.'"[34] The CWC's concept was supposedly modeled after the Tivoli Gardens in Copenhagen and the Piazza San Marco in Venice. Embarcadero Gardens included an amusement area, a boardwalk of theaters, galleries, bars, berths for 150 boats and, inland, space for offices. In its scope, the concept harkened back to some of the "grand plans" of earlier decades, but its focus was quite different; that is, it was geared primarily to bringing people out to the water, and its uses were envisioned as attractions to San Francisco residents, not just tourists or downtown workers. Indeed, half of the area was proposed for open space. The CWC envisioned structures that jutted out over the

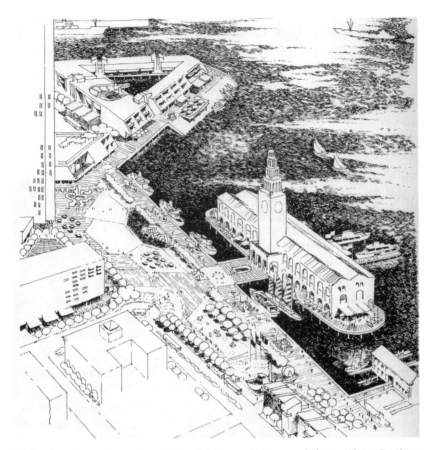

5.1 Development concept for part of the Ferry Building area. Livingston and Blayney, *What to Do About the Waterfront*, Citizens' Waterfront Committee, 1971.

water, removing activities from the freeway's dominating presence.[35] As a concept, it was generally well received by Cyril Magnin, the port commission, SPUR, the Telegraph Hill Dwellers, and Mayor Alioto's Port Committee. However, although Goldman asserted that the project would not need money from the city, and the CWC's economic consultants projected substantial revenue, the project did not materialize.[36] What it did do, however, was force the port to engage seriously with the proposal, and it helped create more widely held public expectations about what might be done with that particular stretch of the waterfront.

So, even though the Embarcadero Gardens was not to be, it was important in that, as CWC's planning consultant George Rockrise commented, "'a remarkable feature of the plan' is that for the first time a civic group, the

Citizens' Waterfront Committee that commissioned the Gardens, has made a 'truly positive contribution to a development project.'"[37] While activists were not successful in getting their development proposals implemented or in forcing immediate change in planning policy, their involvement did buy them a place at the new table and thus another opportunity to voice concerns and influence policy—as reflected in later versions of the Planning Department's *Northern Waterfront Plan* and in BCDC's *Special Area Plan*.[38] For example, Richard Goldman, chair of the CWC, was chosen as one of the thirteen members of Mayor Alioto's special citizens' committee.[39] Frustrated by the port's decline and not provided with an agreed-upon strategy for its revival, the mayor formed the Port Committee in 1972. Its charge was to "satisfy both economic and esthetic considerations in proposing future uses of the city's Northern Waterfront."[40] The creation of this committee, which included representatives from the planning department, the board of supervisors, BCDC, SPUR, advocacy groups, labor, and private business, clearly signaled the influence that activists and neighborhood groups concerned with the environment and public access now had in shaping the debate over the waterfront. In his statement to the new committee, Mayor Alioto admitted that the port's northern waterfront could support more public use. As he noted, "Right now . . . the people cannot get to the bay. In times of the ferry boats, everyone had a consciousness of the water . . . now we simply have no physical or visual contact with the bay. Right now, what you have is a slum."[41] The committee itself concluded that "subsidization of the maritime activities of the port by income from its non-maritime properties should not be allowed to lead to poor exploitation of the non-maritime properties."[42] The mayor's committee began its work with the notion that the port's cargo operations might no longer be important to San Francisco, but ended by concluding that in fact these activities were very important to the city. This led the committee to warn that unless the port overhauled its facilities, it would not be able to compete with other West Coast ports.

Alioto also created a committee to prevent Fisherman's Wharf from becoming a "plastic Disneyland" and to preserve the "original spirit of Fisherman's Wharf," an unsurprising move given his family's restaurant business and the many friends and political connections he had in and with the wharf. His particular concerns were Piers 45 and 47, then used for storing newsprint (not what the mayor considered the highest and best use), improvement of conditions for the fishing fleet, and the creation of a promenade from the wharf to the Ferry Building.[43] Unfortunately, he and the committee were unable to prevent the production of a space of intense consumption in the wharf, epitomized by the now world famous Pier 39. However, ideas very similar to Alioto's would be implemented as part of more recent changes to the waterfront. In fact, some of these improvements have helped remove at least a little of the plastic, Disney-like quality that has characterized much of Fisherman's Wharf. The committee eventually decided that its focus should be on restoring the fishing fleet, and in that regard, securing long-term leases for fishing and related businesses was critical.

Three final observations can be made with regard to the proliferation of citizens' advisory groups. First, their support for improved shoreline open space and water access were difficult for the port to accommodate because such public benefits are expensive, often necessitating substantial, high-rent development to support them. Moreover, citizens' advisory groups were also generally skeptical toward office and commercial development—the kinds of land uses that generate sufficient income to provide those public benefits. To make matters worse, by the mid-1970s state and federal subsidies and grants for development, including parks and open space, were increasingly very hard to come by. This situation created tension over the disposition of scarce resources, intensified by the need to decide how to use income from development, should it be forthcoming, for competing purposes. If the income from the commercial "economic engine" of a project were to be diverted to providing recreation and public open space, then there would likely be nothing left to support commercial maritime uses—the port's main impetus for developing its real estate holdings. Second, the development dynamic was now much more complex. As more groups became involved, more voices were added to an already large chorus. In later years, differing opinions about what should happen on the waterfront, and even how particular projects should be configured, would help delay the development of plans and even kill development proposals. There was and still is an irony at work. Planning documents were intended to help make decisions about how and where development should occur but the plans, and the processes of developing them, came to include and empower many voices, which often resulted in a tangle of argumentation and fractured purposes.

Third, citizens' advisory committees convened by public agencies to participate in setting goals for policy documents and redevelopment plans were created by selection not election. The community as a group did not offer candidates for appointment or vote on representatives to participate in the planning process. So, a small handful of self-selected or autocratically appointed people represented and acted on behalf of the wider community. Furthermore, certain people were selected repeatedly to serve on different groups (a practice that continues), reducing the depth of representation that the term *citizens' advisory committee* implies. Thus while citizens' advisory committees help make the public planning process more manageable and focused, they tend to empower individuals with strong personalities or those people who have the time and desire to be actively involved but who may not in fact share the concerns of a majority of the community and may not represent their many views and opinions in a public forum. It is not uncommon for community members who are not part of a citizens' advisory committee or citizens' advisory group to testify at public hearings in opposition to those groups.

By way of a summary, the 1970s and early 1980s found the port on the defensive. It had administrative difficulties, it lost shipping lines, the LASH technology it adopted failed, it all but lost the fight for container cargo, and its attempts at commercial development were sensational failures. Publicity was not favorable. This made the port's absorption into San Francisco's body politic a difficult process. Even so, the port's new political context deeply influenced the planning process that would become a critical factor in the waterfront's evolution. A diverse and vocal group of stakeholders would influence public agencies as they began to plan feverishly for the embattled port's future. Yet, as we have seen, bottom-up or local forces have many voices; it is a chorus whose members change, and in which some voices may be louder at times than others. Local actors and agents that comprise bottom-up forces may compete with one another, and may switch positions depending on circumstances. This underscores the complex nature of interactions among agents and agencies that, while they affect the landscape, do so in ways not necessarily apparent in the built environment.

Another way to view the relationship between and among neighborhood groups, activists, business interests, and the port is as a struggle to establish a dominant discourse and in turn leverage a rhetoric powerful enough to influence the decision making process. Indeed, empowered by new policy, regulation, and public processes, environmentalists and community organizations were able to frame a new, competing discourse in opposition to the mantra of development coming from the port and supporters of real estate development. Tussles over discourses can occur even within agencies or organizations. The port commission's relationship with its director during this period resulted at least partially from a desire to control how the agency would establish its own discourse over development and ensure that it sent a single message to the public.

But inasmuch as a discourse can be thought of as the purposeful manipulation of language, or argumentation, in an attempt to exercise power or control over a situation (or group of people), or as a form of legitimation, the port's attempts at establishing one could only have limited success given the circumstances. The port was in the difficult position of having to assert that maritime activity was its main activity and that real estate development was just something that had to be done to support its primary mission. The reality was that commercially based redevelopment had become one of two primary missions, and actual attempts to do what it argued was necessary ran into a discursive framework of another kind—policy and regulation.

The next chapter turns to a discussion of some of the most important planning documents to evolve during the 1970s and early 1980s. These plans were the creations of agencies that took on the responsibility for establishing the vision of what the waterfront should and could be. With the exception of the port, these agencies had the tools to frame this vision and, in some instances, to implement it. They were also responding to demands from the public and therefore reflected public interest, which increased the power of local agencies and actors to influence the landscape. As planning strengthened and policies generated through planning policy evolved, the ability of local entities to negotiate with larger forces, especially the pressures of capitalist development, was also enhanced. These plans then, along with an increasingly active and knowledgeable citizenry, represented a solidification of local power.

6

The Best Laid Plans

PLANNING, AS THE apothegm of practitioners goes, is best done in a down cycle. The idea is simple: when the economy is stuttering along there is less pressure on land markets and the flow of building permits eases. This means, theoretically at least, that planners have more breathing room to consider new policy or to implement new zoning. When the economy is booming and projects are coming in fast, there is much more political pressure to approve development and to grandfather projects already in the pipeline so they are subject to the older, possibly more lax rules. During up cycles, planners are warned not to kill the goose laying the proverbial golden egg.[1]

However, during the 1970s and 1980s in San Francisco—a period of significant economic growth—planning progressed in significant ways. Rather than honing in on specific issues generated by particular proposals, the focus was broadened, largely by community activists, to address what planning's purview should be, how the planning process should be managed, and who should participate. Much of this played out in battles over the transformation of downtown as the anti-growth movement engaged the entrenched growth regime. Rampant office development led activists to emphasize the socioeconomic effects of such growth, not just its aesthetic and environmental impacts.[2] The case was made that new offices brought more employees into the city, which strained the public transit system, increased demand for housing (driving housing costs up), and did not provide jobs for the people in San Francisco who needed them most. A rising tide, it was strongly argued, did not lift all boats.

Over a period of about fifteen years starting in the early 1970s, activists became increasingly organized and expanded their coalition to include a range of neighborhoods and ethnic communities. They also adopted several effective strategies to advance their cause. Groups such as San Franciscans for Reasonable Growth (SFRG) were adept at using the information and public process mandated by CEQA to their advantage. Data in environmental impact reports (EIRs) were used to help substantiate the nexus between office development and negative social and economic impacts on the city. Lawsuits were filed to stop projects that did not publish sufficient EIRs.[3] When faced with a recalcitrant bureaucracy, ballot-box initiatives helped bring their concerns into the public spotlight and, even when they failed, forced officials to acknowledge that uncontrolled growth could have undesirable consequences. Urban growth was made a political hot-button issue.

Eventually anti-growth forces were quite successful. The landmark 1985 Downtown Plan was adopted in response to their concerns. While it did many positive things, such as protect historic structures through transfer of development rights and require fees from developers to support public art, open space, transportation, and housing, its critics argued that it did not slow growth sufficiently. Thus SFRG spearheaded an effective grassroots campaign to put Proposition M on the ballot in 1986. It passed, and the nation's first annual limit on office construction was implemented.[4]

As the planning process became the prime venue for these struggles, and more generally for hammering out political bargains that could alter the course of urban change, the port was sucked into the maelstrom, pushed and pulled by top-down pressure and local resistance. While downtown the outcome of struggles over development was that growth continued in a more or less managed fashion, on the waterfront the result was different. There, the engagement between larger forces (and their local embodiments) and local resistance resulted, for the most part, in a standstill.

Another Cycle of Top-down Forces

By the end of the 1970s, containerized cargo had become the standard method for moving most goods. The reduced cost of transporting goods in

SAN FRANCISCO EMPLOYMENT AND ESTABLISHMENTS FOR SELECTED 2-DIGIT SICS, 1970 AND 1990				
	1970	1990	Difference	% Change
Manufacturing	58,911	36,351	-22,560	-38%
Transportation and Utilities	53,015	40,690	-12,325	-23%
Wholesale	43,163	29,937	-13,226	-30%
Retail	58,229	83,503	25,204	43%
Services	65,574	79,987	14,413	22%
FIRE	97,211	207,969	110,758	139%

6.1 San Francisco employment for selected 2-digit SICs, 1970 and 1990. U.S. Census, *County Business Patterns.*

containers helped speed the relocation of industrial production, which in turn helped set the stage for the transformation of urban economies and the rise of the postindustrial city. So, as the port was in decline, the rest of San Francisco was on the rise. Between 1970 and 1990, the total number of employees in the city grew from 401,863 to 520,059, an increase of 118,196 or 29.4 percent (Fig. 6.1).[5] The finance, insurance, and real estate sector itself more than doubled to 110,758 employees, accounting for more than 90 percent of the total growth in employment. Together, the retail, service, finance, insurance, and real estate sectors grew from 55 percent of the city's total employment to 71 percent. These same sectors added 9,402 establishments—84 percent of the city's total increase in businesses. Such growth continued to put pressure on the downtown to expand. So, while part of the city's economic growth could be met by vertical expansion, it also spread horizontally into SoMa, adjacent to the downtown financial district.[6]

Between 1965 and 1983, downtown office space doubled, adding 36 million square feet.[7] During the 1970s, San Francisco's annual economic growth rate of about 3.5 percent exceeded the national average and the 1980s saw a decline in unemployment.[8] These figures are indicators of what many urbanists have identified as contemporary global capital working to reform cities, especially their downtowns, as transnational and multinational corporations seek to diversify investment through real estate and to establish nodes in the global financial and information network; essentially, real estate was being integrated into global capital markets.[9] And of course, globalizing cities function as command and control centers, and not just of transactions speeding through the ether. They are emplacements—they have to be situated some*where*, and that place, the locale or region, deeply affects a city's globalized character.[10]

Another top-down force affecting cities during the 1970s and 1980s was a shift in federal funding for urban development and redevelopment from direct grants to programs such as the Urban Development Action Grants (UDAG) that required the inclusion of private funding. The Reagan administration emphasized defederalizing urban programs, which served to increase privatization as both a factor in and a result of urban redevelopment (for instance, helping generate an era of public-private partnerships). The resulting change in the character of urban space can be seen literally in the streets of downtown San Francisco, where placards embedded in some sidewalks announce that the right to pass is granted by the building's owner. It is also seen in the nature of open space provision. Through its Downtown Plan, San Francisco requires open space for new major downtown construction, but it is often incorporated into rooftop areas, making it accessible only to those who know where it is—usually just employees in the building itself. At the street level are many examples of open spaces with features that degrade the public realm: they are designed defensively, are not well connected to the street, or their insufficient size or arrangement makes them unsuitable for public gatherings.

The privatization of public space (where the private sphere is seen as a more efficient regulator of space than government), the devolution of government responsibilities from the federal to the local, and tightened funding for social programs are all elements of neoliberalism. Neoliberal urbanism produces other features in the built environment including reductions in the number of affordable housing units produced; increased control over and surveillance of public space; the spread of privately developed public land; business improvement districts; enterprise zones; certain forms of gentrification; and support for heritage districts and place-marketing (which emphasize spectacle for the middle and upper classes as opposed to services and facilities for the poor and marginalized).[11] The most fundamental of these represent challenges to one's right to the city; that is, the right to live in, work in, and participate in its continual creation.

Starting in the 1970s, however, large-scale forces that influence development and the politics surrounding it, such as postindustrialization, increased globalization, and the dawn of an age of neoliberal urbanism, were met at the waterfront by the powerful counteractive effects of a bevy of new policy documents and land-use plans. They represented the success of members of the public and a spate of organizations to leverage three related points to their advantage as they sought to manage the planning process and direct its outcomes: 1) that it was important to preserve the city's remarkable and beautiful setting; 2) that unconstrained development meant further degradation of the environment, of the regional ecology; and 3) that everyone should be able to enjoy the natural, historical, and cultural resources associated with the waterfront. The second point lifted the argument from one of aesthetics and NIMBYism to something more substantial and pressing, while the third made the debate immediately relevant to the public at large.

But it takes more than pressure from the public to produce policy and land-use controls; the local state—government agencies and decision-making bodies—must have the will and wherewithal to follow through. The first step was to recognize that both the 1969 *Northern Waterfront Plan* and the *Bay Plan* needed to be updated to address issues raised by the fight over development near the Ferry Building. There was also an urgent need to clarify BCDC's role in determining the use of port property and to reimagine how the city should relate, physically and functionally, to its newly acquired waterfront, especially in the northern reaches. What follows is a discussion of the most important changes and updates to the policy documents that applied to the waterfront. In the end, these plans most directly settled the question of "What to do with the waterfront?"[12]

Winds of Change: New Planning Policy Documents

The importance of the waterfront to the total community is recognized
through the planning procedures which have been adopted.[13]
—Port of San Francisco, *Port and Shipping Handbook 1988–1989*

During the 1970s and 1980s, while the port was adjusting to its new circumstances, the planning department, SFRA, and BCDC embarked on intensive planning efforts that would further affect the port's ability to dispose of its property.[14] These plans presented a new level of detail and comprehensiveness in their determinations about where the port could pursue particular activities, and established a more complex set of requirements to be met for any potential development. The evolution of the planning and regulatory environment took the port full swing from an essentially open field in the 1950s to a tangled jungle of policy twenty-five years later. The port's position was not helped by the lack of its own solid vision for its future, particularly with regard to land use. In fact, the port did not even have a professional planner on its staff before 1982. A Planning and Community Affairs Division, later renamed Planning and Development, was created by Michael Huerta after he became the port's executive director in 1989. This meant that while the port was involved in the development of plans and planning concepts for the waterfront, other agencies took the helm when it came to writing policy. Ironically then, even though the port was semiautonomous, unlike other city agencies it would have only limited control over its own fate—at least as far as non-maritime activities were concerned. The best the port could do was participate in various planning efforts, continue to maintain its facilities, try to improve its maritime business, especially shipping, and, as will be seen later, pursue more modest projects in an effort to meet the conditions placed on it.

Policies in the plans that were published and updated during the 1970s and 1980s generally favored protection of existing maritime uses and support for shipping. For our purposes, though, the most important focus was on areas of the port no longer used or needed for maritime activities, nearly all of which were in the northern waterfront. The northern waterfront had been transformed by years of decline and neglect; few piers were in active use and by the late 1970s, many were abandoned or falling apart. As it was often described, much of the waterfront north of China Basin Channel was becoming blighted. Given the port's history of proposals for monumental projects that showed little consideration for existing urban form, that all but ignored the public realm, and that treated the bay as potential landfill, conservationists, activists, and public agencies recognized that to make the most of the opportunities presented by disused port property, plans for revitalization that reflected their concerns had to be formulated.

THE PLANNING DEPARTMENT'S REVISED NORTHERN WATERFRONT PLAN

The planning department acted first with amendments to the *Northern Waterfront Plan* in 1971.[15] The essential policies were not significantly altered; it retained objectives and policies pertaining to land use, transportation, and urban design for the waterfront and land-side areas within its boundaries, but it did not include a section on implementation. It also remained rooted in John Bolles' 1968 work, much to the consternation of environmentalists, who were unhappy that policies for expanding commercial development over the water were retained. At the time, the city was suing BCDC over the Ferry Port Plaza project with the hope that it would be able to maintain control of the nature of waterfront development. The suit failed, but to activists like Richard Gryziec of San Francisco Tomorrow it appeared that such legal action and the "weak" *Northern Waterfront Plan* were part and parcel of the city's attempt to foster the commercialization of port property and nearby land, not sufficiently recognizing the waterfront as a unique natural resource.

The purpose of the *Northern Waterfront Plan* was to "guide the future development in all areas on and contiguous to the harbor in a manner consistent with the interests of San Francisco."[16] These interests were narrowly defined, as many critics vocally argued, and with the advent of BCDC's plans for the San Francisco waterfront in 1969, the plan was in need of an update. In fact, the next major set of amendments to the *Northern Waterfront Plan*, adopted six years later in 1977, changed its title to the *Northeastern Waterfront Plan* and were conceived largely to bring it into conformity with BCDC's 1975 *Special Area Plan* (discussed below), which itself was simultaneously amended "to ensure congruency with the City's plan."[17] Perhaps most important, the *Northeastern Waterfront Plan* was amended to reflect BCDC's prohibition of office and housing on new replacement fill. The 1977 version was much more attentive to the public's interest—the right to the waterfront—especially with regard to access to the bay, sensible transit, and the promotion of coherent urban design framework for the area.[18] It also more carefully focused visions for commercial development, especially by removing ideas of building the city out over the water, thus excising much of Bolles' earlier work.

An important cause for these changes was the input of a planning advisory committee, which included what was fast becoming a familiar cast of characters: William D. Evers (who had left BCDC and now represented SPUR), Supervisor Dianne Feinstein, James Herman (ILWU), Richard Goldman (CWC), and Jean Kortum (of SFT, and Karl Kortum's wife). Such committees were not required, however. Rather, they reflected the influence of neighborhood activists and advocacy groups. They have no legal

authority but are important because they can lend legitimacy to the planning process, especially by ensuring that it does not occur "behind closed
doors." One limitation, however, is the choice of members. As noted earlier, they tend to be from a partially self-selected group of people who are
interested and active in planning issues. Even so, the development discourse was changing and becoming more inclusive.[19] The SFRA, however, is
required to create a citizens' advisory committee or project area committee
when establishing a redevelopment area. Naturally, the role and tenure of
these two kinds of committees and similar groups varies based on many
factors. The advisory committee for the 1977 *Northeastern Waterfront Plan*
was similar in composition to the WAC and the Northeastern Waterfront
Advisory Committee (discussed below), making committee members an
influential coterie. In a similar vein, the same consultants are hired for
many different projects. For instance, the port and Boris Dramov of the
design firm ROMA have had a decades-long relationship.

New priorities resulted in a plan with the clear intention of responding
to community concerns. As the plan's authors noted:

> The San Francisco community, in general, has changed its interests and
> desires for the northern waterfront such that significant concerns for pre-
> serving maritime uses, creating open space and controlling traffic have been
> expressed since the adoption of the existing Northern Waterfront Plan.
> These concerns are reflected throughout the Objectives and Policies of this
> Plan for the Northeastern Waterfront.[20]

The new plan offered a vision quite different from the massive development proffered not so long before, one that revealed a new consciousness of
the water and thus a more public role for the northern waterfront, as can
be seen for example in Policy 1, which called on the city to "preserve the
physical form of the waterfront and reinforce San Francisco's distinctive hill
form by maintaining low structures near the water, with increases in vertical development near the hills or the downtown core area"[21] and Policy 5,
which permitted "non-maritime development bayward of the sea wall only
if . . . maximum feasible public access is provided to the water's edge."[22]

The complement to the plan's more cautious and focused stance toward
commercial development was its support of the port's maritime activities.
For example, Objective 1 called for "retain[ing] and enhance[ing] maritime
activities, reserving as much of northeastern waterfront as is realistically

required for future maritime use, and providing for efficient operation of port activities,"[23] and Policy 2 called for "continu[ing] maritime activities on Pier 45, Piers 35 through 9 and Piers 26 through 32 as long as practical.[24] The plan also required that non-maritime development on the bay side of the seawall, east of the Embarcadero, provide maximum feasible public access, protect views, and retain historic structures. Finally, the plan recognized that it was important to "diversify activities to encourage the use of Northeastern Waterfront by a *broad spectrum of the population*," and that it should have "recreation facilities attractive to residents and visitors of *all ages and income groups*."[25] Policy statements like this cannot force inclusion or prevent exclusion, but they go a long way to putting the public in public space.

Like the 1969 version, the 1977 plan applied to an area several blocks inland, beyond the port's waterfront jurisdiction. This brings up one nearly constant source of friction between the planning department and the port. The port was ever focused on the area under its jurisdiction and with its need for income-earning development. The planning department, however, was concerned with the larger issues of how the city and its waterfront should relate together. This difference in perspective led to variations or conflicts in priorities regarding land use, transportation, urban design, and open space. The imposition of the 40-foot height limit along most of the waterfront is an example of the Planning Department's broader perspective, at least at the time. The height limit reflects concern for public view corridors from inland to the bay, and with preventing the construction of a physical barrier between the city and the water, instead of just maximizing development potential.

The *Northeastern Waterfront Plan* was amended again in 1980. New language fleshed out many of the basic principles reflected in its objective and policies, including those pertaining to the environment, and the relationship between the city and the water. For instance, with respect to the Ferry Building Area, the plan stated that "contrary to previous proposals for extensive bay fill, the Plan calls for open water as a relief to the intensely developed downtown and to ensure the continued prominence of the Ferry Building and its tower. The Ferry Building would be reestablished as . . . a major entryway to the City from the water." And from its Commerce Objective, Policy 1: "Except on new or replacement fill, permit additional office space development adjacent to the Downtown Office District which complements the downtown but which is of a lesser intensity and which reflects the transition between city and water."[26] There were also more substantial changes. First was the addition of policies that supported the intent to develop the area just north of the China Basin Channel, known as South Beach, as a mixed-use residential area, as suggested in the SFRA's *Northeastern Waterfront Survey* and echoed in the *Total Design Plan* and the port's own *Maritime Strategy* (discussed below). Second revisions created a policy document more pointedly interested in reducing the impact of the automobile on the waterfront. Perhaps the single most significant aspect of the 1980 plan was the inclusion of a new section on the so-called Embarcadero Corridor. Planners took aim at the general mess created by the Embarcadero (or rather, how it was used) along much of its northern waterfront alignment. With the maritime-industrial character of the northern waterfront all but gone, both the Embarcadero freeway and the surface road stood as effective barriers to creating a new waterfront. The freeway itself was the single most disruptive element preventing good public access to the waterfront, especially at its most publicly important section—the Ferry Building area. Parking underneath the freeway, at intervals along the Embarcadero roadway, and on piers themselves (parking is very lucrative), in conjunction with an almost dead State Belt Line only added to the increasingly moribund feeling of much of the waterfront between Fisherman's Wharf and China Basin Channel (Figs 6.2 and 6.3).[27]

With a new Embarcadero would come a new northern waterfront. The 1980 plan called for the removal of the freeway and presented a series of policies for rejuvenating the Embarcadero, including pedestrian walkways along the water, the extension of transit services along its length, and rerouting the roadway to accommodate open space and water-related activities. Policies in the plan also stated that these improvements should be carried out without disrupting remaining maritime activities. The impetus for the Embarcadero Corridor proposals was the expectation that federal money would be available to remove the freeway. Instead, it would take ten years and an earthquake before the visions of a new Embarcadero could materialize. In a final break with past thinking about the range of uses appropriate for a new, "modern" waterfront, the plan included a policy to "prohibit heliports or STOL ports," which had been part of earlier proposals. This, plus a stronger stance against prioritizing the automobile, resistance to monumental development, and new concern for the preservation of historic aspects of the waterfront, most practically through

6.2 The Ferry Building isolated by the Embarcadero Freeway. Mayor's Economic Development Council, *San Francisco Central Waterfront Adjustment Strategy*, 1978.

6.3 Decrepit and mostly removed piers north of the Ferry Building. Port of San Francisco, *An Action Plan for San Francisco's Waterfront*, 1979.

adaptive reuse of old warehouses, signaled the end in San Francisco of waterfront planning in the age of the modern.

BCDC'S SPECIAL AREA PLAN

BCDC was not idle after the adoption of its *Bay Plan*. The mandate to regulate bay fill had been reaffirmed by the failure of the city's lawsuit over Ferry Port Plaza, and so the agency moved to solidify its role by creating detailed and geographically specific guidelines regarding the nature of development that could occur within its San Francisco jurisdiction. It also wanted to put to rest any concerns left over from the adverse reactions to Ferry Port Plaza and U.S. Steel, and, perhaps, demonstrate that it was not callous about the port's difficulties. In essence, BCDC was able to transform its regulatory power into land-use planning policy. In 1973, at the behest of Chairman William D. Evers, BCDC established a committee whose particular focus was the San Francisco waterfront. The committee would quickly become a powerful voice in the debate over waterfront development. The purpose of the committee, referred to as the waterfront advisory committee (WAC), was to devise a way to satisfy BCDC's mandate to preserve the bay while supporting the port's need to generate income to bolster its maritime activities. Its members represented a cross-section of interests and included Supervisor Diane Feinstein, Cyril Magnin, Richard Gryziec (SFT), and Richard Goldman (WAC), as well as representatives from the planning department, environmental and residents' groups, and SPUR. The WAC worked for two years to develop what it believed was a solid policy document for the port's waterfront. The fact that consensus was reached led one member to refer to the plan as a "miracle between paper covers."[28] Entitled the *San Francisco Waterfront Special Area Plan*, it was adopted as an amendment to the *Bay Plan* in 1975.

The *Special Area Plan* signaled BCDC's evolution from an agency concerned generally with the protection of the bay into a regulatory agency with broad planning powers particular to San Francisco. The commission is able to enforce its policy because at its core BCDC is a permit-granting agency, and can thus deny developers entitlements if it determines that even a part of a proposal is in conflict with the *Bay Plan* and the McAteer-Petris Act, and by extension the *Special Area Plan*.[29] As we shall see, however, the *Special Area Plan* became another source of conflict in defining goals for port development. One important aspect of the plan was that it confirmed the preclusion of housing and office on replacement fill, ending any lingering hope for a rule of equivalencies. Yet city officials and members of the port and planning commissions seemed to hold out hope that the *Special Area Plan* would provide some exceptions to the restrictions on office and housing. That it did not was a source of intense contention. Such constraints did not sit well with the port commission or with planning director Allan B. Jacobs, who noted that "San Francisco is the only location on the bay where intense urban uses come down to the water's edge and where continuation of such development is so logical."[30]

So, despite the fact that the *Special Area Plan* was devised by a broadly based committee, including representatives from the port, and was described at the time as the resolution of years of conflict between conservationists and proponents of development, the port commission flatly rejected BCDC's plan. Members of the port commission expressed serious concerns over the potential impact of the plan on the port's ability to dispose of land as it saw fit. In a special public meeting held by the port to discuss the *Special Area Plan*, Commissioner Arnold criticized the plan and its implications. His opinion was that BCDC would be, through its plan, overextending its mandate by assuming jurisdiction over the economics of port development. Addressing BCDC's William Evers, who was present at the hearing, the commissioner bluntly described the situation, saying that "without the BCDC we could fill in the Bay and do just about anything we please . . . so you see, you're antagonistic to us to the extent that you are depriving us and limiting us on the use of our property."[31] Commissioner Arnold tried to delay BCDC's approval of the plan by arguing, not entirely unreasonably, that new port director Tom Soules should at a minimum be allowed to perform his own analysis of what port property should be retained for maritime uses and what could be used for other purposes. For his own part, Soules said of the *Special Area Plan*, "I believe that it is a type of restriction that no other port director in the United States has had imposed on him." He further commented that "[I] know of no seaport which has had success under similar conditions of restriction or compromise, however well intentioned, and we believe that the port cannot be made competitive by this means."[32] San Francisco Tomorrow's representative Richard Gryziec was unconvinced by anything the port said, commenting that "the real waterfront obstructionists are Joe Alioto and his Charlie McCarthy commissioners."[33] In his support for the *Special Area Plan*, Robert Katz, who represented the Telegraph Hill Dwellers

Association, took the opportunity to criticize the port's strategy to use commercial development to support maritime. Katz explained, "If you had a wall of U.S. Steel buildings here, it wouldn't have brought one more ship into the Port of San Francisco."[34]

Support for BCDC's plan also came from Supervisor Feinstein. Anxious to see some form of development move forward, she said that "failure to adopt the plan would 'condemn the waterfront to total stagnation.'"[35] As the *Chronicle* pointed out, her assertion was based on the "long history of wrangling over non-shipping projects proposed for the Embarcadero."[36] Indeed, it was commonly held that this "wrangling" had everything to do with the state of the waterfront, as succinctly put by a member of the League of Women Voters who testified at the April 1975 hearing that "for years the shores of San Francisco have been suffering from the decay of inaction. The League of Woman voters feels that a living port is essential to the life of San Francisco. Now, more than ever, we need the legislative controls of the Bay Conservation and Development Commission, including its power to make special area plans."[37] Feinstein was not alone in suggesting that development could not occur without a clear set of policies as articulated in a plan for the waterfront. In the port's special hearing on the *Special Area Plan*, Richard Gryziec and John Williams, the port's commercial property developer, argued to a combative port commission that a project like the Embarcadero Gardens could only move forward if there were first a *Special Area Plan* to support it.[38] Without a plan, such proposals could not be considered because the proper tools to guide developers and to help decision makers in their evaluations would not exist. Moreover, project sponsors would have no clear legal authority to commence. SPUR's representative at the meeting also argued that the plan was necessary for basic economic reasons. For instance, if the SFRA were to take over the area to initiate a redevelopment project, then the port would not be able to assess accurately its land value and back up its estimates. If there is no plan that establishes potential uses, there is no way to determine property value. In the end, BCDC chairman William Evers responded to the port and his agency's other critics by announcing that the plan would be adopted by the BCDC regardless, and it was.[39] Neither the port nor the city had any practical means to contest the decision.

The plan analyzed the port parcel by parcel. After establishing which portions of port land did not or would not support shipping or maritime-related activities, the WAC assigned them a range of possible new uses. Committee decisions pertaining to what kinds of development could occur, and where, were based in part on conclusions reached by Mayor Alioto's Port Committee, which suggested that the port needed an income of $3 million per year from its non-maritime property. Thus, for instance, to enable the port to generate enough income to meet that goal, a hotel was added as a possible use for one piece of port property.[40] Whether the target income recommended by the mayor's Port Committee was reasonable and whether BCDC's take on what would generate that income was realistic are debatable.

Even though it was based on a very detailed analysis, at its core the *Special Area Plan* was quite straightforward. It focused on the areas determined by the Port of San Francisco likely to be surplus to maritime needs. Of less concern were maritime uses themselves because they were supported by the McAteer-Petris Act through BCDC's *Bay Plan* and in planning department policy and zoning code. It was assumed that the port was already doing everything it could to utilize and improve property dedicated to its maritime and shipping industries, and so this did not need to be addressed at the same level.

The plan also clearly identified what the permitted uses were on new or replacement fill, tailored to a group of sub-areas around which the document was structured. It also included policies that helped illuminate the rationale BCDC would use in making decisions to grant permits, or not. It thus served as an advisory document to the city because it indicated the kinds of projects or improvements that might be approved by BCDC, and therefore what features would make projects worth spending effort on. In general, the plan aimed at limiting fill, improving the shoreline, and providing public access to, and views of, the water. Following are a few of the plan's main points.

First, neither office nor housing could be permitted on new or replacement fill without amendments to the McAteer-Petris Act.[41] Second, piers removed could only be replaced within the same general area (the plan defined three such areas). The plan also allowed for 'fill credits' equal to the area of fill (for instance piers) removed. However, 50% of the replacement fill must be devoted to open space and public access to the bay, quite severely limiting the parameters of any development thereon. Fill credits were a variation on the "rule of equivalencies." Third, a detailed 'Total Design Plan' was required to guide replacement and reuse of finger piers north of the Bay Bridge, in the area between Piers 7 and 24 (completed in

1980). No replacement fill was to be permitted in this area unless it was consistent with that plan. Finally, uses allowed on new or replacement fill generally included maritime, public recreation, and in limited areas hotels, shops, and amusements.

Despite these parameters, the plan's authors felt that it was sensitive to the port's economic needs, asserting that "the Plan the committee came up with was based on a blending of interests. It was responsive to the financial needs of the Port, the environmental constraints of the Bay Plan and McAteer-Petris Act, and strong public desire for an accessible, usable waterfront."[42] But even though they recognized that the port should not be overly restricted in the use of its property, the limitations that were imposed would prove to be a severe burden on the port. Not only were issues of good urban design at stake, but the port's ability to generate income from development to pay for open space or new shipping facilities also was constrained by its inability to promote housing or office development. For the port, a few allowances for hotels and commercial recreation did not cut the economic mustard. Even though the *Special Area Plan* did not restrict housing or office on *existing* fill, there were few such opportunities of which to take advantage. Not many existing piers could accommodate significant development, and shoreline opportunities for housing were limited. Pier 45 was a notable exception, and was called out as site that could be developed for residential and hotel use. The general upshot of the plan was that if developers could not make what they consider to be sufficient return, and if the port could not derive income from development, there was little chance of any change. In this regard, the *Special Area Plan* contributed to several decades of relative inactivity—quite opposite to the expectations held by Supervisor Feinstein and others.

The adoption of BCDC's *Special Area Plan* imposed a layer of regulation in addition to existing policy established by the Planning Department's *Northeastern Waterfront Plan*. Even while the *Northeastern Waterfront Plan* was amended in 1977 to ensure that it conformed to the *Special Area Plan*, it differed from the *Special Area Plan* in that the range of its policies was wider and it included inland areas beyond BCDC's jurisdiction. Furthermore, the planning department maintained its own land-use policies, building-form restrictions, and the authority to grant entitlements. Finally, as its authors pointed out, the *Special Area Plan* had to be read in conjunction with the *Bay Plan* and the McAteer-Petris Act, as it was technically just an amendment to the former.

THE 1979 *NORTHEASTERN WATERFRONT SURVEY* AND THE RELATED
1981 *RINCON POINT-SOUTH BEACH REDEVELOPMENT PLAN*

Sometime around 1974, Supervisor Diane Feinstein began to work with
the San Francisco Redevelopment Agency to pursue development of moribund port land near the Bay Bridge. Feinstein, who had cut her teeth on
waterfront issues early in her career protesting the U.S. Steel proposal, saw
different possibilities for development, especially given the city's need for
new housing. The idea of turning over revitalization efforts of the financially strapped and, so far, ineffective port to the SFRA was not whimsy.
After all, "renewal" was what the agency did best and it had the mechanisms to make things happen, as demonstrated by the Golden Gateway
and the Embarcadero Center. As Feinstein put it, "'I believe this can be
sold to the citizens . . . because it means the difference between doing
nothing (on the waterfront) for two decades and doing something.'"[43]

The idea was not entirely new. Consultants had suggested in a report
prepared for the Citizens' Waterfront Committee in 1971 that a redevelopment project area would put in place a financing mechanism for marine
parks and other public uses that would not otherwise be affordable.[44] In
order to make the possibility a reality, one step was to get BCDC to agree to
the concept. As a member of BCDC's waterfront advisory committee, Feinstein had a direct line of communication with BCDC Chairman William
Evers. When the *Special Area Plan* was published in 1975, it included policies that supported the kind of mixed-use development Feinstein envisioned.[45] Working also with Robert Kirkwood of SPUR gave the concept
of pursuing redevelopment real momentum, given that organizations' history and its evolving role in development issues.

Feinstein and her cohorts had an even more significant hurdle, however,
in that they had to convince the state legislature that several parcels of port
land were no longer needed for maritime purposes and were surplus to the
needs of the public trust, which became an issue in the early 1980s. The city
took its case to Sacramento, arguing that port's seawall lots in the area were
part of an old industrial district of abandoned rail yards and warehouses
that would never again serve shipping activity. After a long legal and legislative process, the request was granted. This is one of only two places on San
Francisco's waterfront that the SLC has made such a finding.[46]

The board of supervisors approved the Northeastern Waterfront
Survey Area in 1977. The results of the survey were published in 1979, and

the project area eventually selected from within the survey area was named the Rincon Point-South Beach Redevelopment Area (Figs. 6.4 and 6.5). The plan for it was adopted in 1981. The 1979 survey was a joint effort of the redevelopment agency, the port, and the planning department, with citizen review and comment provided by a Northeastern Waterfront Advisory Committee (NEWAC). In part, the survey was undertaken as a step toward implementing some of the public policy established by BCDC's *Special Area Plan* and the planning department's *Northeastern Waterfront Plan*. But one of the main purposes of this survey was to identify where on the waterfront housing, among other things, could sensibly be developed. It was in fact a bit unusual in that it included a set of specific policy goals, or visions, for what should happen in the area of the northern waterfront covered by the survey. The survey identified a set of sub-areas for which different goals were established. It addressed job creation, housing development, transportation improvements, open space, and urban design. Generally, the survey, and subsequently the redevelopment plan, called for a mix of hotels, shops, open space, housing, and a marina between the Bay Bridge and Townsend Street, just north of China Basin Channel.

The survey was an important document because it was the legally necessary first step in the SFRA's particular process and it established a framework for change between Pier 7 and China Basin Channel that reflected the goals of all of the major agencies involved—BCDC, the planning department, the port, and the SFRA. It was created, and was ultimately quite successful, because of the unprecedented cooperation and rare political momentum that supported it. Allen Temko concluded his praise of the survey by pointing out what might be its most meaningful contribution (other than the development it would enable), noting that "thus far citizens have accomplished democratically what princes and popes did in the days of autocratic planning. The result has not been a patched-up popular compromise, but a lordly urban vision."[47] The survey itself made a point of describing the unusual circumstances of its creation:

> The planning and design of the Northeastern Waterfront requires an approach which goes beyond problem solving to create a new vision of what the future might be like. The vision is not one imposed upon the planning process, but rather one which has evolved out of it and resulted from the active participation of the Northeastern Waterfront Advisory Committee, City officials, professionals of various disciplines, and the general public.[48]

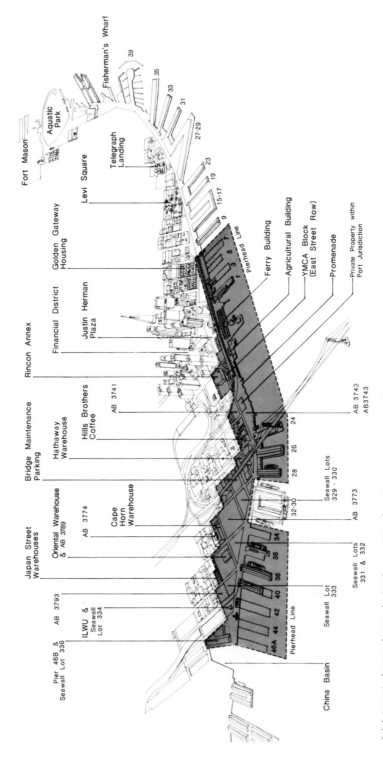

6 4 Axiometric drawing showing the *Northeastern Waterfront Survey* area boundaries (dark grey) and various landmarks, including Assessor's Blocks (Abs). Roma Design Group. San Francisco Redevelopment Agency, *Northeastern Waterfront Summary Report*, 1979.

Fort Mason

Aquatic Park

Fisherman's Wharf

39

35

33

31

27-29

Levi Square

Telegraph Landing

23

19

15-17

9

Golden Gateway Housing

Financial District

Justin Herman Plaza

Pierhead Line

Ferry Building

Agricultural Building

YMCA Block (East Street Row)

Promenade

Private Property within Port Jurisdiction

Rincon Annex

Bridge Maintenance Parking

Hathaway Warehouse

Hills Brothers Coffee

AB 3741

AB 3742

AB3743

24

26

28

Seawall Lots 329 - 330

AB 3773

32-30

Japan Street Warehouses

Oriental Warehouse & AB 3789

AB 3774

Cape Horn Warehouse

34

36

38

Seawall Lots 331 & 332

Seawall Lot 333

Pier 46B & Seawall Lot 336

AB 3793

ILWU & Seawall Lot 334

40

42

44

46A

Pierhead Line

Seawall Line

China Basin

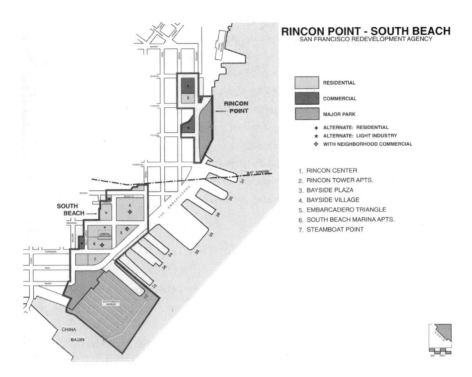

RINCON POINT - SOUTH BEACH
SAN FRANCISCO REDEVELOPMENT AGENCY

RESIDENTIAL

COMMERCIAL

MAJOR PARK

✦ ALTERNATE: RESIDENTIAL
★ ALTERNATE: LIGHT INDUSTRY
✤ WITH NEIGHBORHOOD COMMERCIAL

1. RINCON CENTER
2. RINCON TOWER APTS.
3. BAYSIDE PLAZA
4. BAYSIDE VILLAGE
5. EMBARCADERO TRIANGLE
6. SOUTH BEACH MARINA APTS.
7. STEAMBOAT POINT

6.5 Rincon Point-South Beach Redevelopment Area land use program. San Francisco Redevelopment Agency, *San Francisco Redevelopment Program*, 1996.

Temko attributed much to the involvement of environmentalists, who, he suggests, were responsible for the overthrow of the "city's own foolish northern waterfront policy—I won't call it a plan—that consultants . . . concocted some years back under the gaze of our beauty-loving former doge, Signor Alioto."[49] Temko observed that the plan, as outlined in the survey, brought the city back to the water not by proposing massive development along and over the bay, but rather "simply and sanely" by demolishing the freeway and proposing good public access to the bay.

Writing the actual plan was the next step in the redevelopment process, followed by pursuing specific development projects that would implement the plan, though in an incremental fashion. The *Rincon Point-South Beach Redevelopment Plan* has led directly to significant changes along a very visible part of the waterfront. With this plan the SFRA essentially took over development of much of the waterfront from south of the Ferry Building to China Basin Channel, although it did so in a way that jibed with existing thinking for the area. The critical difference between the planning department and BCDC, or any other agency's policy plans and regulations, and those of the SFRA is that the former are prescriptive or reactive; they do not cause anything to happen. However, once a redevelopment plan is in place, the SFRA has the ability to pursue development; it can act very much like a project sponsor or housing developer. A major difference, though, is that redevelopment agencies are not expected to generate profit for themselves; technically, they service debt issued against tax increment (that is, on bonds floated against the future value of newly developed property). Furthermore, a substantial portion of the bond money received is, in California, required to be "set-aside" for low-income housing.[50]

THE PORT'S *MARITIME STRATEGY* AND THE *TOTAL DESIGN PLAN*

Two other documents were created as part of the process that resulted in the 1979 *Northeastern Waterfront Survey*. First, the *Maritime Strategy* was prepared by the port during the early stages of the survey. This was the port's effort to state succinctly its basic needs and goals, which, it hoped, would be reflected in planning documents both extant and underway, especially the *Northeastern Waterfront Survey* and the *Total Design Plan*. The *Maritime Strategy* was not adopted by any governing body and so did not carry the legal weight of an ordinance or resolution. However, it was important as a general statement of the port's intentions. The scope of the report was the entirety of the port's jurisdiction, within which the *Northeastern Waterfront Survey* area fit. In stating its basic land-use objectives, the port acknowledged, though somewhat grudgingly, the new obligations being placed on its property, stating that "piers and seawall lots no longer to be retained for maritime uses will be developed at their highest and best uses. No efforts, however, have been made to distinguish public recreational and open space uses from highest and best uses. It has been assumed that a successful commercial development program will include sufficient new public open space, open water, and recreational uses for the enjoyment of the residents of San Francisco."[51]

The port's basic decisions regarding what to do with its land reflected the obvious changes to its activities, most essentially that cargo moving through the port was going through a radical redistribution. In 1971, the northern and southern waterfronts handled about the same amount of cargo, but by 1977, the piers south of China Basin Channel were handling more than two-thirds of the cargo.[52] Of course, it had been clear for some time that the northern waterfront was not going to be where the port made its stand, but some break-bulk general cargo, such as newsprint, continued to come across its more modern finger piers. The *Maritime Strategy* listed all such facilities, perhaps in an attempt to place a check on the pressure to chase maritime operations completely out of the northern waterfront. Even now, the maritime operations side of the port struggles to convince critics and doubters that it needs to keep some areas in reserve for potential future maritime uses. However, this debate is now focused entirely on the southern waterfront, at least with regard to shipping.[53]

The second document to come out of the survey process was the *Total Design Plan*, which covered the area between Piers 7 and 24, essentially the Ferry Building Area. According to the plan, the *Special Area Plan* had recognized that this area "needed more detailed planning by the San Francisco community."[54] Added incentive to write the document came from the Rincon Point-South Beach Redevelopment Project, which could lead to the addition of fill (the slips in a marina, for instance, might be considered fill) in the area covered by the *Total Design Plan*. The BCDC still uses an updated version of the plan to evaluate all proposed projects in the area requiring a permit from them.

The same agencies and citizens' committee involved in preparing the *Northeastern Waterfront Survey* were involved in preparing the *Total Design Plan*, although the *Total Design Plan* was primarily a joint effort between the port and BCDC.[55] In fact, authors of the plan repeated verbatim the assertion from the *Northeastern Waterfront Survey* that its roots were in a community-based process. The plan was endorsed by the planning and port commissions in January 1980, and adopted by BCDC that June.[56] The purpose of the *Total Design Plan* was to set forth specific policy and criteria for development on port property in the area between Piers 7 and 24 under the jurisdiction of BCDC. It also intended to "create a major recreational resource for residents and visitors of all age and income groups."[57] Particularly, it included "the approximate location, amount, height and bulk of proposed uses"; "the location and design of parks, open space, public access areas, and view corridors"; "the amount of parking to be allowed for permitted uses"; and "the means by which public recreation, open space, and public access were to be provided and maintained." Furthermore, the plan confirmed the role of city agencies in the review process: "Detailed designs prepared for specific projects shall be in accord with these Guidelines and

Program and subject to approval by the San Francisco Port Commission, and planning department and Art Commission, and the San Francisco Bay Conservation and Development Commission. Detailed landscaping and materials plans and signs shall be approved by the San Francisco Department of City Planning prior to approval of any new non-maritime development in this area."[58]

That these agencies, and often others depending on the project, were all to have a say in evaluating development proposals generated a thicket of bureaucratic red tape, especially for the area around the Ferry Building. While this condition proved too difficult for privately sponsored (and thus profit-oriented) projects to overcome, some of the changes encouraging public use were implemented with federal grants and through the formal financial mechanisms available to the SFRA as implemented through the *Rincon Point—South Beach Plan*. Some of them will be described in the final chapters.

THE *CENTRAL WATERFRONT PLAN* AND THE *BAY AREA SEAPORT PLAN*

With plans in place slating much of the northern waterfront for new uses, some effort had to be devoted to establishing policies for those areas where the port's maritime and shipping activities would be concentrated. While BCDC's *Special Area Plan* covered the length of the waterfront, the Planning Department's efforts had stopped at China Basic Channel. So, in 1980, the planning department released the *Central Waterfront Plan*, which covered the area between China Basin Channel and Islais Creek, including a significant inland area beyond port jurisdiction. The city had for some years been concerned with the decline of the central waterfront. The concentration of abandoned rail yards, warehouses, contractors' open storage areas, and truck depots led some to characterize this area as a place of underutilized land and of lessening economic importance because it supported only modest job density. While the downtown prospered from the increase in finance, administration, and service jobs, the central waterfront was suffering from severe declines in waterborne commerce, manufacturing, and wholesale trade.[59] Nevertheless, the city reasoned that "there is a danger stemming from over reliance on a limited number of economic sectors to provide jobs, especially during recessionary periods."[60]

The purpose of the *Central Waterfront Plan* then was not just to establish policy pertaining to port activities but more broadly to address the transition of an old industrial area into a place of mixed uses, with the idea that industrial land needed to be preserved. The latter policy was linked to conclusions drawn by the city's economic consultants, who indicated that there were bright spots in the city's industrial and maritime future. According to them,

> The overall goal of the plan is to create in the central waterfront area a physical and economic environment conducive to the retention and expansion of San Francisco's industrial and maritime activities. This goal is set forth in order to reverse the pattern of economic decline in the area and to establish a land base for the industrial and maritime components of the San Francisco economy.[61]

Policy statements about the retention and expansion of maritime activities were fairly explicit, for example, policies 1 through 4 required, respectively, that the port, "retain all existing maritime general cargo facilities along the central waterfront (Piers 48, 50, 70, 80)"; "retain all existing ship repair operations along the central waterfront (Pier 54)"; "encourage the expansion and modernization of maritime cargo handling facilities and the development of container facilities along the central waterfront"; and "reserve land adjacent to the waterfront as required for maritime support use."[62] With these policies, the planning department anticipated some of the requirements established in the *Bay Area Seaport Plan* published jointly in 1982 by BCDC and the Metropolitan Transportation Commission (MTC), the region's transportation agency. For the purposes of this discussion, the most important part of the *Seaport Plan* is that it established "port priority areas" within which marine terminals and directly related activities were to be set aside by the port and protected. The requirement remains today that any land within the areas, even if not currently used for shipping, is to be kept in reserve should it be needed in the future. Non-maritime interim uses are permissible as long as they can be easily replaced if a marine terminal or related use is called for. With the *Central Waterfront Plan, Bay Area Seaport Plan,* and parts of the *Special Area Plan*, there was now a collection of policy documents that reflected and encouraged the polarized nature of the waterfront.

Caught in Irons: The Morass of Plans and the Struggle Over Revitalization

The 1970s brought the port fully into San Francisco's political arena. Faced with decaying piers in the northern waterfront and a nearly continual decline in shipping and maritime activity in the central and southern waterfronts, the port found itself in a much more complex environment in which to pursue revitalization than before the transfer. Its position as a city agency exposed the distressed port to intense scrutiny and subjected it to a complex and burdensome array of policy plans and regulations as well as increased public activism.[63] By the end of the 1970s, the port and any project sponsor submitting proposals for development would have to navigate policies and regulations set forth in the Planning Department's *Planning Code*, the *General Plan*, of which the *Northeastern Waterfront Plan* is part, and BCDC's *Special Area Plan*. By the 1980s, depending on the area for which the project was proposed, more specific documents applied, including BCDC's *Total Design Plan*, the *Rincon Point-South Beach Redevelopment Plan*, and the *Seaport Plan*. After 1982, projects also would have to negotiate newly empowered public trust requirements. Furthermore, each plan and each agency has different but overlapping areas of jurisdiction, and often differing priorities. While many of the goals and policies in these plans were quite similar, especially where public access to water, open space, parking, and general building programs were concerned, there were also many variations. Some differences were obvious, for instance the *Northeastern Waterfront Plan* did not allow housing on Pier 45 whereas the *Special Area Plan* did (an inconsistency resolved later). Other variations, because of the flexibility in how similar goals and policies might be interpreted, were more subtle.

An especially important difference is found in the agencies' sometimes quite territorial natures. One difficulty, which continues even today, has been the contention between the port and the planning department over the application of *General Plan* policies, which includes the *Northeastern Waterfront Plan*, to port property. The port agreed that it was subject to the controls established by the *Planning Code* and its associated *Zoning Maps*, but did not confirm that it was necessarily governed by the *General Plan*. The port argued that, according to the Burton Act Transfer Agreement, the board of supervisors can vote to approve funds for capital projects even should they not conform to the *General Plan*.[64] What makes this a particularly contentious point is that the *Planning Code* is the specific implementing document of the *General Plan*.[65] The implication for the planning department, and a large part of the disagreement, is that if one must comply with the *Planning Code* then by default one must also comply with the *General Plan*. However, as a practical matter, the port does not disregard planning policy and, in fact, seeks to cooperate in policy development. This is logical because the port relies on the planning department and its commission for zoning and related approvals. If the port were to reject planning department policies, the chances for receiving conditional use permits for development projects, for instance, would likely be jeopardized.

BCDC's *Special Area Plan* has also been a source of friction among the port, the city, and BCDC because it has extended BCDC's purview beyond simply regulating land uses to control over the detailed design aspects of projects. This has been seen by some as an imposition from an agency working beyond the intent of the legislation that created it. Of course, interagency squabbling does not play well to the public, so the port went to some effort, at least initially, to present a less realistic but more politically expedient view of situation to the world at large. Its 1988-1989 *Shipping Handbook*, a sort of combined fact book and advertising brochure included this statement: "Planning for waterfront development is handled through a joint effort of the City and the Bay Conservation and Development Commission (BCDC) which assures co-ordination and consistency in project implementation."[66] This was in stark contrast with a statement made a year earlier by Randall Rossi, a port planner, about planning efforts in Fisherman's Wharf. As Rossi noted, "It's paralyzing because all of these agencies don't talk to each other. . . . And by the time you add up all of the restrictions, you wind up with a situation where you can't do anything."[67] Ten years later, in 1997, the adoption of the port's *Waterfront Land Use Plan* finally provided an opportunity for the port, the planning department, and BCDC to work through some of their respective differences. Nevertheless, such interagency disagreements over development goals and general policy direction and interpretation have created a difficult and intimidating planning and development process. On the whole, this makes for an arcane and sometimes acrimonious bureaucratic environment and one very much influenced by individual staff members and the attitudes of department heads—another quality that contributes to a place's uniqueness, and which, of course, is a factor in how a place changes.

Planning in Place

Even though they both reflected and generated interagency difficulties, the plans discussed here were a source of empowerment in that they addressed many, but not all, of the concerns of a multitude of stakeholders, especially environmentalists, citizen committees, and organizations like SFT. The public was able to affect port land use by getting a place at the table as planning policy was being considered, thereby influencing the content of policy documents, and ultimately, the character of the water-front landscape itself.

The degrees of freedom or the latitude staff had in penning such documents was related, as it is even now, to the effectiveness of activists (or the strength of real estate moguls). Of course, once the basic thrust of policies was established, staff members were the final authors; they structured the documents, focused on finer points, and refined methodologies. So, it was more than just pressure from citizens and activist groups that generated the new policy and regulatory regime. The planning department's director, its staff and the staff and directors of other agencies, especially BCDC, where not merely receptors, incorporating ideas and attitudes debated in public into their work. Rather, the people in these agencies were some of the original thinkers who brought to the profession certain sensitivities and helped shape what might be called an enlightened bureaucracy.[68]

Ultimately, what was taken to commissions or elected bodies for approval represented not only staff members' abilities, judgments, and predilections but also their ability to negotiate both internal politics and relations among agencies. In fact, the sometimes-contentious nature of interactions among BCDC, the port, and other city agencies is an example of how fractious "the local" can be. Nevertheless, through the entitlement process and by monitoring compliance with policies, controls, regulations, and environmental reviews, plans and regulations provided local actors with more ways to challenge, appeal, and simply criticize proposals for development.[69] Having to deal with and be subject to this kind of interplay brought the port more fully into the local planning and development process, another step in the evolution of planning policy and regulation and their articulation in the changing waterfront.

But while the public interest was more wholly incorporated into the planning process, and policies were established with the intention of saving the bay and improving potential development through sound urban design policy, the result was a waterfront that remained largely static for decades. The port's ability to pursue commercial development projects and generally to revitalize the waterfront was hampered by layers of planning policy and bureaucracy and by a more powerful and proactive public, not to mention its own underlying financial and administrative difficulties. Perhaps the two conditions that most limited potential development were, first, the restrictions on what could be developed and where, and second, requirements for what had to be *included* in any given project. Any program for revitalization now had the financial burden of supporting two kinds of goals: public access, open space, and publicly oriented uses on the one hand and maritime activities on the other. Given that two of the most lucrative land uses, housing and office, were not acceptable, it was difficult to finance development. Additionally, the red tape, time delays, and sunk costs (for example, fees to agencies or architects) that were associated with project reviews conducted by several agencies guided by multiple planning and regulatory documents tended to intimidate or thwart even the most stalwart of developers.

The role of public policy, specifically land-use policy, is not to cause development but rather to affect the pace and nature of change.[70] Policies and regulations dictate the possible range of land uses and activities along the waterfront and establish the basic physical parameters and design of structures. In this way, they define and direct the potential of market forces. The plans adopted in this period had, and continue to have, a tremendous impact on the waterfront by directing and even limiting the spatial flow of capital.

In cities that have a relatively robust planning function, policy documents, zoning codes, regulations, ordinances, and even ballot propositions are the creation of interactions among people, organizations, and bureaucracies. Thus planning, and the process by which planning is carried out, is embedded in and reflects the character of the broader political, cultural, and socioeconomic character of a place. Put another way, planning is a fundamental aspect of the local conditions that affect actors and agents in their attempts to create change, and is particular to the locale in which it is practiced. Such conditions are more than situation; they create localness and are an intimate part of what makes places different from each other. So, understanding something about how planning works in a place is basic to assaying a landscape and provides it with more meaning than could be derived just from the visible, tangible surface features of the built environment.

In our case, new planning policy, land-use controls, and development requirements washed away modernist visions of urban development on the waterfront with a concern for the water itself, both as a fundamental part of the natural environment and as new kind of cultural and economic amenity and a source of civic space. An emphasis was placed on incorporating the water, or access to it, into the design of new commercial development, encouraging it to benefit more symbiotically from the unusual, often dramatic location, as opposed to overwhelming such settings with massive buildings. Public policy began to reflect the public's consciousness of the water, and that the bay was a resource that should be accessible to and enjoyed by everyone. The policies established by BCDC and the planning department promoted activities based primarily on leisure and entertainment, from shopping to sport boating, and which achieved their fullest expression in Pier 39. While the benefits of this kind of policy focus are debatable—after all, they resulted in Pier 39—they nevertheless encouraged more publicly oriented rather than completely private uses of the waterfront.

A key aspect of struggle for the waterfront has become how to take advantage of its natural and cultural qualities like its watery setting, topography, views, history, and unusual locale for play and movement. Such features can attract and enhance new economic functions and capital investment (exchange value), or be preserved and respected for their intrinsic value to the public (use value). Since the planning process, itself a negotiation and adjustment among competing forces, is an attempt to resolve or mitigate such conflict, it can be seen as a potential check to the power of capital, neoliberal urban change, and the pressures of a globalizing city, not just as an instrument tuned to the needs of growth.

7

Questionable Results

The Northern Waterfront in the 1970s and 1980s

What this port should have is an over-all plan for its future and then
let the public look over it and understand it. Then when a development
comes up, we'll be able to see where it fits in, instead of taking it as one
project by itself.[1]

 —John Williams, the Port's commercial leasing manager,
  upon quitting his job in 1976

DESPITE THE STIFLED atmosphere created by the port's new situation
and the policies and regulations that helped create it, pressure to
develop port property had not eased. To pursue commercial development on the northern waterfront was a fundamental necessity.
First, the port had to comply with the conditions of the transfer,
which called for maximum return—in other words, the highest and
best use, on land no longer required for maritime activities. Second,
in addition to supporting shipping activities, the port needed to
generate income to respond to new demands for public improvements and access to the waterfront.[2]

 But the port's chance to redevelop its northern waterfront with
even postmodern large-scale, mixed-use projects capable of generating revenue sufficient to support its maritime operations was
all but gone. Any argument that the port could "save" most of the
northern waterfront if it could just develop one or two major projects became moot; the morphology of revitalization would have to be

different. There would be no bold extension of the city or new visionary urbanism to send San Francisco jutting out over the water and into a neo-Le Corbusian future. The waterfront's renewal would have to be of a gentler form. More modest projects would have to be pursued, and these projects would have to address concern for the environment, open space, and public access to the water. While these publicly minded features were now mandated, they were more difficult than ever to implement because of the restrictions on income-generating development. While developers and real estate capitalists had to be strong-armed out of downtown, few could be attracted to the waterfront.

Nevertheless, a slow metamorphosis began to take root along the northern waterfront. A few significant projects were completed and publicly oriented changes along the waterfront began to blossom. The old morphology of finger piers was also affected; several crumbling and decaying piers had to be removed. By the end of the 1980s, the waterfront took on a gap-tooth appearance. Though few, these changes were important because they suggest a landscape that had started to evoke a negotiation between the process of capitalist urbanization and locally situated actors and agencies determined to protect the environment and resist threats to public resources, especially through privatization.

With the exception of those piers that still operated to receive break-bulk cargo, newsprint paper for example, the northern waterfront was for the most part reduced to serving as the home for ferries, tugs, and miscellaneous, non-cargo-related activities. Reflecting this spreading maritime decline, the "northern waterfront" was not a static delineation; it edged southward. Initially, the southern boundary of the northern waterfront was the Bay Bridge, but as finger piers more obviously stuck out as decaying relics of another time, the boundary crept farther south. By the early 1980s, largely as a result of the push to develop South Beach-Rincon Point, China Basin Channel became the southern boundary of the northern waterfront. So, the polarization of port activities that began to appear in the 1960s was cemented by the 1970s. By the 1980s, however, the balance began to tip more so that shipping and traditional industrial maritime activities were relegated to a smaller and more remote part of the waterfront.

Yet, as shipping sank farther out of site, a few particularly important enterprises buoyed the port. Thus we turn to Fisherman's Wharf and then move south to the Bay Bridge and the site of a well-regarded redevelopment project. In the shadow of the bridge was also the site of a hotel proposal that, although ultimately a failure, was critical to the transformation of the waterfront by provoking clamorous public opposition and pushing the contention over the future of the port to something of a crescendo in 1990. It was then that voters passed Proposition H, a ballot measure that forced the struggling agency to come up with its first real planning document.

Fisherman's Wharf: Place and Placelessness

The Wharf's problems lie in a . . . world of politics, real estate economics and a planning process gone seriously awry.[3]
—Niels Erch, *San Francisco Business Times*

If any place on the waterfront exhibits the synergy of differences that characterize the (post)modern condition, surely it is Fisherman's Wharf. The 1970s and 1980s were a time of ostensibly competing demands for the wharf: promote tourism, but protect the activities that gave the wharf its charm to begin with (which in turn generates more tourism); concentrate consumption in a place established by production (fishing and fish processing, canning, and food preparation); and develop new activities on port property that would make the area more palatable to residents of the city, but do so in ways that would maintain the wharf's authenticity (thereby making it even more intriguing to tourists and in turn making it less appealing to residents). While fishing, fish processing, and marine services such as boat repair and fueling did indeed occur at the wharf, and still do, the surrounding area's historic relationship to the water was being transformed. Warehouses, food processing, and other activities beyond port jurisdiction that had connections to the fishing operations, cargo handling, and other maritime businesses using the piers in Fisherman's Wharf were replaced by land uses that supported tourism. Yet, instead of clashing, the different aspects of the wharf settled into what in many ways was, and is now, a mutually supportive relationship.

The transformation of the connection between waterfront activities and land-side development that began in the 1960s and continued through the 1970s and 1980s was fueled by a feedback system that evolved between them. The port side provided the attractions, from historic boats moored at Hyde Street Pier to a working fishing fleet, processing facilities, and restaurants, that would draw tourists and visitors from around the region and beyond. Outside port jurisdiction, the land side provided the hotels to locate consumers within easy reach of that which was to be consumed: the bay (from cruises on it and views of it to the fish in it) and local history based on using and consuming the bay (historic ships and buildings, a maritime museum). The land side also included sites of consumption "themed" by their historic link to water—former sites of production whose raw materials came across San Francisco's piers. These are exemplified by the adaptively reused old Ghirardelli mustard and chocolate factory and former Del Monte Cannery, as well as "curiosity shops." The fate of Ghirardelli in particular was strangely karmic. The Golden Gate Macaroni Company bought the specialty food manufacturer and moved it across the bay to San Leandro. The empty complex was then bought and rescued in the early 1960s by William Matson Roth, an heir to the Matson shipping line fortune, to save it from being replaced by apartment towers.

In the late 1970s, a shopping and hotel complex called The Anchorage was constructed. Its relationship to the waterfront was, and is, in name and proximity alone. Its opening signaled the need for only the weakest association with the waterfront to generate consumption, and even in this unusual and potentially evocative setting, the capitalist development market could only spit out an epitome of homogenized spectacle.

As the wharf area began to take on new functions, most non-fishing-related maritime operations faded away: the Foreign Trade Zone was relocated from Pier 45 to piers farther south; Crown-Zellerbach moved its paper-handling facilities from Pier 45 to Piers 27–29 (only to relocate them again later); Pier 41 was removed from maritime use by 1972; only Piers 37 and 39 were left with a few tenants, and the former was badly damaged by fire in 1976. The infrastructure that had supported industrial and heavy commercial activity, especially the physical connections between land and water, also changed. Improvements were made to Aquatic Park and the cable-car terminus, open space was created between Ghirardelli Square and the Cannery, the area's parking capacity was increased, and eventually, pedestrian access to the bay was expanded. All of this supported the tourist enterprise—recreation and shopping—rather than industry and the movement of goods. The mix of port and land-side activities combined to create an intoxicating atmosphere; it was, and is perhaps even more now, a kaleidoscope of consumption.

Tourism-based consumption is not something readily categorized as either local or global, top down or bottom up. The role of consumption in (and of) Fisherman's Wharf can be seen partly as a top-down force in much the same way that growth of San Francisco's downtown represents the larger forces of capital at work in the city, that is, as the result of broad economic and cultural trends. In the case of tourism, they are rooted in the relative ease of travel, increases in leisure time and disposable income, and attraction to the exotic (increasingly rare in a shrinking world). But tourism is also generated by or focused on a local scene and is reliant upon the character of a locale. In fact, local differences become exceedingly important in the competition not just for global, but national and even regional, tourism.

Fisherman's Wharf benefits from a location that combines natural and urban settings in a dramatic fashion. It is nestled under San Francisco's famed hills, there is a sandy beach nearby, Alcatraz Island is a short ferry ride away, and across the water in the mid-distance, the Marin Headlands loom visibly. The wharf is clearly part of the city: buses, cable cars, and streetcars ply the routes to the wharf and the hills at its back are full of houses and apartments. Fisherman's Wharf is also successful because it contains an unusual mix of activities, including a real fishing industry and the fantasy provided by shopping and entertainment in an unusual setting. It also capitalizes on local history, reflected in historic structures (some the adaptivele reused), museums, and even in the "living history" of the fishing fleet. This unusual combination of features—the local flavor— is what makes the wharf alluring to travelers from around the world. The wharf attracts business ventures and the city thirsts for the tax revenues all this activity generates. Global and national concerns seek investment opportunities and corporate expansion by serving tourists through, for instance, hotel construction. But, some locals have also wished to trans- form Fisherman's Wharf into a globally known tourist destination, hoping to benefit from retail activity, business opportunities, and job creation. Both outsiders and locals have attempted to take advantage of the unusual nature of the place. Thus the wharf experienced sustained pressure to change from both external and local sources, change reflected in both its built environment and in its socio-cultural characater.[4]

While many San Franciscans criticized the wharf's overly touristic nature, plans and regulations developed with much public input encour- aged it, both by supporting the activities that lent it authenticity and by promoting recreation. The Planning Department's 1969 *Northern Waterfront Plan*, updated in 1971, stated that "all industries which support the fishing fleet, such as fish processing and boat repair services, should be encouraged to remain in close proximity to Fisherman's Wharf" and that "water-oriented retail, restaurant, and commercial recreation activities should be expanded in the Fisherman's Wharf area. Hotels should be developed in the eastern portion of the Fisherman's Wharf area where supporting services can more easily be provided."[5] Similarly, BCDC's 1975 *Special Area Plan* called for maintaining and enhancing facilities for the fishing fleet and fish processing while also encouraging "Bay-oriented commercial recreation," which is defined as "facilities specifically designed to attract large numbers of people to enjoy the bay and its shoreline, such as restaurants, specialty shops, and hotels."[6] In this context, the port approved development of Pier 39, a festival market that would cement the wharf as a "world-class" tourist-shopping destination. Whether it was a success is largely a matter of opinion.

PIER 39: PRODUCING CONSUMPTION

> Corn. Kitsch. Schlock. Honky-tonk. Dreck. Schmaltz. Merde. Whatever
> you call the pseudo-Victorian Junk with which Warren Simmons has festooned Pier 39, this ersatz San Francisco that never was—a chef d'oeuvre
> of hallucinatory clichés—is a joke on the port and planning commissions . . . and an especially bad joke on the whole unfortunate city, which
> must live for the next 60 years . . . with this childish excrescence, which
> was stupidly allowed to deface the northern waterfront.[7]
>   —Alan Temko

The southernmost part of Fisherman's Wharf was by the 1970s an area in transition, flanked on the north by the wharf proper and on the south by the port's cruise terminal and what was left of the real working waterfront north of the Bay Bridge. The three main piers in the area, 41, 39, and 37, were being used for little more than warehousing, water taxis, tugboats, tour boats, and ferries.[8] By the second half of the decade, only Pier 39 was in use. As early as 1966, Arthur D. Little had concluded that these piers could be removed from maritime use, and BCDC's *Special Area Plan* reflected as much. If any area of the waterfront had the potential for redevelopment, this was it.

In fact, as the *Special Area Plan* was being prepared, Warren Simmons, owner of the local chain of Tia Maria Mexican restaurants, was looking to sell his idea for a mall/entertainment/park complex at the site of the three piers. By the time the *Special Area Plan* was published in 1975, permitted uses on new or replacement fill for this area included an explicit reference to Simmons' "North Point Park" (what would later be called simply Pier 39).[9] The *Special Area Plan* described it as "bay-oriented commercial recreation that is complementary to park use."[10] The Planning Department's 1977 *Northeastern Waterfront Plan* also included policies that anticipated development there, and even included a detailed, accurate plan-view of a possible Pier 39 development. One policy stated that "permit additional water-oriented commercial recreation development of restaurants, entertainment and specialty shops in the Pier 41 to 37 waterfront area in conjunction with a major waterfront park along the seawall."[11]

Simmons was an ex-Pan Am pilot who had managed to make a few connections in San Francisco because of his restaurants, which he later sold to finance the Pier 39 project. His connections allowed him to present his ideas almost directly to port commissioners and thus to avoid competitive bidding (which anyway was not then mandated). Such relationships were critical, and Simmons later mused that he could not have pushed the project forward without the friendship of people such as Mayor Moscone.[12] Such connections emphasize the local rather than the global character of real estate investment and development. Of course, being able to pursue a project in such a fashion opened up the process to criticism, which even port director Soules, typically anti-development, tried to deflect by arguing that it would not be fair for other developers to bid on Simmons' own idea.[13] This put him at odds with some members of his commission, which was not entirely deaf to the project's critics. Commissioner Rudden even offered that "if anybody cares to come in with something better that would serve ecological and environmental ends," then they should do so.[14] His comment, along with the policy requirements for open space and access to the water as part of the project, are an indication of the increased influence that activism and environmental preservation wielded in the planning and development processes.

Simmons' proposal adhered to the various land-use policies applicable to the site. It could be permitted under existing regulation without any special requirements, its development was not contingent on development elsewhere, making it more straightforward than other recent proposals, and it fit within the 40-foot height limit.[15] Compared with other projects proposed for port property, the Pier 39 idea was relatively warmly received. The port commission voted 3-2 to proceed with negotiations, and thus launched the process that would create one of the country's most popular destinations.

Pier 39 was not just a jewel in the eye of a commission desperate to do something on the northern waterfront. The San Francisco Chamber of Commerce, the boating community, and real estate professionals also thought it was a fine project. In fact, Simmons won significant support by readily agreeing to demands that a marina be included in his designs. Karl Kortum, a usually persistent critic and protester, actually praised it saying that it was "the first waterfront development with public access since Fisherman's Wharf came into being at the turn of the century."[16] Even most of the vocal activist and grassroots organizations that vigilantly watched over the port were relatively quiet, though none openly supported Simmons—a far cry from the protest against U.S. Steel.

The criticisms aimed at Pier 39 were fundamentally different from those leveled at the port's previous development schemes. Instead of attacking the basic mix of activities or the mass of the structures, critics focused on the project's architectural character and its potential to generate a traffic nightmare on the Embarcadero, partly because of proposed alterations to the roadway itself. In similarly modest criticisms, nearby residents and Fisherman's Wharf merchants worried about potential parking problems. Simmons' mollifying response was to include a multistory garage, which was built, unfortunately, even though its inclusion was questioned by several city planning commissioners as well as by Robert Katz and Richard Gryziec at a hearing regarding the project's environmental impact report.[17] Naysayers also claimed that Pier 39 would simply create a second Fisherman's Wharf. One person described it as a "goddam vacationland for tourists who come down here and spend $2 and then go home."[18] The last bastion of protest against the project was the San Francisco Art Commission, which saw its role as that of a defender against honky-tonk. The art commission actually managed to stall the project for a while, but political pressure easily overwhelmed resistance based on aesthetics.[19]

Given the constraints placed on the port, Pier 39 was one of very few permitted developments that could afford to pay for required public improvements such as open space and access to the water and also generate income to help the port run its operations and modernize its shipping facilities. As such, it was almost guaranteed to succeed, especially when the developer altered elements of the proposal to meet local demands.

7.1 Pier 39 c. 1978. A site for consumption. San Francisco Planning Department, *The North-eastern Waterfront Plan*, 1980.

As initially constructed—although it has since undergone modifications and tenant changes—Pier 39 included a five-acre stretch of open space, a perimeter promenade to satisfy the requirement for public access to the bay, tens of restaurants and more than a hundred specialty shops and boutiques, a large marina, and across the Embarcadero on seawall lots, a thousand-car parking structure. Its low-profile buildings were built partly with weathered wood and other remains of old piers 39 and 41. Pier 39 was the first large project north of the Bay Bridge since the mid-1960s, the last being the upgrade of Piers 27–29. After six years, including thirty months to secure all of the necessary permits, Pier 39 was opened on time in early October 1978 (Fig. 7.1).[20] But while the project was successfully

completed, it has not been entirely successful, at least from the local public's perspective. After its opening, critics found another fault—that the
port was more concerned with creating a place for tourists than for San
Franciscans. The port was also accused of being a purveyor of bad taste and
shameless consumerism. Pier 39 was savaged early on by Alan Temko, the
Chronicle's redoubtable architecture critic, for its unabashedly "faux" character. Unlike the romanticized, softly historic consumption found elsewhere in Fisherman's Wharf, Pier 39 was a "contemporary mass-feeding,
hard-selling operation."[21] His criticism had crescendoed by the time Pier
39 opened. He referred to it as "a kind of 'post-modern' or 'ad-hoc' pop-
ulism—that is, the vernacular building of mass-consumption merchan-
dising," accusing the port of creating "a false city-scape of modernist
contradiction—a meandering pattern, seemingly free, but in fact cleverly
controlled"—a place where "mass-feeding and sleazy entertainment are
'water-related' if they occur in a pier."[22]

The irony of Pier 39 was that the land-use policy and regulations that
were in place to protect the public interest, and the environment, when
combined with the port's financial imperatives, ended up producing a site
of consumption that was of little interest to many, probably most, residents of San Francisco. In attracting people from elsewhere in the Bay Area
and beyond, the port managed to alienate this part of the waterfront from
its city. In an instant city, Pier 39 was a flash of dystopian morphogenesis
that did not result from the power of capital alone to reform the landscape. Pier 39 did not spring from a national or international investment
trust or other corporate financial interest, and it did not come from the
boardroom of a giant mall developer at the forefront of the globalization
of material culture. Rather, the pier was the project of a local entrepreneur
who responded to local regulations and policy related to environmental
protection, land use, and urban design, as they reflected, albeit imperfectly,
local values and local conditions.

Simmons had a particular vision for a place, and he was not driven
by external pressures or an overt desire to expand an empire. He sold his
restaurant chain to finance the project, so while it is possible that some or
all of the capital that he generated for the project came from or ultimately
flowed into national or global financial networks, Pier 39 is hardly the
high symbol (literally and figuratively) of globalization that a downtown
corporate skyscraper is. However, Simmons' monument of shopping and
eating is, even if incidentally, part of the global phenomenon that perpetu-

ates landscapes of consumption. Pier 39 is simultaneously unusual and an example of placelessness, rendered such by being similar in its basic function to malls everywhere, but in the form of low-slung buildings propped over the cold water of San Francisco Bay.

A CATCH-22

Pier 39 was not the only way that consumption became the defining element of the Fisherman's Wharf landscape. While exactly what should happen in Fisherman's Wharf has been and still is a subject rife with contention, there has been one clear goal, sought after by the port, reflected in policy, and supported by regulation—the encouragement of the fishing industry and its associated businesses, including restaurants.[23] Debate has raged over how this should be done. The fishing fleet, fish processing, and other activities supported the port and the city economy in two fashions: directly, in terms of employment and revenue associated with the fishing industry, and indirectly, by tourism attracted to the wharf because of the working character and "genuine flavor" those activities imparted. Policies and regulations support this and therefore are key factors in why the wharf is as it is today. To protect these activities, improve the physical condition of buildings and infrastructure, and to ensure that new development maintained its character were considered so essential that a separate plan was written just for the wharf area.

After some unsuccessful proposals for development, and with the wharf increasingly in need of upkeep, the port decided that it had to outline a coherent strategy for the area and hired the design firm ROMA to lead the effort. The port commission adopted the *Fisherman's Wharf Action Plan* in 1981.[24] The plan was a cautious document that addressed some of the criticisms leveled at past development proposals by including basic use and design standards. Its main goals were to maintain the authenticity of the wharf's maritime character, to enhance its attractiveness to residents and tourists, to protect and improve commercial fishing activities, to encourage development of the Hyde Street Pier and Pier 45, and to encourage minimization of parking and traffic problems. The plan was concerned that over-commercialization of the wharf, which threatened its "authentic character," made it increasingly unattractive to San Francisco residents. The idea was that if Fisherman's Wharf could be made appealing to residents, then activity would be less seasonal, which would help buoy local businesses.[25] The plan also called for certain critical infrastructure and public improvements, including a new breakwater, repairs to the Jefferson Street seawall, and improvements to Fish Alley, which was suffering from prolonged physical deterioration. The oft-maligned visual character of the wharf was also identified as needing much improvement.

An important outcome of the *Fisherman's Wharf Action Plan's* adoption was that it generated a few key amendments to the 1980 *Northeastern Waterfront Plan.* The 1980 *Northeastern Waterfront Plan,* and its predecessor, contained policies for Pier 45 that were contrary to those outlined in the *Fisherman's Wharf Action Plan.* Specifically, Objective 1, Policy 4 stated that the port should "permit only those Bay-oriented commercial recreation and public assembly facilities on the Hyde Street Pier, along Fish Alley and on Pier 45 which are incidental to their primary commercial fishing use. Prohibit commercial office (not related to the fishing industry), hotel and residential uses on Pier 45."[26] Recognizing the potential of the site, and knowing that BCDC had agreed that mixed-use development on at least part of the pier was allowable, the planning department adopted changes to the *Northeastern Waterfront Plan* in 1981. The incongruent policy was struck and replaced with one that supported the possibility of housing and office.

Two of the most important physical improvement projects the plan called for were implemented. First was the construction of a new breakwater considered critical for protecting the fishing fleet and historic ships moored at the Hyde Street Pier. The Hyde Street pier itself had served as a breakwater but over time had been largely reconfigured, and parts of it had been removed. A new breakwater had been a priority for years, but it was not until 1985 that federal funding through the Army Corps of Engineers was approved.[27] The breakwater, including a promenade, was completed ahead of schedule in 1986. Second was repair of the Jefferson Street sea wall, on which many businesses, especially restaurants and crab stands, had been built.[28] Over the years, these projects, along with some of the open space improvements and completion of the cable-car terminus (which completed the line to Union Square), served to strengthen the wharf's twinned characteristics—its authenticity and its attractiveness to tourists.

Yet one of the most significant ideas supported in the plan never came to fruition, underscoring the port's conflicted position. The *Fisherman's Wharf Action Plan* called for the construction of a "Fisheries Center" as

7.2 Pier 45, bottom center, and the Hyde Street Pier, bottom right c. 1975. Port of San Francisco, *Ocean Shipping Handbook*, 1975/1976.

part of new Pier 45 development. In turn, improvement of Pier 45 was linked to the redevelopment and improvement of the Hyde Street Pier, to which fishing facilities were to be relocated so that much of Pier 45, a large, 11.5-acre structure, could be devoted to new uses. In 1981, Pier 45 presented a unique opportunity because a portion of it was built on landfill prior to passage of the McAteer-Petris Act, and BCDC regulations at the time allowed housing on existing bay fill (Fig. 7.2). The potential to build housing was important to the port because it believed that bringing residents to the wharf would help counterbalance the seasonal nature of commerce in the area and make the wharf more appealing to San Franciscans, thereby softening its tourist-hardened image. SPUR considered housing on Pier 45 a lynchpin for the future success of the *Action Plan*.[29]

Actually, the port's first efforts to attract development in Fisherman's Wharf at Pier 45 had preceded the *Fisherman's Wharf Action Plan*. Around 1972, the port commission actively sought proposals for mixed-use development to include hotels, retail, and housing. In 1974, the concept of development on the pier was officially sanctioned by the port's commission, which was "optimistic that plans for Pier 45 will escape much of the controversy that has stalled or eliminated development elsewhere on the waterfront."[30] However, mixed-use development at Pier 45 was doomed to fade away, but not until after nearly a decade of struggle to make something work.

The official call for proposals got five responses that all included various mixes of luxury housing, garages, shops and restaurants, hotels, and open space. A familiar tension gripped Pier 45 as local merchants, neighborhood activists, and officials reacted to the project. The range of concerns about the project varied from traffic congestion to finances.[31] Traditional waterfront workers remained resistant to the idea that the northern waterfront's time had come. One retired longshoreman accused the port of being interested only in "hotdog stands and hotels" and not cargo.[32] The port's commercial property manager, John Williams, at the center of many development debates, responded by pointing out that the critics were clearly "not aware of the facts of life on this project."[33] And accusations of conflict of interest flew because Frank Alioto, the mayor's cousin, and former port commissioner Cyril Magnin had connections with various entities that had responded to the development opportunity.[34]

The port weathered all of these criticisms, helped partly by the mayor and planning director Allan Jacobs, who had consistently supported bringing housing to the water's edge.[35] The two leading contenders for the opportunity were a locally based firm, Forty Five Associates, which proposed a festival-housing-retail complex dubbed "Villamarina" and a Houston firm, Gerald D. Hines Interests, which proposed a combination of residential, hotel, and office uses (Fig. 7.3).[36] While Forty Five Associates was thought to have the best design, the Hines project had better money-making potential. The port selected Hines and in May 1975, the port commission granted the firm a sixty-year lease. More importantly, however, Hines was not bound to the lease agreement until all of the necessary permits and approvals were granted—an arrangement that clearly indicated the difficulty of securing them.

Yet Hines was facing more than permitting difficulties. SFT threatened lawsuits, and protests came from many directions. Such hurdles are par for the development course, but with restrictions on building height and requirements for open space that limit design flexibility and potential profit, the development game becomes very difficult. Profitability may have been of particular importance as Hines was apparently experiencing

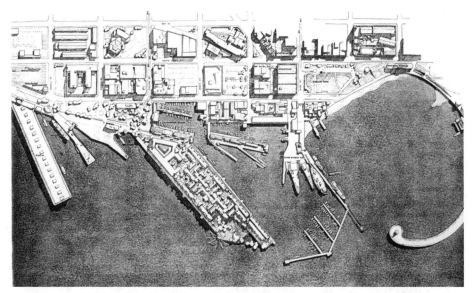

7.3 Drawing of Villamarina. Forty Five Associates, *untitled proposal*, 1974.

some corporate financial hiccups back home in Houston.[37] How that would have had an effect on whether Hines pursued the project is hard to say, but if a development proposal results in a good bottom line with modest risk, it is hard to imagine a developer deciding against the opportunity. This underscores the importance of restraints to development on port land: local policy, regulation, and civic protest made questionable what would otherwise be an incredibly lucrative opportunity.[38]

Nevertheless, what finally sank the project was that it ran into a recessionary period, not the first time or the last that a project would be jeopardized by the time it took to wend its way through the planning process. To make things worse, the port commission approved the proposal for development at nearby Pier 39. The *Chronicle* reported that "the award to Simmons was the 'last straw' for the Hines Associates."[39] According to Hines, because Simmons' project was partly a retail and entertainment development, it would compete directly with similar components of their own project. All of these things would add up to unappealing circumstances for any firm; it was too much for Hines, which subsequently pulled out of the deal. Not one to give up easily, in 1975, at the end of his term, Mayor Alioto convinced Hines to give the project a second chance, but Simmons' Pier 39 was moving determinedly forward, and the initial issues remained.

The project was dead by March 1976, but efforts to do something at Hyde Street Pier and Pier 45 would continue for fifteen years.

The port temporarily gave up hope that commercial and housing development could proceed at least on part of Pier 45 and so, in 1979 it instead solicited bids to develop fishing-related facilities and a "fisheries center." The port received no responses. Concluding that the fishing industry could not be supported without some commercial venture, the port resuscitated the idea of building condominiums on the pier. With plan in hand the port was able to generate interest in development at Pier 45, which included housing. After several years of work, and in the midst of discussions over a potential housing development, the rug was pulled out from under the port. In 1984, in discussions with SLC, the city was informed that housing on Pier 45 was not a permissible use pursuant to the doctrine of public trust, even though BCDC had deemed it acceptable. The SLC's declaration was something of a surprise to local officials, although the potential for the public trust to become an issue had loomed for years. In a piece on the newest condo-less hotel-based proposal, the *Chronicle*'s Alan Temko reported that even port director Eugene Gartland could not explain why the state's decision had not been anticipated.[40] Given that the attorney general had made a significant finding regarding trust uses in 1982, it is surprising that the city was caught off guard.

What had occurred was an unexpected reassertion of state power not through the legislative process but through legal interpretations and judicial intervention. In 1982, the attention of the California Attorney General's office was drawn to a controversial development proposed by the Port of Los Angeles/Long Beach and its developer partner, Wrather Port Properties, Ltd. The southern California agency and its developers were pushing a scheme reminiscent of the kind San Francisco had been forced to abandon. Their intention was to fill sixty acres of tideland to support 2.5 million square feet of office space. An opinion written by deputy attorney general Nancy Saggese quashed the project. Her main conclusion was, essentially, that office buildings could only be constructed on trust land if they directly supported trust (port) activities; specifically, "leases of tidelands trust for the promotion of commerce must benefit Long Beach Port commerce and not 'commerce' as defined for Federal Commerce Clause purposes."[41] This was one of several decisions that asserted the public trust doctrine in new ways, in particular cementing the prohibition of office and housing on trust land. The result has been of fundamental importance to California's coastal waters, and spurred the SLC's rapid transformation into a powerful state agency.[42] The determination from the SLC for Pier 45 altered the framework for development on port property in a dramatic fashion in another way: as a "trust agency," BCDC had to become more careful in implementing its policies and administering its jurisdiction.

In 1985, desperately needing income and facing pressure to support the fishing industry, the port decided that a hotel and convention center-based development on Pier 45 was the only way to generate the required funding to refurbish and extend the Hyde Street Pier and retain a working wharf. A year after starting the search for sponsors for this new development configuration, the Office of the Attorney General only added to the port's troubles. In 1986, executive director of BCDC Alan R. Pendleton requested an opinion from California's attorney general regarding repair or modification to existing piers. The issue was this: if piers that predate the McAteer-Petris Act were substantially altered, would the area affected be limited in use to water-oriented activities? The answer was yes.[43] This meant that if an older pier needed to be upgraded to support the weight of new development, as was the case for Pier 45, that development could not be general office or housing, or any other non-trust use. Even in areas where BCDC had reached agreement with the port that such uses were permissible, including on new structures that used fill credits, the trust now prohibited them. Hotels were the only substantial revenue-generating uses left on the table; the convention center, for which Pier 45 would have needed retrofitting, was no longer possible.

One aspect of the struggle over Fisherman's Wharf that was different from many of the others along the waterfront was that everyone agreed on the fundamental issue—the need to preserve and even to enliven the fishing industry. The problem was how to do that. Fishermen and seafood businesses like packers and processors wanted to remain on Hyde Street and near Fish Alley, while some merchants and neighborhood residents wanted at least some fishing activity to be moved to Pier 45. Others felt that congestion was an issue, and that a hotel and improved fishing facilities would clash. In an attempt to ensure as smooth a process as possible, Port Director Gartland formed a citizen advisory committee headed by Chris Martin, manager of the Cannery and president of the Fisherman's Wharf Merchants Association. But even this gesture of consensus building did not help much. The port pushed forward with its request for proposals and received four bids by early 1987. What it really got was a debate that roiled for the next several years, until an earthquake finally loosened things up, literally and figuratively.

By May 1987, the first hitch appeared in the port's plans. A study was released that revealed it would be too expensive to upgrade and expand the Hyde Street Pier, taking it out of the picture. This meant that Pier 45 would have to accommodate fishing activities, which in turn meant that hotel-based development would have to be scaled back or scrapped altogether. To many this was not bad news as the idea of hotel beds and fish heads in close proximity seemed impractical, and what really mattered was the ability to maintain efficient operations for the fishing industry. Yet the port clung to the hotel, arguing that it simply could not do everything needed to support wharf activities without the added income. This assertion raised ire and doubts. A letter to the editor of the *Chronicle* by one articulate critic is worth reproducing in full:

> The painful sore of the 500-room hotel proposal for Pier 45 at Fisherman's Wharf is coming to a head like a boil ready to be lanced. Let us hope that the ensuing suppuration will not kill off our north waterfront and turn it even more into a tourist play zone uninhabitable by residents or the fishing industry.
>
> The claim by port officials and their out-of-town hotel developers that this is the only way to save the fishing uses of the waterfront only exhibits their poverty of investigation and imagination.
>
> It has properly been said by many, including Art Agnos, that the reason people come to Fisherman's Wharf is to experience the real-life drama of a working waterfront in action. To deliberately obliterate this magic by tourist glitz and upscale rooms by the night in our Bay is a folly of inexcusable magnitude. San Franciscans should let the Port Commission know in no uncertain terms that they will not tolerate this non-maritime pillaging of our historic waterfront.[44]

Facing stiff resistance, the port decided to reconsider its position and to investigate more fully non-hotel projects and possible sources of public and private funding. Calls to reconsider housing were quickly rebuffed by Randall Rossi, the port's first planning director. "We've been down that road more than once. . . . I don't think that's very productive."[45] In July 1987, the port commission moved away from the hotel project and endorsed the possibility of using $14 million cobbled together from loans, fees, and rents to repair and upgrade fishing births and related facilities. As port commissioner Ann Halsted noted, "There is a lot of public support for anything that's real and maritime there, that has to do with the water," but not, is the obvious implication, for much else.[46] And so, in late August 1987, the commission formally voted to reject the four bids for hotel-based projects and asked the planning department to help decide what could be done instead. Simultaneously, they committed several million dollars to build a new marina at the Hyde Street Pier and to reserve the west side of Pier 45 to commercial fisherman and seafood businesses. Nevertheless, this would not be the last time that the port would attempt to use hotels, its last best hope for profitable commercial ventures, as the anchors for development proposals and as the source of funds to implement policy and meet public interests.

As the commission was coming to terms with its hotel problem, Mayor Diane Feinstein stepped into the arena. Never a supporter of the hotel, she too wanted to prevent a "honky-tonk" on the wharf.[47] Perhaps inspired by success in South Beach, her contribution was to suggest the establishment of a redevelopment area in the wharf. This would make available the financial tools to pay not just for a modernized fishing industry but a public market as well, or so it was argued. Feinstein also took pains to assure nervous onlookers that unlike other SFRA projects, this would not take over privately owned land. Initially, the idea was greeted with enthusiasm from all quarters. Feinstein worked assiduously to broker a deal and was, by all accounts, admirably successful given the context described by the *Chronicle* as one of "warring fishing, retail, and civic groups."[48] James Haas, attorney for "out-of-town" developers who still clung to a reduced hotel concept, humorously observed that "for the first time in the memory of man or fish, everyone at the wharf seems to agree on something."[49]

This state of affairs did not last long. The financial realities set in first. Part of the package included taking money that the Golden Gateway contributed to the city's general fund and redirecting it to Fisherman's Wharf. Supervisor Doris Ward, while excited by the idea generally, was very skeptical about siphoning money in that way. And then the quagmire of local politics spread its undermining ooze. As a result of sudden opposition to the idea of a redevelopment area, the board of supervisors voted to shrink it by a quarter. Pier 39 was thus removed from the equation, which set off a chain reaction of pullouts. According to the *Chronicle*, Richard Hongisto, the lone vote in favor of the original redevelopment area, accused his colleagues of "gutting the plan to please the renegade wharf interests because many of them are big contributors to political races." He was quoted as saying, "It smelled, it stunk and I didn't like the biggest wheeler dealers around collecting their favors."[50]

A hodgepodge of lobbyists, including supervisorial campaign managers, lawyers, and ex-officials, were involved in stirring up the mud. According to Chris Martin, they nearly outnumbered audience members at the board hearing.[51] Rumors also circulated that new port director Michael Huerta did not want to see the SFRA gain control of its piers and that Huerta worked with Pier 39 managers to help sink the idea. Still, it was not until 1991 that the port formally aborted its attempt to work with the SFRA, which had already spent hundreds of thousands of dollars on geotechnical and engineering studies and urban design analysis. Perhaps the final nail in the coffin was the city's budget crisis. Had the redevelopment area been established, the resulting tax increment dollars would have supported the wharf instead of going into the general fund. Planning director Dean Macris put it succinctly: "That's good when your budget is balanced, and it's not good when your budget is not balanced."[52]

In the midst of the argument over the possibility of a redevelopment project in the wharf, Mayor Feinstein was termed out. She was replaced in 1988 by progressive Art Agnos, who had just ended a term as California assemblyman representing the San Francisco district.[53] Agnos was not new to the issues in the wharf and, like Feinstein before him, was interested in preserving maritime activity at the port. In 1986, as an assemblyman, Agnos championed the idea of a fisheries center to be modeled after similar facilities in Denmark. Agnos took his cause to Sacramento in the form of a request for money from the legislature to study the feasibility of a fisheries center. His argument was straightforward: "This center . . . would keep Fisherman's Wharf a genuine fishing wharf. You can't expect that tourists would want to come from across the country here just to buy a T-shirt and push a pin ball around. They want to see a working fishing port."[54]

The idea of a convergence of tourists and the "real" wharf had been first imagined literally as a glass wall on the Hyde Street Pier through which visitors could peer at the catch being iced, packed, and shipped. The center proposal was more active in its program, and included a research facility that would focus on practical things, such as improved fishing gear, processing techniques, and marketing strategies, and would also address environmental problems and fisheries issues. The center was supported by a coalition of seafood companies, fishermen, environmental organizations including the California Coastal Conservancy, and politicians; Agnos came to refer to it as "his center."[55] Although the amount Agnos requested was quite small, a matter of several hundred thousand dollars, Governor George Deukmejian refused to sign Agnos' bill, arguing that it would not be equitable to other jurisdictions if money were set aside just San Francisco. Agnos repackaged the bill, which the governor signed in 1987. But by the time Agnos was ushered into city hall, conditions had changed in the wharf, and the fisheries center concept, felt to be impractical, was abandoned.

Despite the setback, Agnos' commitment to a working wharf did not diminish and he continued to push for renovations and improvements, which were begun in 1988. This also marked a minor turning point for the port. Port director Michael Huerta agreed with the conclusions of a consultant study calling for all of Pier 45 to be devoted to the fishing industry. The idea that a purely touristic enterprise would expand onto the pier, bringing with it the "festival" feel of much of the rest of the wharf was nearly over. Instead, as Mayor Agnos had hoped, Pier 45 was to be home to the fishermen and related businesses, a "realness" of activity, it was thought, that would make the rest of the wharf more attractive as a place for diversion, perhaps even to locals. Indeed, when a place like a fisherman's wharf retains some of its original functions, the area as a whole is made more intrinsically interesting; the local color takes on more depth. However, the issue of financing improvements again plagued the port, whose only alternative was to rely on the success of local representatives in Sacramento in obtaining funds for San Francisco.

But then, in October 1989, the ground shook. The Loma Prieta earthquake did about $20 million worth of damage to port property. Pier 45's foundations were wrecked and its large sheds were severely damaged, forcing the port to evict a number of fish-processing businesses. Turning the tremor to its advantage, the port managed to secure enough state and federal funds, including Federal Emergency Management Agency money, to repair the damage and reconstruct fish processing facilities in two of its huge sheds.[56] After two years of work, the upgraded and modernized pier was fully reopened in 1995. Finally, the port's fishing facilities were unstuck from the 1930s, the decade with which some people had associated their functionality.

Since the opening of Pier 39, the underlying character of Fisherman's Wharf has changed little. It is still a major tourist area generally shunned by San Franciscans. Now, however, the fishing industry that is the foundation of the wharf's popularity is in much better condition, especially in terms of facilities. Additionally, new berths for the fishing fleet at the Hyde Street Pier were completed in 2001. The two rehabilitated sheds on Pier 45 are home to processors, wholesalers, and distributors that now comprise one of the largest concentrations of seafood businesses on the West Coast. Fish handling and processing is busier on Pier 45 than anywhere in northern California and Oregon.[57]

Regulation and planning policy have done much to help establish the character of Fisherman's Wharf as a place of mutually reinforcing activities—production and consumption. From the state, the strictures of the public trust have been instrumental in limiting commercial and housing development. In this context, local processes have further etched the landscape, creating both place and placelessness, the latter derived from the hackneyed experience of shopping that pervades much of the wharf—one of the few major income-generating activities permissible on land burdened by the trust. That Fisherman's Wharf has not changed substantially in twenty-five years can be attributed to a set of conditions characterized by state and local planning policy and regulatory restraints on development that limit potential profitability; a planning process and political environment that delayed projects until conditions ceased to be favorable to developers; and intense and effective protests by neighborhood associations and advocacy groups.

As noted, the single major exception was Pier 39, an example of a project that, for better or worse, conformed to planning policy and regulation and was successfully implemented. The practical difference between it and projects proposed for Pier 45 was local political support. Even though the port's later, hotel-based attempts at revamping Pier 45 technically conformed to established policy and were intended to achieve a goal that most people agreed with—support for the fishing industry—the agency still ran into severe difficulties. In this case, planning and regulations did not directly dictate what happened at Pier 45, although they certainly limited the port's choices. Rather, because the port was a city agency, it was subject to the politics of planning, which stymied its efforts to transform this very visible part of the waterfront. Where public disgruntlement is so intense and the profitability of a project is so marginal, politicians are not wont to commit themselves, especially to support an agency so often criticized. And if the mayor or the board of supervisors do not support a project, its chances for success are greatly reduced.

The port's attempt to capitalize on the seemingly vast potential of the tourist industry created a visceral response from locals who saw it as another effort by the port that would further alienate the citizens of San Francisco from their waterfront. For members of the public who wanted the wharf to become more appealing to them, and for local businesses who were concerned with the everyday functioning of the wharf, a hotel was anathema. So, the port's inability to reorganize and redevelop Pier 45 and the Hyde Street Pier is an example of how both bottom-up and top-down forces (in this case, from the state) can mix with local conditions to stymie potential change in a landscape. Limits on development, local resistance, competing ideas, delays created by the planning process, the vicissitudes of financing, investment, and ultimately, economic recessions, combined to squelch change. This interplay is not easily read from the landscape because it did not produce material change. One could not look at the new berths for the fishing fleet and discern the struggle over placemaking that had occurred before an earthquake made outside funding available for improvements. Indeed, the appearance of the harbor might lead one to think that San Francisco acted in a moment of unified purpose and interest. While the built environment appears to manifest societal cooperation and coherence of purpose, it hides struggle and conflict.

Office Interlude

In 1968, just before the transfer of the port became effective, the port commission initiated an office development project that was completed in the mid-1970s. Far different from U.S. Steel and Pier 39, the Francisco Bay office park and Blue Shield building were proposed to be located on a series of seawall lots beneath Telegraph Hill across from Piers 35–27. Little of the acrimony associated with other proposals was directed at this suburban-like development, although it did generate some comment.

At a hearing on October 9, the commission passed a resolution declaring that a collection of seawall lots in the northern waterfront were no longer needed under Sections (a), (b), and (c) of the *California Harbors and Naviga-*

tion Code, and could be devoted to uses allowed by Section 3000(d). These seawall lots, numbered 317, 318, 319, and 320, were for the most part undeveloped and underused. The State Belt Line Roundhouse, a major exception, occupied 318. It was preserved, eventually to be an early example of successful historic preservation through adaptive reuse. Seawall lot 317 was used by Western Pacific Railroad Company and for parking, 319 was occupied by an "old-time waterfront restaurant" and more parking, and 320 was used by a tire company.[58] Seawall lot 315 was later added to the project area.

A few people attended the hearing on the proposed development to voice what were relatively mild concerns. Jean Kortum, for example, did not like that the port was abandoning shipping in the area, contrary to the advice of Arthur D. Little. If the port dismissed part of their report, she argued, then the whole thing should be redone. Magnin, who bristled at her accusation that the port *wanted* to abandon shipping, pointed out that piers in the area were to be reserved for maritime activity, and that the hearing was about seawall lots that no longer supported the users of those piers. Robert Katz of the Telegraph Hill Dwellers was also there, but was circumspect with his comments, having voiced his opinion at a previous planning department hearing related to the proposal. His main admonition was that the port should be conscious of the potential for any project to increase congestion, especially given construction of the Embarcadero Center to the south.

A few people suggested that the port wait until after the transfer to the city make their determination, believing that more people throughout San Francisco would become aware of the proposed project as a result and could participate in planning for it. Magnin declined, stating that members of the public were welcome to participate in the future. He added that the port commission's composition and powers would be essentially the same after the transfer—an implication that the planning process would be no different as a result (an incorrect assertion, of course), to which one attendee replied, "there will be a change in psychology . . . the authority will be more attuned to the people of San Francisco." Magnin's gentle riposte was that for as long as he had been a member of the commission, the port had always "been sensitive to the needs of the City," citing as an example the accommodation of a heliport that the port did not want. Finally, a veteran of the Russian Hill height wars warned that, while glad that the port was not acting in haste, "[our] people will be watching you."[59]

Fears about heights were unfounded, as the buildings that were eventually to occupy the site had to adhere to the 40-foot limit imposed by the Planning Department's zoning.

The project was an easy one for the port, and it was pursued and implemented quietly. Advertisements for bids were placed in local papers, the port's selection of its developer did not seem to worry the usual watchdogs, and the development was approved by the planning department. Perhaps most important, because the project was located inland of the Embarcadero, it was not caught in BCDC's jurisdictional gravity well. Little has changed on the seawall lots involved since the buildings were completed. And the port has yet to repeat this kind of success.

Ferry Building Area Redux

Just a few years after the U.S. Steel failure, the port renewed its efforts to transform the Ferry Building area. In 1978, the port placed a full-page ad in the *Wall Street Journal* and began a national search for firms to redevelop the Ferry Building. In 1980, the port commission selected Continental Development Corporation (CDC) based in El Segundo, California, as its developer.[60] Because proposals for projects to improve the Ferry Building area now had to comply with land-use and building-form restrictions, the port's request for proposals was primarily for restoration and adaptive reuse of the Ferry and Agriculture buildings, and, just to their north, development of Pier 1, which at the time was covered by a large shed used for parking. Undaunted, CDC embarked on a lengthy effort to achieve the port's goals for revitalization. The many-year effort would end in nothing more than lawsuits.

Most important about this proposal was its scope and scale and how developers responded to criticism that it was overly commercial. Initially, the project encountered stiff resistance from Fisherman's Wharf businesses. Their area of concern had begun to creep south along the waterfront in tandem with proposals for development that might draw business away from them. Thus, as with Pier 39, they protested that the Ferry Building proposal would threaten their livelihoods. Quickly launched criticism also came from SFT and the Telegraph Hill Dwellers, who claimed that the project did not respect the historic and architectural importance of the landmarked building. In fact, even the port commission rejected their developer's initial ideas. CDC responded by pairing with renowned architects I. M. Pei & Partners and by offering to compromise with a scaled-back program. These two moves on the developer's part garnered support from the port commission and a cessation of overt opposition from activists and businesses. "We are still keeping an eye on you," warned one neighborhood association member.[61]

CDC's proposal included shops, offices, and restaurants, and a "Viennese-type coffee house that promises to become the new social hub of San Francisco."[62] An expanded World Trade Center also was slated for Pier 1 (Fig. 7.4). As stipulated by BCDC's *Bay Plan*, offices were permissible if they were maritime related (for the port itself, for instance) or if they were placed in existing structures and not new fill (the Ferry Building). Overall, the developers promised a "total experience of work, trade, leisure, and recreation" that would enable the Ferry Building area to "once again serve San Francisco as it did in the past—as the city's crossroads and market plaza. Its central place."[63] Despite its pretensions, the program was dramatically subdued when compared to earlier grand schemes that would have overwhelmed the Ferry Building area. The scale of the CDC's Ferry Building complex proposal reflected both the limits placed on development in the area by the *Planning Code* and BCDC's *Special Area Plan* and *Total Design Plan* and the commercial and recreational uses encouraged by policy. Yet even though the proposal got as far as construction scheduling, it was not a done deal.

CDC encountered two related problems. First, the permitting process was difficult and slow. Second, further delays were attributed to several tenants of the Ferry Building who did not want to be temporarily relocated during construction and who claimed that the CDC was not going to sufficiently compensate them for the inconvenience.[64] The port lost patience with CDC and sued to remove them from the project, claiming that the firm failed to obtain permits according to the agreed-upon schedule. CDC suggested that the port that did not want to continue with the project because the commission realized it could have arranged a better financial deal.[65] Their argument was punctuated by filing a countersuit to continue with the project. The port eventually settled by paying CDC several million dollars for its time and effort, but ultimately the deal was terminated. CDC's project was yet another development to be scuttled by the difficult local planning and permitting process, and peculiar local conditions.

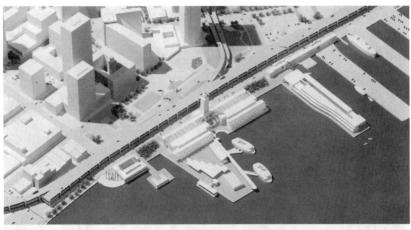

7.4 Two views of CDC's model of proposed development of the Ferry Building and Pier 1. Continental Development Corporation, *San Francisco's central place. Reestablished.* Model design by Pei Cobb and Freid, 1980. Top photo courtesy of Gerald Ratto. Bottom photo courtesy of Peter Xiques.

Another development was proposed for the area before the close of the 1980s. Pier Plaza, an even more moderate vision of waterfront revitalization, was proposed for Piers 1½, 3, and 5, just north of the Ferry Building. Submitted by Pier Associates, a joint venture of maritime firms, design agencies, and developers, this project included remodeling the existing bulkhead buildings, construction of 120,000 square feet of office on Pier 3, a restaurant, moorings for historic ferries, and extensive public access improvements (Fig. 7.5). The project, like the Ferry Building complex, generally seemed to conform to existing policies and regulations; its design seemed promising. Allen Temko even commented that "the Port of San Francisco has a history of grandiose projects that never get built. But its latest scheme to transform three old piers north of the Ferry Building into offices, cultural facilities and recreational open space has a real chance of

7.5 Model of Pier Associates' proposed development. Port of San Francisco, *Wharfside*. September/
October 1982.

7.6 A stretch of the Promenade today. Photograph by author.

7.7 Pier 7 as seen today. Photograph by author.

success."[66] However, as part of the permit review and approval process, the SLC examined the project and determined that its office element had to be maritime related, as opposed to "general office," in order to satisfy public trust requirements.[67] What happened exactly is unclear; however, Pier Associates likely was concerned they might not be able to attract solely maritime-related firms to lease the office space, and this project too sank quietly out of sight, sometime after 1986. Coincidentally, the mid-1980s were marked by a recession, making it more difficult to secure financing and pursue such projects.

Overall, the result for the Ferry Building area was that, for a quarter century between the late 1960s and the early 1990s there were only four changes to its morphology: construction of a concrete platform to protect the BART rail tube, but which is also home to a restaurant, open space, and a fishing pier; removal of a half-dozen dilapidated finger piers during the early 1980s; and two public access projects, one to construct the roughly 1,600-foot promenade (which would become part of Herb Caen Way), completed in 1982, and one that replaced the old Pier 7 with a new public strolling and fishing pier, dedicated in 1990 (Figs. 7.6 and 7.7).[68] The condition of the piers in the area had been evaluated as part of the *Northeastern Waterfront Survey*, which had also suggested that a public promenade be built nearby. Policy supporting these changes was also contained in the

Northeastern Waterfront Plan, Special Area Plan, and *Total Design Plan.* An Economic Development Administration grant primarily provided funding for these projects, demonstrating that while planning policy does not cause things to happen, as has been pointed out, it can direct how public funds should be used.[69]

At least in the Ferry Building area, public access to the waterfront was being improved, and the value of public space was being asserted. Planning policy, bureaucratic initiative, and public intervention were beginning to assert use value, not just theoretically but physically. This was not the only part of the waterfront where hints of the future were beginning to materialize. South Beach was also on cusp of becoming something new.

South Beach—The Redevelopment Project

$400,000 condos and container terminals do not mix.[70]
    —Port director Edward L. David

South Beach, the area between the Bay Bridge and China Basin Channel, has over the last twenty-five years, experienced perhaps a more dramatic transformation than any other part of the San Francisco waterfront (Fig. 7.8). Parts of it have also proven to be as difficult to revitalize as anywhere on the waterfront. The changes visited upon South Beach are attributable largely to the work begun in the 1979 *Northeastern Waterfront Survey,* which culminated in the *Rincon Point-South Beach Redevelopment Plan* and a companion document called the *Design for Development,* standard issue for redevelopment projects providing details of the physical aspects of the proposed development program.

The board of supervisors and mayor approved the program in 1981. Its implementation was begun soon thereafter and is now essentially complete. As described by the SFRA, "The purpose of the project is to transform a blighted area into a new mixed-use waterfront neighborhood incorporating rehabilitation and new development."[71] The main elements of the project include mixed-income housing, historic rehabilitation, waterfront parks, a boat harbor, Embarcadero roadway improvements, and, added later, a "corporate office building," and, finally, a ballpark.[72] The project also included various infrastructure improvements, such as sidewalk and street reconstruction, landscaping, and the provision of utilities. Funding for

7.8 Aerial photo of South Beach and its finger piers. San Francisco Redevelopment Agency, *Northeastern Waterfront Survey*, 1979.

the project has been through a combination of private investment, community development block grants (CDBG), tax-exempt revenue bonds, and tax-increment financing.[73]

Most of the changes generated by the project have been to land-side areas, but it has also led to unique uses of three of the port's seawall lots. On the land side, several large, mixed-use projects and high-density housing developments have been completed as have several smaller projects involving the adaptive reuse of historic warehouses. The area is also home to the Gap's headquarters, completed in 2001. Several of the port's seawall lots now accommodate low-income housing developments sponsored by the Delancey Street Foundation and BRIDGE, a nonprofit housing corporation.[74] A 700-berth marina replaced Piers 42–46 in 1986, and two waterfront parks were completed in 2003 and 2005, respectively. The Giants' ballpark, built on port property after an amendment to the redevelopment plan allowed for it, is also here.

While several piers in the area were condemned, others supported a variety of maritime uses. Pier 22½ was home to the port's fireboats,

Guardian and *Phoenix* (where they are still berthed); parts of Piers 26 and 38 were leased to divers, underwater construction services, and emergency spill cleaners. Piers 30–32 served as a layover berthing facility and were leased for special events. These uses, a number of which continue today, were all considered compatible with the residential and mixed-use neighborhood rising from an otherwise derelict part of the waterfront.

However, the conversion of piers 42, 44, and 46a into a yacht harbor was a watershed moment for the port. The proposal was actually made in 1979, several years before the redevelopment plan was adopted, and contention over it represented some of the last resistance by port officials to forsaking the possibility of maintaining shipping on land north of China Basin Channel. Port Commissioner Morrison, ever a defender of cargo-related maritime uses, said that the decision to convert those piers could prove to be a serious mistake. He warned his fellow commissioners that, "if we're not careful this could be a signal to the community that we have given up maritime uses."[75] One can understand his concern, given public animosity to previous development proposals and past public support of bond measures intended for maritime operations; the citizenry clearly shared Morrison's ideas about the port's role. In this case, however, the impossibility of converting the area to container terminals was easily demonstrated. In a 3–1 vote, the other commissioners rejected the idea of preserving what were determined to be outmoded piers and "banking" them for future cargo-related use. The SFRA was pleased with the decision, interpreting it as a significant endorsement of the concepts outlined in the *Northeastern Waterfront Survey* by incorporating them into the redevelopment plan then underway.[76]

Initially, public support for the Rincon Point-South Beach redevelopment project was mixed. The agency's reputation made some people leery of the plan, and some members of the board of supervisors were concerned with how the project would be funded. For Mayor Feinstein this was a pet project, so her office strongly advocated it. The *Chronicle*'s editorial board found the proposal to be "interesting and exciting," but Supervisor Kopp and the board of supervisor's budget analyst Harvey Rose were quite critical of the project.[77] However, because the project promised to build a large number of affordable housing units, support for it grew. As the *Chronicle* observed "the idea of creating a new living area within walking distance of downtown has drawn few critics."[78] That the project was part of a plan to reinvigorate what was generally seen to be a functional backwater of disused railroad tracks and warehouses did not hurt the cause.

An important piece of the puzzle was incorporating port property into the development program. The marina, waterfront parks, and housing were all supported in the city's and BCDC's policy documents, and as indicated above, the port eventually agreed that South Beach could not reasonably be reserved for cargo operations. The challenge, then, was to convince the newly powerful SLC and the legislature that the seawall lots incorporated into the project area were no longer able to support trust purposes other than revenue generation. After intensive lobbying by the city, with pivotal (and rare) cross-agency cooperation, legislation made its way through the state capital. The legislature passed Assembly Bill 2659 in 1987. The bill stipulated the conditions under which housing would be permitted on the three seawall lots in question. Essentially, it required that the land continue to be held in trust, but removed the requirement that it be used for maritime-related activities.[79] Furthermore, revenue generated by developing the land, which itself could only be leased to the SFRA, had to be used to support other trust purposes, such as providing open space or water-oriented recreation. The difficulty of removing land from the burden of the trust is one of the reasons that San Francisco is unlike so many other cities that have turned to housing in efforts to revitalize their waterfronts.

The transformation of port land in South Beach occurred because there was agreement regarding what should happen to the area; several policy documents supported it; the powers of the redevelopment agency were brought to bear; and the public approved of the project in its specifics. These conditions were so favorable that developers, their financial backers, and project sponsors continued to move forward with construction even during the early 1990s, when real estate development in the rest of the city was grinding to a halt. Here, the port, and in particular the redevelopment agency, acted as investment magnets. Contrary to what had happened at Pier 45 and the Ferry Building, local conditions, and the active efforts on the part of the local and state governments, created an environment that was attractive to capital investment, and more specifically to the kinds of firms that, together, constitute a capitalistic force that was, and is, at once top down and bottom up.[80] While change in this part of the waterfront has many of the characteristics that can help a city navigate upward in the global hierarchy, it was not part of a wave of globally originated transformations.

The overall result has been that, despite some poor urban design decisions and architectural treatments, the redevelopment project has managed to reconnect the city and its waterfront both in ways that have responded to larger pressures facing the city—for instance, its desperate need for new affordable housing—and in ways that maintain important public goals for waterfront use, especially in term of open space and access. Conversely, as will be discussed next, Piers 24–26 and 30–32 were prevented from being reused by bottom-up forces, largely because proposals were for developments that would have done much to separate San Franciscans from their waterfront.

No Room for Hotels

> The decades-long building boom that reshaped San Francisco's skyline is now inching toward a mile-long strip of dilapidated piers and bulkheads, creating an emotional debate.[81]
>
> —Doyle and Massey, *San Francisco Chronicle*

As the old warehouses and rail yards of South Beach were being converted into a new urban neighborhood, a residential extension of San Francisco's downtown, the port was pursuing options to redevelop Piers 24–26 and 30–32. With a vote to allow the marina at Pier 40 and with three seawall lots devoted to housing, the port could now concentrate on what it felt would be appropriate and lucrative uses given the evolution of the neighborhood. Residents and activists strongly rejected the decision, however.

Piers 24–26, which lay partly under the spans of the Bay Bridge, were deteriorating and presented an obvious possibility for reuse. Pier 24 was condemned, and Pier 26 housed a few offices and miscellaneous small industrial business. The first suggestion for revamping the double pier came in 1987 from a Sausalito sailor named Robert Scott, who brought to the port commission a proposal for a sailing center and conference facility dubbed Gateway Center. Scott "thought his project was a shoo-in because the Port . . . accepted it as a reliable moneymaker that would open the piers to San Francisco residents."[82] However, when Art Agnos was elected mayor, he pressured the port to open the project to competitive bidding—not surprising given the problems that had plagued the port under Director Gartland.[83] The result was intense controversy over the new submissions that would vex Michael Huerta, whose appointment as port director in

1989 was much covered in the press.[84] Only two other proposals were received, which *Chronicle* columnist Thom Calandra interpreted as being the result of difficulties other developers had encountered elsewhere on the waterfront.[85] This points to another characteristic of local conditions that influence the potential for change. A place can acquire a reputation that becomes part of the local character and can create a disincentive or even barrier to capital investment.

The proposal recommended by port staff was from the Koll Company, a firm from Newport Beach in southern California (Fig. 7.9). Not new to the area, they were sponsoring the adaptive reuse of the old Hills Brothers Coffee building and associated new construction across the Embarcadero from the piers. Koll's project called for a sailing center and marina similar to Scott's Gateway Center, as well as a convention center, shops, offices, and a museum. But the lynchpin of their development was a hotel. Even though height limits restricted the hotel to four stories, ILWU leader and port commissioner James "Jimmy" Herman said it could become part of a "wall of hotels," the second time in a quarter century that this image had been used to describe potential development on the waterfront. Herman chafed at what could become the first hotel built on port property, saying that it would represent "a turning point in the port's history."[86] Public outcry over the hotel came fast and furious; many argued that such a development would block views, encourage tourism, create congestion, and separate San Franciscans from the bay. Others worried that "the city is rushing ahead without a clear vision of what the waterfront should be" and that what was needed was an overall plan for the waterfront.[87] Port director Huerta responded with the familiar argument that the port had to find ways to pay the bills for new open space, to refurbish its fishing facilities, and to upgrade cargo operations; it continued to fall on deaf ears. For their part, the developers responded by saying that the hotel was needed to generate profit and pay for the amenities included in the development program.

At a packed hearing on December 12, 1989, the port commission voted on the proposal. Commissioner Herman made one last plea, repeating his earlier warnings that the proposal was "a pig in a poke; it can't work out, and it will lead to what I'm concerned about—a wall of hotels along the southern waterfront."[88] Many people believed that the project would be stopped because of a deadlocked commission. To audible gasps, however, Commissioner Coleman, who had earlier voiced his strong opinion that a hotel on a pier was a bad idea, switched his vote; the project was approved

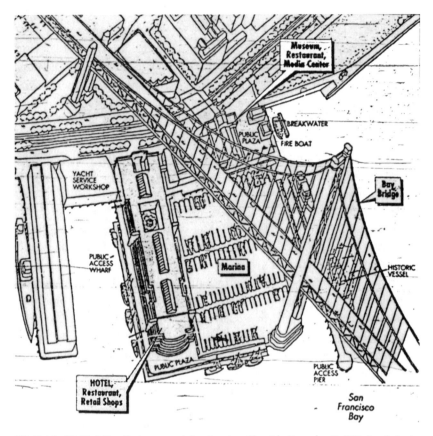

7.9 Sketch of Koll's Sailing Center proposal. San Francisco *Chronicle*. December 11, 1989. Permission to reproduce kindly granted by the San Francisco *Chronicle*.

3–1. Apparently, Coleman had been convinced that the port needed the money. After the vote, the *Chronicle* quoted him saying that "there has to be some balance between public interest and economic viability" and that one hotel on the waterfront would not be fatal to it.[89] For many, the vote also represented a broken promise by Agnos, who had said during his mayoral campaign that he would stop all development on the waterfront until guidelines for its future were established.[90]

As Alan Temko pointed out, such proposals in the end would "create a phalanx of view-blocking hotels and other tourist-shearing operations" and thus "sell the public interest short." But Temko carried the point farther, lamenting that because of restrictions enforced by public agencies like BCDC, "developments must be cloaked in a nautical aspect, real or ersatz," and "blithely enlivened with sails."[91] His evaluation was that these proposals maintained a veneer of compliance by including such elements as sailing centers, harbors, docks, repair centers, and other maritime amenities. Underneath, however, they were commercial developments that could have been built anywhere on dry land. Temko's criticism started to get at the underlying issue facing the port, that restrictions on development intended to support public goals did not always produce successful results. In fact, they were seen by many to stymie possibilities for development that could respond to a variety of interests, public and private. However, allowing housing, offices, and hotels would not necessarily solve the problem, as we will see in the next chapter. In this light, it is not surprising that the Koll Company's proposal, based on a hotel-on-a-pier idea drew such fire, and that a frustrated public would turn to the ballot box in an attempt to stop the port.

At the same time that Koll's Sailing Center was being pushed by Huerta and the port at the end of the 1980s, Erik Norgaard, an executive of the Danish firm Kampex Pacific, was looking to build a Scandinavian Center, cruise terminal, and hotel (Fig. 7.10). Norgaard was not new to the port, having been earlier involved in attempts to pursue the fishery research center at Pier 45. As part of this proposal, he agreed to fund the fishery center at Pier 45 that the port had tried unsuccessfully to build. As the fishery center idea was a favorite of Agnos', when Norgaard and his team identified Piers 30–32 as a good site for their project, the mayor had another reason to hedge his promise of no waterfront development. Norgaard worked hard to locate financing for his project. He convinced Scandinavian banks, pension funds, and small investors looking for tax shelters to participate—not exactly a global capital battering ram forcing an opening to port development. With promises of 1,300 new jobs and millions in revenues to the port, Agnos mentioned the project in speeches, even suggesting that he would fly to Scandinavia to demonstrate his seriousness about pursing the idea.[92] Yet the proposal moved forward slowly. The *Chronicle* editorial board expressed concern that the Pier 30–32 project had been allowed to simmer on the back burner too long—well over a year had gone by—positing that the controversy over the vote on the Sailing Center must have "shell-shocked" the port and mayor's office. They also complained that "officials tend to pay so much attention to complaints of small and special interests that plans that would enhance the common good are sometimes set aside."[93]

7.10 A model of Norgaard's Scandinavian Center proposal. Port of San Francisco, *Wharfside*, Marche/April 1991.

Amidst the roiling criticism, Commissioner Herman and Mayor Agnos reversed their respective positions on hotels at Pier 30–32. Agnos voiced reservations, suggesting that a hotel was not appropriate for a pier, and Herman acknowledged that substantial benefits might accrue if a hotel were allowed. In what must have been a very familiar refrain, Norgaard insisted that the hotel had to be part of the project, otherwise it would not be financially possible. "We have scratched our brains for two years with the best consultants and there are no other uses that produce income," he concluded.[94] The proposal came to a vote at the port commission at the end of May 1990. Supporters packed the hall and the commission voted unanimously to approve the project. This drew fire from Telegraph Hill residents and SFT, which again threatened that a ballot initiative would be part of the fall elections.[95] Clearly, they were unimpressed with a resolution passed earlier by the commission that barred more than two hotels from the waterfront.

Proposition H Lowers the Boom

Incensed at what they saw as another boondoggle in the making, and one that slipped through planning documents and regulatory protections, former supervisor Robert Scott, ex-port commissioner Jack Morrison, SFT, and the Sierra Club vowed to go to the ballot box. San Franciscans would determine by direct action what should happen on the waterfront; Proposition H was placed on the November 1990 ballot.[96] As one member of Save the Bay commented, people wanted, "some kind of guarantee that hotels do not pervade the waterfront. We'd like to see an overall plan for the waterfront rather than just a catch-as-catch-can philosophy of entertaining developers' proposals that happen to come in."[97] Proposition H required a moratorium on hotels and any other non-maritime development within a hundred feet of the water's edge until the port completed a waterfront land use plan. The measure passed with just 51 percent of the vote.[98] The successful passage of Proposition H killed Koll's Sailing Center project for Piers 24–26.

In response to Proposition H, Norgaard and his team actually reconfigured their proposal for Piers 30–32 to place the hotel on land across from the piers. This won strong support for the project, even from skeptics like Jack Morrison. Fortune was not smiling on Norgaard, however. His ambitious project, which now also included a "World Centre," was required to include at least one local financial backer (further complicating where to place such projects in the local-global continuum or top-down/bottom-up framework). Norgaard requested an extension to his agreement with the port, which the commission agreed to "given the current difficult economic development climate."[99] A year later, the port severed ties with Norgaard because he was unable to pull together financing. His project, along with Continental's proposal for the Ferry Building, are examples of projects that adhered to basic planning policy and regulation and worked their way through controversy, only to be delayed by the politics of planning long enough to skid into the trough of an economic cycle, which then prompted the port to cut ties with them. Local conditions again conspired to frustrate waterfront revitalization. The lack of change along this part of the waterfront can really only be understood in this context.

Whether either project would have successfully navigated the permitting process or even produced well-designed development is impossible to say. What is clear, though, is that hotels were deeply problematic for many waterfront watchdogs, making the policy that allowed them suspect—even though neighborhood associations and organizations like SFT had a hand in creating that policy. That hotels "slipped" through as plans were being written is because planners and bureaucrats believed that they would bring a wider public to the water than would offices or housing. And if the public trust and BCDC could abide them, the port would certainly not preclude them unless forced to do so. But because the port was a city agency and subject to local initiatives, activists and neighborhood organizations were able to patch the perceived breach in planning policy created by allowing hotel development. Notably, as an agency exercising some state powers, the port cannot necessarily be affected by local initiatives, so in this case, the initiative applied to the board of supervisors, which was prevented from approving hotels on port property through changes to the zoning and administrative codes.

In his analysis of Proposition H, Richard DeLeon suggests that what made the initiative appealing was not just that it required the port to write a detailed plan based on a parcel-by-parcel analysis, but that the planning process "had to make room for citizens as active participants; traditional methods of deal making had to be discarded."[100] As we have seen, however, citizens had been deeply involved in waterfront policy and development issues for twenty years. So, a slightly different interpretation is offered here regarding waterfront development; planning policy and activism had already demonstrated their strength. With Proposition H, people were reacting instead to planning policy and regulation that, despite being a complex tangle of jurisdictional requirements, and despite public input, still allowed an undesirable use to be proposed nearly anywhere on the northern waterfront. What San Franciscans recognized was that the port needed its own clear policy statement, a detailed vision for the use of its land that would represent some level of consensus among competing local interests about what the future of the waterfront should be. This would happen after six years of community-based planning with publication of the *Waterfront Land Use Plan*.

8

A Waterfront Planned

The 1990s and the New Millennium

> The Port's real value to the city isn't financial. It's the sheer beauty of it.[1]
> —Port director Dennis Bouey
>
> Determining the role of the port is crucial to saving it.[2]
> —Tibbet L. Speer, *San Francisco Business Times*

THE END OF our story brings us close to where we started, with San Francisco's contemporary waterfront. Much of what one encounters when strolling along Herb Caen Way and the Embarcadero was ushered in by an earthquake, a new planning policy and regulatory regime, and new approaches to public-sector financing. For decades, the waterfront was shut off, partially barricaded by an elevated freeway, parking, keep-out signs, crumbling piers, and activities and work sites not publicly accessible. Years of failed projects and an extended period of decay set the stage for recent changes along San Francisco's waterfront. Now, in many places and in many ways, people are welcomed to it. This transformation has been guided for the most part by local conditions, from San Francisco's planning culture and environmental activism to the nature of the site itself—a beautiful, but shaky, hilly peninsula.

Excepting the removal of piers and the projects addressed in the last chapter, most of the significant changes that have helped define the current lineaments of the port's property north of China Basin Channel commenced in the mid-1990s. What follows is a short discussion of the most important of these, and, for the sake of coming to a conclusion, a very brief outline of key events that have unfolded early in the new millennium. The port's *Waterfront Land Use Plan* figures prominently in this new era of waterfront transformation. We start, however, with one last status check on the port's shipping operations, once the agency's core purpose. Although the port no longer functioned as an important center for the movement of goods, the agency continued to pursue any new glimmer of hope for maritime business and to protect doggedly what maritime activities it still had. In fact, maintaining a working waterfront is even now a major planning and development goal, and the mantra of many parties interested in the fate of the waterfront.

Out with the New, In with the Old

During the 1980s and into the 1990s, the port made efforts to modernize its shipping facilities, spending tens of millions in bond money, but to no avail. The port also sought to underbid its rival in Oakland for shipping lines, but that strategy proved fruitless as well. Between 1995 and 1996, just after millions were spent on upgrades to Pier 80, containerized shipping at the port dropped to a trickle, pushing San Francisco to the bottom of port rankings in the United States. The mid-1990s also saw four shipping lines move to Oakland, including Evergreen and Nedlloyd. It is no surprise, then, that the total number of container units crossing the port's piers dropped precipitously, from about 116,000 to 13,000 between 1991 and 200.[3] In 1994, the port nearly fell into bankruptcy, averted only by staff layoffs. Although its financial situation improved, the condition of its shipping operations were so bad that the port turned down federal grants to improve a major bottleneck in the transshipment of containers.

As part of the port's program to modernize its facilities, Piers 94–96 had been developed with an "intermodal container transfer facility," which meant rail tracks were brought onto the piers, allowing containers to be loaded directly onto railway cars. The problem was that the route into and out of San Francisco is through a pair of half-mile-long tunnels used by commuter lines running up the peninsula. These tunnels, bored in the early part of the twentieth century, could not accommodate cars double-stacked with containers (the standard way to load trains). Cargo that could not be moved through the tunnels efficiently was put on trucks to cross the bay where they were then loaded onto trains—not very competitive! The port's decision to turn down millions in federal funds to enlarge the tunnels was based on several factors: loss of shipping lines, which according to the port was not related to the tunnel; additional costs for dredging that would be required to accommodate the new super-sized vessels too wide for the Panama Canal; the need for new cranes; and that the money would be better spent elsewhere, such as on improvements to Fisherman's Wharf and the cruise terminal.[4]

On the upside, however, the port announced that it was going to focus on break-bulk shipping. Not everything fits in a container.[5] The Port of Oakland had all but devoted itself to containers, allowing San Francisco to develop a niche market, modest as it is. This shift in focus did not mollify the ILWU or Seafarers Union. The ILWU president referred to the tunnel decision as "just another political nail in the coffin of the port's cargo industry" and that it was an "absolute message to the world that the San Francisco port has no maritime future."[6] John King, a reporter for the *Chronicle* and later its urban design critic, pointed out that Mayor Frank Jordan, elected in 1992, in his support for commercialization of the port represented a break from Mayors Feinstein and Agnos. The general sentiment was that this orientation was in part the reason for shipping's decline, or at least the port's seeming unwillingness to go all out to support it. King wrote that "each [Feinstein and Agnos] treated shipping as the backbone of the port—partly for the jobs it provides, but also because of the city's self-image. In a city where diversity is proclaimed as the greatest civic asset, a strong working port would show that blue-collar workers still had a place, and tourism had not conquered the waterfront."[7]

Still, between 1999 and 2005, the port's break-bulk traffic increased from 14,000 to 237,000 metric tons and its dry-bulk tonnage increased from about 900,000 to 1.5 million. Amounts like this are not insignificant. According to the port, the additional traffic in bulk cargo created two thousand jobs, generated $15 million in taxes, and spurred $95 million in purchases of local goods and services.[8] The uptick even caused the port to reopen Pier 80 early in the new century; it had been mothballed for much of the 1990s. By 2000, the port had gone from a low of one carrier to a dozen shipping lines making it a port of call. [9]

So, the Port of San Francisco cleaves to its working roots as much as it can and involves labor organizations in making decisions about development that may affect existing and potential maritime work. And it continues to evaluate its markets for cargo operations and has devoted resources to a few capital projects. For instance, in 2008, the port dedicated the multimodal Illinois Street Bridge linking the Pier 80 "Omni Terminal" to the intermodal facility across Islais Creek at Piers 94–96. The bridge was a solution to requirements in the *Seaport Plan* that the port maintain rail access to its maritime facilities in "maritime priority areas." It also helped the port deal with impediments to rail operations due to development at Mission Bay and the construction of the 3rd Street extension of the city's light-rail system. The bridge enables the port to take on heavy-lift cargo jobs and it generally expands marketing possibilities due to increased functionality. Yet in recognition of changed times, the bridge accommodates pedestrians and bicyclists as well. The port has also worked to support the dry-dock operation at Pier 70, which has seen significant increase in business from cruise lines. Finally, as it turns out, the tunnel expansion is still listed among the possible capital projects the port is considering.

There was one missing element in the port's pursuit of shipping and maritime businesses. During the 1990s, it had become obvious that the old argument that commercial development was needed to support shipping and maritime development no longer held water—there just was not much to support. This was underscored by Mayor Jordan, who asserted that commercial development should instead be used to bring people to the water, especially through shopping, entertainment, and recreation, and to finance maintenance of piers and other facilities. A few years later, this was a generally agreed-upon strategy, and was incorporated into the 1997 *Waterfront Land Use Plan*. So, the pursuit of industrial maritime activities has not been able to rely on potential income generated from commercial development; cargo operations in particular have had to fend more for themselves, financially speaking, and not on what happens in the northern waterfront. This also meant that the port could solicit commercial projects and focus on making the project work internally. That is, if the project met design parameters and could pay for required open space and other mandated features, then "go for it" was often the attitude. But even this loosening of the financial noose would not be enough to jigger free some of the creative capacities of capital. That would take public-private partnerships, historic preservation tax credits, other public support for private enterprise and an earthquake.

The Embarcadero Reborn

A year before Proposition H was passed, the 1989 Loma Prieta earthquake severely damaged the Embarcadero Freeway, thus providing the opportunity to rethink the relationship between the city and its waterfront and to implement policies that had been in place since 1977 as part of the *Northeastern Waterfront Plan*. Furthermore, the city had for years maintained as official policy that the Embarcadero Freeway should be removed. The original concept to carry out these policies was developed during the 1980s as the *I-280 Transfer Concept Plan*. Elusive financing and jurisdictional issues, especially with the California Department of Transportation (CalTrans), were barriers to its implementation. And in 1986, San Franciscans actually voted against removing the freeway. The watershed moment came with the state's evaluation that the Embarcadero Freeway was too severely damaged by the 1989 quake to repair; it would have to be rebuilt. The city, whose opinion of the freeway had changed in the intervening years, gasped collectively at the thought and Mayor Agnos organized to fight Sacramento. The board of supervisors joined the mayor by adopting an anti-freeway stance, and an unusual sense of common purpose brought various city agencies together. The city prevailed in its demand that the freeway be removed and replaced with surface transportation elements that reflected city policy.[10]

The design for the new Embarcadero roadway included a significant amount of port property, and only a few general policies existed pertaining to its reuse and reconfiguration. So, planning for the new roadway was undertaken in a multiagency effort coordinated by the city's Chief Administrator's Office under the rubric of the Waterfront Transportation Projects Office (WTPO).[11] Then began a ten-year planning effort that involved substantial community input, a citizen's advisory committee for the Embarcadero Project, and many, many consultants, with the design firm ROMA at the forefront. As described by the WTPO, the city had been "presented with an unprecedented opportunity to realize its vision for a tree-lined boulevard with rail, bicycle, pedestrian, and public art amenities along the northeastern waterfront and [to] create a civic plaza that acknowledges the importance of the Ferry Building, the terminus of Market Street, and the city's historic relationship to the waterfront."[12] Funding for the massive project was secured from a variety of federal, state, and local sources. The

8.1 Looking south along the Embarcadero. Photograph by author.

$700 million collection of projects was immense and immensely complex; it is not possible to address them fully here. Let it suffice to summarize the main components, all of which were completed by the early 2000s: a new alignment for the Embarcadero boulevard that incorporates bicycle lanes and an exclusive right-of-way for an extension of the F streetcar line from the Ferry Building to Fisherman's Wharf (service started in 2000) (Fig. 8.1); a water-side pedestrian promenade that runs from Fisherman's Wharf to China Basin Channel (Herb Caen Way); an extension of MUNI's light-rail system south of Townsend Street along an exclusive right-of-way in the center of the Embarcadero, completed in 1997; an underground MUNI switching yard that was originally to be placed under the elevated freeway; several open-space improvements; and lots of Canary Island palm trees (without dates, so no messy cleanup). The port described the impact of these projects in no uncertain terms: "Together, they singularly changed the character of the northern waterfront from an industrial service corridor to an outdoor living room for San Francisco."[13]

Of particular interest to the port was a subset of this program, referred to as the Mid-Embarcadero Roadway project, initiated in 1998 and completed in 2000. Its main piece is a large plaza that connects the Ferry

8.2 The Ferry Building and plaza as seen today. Photograph by author.

Building to the foot of Market Street and the Embarcadero Center. From it jut spiky "light cannons" that beam their lumens into the night sky. The port linked the success of the then nascent Ferry Building rehabilita-tion and related Downtown Ferry Terminal projects, mentioned below, to the new open space (Fig. 8.2). The concept had evolved from the larger Embarcadero program, and in 1995, officials were already speaking of it in near-giddy terms. "This is a singular opportunity to make the most impor-tant space in the city," enthused the director of the planning department, Lucian Blazej. ROMA's Boris Dramov was broadly categorical in his asser-tion that "the crossings of people will make this place unlike any other place. . . . The historic city front will be reinstated. People will want to feel it."[14] But these were not necessarily exaggerations. To underscore its public importance the plaza was named for Harry Bridges, famed water-front labor leader, and was paid for with public funding, including Fed-eral Highway Administration grants and local voter-approved sales taxes earmarked for transportation. However, the plaza design was the subject of an intense battle over whether to put the roadway underground, and then whether to split the north and south bound lanes. Costs and safety concerns led to a surface roadway split around a plaza, making an island of the open space. The end result leaves much to be desired from a physical design perspective, but it involved much compromise and hand-wringing.

The overall effect of the Embarcadero projects has been to reunite the city and its waterfront in ways that benefit a wide public. In 1995, before the Mid-Embarcadero project was begun, SFT member Norman Rolfe repeated what was becoming a common refrain, that "the waterfront should not be set off from the public by private clubs, hotels, and high-rises. We'd like to see esplanades and maritime uses, things that connect people to the bay and the ocean." His wish, shared by many others, was starting to coming true, and the *Waterfront Land Use Plan* provided the well into which the public could throw its coins, and not just metaphorically speaking.[15]

The *Waterfront Land Use Plan:* Its Success and Failures

> The Waterfront Plan should not be prescriptive . . . it should be designed
> to embrace discussions of different ideas and ways in which its policies
> could be achieved, based on the give and take of rigorous public review
> and debate that San Francisco is known for.[16]
>
> —Port of San Francisco, *Waterfront Land Use Plan*
>
> There's the potential for something beautiful that also creates jobs.[17]
>
> —Don Beck, retired fireman

In response to Proposition H, the port initiated its public planning process in January 1991. An important initial step was the formation of a twenty-seven-member Waterfront Planning Advisory Board (WPAB) based on recommendations from the board of supervisors, the mayor, and responses to a general request for participation sent to interested citizens, organizations, planners, maritime businesses, labor, and a variety of professionals. After many public workshops, draft documents, and board meetings, the port commission approved the final *Waterfront Land Use Plan* in 1997, which has been amended several times since. The work of the WPAB was critical to the plan's success. It is a testament to the WPAB and the importance of the undertaking that its members, representing often-adversarial groups, could reach consensus. Of course, the process had its bumps. For example Jane Morrison, wife of ex-supervisor Jack Morrison took a rather extreme position, saying that "the waterfront should be for maritime or it should be left as open as possible. . . . It isn't there to be 'used.' It's there to be seen. . . . It wouldn't be a great disaster if nothing happened. Piers may fall into the bay."[18] But the WPAB was able to work around such difficulties, thanks in part to its chair, Robert Tufts, who was appointed by Mayor Agnos. Tufts, an attorney, and at the time, chair of BCDC, was later honored by the port for his contributions. So, the result of four years of coordinated planning by BCDC, the port, Save the Bay, the San Francisco Planning Department, the WPAB and the waterfront community, led the port to describe their success as a historic achievement.[19] Indeed, the *Waterfront Land Use Plan* has been hailed as a resounding success by nearly everyone involved in or concerned with the waterfront.

During the course of its work, the WPAB recognized that urban design, open space, and public access issues would be better dealt with separately by a special technical committee. The Urban Design Technical Advisory committee was composed of representatives from the port, the SFPD, BCDC, and Save the Bay and it produced the *Waterfront Design and Access* element, which became a part of the *Waterfront Land Use Plan* and adopted with it under separate cover. Now all major projects are reviewed by a Waterfront Design Advisory Committee (WDAC) and analyzed for consistency with the *Waterfront Land Use Plan* and *Waterfront Design and Access Element.*

The *Waterfront Land Use Plan* is important for several reasons. First, it is an excellent example of a publicly informed planning process. As Diane Oshima, the port's assistant deputy director of planning recently wrote: "The Port also recognized the essential importance of creating a public process for developing the Waterfront Plan that was thorough and rational, and which incorporated authentic and meaningful public debate and participation."[20] Its creation has involved representatives of many interested publics, from labor unions to neighborhood activists to shipping line officials. It is in many ways the acme of land-use and policy planning—a consensus document. Public participation did not end with the adoption of the plan. The port also established four advisory groups responsible for different parts of the waterfront and a fifth whose concern is specifically maritime commerce.

Second, and related to the first, the plan was an incentive to coordinate policies contained in disparate documents. To this end, in 1998, the planning commission unanimously adopted conforming amendments to the *General Plan, Planning Code,* and *Zoning Maps.* Approval from the board of supervisors quickly followed. Changes to the *Planning Code* included removal of the requirement for conditional use permits for non-maritime use, ending a condition that had enforced a repetitive and inefficient form of project-by-project analysis. The port still has to obtain CUs that would be required in normal circumstances, for instance to allow housing in an area zoned for industry. Building height and bulks limits were unaltered.

After several years of sometimes-strained negotiations, amendments were also made to BCDC's *Special Area Plan*, which, along with an updated *Waterfront Land Use Plan* were approved in 2000. The final vote occurred in city hall to applause from the staffs of both agencies. Coordination with BCDC was especially important because it meant that areas where commercial development could be pursued were mutually agreed.[21] As part of the agreement, Piers 24, 34, and 36 were identified for removal and changes to several other piers and buildings were included to increase access to and views of the bay. Additionally, BCDC agreed to relax some of its restrictions on what land uses were appropriate along the waterfront in return for the port's preservation of more open land and public access as part of the *Waterfront Land Use Plan*.[22] The goodwill and feelings of relief that pervaded the conclusion of the process did not spread to labor. Representatives of the ILWU and the Inland Boatmen's Union of the Pacific continued to voice concerns that nothing be done to disrupt facilities then being used for maritime activities and warehousing. They were not wrong in observing that "we're getting squeezed into a smaller and smaller area of the Port of San Francisco."[23]

Third, the *Waterfront Land Use Plan* is the first comprehensive vision for the future of the waterfront produced under the aegis of the port. As the plan itself comments, "Although many elements of the existing plans, policies, regulations and financial objectives are worthy of retention, a new approach is required to halt the continuing deterioration of Port property and to revive the debilitated state of Port finances."[24] The goals of the plan are to create: a working waterfront; a revitalized port; a diversity of activities and people; access along the waterfront; an evolving waterfront, mindful of its past and future; urban design worthy of the waterfront setting; and economic access that reflects the diversity of San Francisco.[25] The *Waterfront Land Use Plan* also helps clarify, for example, issues pertaining to public trust requirements, how piers are subject to BCDC's differing restrictions, and the use and definitions of maritime terms. The plan contains policies pertaining to three main categories—maritime uses, open space and public access, and commercial uses. Perhaps the plan's most significant element is that it identifies acceptable land uses according to a number of categories for every seawall lot and pier in the port's jurisdiction. This was far beyond the mandate of Proposition H, which only required the port to plan for areas subject to BCDC's authority. It was the result of a bureaucratic epiphany of sorts, one that led the port to realize the importance of the opportunity it had and of its responsibilities to the public.

So, forty years after the port started thinking about redeveloping its property, it had a document that answers the question, at least in general terms, "What to do with the waterfront?" Still, the *Waterfront Land Use Plan* does not apply rigid limitations with respect to possible development in its main opportunity areas. As a result of this approach, what exactly the waterfront will become is, for the time being, unknowable. The WPAB adopted this somewhat flexible framework because its members feared the possibility that detailed site-specific restrictions would fail. Instead, most important sites can accommodate a variety of uses.

Fourth, the plan served as the impetus to seek funds for and carry out a series improvements and commercial developments. In part, this was achieved by identifying sites along the waterfront that would offer opportunities for mixed-use development. These areas were carefully negotiated with BCDC and city agencies to allow revenue-generating projects if they supported other public goals. For instance, a project could conceivably include non-maritime office if other trust goals were met as a result, such as the preservation of a historic resource. In an update to the port commission, director Douglas Wong pointed out that adoption of the *Waterfront Land Use Plan*, "along with the current real estate market and other factors, has spurred considerable interest by private developers, public agencies and citizens in revitalization of Port property."[26] His comment serves as a reminder that when opportunities and resources are available to real estate firms and developers, and other agents of top-down forces seeking to imprint their plans on the landscape, they are also available to local entities, enabling the pursuit of visions for change defined and fought for from the bottom up. The plan does more than invite development, it instead focuses on establishing the waterfront as a civic space, serving a broadly identified societal need. Thus it requires private capital to incorporate public needs into its venturing, as opposed to allowing the market to produce whatever it wants with the expectation that public benefit would trickle down. The plan optimistically emphasizes the public in its public-private partnership foundation.

Two years after his update to the commission, with successes in hand and the hope for more, Director Wong expressed his enthusiasm for the *Waterfront Land Use Plan*, exclaiming that "as promised, it has reawakened and revitalized the Port through an intricate series of programs that have expanded maritime operations and created new public access, entertainment, and open space along the Bay."[27] His statement was not just optimism. A number of projects that implement policies in the *Waterfront Land Use Plan* have been completed, and others are at various stages of development. Perhaps most significant among them has been the stunning transformation of Pier 1 and its stately neighbor, the Ferry Building. Pier 1's large shed was originally used as a sugar and dry goods warehouse. When shipping relocated, it suffered the indignity of becoming a parking garage. The rehabilitation of Pier 1 was the first modern full-scale renovation of a pier shed building and the first major project subsequent to the adoption of the *Waterfront Land Use Plan*. It was successful because the developer, AMB Properties, an industrial real estate firm, was able to use tax credits to pay for a substantial portion of the historic rehabilitation costs and because they were able to lease some of the building as general office space. This was allowed as part of negotiations with the SLC, which agreed that to satisfy public trust requirements, in this case historic preservation and public access, development of some office space was justifiable. The pier's apron is fully accessible to the public and bronze rail lines run through the new shed's public corridor as a reminder of its past. The building renovation, designed by local architecture and design firm SMWM, has won several awards for the quality of its historically sensitive rehabilitation. Its Class-A office space is home to the port (clearly a maritime use), AMB's headquarters, and a couple of financial and legal firms.[28]

After several years of complex and difficult negotiations and financial prestidigitation, the renovation of the Ferry Building was completed in 2003. It also benefitted from an agreement to allow office space in order to pay for historic rehabilitation; however, allowing office development in order to support such trust goals has been far more difficult to arrange elsewhere. The port selected local developer Wilson-Meany and partners SMWM to undertake the project. Their success is considered nothing short of splendid. The Ferry Building's historic façade was restored and the

8.3 Pier 14, break water and public space. Photograph by author.

"nave bay" that ran the length of the building, essentially a grand three-story atrium, was recreated. Internal spaces that had been chopped up and isolated are whole once again. The Ferry Building houses a ground-floor marketplace, restaurants, offices, and public uses, including access to new ferry terminals, port commission meeting rooms, and circulation through and around the building. A tremendously popular farmers' market is held on Saturdays on the BART tube platform behind the building, and it is a focal point for community gatherings and civic activities. Of its restoration, the *Chronicle*'s John King wrote, "What's striking isn't simply that a grand landmark has been restored—triumphantly so—but that it is so in sync with the city of today. . . . Now the waterfront is an amenity, a grace note in the harsh grind of city life, and the old icon again plays an active role."[27] In conjunction with the Ferry Building's rebirth, the port has recently completed its Downtown Ferry Terminal. The terminal provides modern facilities for the modest but steady flow of commuters and occasional recreational ferry passengers. To protect the new berths, the port had to construct a breakwater south of the Agriculture Building. This was cleverly disguised as a new public strolling pier, Pier 14, which was opened in 2007 (Fig. 8.3).

8.4 Public walk behind Piers 1½, 3, and 5. Photograph by author.

In 2006, a third major historic rehabilitation project was completed that saved the bulkhead buildings on Piers 1½, 3, and 5 from certain doom, for they had been severely damaged in the earthquake. The project included recreational boating slips and an impressive contribution to the Bayfront History Walk public promenade, which entices the public to walk along the water behind the bulkhead buildings (Fig. 8.4). A modest amount of office space was included, but the public benefits program was also sup-ported by historic preservation tax credits. The project has been described as a "a gift to the city."[30]

The remaking of the Ferry Building Area, including the WTPs, stands in stark contrast to proposals proffered during previous decades. Had any of those schemes been implemented, it is unlikely that the improvements now enlivening the northern waterfront would have been possible. What did not happen in this part of the waterfront, and along the Embarcadero, partly by luck but mainly by active resistance, set the stage for a transformation guided by public policy that resulted in a movement away from privatization and toward the creation of more democratized space.

The *Waterfront Land Use Plan* has engendered many other achievements. The plan served as the basis for the creation of the Embarcadero Historic District, officially listed in the National Register of Historic Places in 2006. Creating the district helped resolve conflicts over development where BCDC policies prevented repairs and seismic upgrades to deteriorating historic structures. Until the *Waterfront Land Use Plan* and *Special Area Plan* were brought into alignment in 2000, BCDC regulations even called for the removal of historically significant resources, such as piers and bulkhead buildings. By contrast, the updated *Special Area Plan* required that the historic district be created.[31]

Many San Franciscans would say that the Giants' ballpark is also a tremendous achievement. The ballpark opened with much fanfare in 2000, but its construction required a ballot initiative, coordination among many agencies, and a significant amount of flexibility and creativity on the part of the team's owners and their developers. Typically, baseball stadiums and similar arenas are associated with raw deals—the public subsidizes much of the cost in return for keeping the team in their city (part of being "entrepreneurial" in the neoliberal urban condition). In this case, the project involved no public funding, although it did require public land. In fact, one issue for the owners was that, even though SLC approved the use, there was no guarantee the trust grant to the port would not be revoked sometime in the future, which meant that the state could reclaim the land.[32] While certainly a grand, material instance of popular culture and spectacle, the stadium also gracefully embraces the waterfront and is a monument to and for the public: a children's area in the park is open to the public in the off-season; large windows overlooking the outfield allow the public to watch a few innings free of charge; the building is surrounded by plazas and open space (adorned with more palm trees); and the team paid for China Basin Park, on the south shore of the channel. The stadium is linked to the East Bay by China Basin Landing, a port-developed public ferry landing and to the rest of San Francisco by a MUNI light-rail stop. Even cynics are hard put to find fault with it.

Other accomplishments of the first decade of the new millennium included the Pier 52 public boat launch; Islais Landing, a shoreline and public access improvement along Islais Creek that features a launch facility for human-powered boats; completion of Rincon Park, funded by the Gap; the South Beach Children's Play Area, part of the Rincon Point-South Beach Redevelopment Plan; Heron's Head Park, a wetlands restoration and environmental education program in the southern waterfront; salt-marsh restoration at Pier 94 near Islais Creek, where part of fill supporting the pier subsided into the bay; and Hyde Street Harbor improvements. Current works in progress include the relocation of the Exploratorium, a children's science museum from the Palace of Fine Arts to Piers 15–17, which is in the entitlement stage; evaluation of proposals for a large mixed-use development at Seawall Lot 337–SW 337 is a 16-acre parcel near Mission Bay that is currently used as a parking lot for Giants games; a master-planning process for the sixty-acre area that includes Pier 70; and a renewed attempt to deal with street-design issues in Fisherman's Wharf. Many of these projects, and others not listed, respond to the *Waterfront Land Use Plan*'s goals to increase public access to the waterfront and the bay by creating a series of linked open spaces and approaches. None was, or has been, particularly controversial, except those concerned with the wharf and one project proposed for SW 351, near the Ferry Building.

The *Waterfront Land Use Plan* ushered in a new stage in the evolution of waterfront planning policy and regulation. Its adoption was an articulation of local power that established a new, more democratic and public-minded discourse for planning waterfront transformation and revitalization. Its inception was the direct result of local grassroots action and a voter-approved initiative, and it was the product of a planning process that involved citizens, professionals, and advocacy groups of many stripes. The *Waterfront Land Use Plan* also owes its success to the hard work and patience of the WPAB, port staff, and the willingness on the part of all agencies involved to rise above bureaucratic territoriality and to create a commonly agreed upon set of conditions for development.

Naturally, no plan can satisfy everyone completely, and no matter how thoughtfully crafted, policy documents usually contain inconsistencies, vagueness, or a measure of uncertainty. The planning department, for instance, has felt that the flexibility built into some of the land-use designations creates something of a "black-box" effect; that is, for some "opportunity sites" the range of possible developments is so broad that a project sponsor could come out of the process with a proposal not supported by the *General Plan*. And initially at least, even the port's own commission was not entirely at ease with the plan. Commissioner Jim Herman expressed concern that it did not guarantee that the port would not become home to "Ferris wheels, roller coasters and Coney Island West."[33]

Nor is the plan an impervious shield from top-down forces, or necessarily even from the adroit politicians and clever developers indigenous to San Francisco. The SLC is still heavily influential and not much can be done to control the continuing variability of shipping and maritime activities. Moreover, though it is a document full of good intentions, the *Waterfront Land Use Plan* relies on public-private partnerships as the primary mechanism for achieving many of its goals. This has presented certain difficulties that have only relatively recently come to a head. So, despite its broad base of support, the *Waterfront Land Use Plan* is not the be all and end all of waterfront planning policy. Its many positive achievements are accompanied by some failures and keenly felt disappointments; a few are discussed below. Dealing with the issues raised by some of these projects has had an impact on the port's more recent approaches to encouraging development.

PROBLEMS OF SEISMIC PROPORTIONS

As one might surmise, the *Waterfront Land Use Plan* has not ended contention over development, or resulted in a magical transformation of the entirety of port property. Nor has it prevented the port from making dubious decisions regarding what projects to pursue. At the turn of the millennium, the agency was fairly well excoriated for choosing to pursue an "interactive" San Francisco history museum/amusement park at Shed A of Pier 45, proposed by Malrite, instead of a marine research center. The former had funding, lobbyists aplenty, and port support. The latter, proposed by the nonprofit Bay Center, a coalition of merchants and environmentalists led by Chris Martin of the Cannery, struggled to raise cash but was favored by most San Franciscans.[34] After nearly a year, the museum proposal, disliked by both Mayor Gavin Newsom and the board of supervisors, died an ugly political death. The research center was never able to secure sufficient funds to move forward.

Since adoption of the *Waterfront Land Use Plan*, two projects in particular—both large and complex, and destined for failure—have frustrated the port. The first was a proposal by San Francisco Cruise Terminal LLC, which was a partnership between Australian giant Bovis/Lend Lease and minority partner Port of Singapore, to develop a cruise terminal and 600,000 square feet of offices, retail, and commercial uses at Piers 30–32 (Fig. 8.5). The project also included seawall lot 330 across the Embarcadero from the piers, originally to be developed with hotel and retail. The basic concept was supported by the *Waterfront Land Use Plan* and enjoyed a fair amount of support from the public and city agencies. The public responded well to the cruise terminal, open space, access to the bay, and other amenities, and to the development team itself, which was considered creative and engaging.[35] However, even with the International Cruise Terminal as its focus, the proposal ran into public trust issues that required special state legislation to resolve. After engineering studies revealed that the cost to repair and seismically upgrade the piers was much higher than expected, the development team proposed that condos instead of hotels be built, but this involved the lengthy process of transferring the burden of the public trust from the seawall lot to property elsewhere.

The developers had all of their entitlements in hand and had secured the right to build the condominium tower first so that profits from that venture could support the cruise terminal and public spaces. However, even though the tower was completed at the height of the real estate boom

8.5 Sketch of proposal for the Justin Herman Cruise Terminal. Courtesy of the Jerde Partnership.

8.6 Sketch of the proposal for Piers 27–31. Courtesy of Johnson Fain.

in 2006, profits were insufficient to make the project financially feasible. Adding office space and a shopping arcade may have been enough to pay the $80 million needed to upgrade the piers and cover increased construction costs, but to do so would have made it un-approvable—politically and legally. Bovis/Lend Lease backed out of the project and actually left money on the table. Per the terms of the agreement, most of the profit from sales of condominiums would go to the port should the cruise terminal not be constructed.[36] This is the second place in which housing has been built on the waterfront. One more attempt was made at getting the cruise terminal built at Piers 30–32. Eddie DeBartolo, former owner of the 49ers football team, took a stab at making a project happen. His proposal shrank the size of the cruise terminal (though cruise ships were getting longer) and increased the amount of commercial space. The port rejected his bid in 2006 and appointed an advisory panel to seek alternative locations. Pier 27 is the current candidate, and the project is advancing.

A similar fate befell a proposal to develop a massive complex at Piers 27–31, at the base of Telegraph Hill. The *Waterfront Land Use Plan* identified the piers as an appropriate location to promote active recreation, retail, and other maritime activities. The port received two bids to its RFP, one from Chelsea Piers, responsible for the waterfront entertainment complex of the same name in New York, and one from Virginia-based Mills Corporation, known as a builder of shopping malls, teamed with the YMCA. After a contentious and politically heated selection process and nearly pugilistic tactics on both sides, the port selected Mills in 2001 (Fig. 8.6).[37] Mills' proposal was to create a mixed-used project to include 145,000 square feet of shops and restaurants, a 110,000-square-foot YMCA facility, boat ramps, and a plaza. Opponents of the project objected that the piers would end up another retail mecca and that transportation along the Embarcadero would suffer. The more dedicated and vociferous among them formed Citizens to Save the Waterfront, which, supported by supervisor Aaron Peskin, successfully pressured Mills to change aspects of its project. The firm did so and the commission approved the revisions in 2004.[38]

The particular recreational uses proposed included indoor basketball courts, soccer fields, and a bowling alley. The SLC determined that these were inappropriate to a tidelands site, revealing an issue with the flexible approach taken in the *Waterfront Land Use Plan* with respect to programming potential land uses. Until specific proposals were made, thus clarifying the exact nature of "recreational enterprises" proposed, it was difficult to know how the SLC would react. This was a lesson learned for the port.

But even after refining the project proposal yet again to respond to SLC concerns, Mills could not rid itself of the controversy that had boiled and simmered for six years. The project also suffered from results of the local election cycle. Mayor Willie Brown, the sponsor's main backer in city hall, was replaced by Gavin Newsom, who was neutral toward the project. At that point, Mills had little political power left. Official support all but disappeared with the appointment in 2004 of Monique Moyer as port executive director. Known for her fiscal prudence, Moyer was cool to the project because it committed the port to a 66-year lease with less than stellar terms. So, after spending $21 million and several years in predevelopment, Mills sold their right to negotiate to a team headed by local real estate giant Shornstein and Company early in 2006. The new sponsors replaced the retail component with office space. Only months after taking over the project, they insisted that it would take at least double the office space to pay for repairs to the piers necessary to support construction—the estimate had risen from $78 million to $145 million. This essentially killed the project because even in the unlikely event that the SLC would approve a major increase in offices (even to pay for trust uses) there would be no money left to provide the required public amenities.[39] The combination of restricted development potential and the cost of seismic upgrades in addition to the requirements for public amenities was too much.

It is not necessary here either to dig into the complexity of the cruise terminal project or the teeth-gnashing, maneuvering, and hardball politics that permeated the Mills project, or reveal the details of their land-use planning and financial intricacies to make the main point. In the port's own words, "it is clear that public-private partnership developments do not work in all instances. On the one hand, the qualities of rehabilitated historic maritime facilities, which incorporate generous amounts of public access and a diverse mix of activities—when they work—do produce enormous public benefits. . . . On the other hand, the balancing act required to contain development costs [for projects that have] relatively low development density and relative high public benefit and regulatory requirements, is very precarious."[40]

In the dozen or so years after the adoption of the *Waterfront Land Use Plan* the port has not been able to produce a single major commercial development using the public-private partnership formula of public real estate for private capital outside of the Ferry Building area. The failure of two difficult projects and the hard-won success of even a noncontroversial one like the Ferry Building forced the port to reassess its approach. In fact, a new paradigm based on public financing has been ushered in. So far, it has met with success. Instrumental have been an energetic and creative staff and the current director of the port, Monique Moyer, considered by some to be one of the best public agency finance people in the country, and who has been extremely effective in negotiations with other city agencies and the state.

The foundations of the future are in a supplement to the *Waterfront Land Use Plan*—the *Ten-Year Capital Plan*. Published in 2006 and updated in 2008, it provides the public for the first time with a clear accounting of the port's maintenance, maritime, and development goals and the costs tied to each. The total for the balance sheet is a staggering 1.9 billion dollars, most of which is for deferred maintenance and seismic work and to clean up Pier 70 and rehabilitate its historic buildings. The port is searching for ways to pay this massive bill, with only some covered by public financing made available by ballot measures, legislation at the state level, and a city administration newly sensitive to the predicament of its port. What follows is a summary of the key components of the new public financing approach.

First, the port was able to convince the city's administration that it should be included in a general obligation bond proposal placed on the ballot. In fact, voters recently passed a proposition that included significant funding for port open space projects. This is the first time the city has used its bonding capacity to support port waterfront improvements.

Second, with support from state assembly member Carole Migden, who represented San Francisco, the port was able to push legislation through Sacramento in 2005 that has enabled the agency to create "Infrastructure Finance Districts." These districts will allow the port to capture tax increments from future developments and, instead of sending the income to city and state coffers, apply it to the provision of public amenities, reinvestment, and historic preservation. Third, in 2007, Governor Arnold Schwarzenegger signed Senate Bill 815. The bill was the outcome of a coordinated effort between state, regional, and local agencies, facilitated by negotiations with local activist organizations. It allows the port to remove public trust restrictions from certain seawall lots that no longer serve maritime purposes so that it will be able to pursue mixed-use projects—as long as return from the development is invested in historic preservation and provision of open space, community facilities, and other public benefits along the waterfront. Fourth, in November 2008, San Franciscans passed Proposition D, a measure that supports land-use planning for and rehabilitation of Pier 70 by allowing up to 75 percent of any new payroll and hotel tax revenue to be use for environmental cleanup, infrastructure improvements, historic preservation, or open space. Without the measure, all tax income funds would have gone directly to the city and the state, never to be seen by the port. Finally, the port recently retired its debt obligations from old revenue bonds, freeing the agency to issue new ones.

These changes in the mundane world of finance have profound implications for the waterfront. The environmental movement, activist organizations, and public policy have shielded the waterfront from many forms of development, but they could not initiate change. Now, the port has the wherewithal to generate funds that will go no small distance in meeting public mandates for open space, access to the water, and historic preservation without the full burdens imposed by public/private partnerships or the imperatives of capital accumulation. Furthermore, the port will be better able to control the character of its commercial development because private sponsors will not have to argue for bigger projects dominated by highest and best uses to pay for public benefits or to retrofit piers. But even with this improved situation, SPUR recently admonished readers of its newsletter that "San Franciscans face hard choices at the Port," and asked, "Can we create a waterfront that people will love and use, or must we continue to watch it slowly rot into the Bay?"[41] At least for now, though current plans and policies may not satisfy everyone and agencies may still skirmish over turf, popular opinion seems to be that the results have been for the better, so indicators seem to be twitching in the direction of "yes we can."

Planning and the Landscape

Clearly, as we have seen, the interplay among forces that affects places varies over time and space. At a basic level, San Francisco's urban waterfront landscape has been formed by two opposing pressures: on the one hand, cycles of economic boom and bust, especially as they encourage or restrain investment in the second circuit of capital (a top-down pressure on the urban fabric), and on the other hand, planning policy and regulation (a bottom-up pressure).[42] Top-down pressures have come, and will continue to come, in many guises, although Richard Walker points out in his discussion of globalization that most such pressures are similar in nature, particularly where they occur in a common context, for instance in the realm of the capitalist economy.[43] Some sources of pressure play themselves out relatively quickly, but change the playing field completely in their wake. This was the case with the impact of containerization on the 1950s waterfront. Others are constant but morph over time. For instance, the state has played a role throughout the history of the port but its role changed when the port was transferred to the city and again once the SLC matured as an agency. To the contrary, the pressures brought by attempts to invest capital in the waterfront have been more or less continual and are homogenous in their basic nature.

Bottom-up forces affecting the waterfront have changed radically in the decades since 1950, as illustrated by the evolution of planning policy and regulation and ever-shifting interactions among the ranks of activists, gatekeepers, associations, committees, and agencies. Initially, bottom-up forces were not at the ready, only coalescing in response to proposals for reuse of port land that were deemed to be misguided, especially if they threatened to degrade the environment by filling the bay, or by limiting access to and views of the water. Paradoxically enough, as the planning process evolved, and local actors took advantage of their new powers, development became more difficult, which contributed to the creep of disuse. Nevertheless, local forces came to prevail in many ways, which has meant for the waterfront that capital's propensity to creatively destroy has been, so far, quite stymied.

Much of the politics of planning, and therefore the politics of urban development, takes place at a local level and within a local framework. One of the most important aspects of land-use planning, policy and regulation is that the process of their development provides a focal point for the cacophony of voices raised in hopes of influencing the course of urban change: many actors and agents have had a hand in the development of policy pertaining to the waterfront. Once plans are completed, they act as structural or formalizing elements in the process of urban transformation, for instance allowing participants to evaluate a potential development against established policy and to present an argument for or against it. Plans can become the nexus of coordinated resistance or advocacy, and the planning process becomes a medium for attempts to frame dominant discourses of development.

But the dynamic of success and failure is one of ebb and flow. It can depend on who has the most access to local power bases, and on the character, personalities, and perspectives of the mayor, elected officials, department staff, advocates, and individual members of the public. San Francisco's political culture may eventually change: its traditional core of environmentalists, anti-growth activists, preservationists, and neighborhood boosters may pass on, like Tolkien's elves, to be replaced by a new generation of residents more likely to support dramatic urban change, who may believe that sustainable development requires office towers and housing on the waterfront. Only time will tell, although recent demographic trends foreshadow a new cultural politics that may engender such a shift. One may venture, however, that what fate befalls San Francisco's waterfront in the future will be the result of the same essential process that has made it what it is today—a series of negotiations. So, while the role of planning is not easily gleaned from the built environment, it is in fact critical to the formation of the urban landscape. Of course, how planning helps to (mis)shape the urban landscape varies with how it is carried out and who, if anyone, engages with it. Our example of San Francisco's waterfront has revealed planning as two sides of a coin—it is both context for processes and it shapes their material outcomes.

Artifacts of the built environment represent different moments in the history of the relationship between sets of forces that affect the landscape. The absence of any obvious change in the built environment is equally revealing and representative, though in a somewhat different fashion. To summarize, the interplay of forces, the conditions and characteristics of the locale in question, and how they all interact are what individuate an area, are what define a place. They come to be expressed in the built environment, but the process and the result of that expression is negotiated, and that negotiation is an essential part of what forms an urban landscape.

A WATERFRONT FOR THE PEOPLE?

The Embarcadero Roadway and other projects catalyzed by the Loma Prieta earthquake and implemented in response to some of the goals in the *Waterfront Land Use Plan* have reunited city and port, and in doing so, have created a new atmosphere along much of San Francisco's urban waterfront. Indeed, it would not be an exaggeration to say that already San Francisco has reclaimed much of its waterfront. But it is still important to ask "For whom?"—a question that began our story. Vendors in the Ferry Building cater to a high-end crowd; organic beef, specialty cheeses, and artisan baked breads await deep-pocketed consumers. The Saturday farmers' market is frequented by latte-carrying hipsters, aging yuppies with children, and foodies willing to spend the money for top-notch goods. Nearby at Rincon Park, two restaurants have recently opened that are not marketed to people on a budget, or for that matter, families with children. The same can be said for the new eatery at Piers 1½–3-5. Giants games are not cheap, and neither is the beer sold inside. And by and large, the active uses along much of the waterfront north of China Basin Channel are, aside from businesses in bulkhead and pier-head buildings, oriented to diversions not particularly water-oriented in nature. Spectacle and entertainment bring cash to the port. And finally, not many blue-collar maritime jobs are left. What remains of the working waterfront, aside from the wharf, is isolated in the south, far from the heart of the city for which it was once the lifeblood. One wonders how often a longshoreman or ship welder sits down at the Ferry Building for oysters and champagne. But they may take their children for a bike ride along Herb Caen Way, stop for ice cream, and watch the sea lions bark at Pier 39.

San Francisco has avoided the affliction of a modernist project of office towers, STOL ports, and other gleaming monoliths of commerce on its waterfront. The rampant privatization and narrowing of purpose that comes with unfettered commercialization has not occurred. The city has not, in a spasm of entrepreneurialism, turned over its waterfront entirely to the spectacular, to éclat. While there is no doubt that the pursuit of leisure and distraction through consumption is part of the waterfront today, it is far from unmitigated. From the remains of a working port and its gritty docks, San Francisco has also created a place of promenades, historic stateliness, long open piers, pockets of green against the blue, access to the water, and evocative vistas. Even commercial developments include features meant to draw people to the waterfront and not prevent them from venturing to the water's edge. The homeless are not forced out of these public spaces in actions tantamount to state-sanctioned violence.[44] Skateboarders and stunt-bike riders are not chased away, nor is the area controlled or surveilled in an attempt to make the place "safe" for certain groups of people (Figs. 8.7 and 8.8).[45] The waterfront is far and away more public and civic in purpose than what was imagined for it in the past, or that one might expect in a world-class city in contemporary capitalist society.

Geogrpaher and preeminent urban theorist David Harvey has averred that "contestation over the construction, meaning, and organization of public space takes effect, therefore, when it succeeds in exercising a transformative influence over private and commercial spaces."[46] The processes outlined in this book provide an example of some successes in a similar struggle, in this case to protect public land against privatization and commercialization. In fact, "transformative influences" along the waterfront have actually increased the amount of civic space in San Francisco, right at the city's front door and smack dab across from a downtown aching to expand. This was made possible by institutionalizing a consciousness of the water—that is, protecting its use value for a wider public. To make the most of the opportunities presented by San Francisco's disused waterfront land has not meant unbridled market-based development in support of positioning the city globally, but as much as possible emphasizing the public importance of the area, asserting its public value. If "going global" is indeed a desirable end, then pointing to the civic aspect of the waterfront would be a different and legitimate way to lay claim to a position at the top of the world's urban hierarchy. An optimistic reading would have the waterfront as a bulwark against the neoliberal urbanization found in other

8.7 Homeless people in Rincon Park, in both foreground and background. Photograph by author.

8.8 Stunt bike riders at the Ferry Building plaza. Photograph by author.

parts of San Francisco—a bulwark put in place by public involvement, a progressive, green, political culture, and relatively enlightened government agencies and staff.

The right to the city, Harvey elaborates, is "far more than the individual liberty to access urban resources: it is a right to change ourselves by changing the city. It is, moreover, a common right rather than an individual right since this transformation inevitably depends upon the exercise of a collective power to reshape the process of urbanization."[47] Society must strive for what would then be a more inclusive city even if, Harvey admits, the result is continual fractiousness. However, bringing together individuals and finding and establishing common cause among disparate groups is very difficult at a practical level. But at some point, to get things done, one must be able to make decisions and strike bargains. San Francisco's waterfront is an example of a relatively successful negotiation to create a place that reflects the interests and hopes of many diverse groups and people.

The story is not over, but there seems to be real promise that use value and a right to the waterfront, and therefore a right to at least part of the city, is being secured for the citizenry, as opposed to a waterfront made primarily into a commodity by the dominance of exchange value and a capitulation to capitalist accumulation strategies. The randomness of play and encounter, the sense of belonging, the very flow of people, tourists, locals, workers, leisure seekers, homeless, skate punks, wealthy diners, and middle-class consumers, together with the myriad activists, agencies, and businesses involved in the waterfront create an instance, even if in a small way, of what Henri Lefebvre called an *oeuvre*—the city as a work, an assemblage of many functions, made by its people (Fig. 8.9). Whether the transformation of San Francisco's waterfront represents hope for and the possibilities of an "urban revolution," or is just an isolated pocket of minor resistance, remains to be seen.

8.9 "Cupid's Span" by Claes Oldenberg and Coosje van Bruggen. Photograph by author.

Notes

Introduction

1. As argued by M.P. Smith in *Transnationational Urbanism* (Oxford: Blackwell Publishing, 2001).

2. Sharon Zukin has argued that because the workings of the market no longer revolve around or reflect the specificity of particular places, the differences among them get lost. As she puts it, ". . . as markets have been globalized, places have been diminished" (*Landscapes of Power* [Berkeley: University of California Press, 1991], 12),

3. Paul Knox, "The Postmodern Urban Matrix" in *The Restless Urban Landscape*, ed. Paul Knox (Englewood Cliffs, NJ: Prentice-Hall, 1991), Paul Knox, "The Restless Urban Landscape: Economic and Sociocultural Change and the Transformation of Metropolitan Washington, D.C.," *Annals of the Association of American Geographers* 81, no. 2 (1991): 189–209; and Michael Dear and Steven Flusty, "Postmodern Urbanism," *Annals of the Association of American Geographers* 88, no. 1 (1998): 50–72.

4. Richard Walker, "Landscape and City Life," *Ecumene* 2, no. 1 (1995): 33–64. This is a mini-theme in some of Walker's work. In another piece, he states that "in seizing upon fashion, we ought not to lose sight of the dialectics of the local and the global and of the importance of place. Local studies still have much to teach us" ("Another Round of Globalization in San Francisco," *Urban Geography* 17, no. 1 [1996]: 6–94, quotation on 60).

5. Leslie Sklair, "The Transnational Capitalist Class and Contemporary Architecture in Globalizing Cities," *International Journal of Urban and Regional Research* 29, no. 3 (2005): 485–500.

6. For criticisms on the use of the concept of dualities, in particular of the global-local variety see: J. K. Gibson-Graham, "Beyond Global vs. Local: Economic Politics outside the Binary Frame," in *The Geographies of Power*, ed. Andrew Herod and Melissa K. Wright (Oxford: Blackwell Publishers, 2002); and Eugene J. McCann, "The Urban As an Object of Study in Global Cities Literatures: Representational Practices and Conceptions of Place and Scale," in Herod and Wright, *Geographies of Power*; and Smith, *Transnational Urbanism*.

7. See, for instance, Doreen Massey, *Spatial Divisions of Labor: Social Structures and the Geography of Production* (New York: Methuen, 1984); Neil Smith, *The New*

Urban Frontier: Gentrification and the Revanchist City (New York: Routledge, 1996); Kevin Cox, ed., *Spaces of Globalization: Reasserting the Power of the Local* (New York: The Guilford Press, 1997); Dolores Hayden, *The Power of Place: Urban Landscapes as Public History* (Cambridge, MA: MIT Press, 1997); and Andrew Herod, "Labor Internationalism and the Contradictions of Globalization: Or, Why the Local Is Sometimes Still Important in a Global Economy," *Antipode*, 33 no. 3 (2001): 407–26.

8. Work Progress Administration, *San Francisco, The Bay and Its Cities* (New York: Hastings House, 1947). John Bolles, planner and consultant to the city and port, wrote that "the waterfront has been San Francisco's principle link to the Bay Area, the nation, and the world--it was the City's 'front door'" (John S. Bolles Associates, *Plan* [San Francisco: City and County of San Francisco, 1966], 21). His remark points to the image of the port held in the city's collective consciousness as being a very public place. Along with the city's activist political culture, it helps explain why there has been so much debate over waterfront development in San Francisco.

9. John Fraser Hart, "Reading the Landscape," in *Landscape in America*, ed. George F. Thompson (Austin: University of Texas Press, 1995).

10. As M. Ball has observed, "The most obvious way that people know they are in a city or town is that buildings are everywhere. . . . It is difficult to see how the creation of the built environment can be avoided when examining housing provision; the cyclical patterns of office development . . . and in comprehending the very shapes and forms of cities and towns" ("The Built Environment and the Urban Question," *Environment and Planning D: Society and Space* 4, no. 4 [1986]: 447–64, quotation on 447).

11. See, for instance, Mona Domosh, "The Symbolism of the Skyscraper, Case Studies of New York's First Tall Buildings," *Journal of Urban History* 14, no. 3 (1988): 321–45; Larry Ford, "Reading the Skylines of American Cities," *Geographical Review* 82, no. 2 (1992): 180–200; and John A. Jakle and David Wilson, *Derelict Landscapes* (Savage, MD: Roman and Littlefield, 1992).

12. Denis Cosgrove, *Social Formation and Symbolic Landscape* (Totowa, NJ: Barnes and Noble, 1984); and Stephen Daniels and Denis Cosgrove, "Spectacle and Text: Landscape Metaphors in Cultural Geography," in *Place/Culture/Representation*, ed. James Duncan and David Ley (London: Routledge, 1993).

13. Some of the older work of American landscape geographers has skirted around, if not directly confronted, this problem. *The Interpretation of Ordinary Landscapes*, a landmark collection edited by Donald Meinig (New York: Oxford University Press, 1979), was celebrated by some but has been faulted by others who question the efficacy of uncritically "reading" landscapes and attempting to interpret culture from material artifacts alone. Cosgrove, *Social Formations and Symbolic Landscape*, was an early and pointed critic.

14. As Knox has put it, "the built environment is both the product of, and the mediator between, social relations" ("Restless Urban Landscape,"182).

15. Cosgrove, *Social Formations and Symbolic Landscape*.

16. Deryck W. Holdsworth, "Landscape and Archives as Texts," in *Understanding Ordinary Landscapes*, ed. Todd W. Bressi and Paul Groth (New Haven, CT: Yale University Press, 1997), 55.

17. Don Mitchell, "Cultural Landscapes: The Dialectical Landscape--Recent Landscape Research in Human Geography," *Progress in Human Geography* 26, no. 3 (2002): 38.

18. Allan B. Jacobs, *Making City Planning Work* (Chicago: American Society of Planning Officials, 1978). It is beyond the scope of the work at hand to enter directly into discussions of planning theory. How planning is carried out, by whom and for whom, is the subject of a voluminous literature. See, for instance, Norman I. Fainstein and Susan S. Fainstein, "New Debates in Urban Planning, the Impact on Marxist Theory within the

United States," *International Journal of Urban and Regional Research* 3, no. 3 (1979): 381–403; Richard E. Klosterman, "Arguments for and against Planning," *Town Planning Review* 56, no. 1 (1985): 5–20; Clarence N. Stone and Heywood T. Sanders, eds., *The Politics of Urban Development* (Lawrence: University of Kansas Press, 1987); Scott Campbell and Susan S. Fainstein, *Readings in Planning Theory*, 2nd ed. (Malden, MA: Blackwell Publishing, 2003); and Susan S. Fainstein "Planning Theory and the City," *Journal of Planning Education and Research* 25 (2008):121–30. Generally, though, it should be pointed out that much of planning until 1960s was a modernist affair, rational and technocratic. As the social sciences reacted to the positivist movement that dominated much of the 1960s and 1970s, planning welcomed new, more participatory, and even grassroots approaches into its practice, epitomized by advocacy planning. See Paul Davidoff, "Advocacy and Pluralism in Planning," *Journal of the American Institute of Planners* 34, no.2 (1965): 544–55. By the 1980s, planning found itself in a sort of middle state, somewhere between the modern and postmodern. Robert A. Beauregard, "Between Modernity and Postmodernity: The Ambiguous Position of U.S. Planning," *Environment and Planning D: Society and Space* 7 (1989): 381–95. Postmodernism in planning has been thought of as potentially offering resistance to market-determined and neoconservative urban development. David Ley, "Styles of the Times: Liberal and Neo-Conservative Landscapes in Inner Vancouver, 1968–1986," *Journal of Historical Geography* 13, no. 1 (1987): 40–56, and David Ley and Caroline Mills, "Can There Be a Postmodernism of Resistance in the Urban Landscape?" in Knox, *Restless Urban Landscape*. Judith Innes has described it as confronting "the challenge of continuous change, not by creating blueprints or rigid regulatory regimes, but by trying to influence the direction of change and preparing to meet uncertainty" in a collaborative process. Judith Innes, "Challenge and Creativity in Postmodern Planning," *Town Planning Review* 69, no. 2 (1998), vi–ix, quotation on viii. Collaboration is part and parcel of the "communicative turn" taken by planning. See Susan S. Fainstein "New Directions in Planning Theory," *Urban Affairs Review* 35, no. 4 (2000): 451–78; and Philip Allmendinger and Mark Tewdwr-Jones "The Communicative Turn in Urban Planning: Unraveling Paradigmatic, Imperialistic and Moralistic Dimensions," *Space and Polity* 6, no. 1 (2002): 5–24.

19. See, for example, Sidney Plotkin, *Keep Out: The Struggle for Land Use Control* (Berkeley: The University of California Press, 1987); and Rutherford Platt, *Land Use and Society: Geography, Law, and Public Policy* (Washington, DC: Island Press, 2004). In the parlance of theorists, planning is a discourse, or the struggle over establishing a dominant one. But it is one that cannot always be fully plumbed from an outsider's vantage point. Those interested in this critical aspect of urban change should be prepared to advance a more participatory research agenda. Few urbanists outside of planning do this, preferring to throw darts from a distance. A notable exception can be found in the work of Eugene McCann who has written ably on urban planning and policy issues as a "participant-observer." Eugene J. McCann, "Collaborative Visioning or Urban Planning as Therapy? The Politics of Public-Private Policy Making" *Professional Geographer* 53, no. 2 (2001): 207–18. Geographers have been particularly quick to dismiss planning as elitist, or as an apparatus of the state co-opted by capital to assist in the accumulation process. In this view, planners are relegated to being little more than bucket carriers for capitalism. This is neither accurate nor constructive, though to suggest that planners may not be constrained by, or even actively perpetuate, conditions that serve class interests or interests other than the public good would be naïve. I point simply to the pivotal and contested role that planning plays in issues of social justice and equity.

20. Much of the authority invested in planning devolves to local bodies and in most ways, it is a local endeavor. Exceptions include state laws that, in California for example,

require certain subjects be included in general (master) plans and that require projects to meet environmental standards, although the California Environmental Quality Act (CEQA) allows broad degrees of freedom in how it is implemented by the local responsible agency.

21. In San Francisco, actions taken by other departments, for instance changing sidewalk configurations or selling property, must go through an administrative review for consistency with the city's *General Plan*. Theoretically, other agencies and departments must also reflect support for official planning policy in their budgets and capital expenditure plans. The practical reality is that this is difficult to do.

22. Formalized evaluation of the potential impact of projects on the environment is another powerful, but controversial, part of the planning toolkit. At the federal level, this is carried out under the National Environmental Protection Act (NEPA), and in California, under the California Environmental Quality Act (CEQA). Redevelopment powers, touched on later, are also important.

23. Michael Neuman, "Does Planning Need the Plan?" *Journal of the American Planning Association* 64, no. 2 (1997): 208–20.

24. See, for example, Don Mitchell, *The Right to the City* (New York: The Guilford Press, 2003); Setha Low and Neil Smith, eds., *The Politics of Public Space* (Routledge: New York, 2006); and Paul Edwards, "Citizenship Inc.: Negotiating Civic Spaces in Post-urban America," *Critical Survey*, 18, no. 3 (2006): 19–36. The link between democracy and the right to the city is ably made by Mark Purcell in *Recapturing Democracy* (2008).

25. Kevin Lynch, *Image of the City* (Cambridge, MA: MIT Press, 1960).

26. Waterfronts may also be thought of as "uniting seams rather than isolating barriers" (Ibid., 65).

27. Depending on the context, the *port* and *waterfront* can connote slightly different things. Port usually refers to the part of a waterfront used for shipping and other maritime functions, or to the specific area over which an agency, for instance the port of San Francisco, has jurisdiction. Waterfront can also refer to the entire port-city interface and can include open space and undeveloped areas as well as inland areas functionally connected to, but not necessarily part of, a port agency's area of authority. In this book, the term waterfront refers to the urban waterfront, and sometimes to areas beyond the port's jurisdiction.

28. Reasons for the decline of traditional maritime activities, especially shipping, are well established. See Sarah L. Richardson, "A Product Life Cycle Approach to Urban Waterfronts: The Revitalization of Galveston," *Coastal Zone Management Journal* 14, no. 1/2 (1986): 21–46; Brian Hoyle, "Development Dynamics at the Port-City Interface," in *Revitalizing the Waterfront*, ed. Brian S. Hoyle, D. A. Pinder, and M. S. Husain (London: Belhaven Press, 1988); Ray Riley and Louis Shurmer-Smith. "Global Imperatives, Local Forces, and Waterfront Redevelopment," in Hoyle et al., *Revitalizing the Waterfront*; and Stephen J. Craig-Smith and Michael Fagence, eds. *Recreation and Tourism as a Catalyst for Urban Waterfront Redevelopment* (Westport, CT: Praeger, 1995). Passenger lines have been similarly affected by technological innovation, especially by the automobile and the jet engine and associated international airlines, see Henry S. Marcus, Nawal K. Taneja, and Paul O. Roberts, "The Impact of Changes in Transportation Technology on the Use of Land in Harbor Areas," in *Urban Waterfront Lands*, ed. National Research Council, (Washington, DC: National Academy of Sciences, 1980).

29. Riley and Shurmer-Smith, "Global Imperatives," in Hoyle et al., *Revitalizing the Waterfront*.

30. Ibid.

31. Ian Tweedale, "Waterfront Redevelopment, Economic Restructuring and Social

Impact," in Hoyle et al., *Revitalizing the Waterfront*. Cheap labor and lax environmental protection laws have dramatically reduced ship repair business on the West Coast. It is often cheaper to sail a vessel to an Asian Pacific port for repairs than to have the work done in the United States.

32. In general, federally generated influences have not been essential to the basic changes along San Francisco's waterfront since World War II, with two notable exceptions: first, as will be mentioned briefly later, the federal government helped subsidize the construction of container facilities in Oakland, and second, the U.S. Navy abandoned its Hunters Point Shipyard, which was recently transferred to the city after massive clean-up efforts. Planning for its reuse is underway, but beyond the scope of this book.

33. Writing on waterfront revitalization has tended to focus on physical changes, with particular attention to architecture and design. Individual projects of major scope have been fairly well documented. The fields of planning and architecture have probably contributed the most in this vein. See Ann Breen and Dick Rigby, *The New Waterfront: A Worldwide Urban Success Story* (New York: McGraw-Hill, 1996); and the periodicals *Urban Land* and *Landscape Architecture*, which regularly include case studies of waterfront development.

34. See, for example, National Research Council, *Urban Waterfront Lands*.

35. Claudio Minca, "Urban Waterfront Evolution," *Geography* 80, no. 3 (1995): 225–34. Minca has made this point regarding waterfronts with reference to the service economy. For discussions about investment in the second circuit of capital, see David Harvey, *The Urbanization of Capital* (Oxford: Blackwell, 1985); Joe R. Feagin, "The Secondary Circuit of Capital: Office Development in Houston, Texas," *International Journal of Urban and Regional Research* 11, no. 2 (1987): 172–92; and Robert A. Beauregard, "Capital Restructuring and the New Built Environment of Global Cities: New York and Los Angeles." *International Journal of Urban and Regional Research* 15, no. 1 (1991): 90–105.

36. Minca, "Urban Waterfront Evolution," 225.

37. Tweedale "Waterfront Redevelopment."

38. Festival malls and heritage sites have been common targets in urban literature over the last quarter century. For their mention with reference to waterfronts, see S. Britton, "Tourism, Capital, and Place: Toward a Critical Geography of Tourism," *Environment and Planning D: Society and Space* 9, no. 4 (1991): 451–78; Patrick Mullins, "Tourism Urbanization," *International Journal of Urban and Regional Research* 15, no. 3 (1991): 326–42; Timothy Sieber, "Waterfront Revitalization in Postindustrial Port Cities of North America," *City & Society* 5, no. 2 (1991): 99–102; John Urry, *Consuming Places* (London: Routledge, 1995); Jon Goss "Disquiet on the Waterfront: Reflections on Nostalgia and Utopia in the Urban Archetypes of Festival Marketplaces," *Urban Geography* 17, no. 3 (1996): 221–47; and B. S. Hoyle, "Urban Waterfront Revitalization in Developing Countries: The Example of Zanzibar's Stone Town," *Geographical Journal* 168, no. 2 (2002): 141–62.

39. John Tunbridge, "Policy Convergence on the Waterfront? A Comparative Assessment of North American Revitalization Strategies," in Hoyle et al., *Revitalizing the Waterfront*; and Han Meyer, *City and Port: Urban Planning as a Cultural Venture in London, Barcelona, New York, and Rotterdam: Changing Relations between Public Urban Space and Large-Scale Infrastructure* (Utrecht: International Books, 1999).

40. The intent of this book is not to compare the story of San Francisco's waterfront with development elsewhere, but we need to have a sense of what has happened in other ports to underscore one of the basic points to be made here. That is, while confronted by top-down forces similar to those affecting other waterfronts, San Francisco has produced a notably different redevelopment pattern as a result of particular local conditions and the role of bottom-up forces. Local power cannot do much about some

top-down forces, especially the influence of new technology, but it can have control over revitalization—what happens once the carpet has been pulled out from under a port. Timothy Butler, "Re-urbanizing London Docklands: Gentrification, Suburbanization, or New Urbanism?" *International Journal of Urban and Regional Research* 31, no. 4 (2007): 759–81; and Ute Lehrer and Jennifer Laidley, "Old Mega-Projects Newly Packaged? Waterfront Redevelopment in Toronto," *International Journal of Urban and Regional Research* 32, no. 4 (2008): 786–803.

41. Ley and Mills, "Can There Be a Postmodernism of Resistance in the Urban Landscape?"

42. Leitner et al (2007, ix) strike a hopeful note in their general assessment that cities are "preeminent sites of resistance and struggle; they are places in which progressive alternative visions are being forged both beyond and outside the restricted modalities of neoliberalism." For an explanation of use and exchange values in the Marxian context, see David Harvey, *The Limits to Capital* (Oxford: Veson, 1999). For our purposes, it is worth noting Henri Lefebvre's somewhat abstract but more pithy take on the concepts: use value is "the city and urban life" and exchange value is "spaces bought and sold, the consumption of goods, places and signs" (*Writings on Cities*, trans. and ed. Eleonore Kofman and Elizabeth Lebas [Malden, MA: Blackwell Publishing, 1996], 86). A gross simplification would have use value as the characteristics of a material object (a commodity or a or part of the city) that meet some human need and exchange value would be the monetized worth of that object (or part of the city)—in other words, a park has a use value in that people use it as a place for relaxation and as a respite from the built environment, and it has exchange value in that it could generate profit for capitalists if it were to be developed.

Chapter One

1. Studies of San Francisco's post–World War II waterfront are virtually nonexistent. A chapter in National Research Council, *Urban Waterfront Lands;* one in Richard E. DeLeon, *Left Coast City* (Lawrence: University of Kansas Press, 1992); and recently, one in Peter Hendee Brown, *America's Waterfront Revival: Port Authorities and Urban Redevelopment* (Philadelphia: University of Pennsylvania Press, 2009), stand out.

2. San Francisco Planning Department (SFPD), *Port of San Francisco Waterfront Land Use Plan, Final Environmental Impact Report* (1997), 111.

3. Ibid.

4. Generally speaking, non-water-related businesses are only allowed under special circumstances, an important fact addressed later in the book.

5. The board of supervisors is the legislative branch of San Francisco's government. The board consists of eleven members elected by geographic districts, with no at-large seats. While it cannot reduce the port's budget, it can prevent the port from using funds.

6. San Francisco's *General Plan* contains two kinds of chapters. There are "Elements" that include objectives and goals that address issues citywide in scope such as housing, transportation, and recreation and open space, and there are "Area Plans" that focus on particular parts of the city. The *Planning Code* is an oft-amended document containing the specific rules and regulations intended to implement many of the policies set forth in the *General Plan;* it is separate from but functionally related to the city's zoning maps. Changes to the *General Plan* are approved by the planning department and ultimately by the board

of supervisors. Debate persists as to whether and how the *General Plan* applies to the port.

7. A conditional use (CU) is an entitlement that, if granted, allows an activity to occur in an area that the zoning would not otherwise allow. For instance, housing in an industrial district is not what is referred to as an "as-of-right" use; it requires a CU. Granting a CU involves a detailed case report by planning staff that is advisory to the planning commission, which ultimately decides whether to authorize the entitlement. Their decision is appealable to the board of supervisors. The specifics of how the *General Plan* and the *Planning Code* relate is beyond the scope of the discussion.

8. SFPD, *Port of San Francisco Waterfront Land Use Plan, Final Environmental Impact Report*, 76.

9. Ibid., 4.

10. Ibid., 121.

11. The Port of San Francisco Embarcadero Historic District was listed in the National Register of Historic Places on May 5, 2006. It includes nearly all piers and structures between Pier 45 and Pier 48 on the waterside of the Embarcadero.

12. Brown died in 1896 at age thirty-six from injuries related to a horse-and-buggy accident, and never saw his building completed.

13. Writing for the *San Francisco Chronicle*, Kenneth Baker (December 23, 2002) said of it, "park visitors may imagine the ships that are said to lie buried under the site, while the feathers far above their heads suggest the sails and rigging which once filled the harbor."

14. The project is being undertaken by Catellus, a real estate firm that spun off from Southern Pacific. For an account of this massive development, see Frédéric Leriche, "Le redéveloppment urbain de Mission bay," *L'Information géographique* 69, no. 4 (2005): 71–87.

15. Charles Hall Page Associates, *Survey of Cultural Resources Piers 14–22½: The Agriculture Building and the Fire Boat House, the Port of San Francisco* (San Francisco, 1977).

16. Gunther Barth was the first to describe it as such in Barth, *Instant Cities: Urbanization and the Rise of San Francisco and Denver* (Albuquerque: University of New Mexico Press, 1980). See also Brian J. Godfrey, "Urban Development and Redevelopment in San Francisco," *Geographical Review* 87, no. 3 (1997): 309–33. In 1848, San Francisco was a hamlet of 840 people. Six years later, the population had swelled to about 50,000. Anne Vernez Moudon, *Built for Change: Neighborhood Architecture in San Francisco* (Cambridge: MIT Press, 1986). During the 1860s and 1870s, several thousand buildings were constructed. Rand Richards, *Historic San Francisco: A Concise History and Guide* (San Francisco: Heritage House Publishers, 2001), 103.

17. William Issel and Robert Cherny, *San Francisco, 1865–1932: Politics, Power, and Urban Development* (Berkeley: University of California Press, 1986), 14.

18. The following account relies largely on an excellent thesis by Gerald Dow, "Bay Fill in San Francisco: A History of Change" (master's thesis, San Francisco State University, 1973).

19. A water lot is surveyed in the same fashion as standard parcels, but is submerged. The lot really only becomes usable once the shoreline is extended and it is filled. It is the subdivision of "land" in a most speculative fashion.

20. Until 1870 or so, the waterfront comprised a confusing mix of ownership and leases. San Francisco's surveyed boundaries did not contain the entire peninsula, they ended at Potrero Point, about half way to the San Francisco–San Mateo County line. To the south of Potrero Point, the tidelands (the area between mean high and mean low tides) and submerged lands (the area between mean low tide and the lowest tide mark)

were the state's. It was in this southern stretch that the state made grants for portions of its waterfront land until 1868. The city leased portions of its waterfront property, most of it above mean high tide, to private entities that then built wharves or engaged in other business enterprises.

21. The first piers were built at the ends of east-west streets and the city itself grew from the waterfront area and spread inland. Part of what makes the interface between San Francisco's city and port particularly distinctive is that the street grid terminates in piers arranged along a curved waterfront. As described by Bolles, "During the first years of the Gold Rush, most ships entering the bay were deserted by their crews and anchors were dropped, and the vessels were then either beached or allowed to remain at anchor indefinitely. Wharves were extended to these ships and cross streets were built on piles; these piers and streets enclosed blocks of water lots and the abandoned ships. . . . Eventually the water lots were filled in with earth and developed for commercial activities (John S. Bolles Associates, *Northern Waterfront Plan* [San Francisco: City and County of San Francisco, 1968], 19).

22. Gerald Dow, "Bay Fill in San Francisco."

23. Felix Riesenberg, *Golden Gate: The Story of San Francisco Harbor* (New York: Todor, 1940).

24. Page and Associates, *Survey of Cultural Resources*.

25. Quoted in Gerald Dow, "Bay Fill in San Francisco," 76.

26. For a thorough account of the evolution of the port's physical character, see Michael Corbett, *Port City: The History and Transformation of the Port of San Francisco, 1848–2010* (San Francisco: San Francisco Architectural Heritage, 2010).

27. Board of State Harbor Commissioners (BHSC), *The Port of San Francisco, One of the World's Greatest Maritime Centers* (San Francisco, 1952).

28. Robert O'Brien, *This Is San Francisco: A Classic Portrait of the City* (New York: Whittlesey House, 1948), 5.

29. Work Progress Administration, *San Francisco, The Bay and Its Cities* (New York: Hastings House, 1947), 260.

30. For an account of sailor towns and their decline, see Davis Hilling, "Socio-Economic Change in the Maritime Quarter: The Demise of Sailortown," in Hoyle et al., *Revitalizing the Waterfront*.

31. State of California, 1951, 114.

32. The San Francisco Bay Area ports are San Francisco, Oakland, Richmond (North Bay), Benicia (North Bay), and Redwood City (South Bay).

33. Works Progress Administration, 1947, 250.

34. Work Progress Administration, 1947, 250; and O'Brien, *This Is San Francisco*, 161. The descriptions of Fisherman's Wharf and the many other areas covered by the 1947 WPA guide are completely without the word *tourist*. Restaurant goers in Fisherman's Wharf were referred to only as *diners*.

35. Quoted in David T. Wellman, *The Union Makes Us Strong: Radical Unionism on San Francisco's Waterfront* (New York: Cambridge University Press, 1995), 38.

36. The Foreign Trade Zone (FTZ) program was started by the federal government in the 1930s to facilitate international trade and make U.S. companies more competitive in the global arena. An FTZ is an area in or near a U.S. Customs port of entry that allows goods in the FTZ to be treated is if they were outside of U.S. Customs jurisdiction. No duties or taxes are paid until merchandise is moved outside of the zone. This allows goods to be assembled, repackaged, or processed while deferring or reducing duties.

37. California State Legislature, *Ports of San Francisco Bay, Commerce, Facilities, Problems, and Progress—Final Report* (Sacramento, 1951), 115.

Chapter Two

1. BSHC, *Quarterly Report*, 3rd Quarter (San Francisco, 1948).

2. The BSHC was composed of three members appointed by the governor and approved by the state senate. It was responsible for running the harbor and for appointing the port's director, who was responsible for day-to-day operations. The BSHC's legally defined jurisdiction was essentially the same then as the Port of San Francisco's is now, although some changes to the amount of physical property under port jurisdiction have occurred over the years.

3. State of California, *Ports of San Francisco Bay*. Liquid cargo, most of which was petroleum, actually comprised the largest part of the total cargo moving through the Golden Gate. But San Francisco had never really served the petroleum market, especially refining, so changes in it were not significant for San Francisco. Most oil went not to public piers but to privately owned and run facilities, of which there were proportionately few in San Francisco.

4. *Coastwise* refers to cargo moved along or between U.S. coasts and *inland waterway* refers to river or canal-borne cargo.

5. Floyd Healey, "Ship Lines Blamed for Cargo Loss," *SFC*, November 28, 1950.

6. George Fox Mott, *A Survey of United States Ports* (New York: Arco Publishing Company), 197.

7. Ibid., 195.

8. State of California, *Ports of San Francisco Bay*, 241. The value of that tonnage only decreased a little, a point made much of by consultants fifteen years later.

9. Demurrage is a fee paid for time spent beyond the scheduled departure of a ship that is loading or unloading cargo at dock.

10. San Francisco Chamber of Commerce, *Promotion and Improvement of the Port of San Francisco* (San Francisco, 1950), 1. Labor disputes and strikes were not restricted to the 1930s. As mechanization evolved, waterfront labor fought to prevent job loss. Labor's efforts culminated in the refusal to handle containers when that technology first appeared in San Francisco. The ILWU was quickly forced to acquiesce to the juggernaut of containerization with the 1960 Modernization and Mechanization Agreement. While the agreement was a boon to workers at the time, in the longer term it represented, probably unavoidably, a real loss of power. For more on labor with respect to the waterfront, see David T. Wellman, *The Union Makes Us Strong: Radical Unionism on San Francisco's Waterfront* (New York: Cambridge University Press, 1995); and for a discussion of San Francisco's general strike, see Richard A Walker, "San Francisco's Haymarket: A Redemptive Tale of Class Struggle," *ACME: An International E-Journal for Critical Geographies* 7, no. 1 (2008): 45–58, http://www.acme-journal.org/Volume7-1.htm.

11. California Department of Finance, *Management Survey for the Board of State Harbor Commissioners for San Francisco Harbor* (Sacramento, 1955).

12. State of California, *Ports of San Francisco Bay*, 243.

13. San Francisco Chamber of Commerce, *Promotion and Improvement*, 1.

14. BSHC, *The Progressive Port of San Francisco* (San Francisco, 1954).

15. According to the BSHC, some "authorities believe that the volume of imports into San Francisco may be increased ultimately by as much as 40 percent, and the advertising value for the Port of San Francisco among world traders in every country will be incalculable" (*Special Report of the BSHC, Port of San Francisco, to the Hon. Earl Warren, Governor, State of California* [San Francisco, 1948]).

16. BSHC 1954 and BHSC, *Ship via the Port of San Francisco* (San Francisco 1956, winter issue,).

17. California Department of Finance, *Management Survey for the Board of State Harbor Commissioners for San Francisco Harbor*.

18. San Francisco Port Authority (SFPA), *Frontiers of the Sea* (San Francisco, 1958), n.p.

19. Ebasco Services, Inc. (Ebasco), *Port of San Francisco Facilities Improvement Survey, Summary Report* (San Francisco: San Francisco Port Authority, 1959), 7.

20. Ebasco, *Port of San Francisco Facilities Improvement Survey*, 79. Roll-on, roll-off (or "ro-ro") is a method of goods movement that involves a vehicle driving onto the ship and driving off with cargo. At the time, this was seen as a method of modernizing cargo movement that took advantage of the increased importance of trucking.

21. State of California, *Ports of San Francisco Bay*. Note that the port did not derive any direct benefit from the value of cargo moving across its piers.

22. SFPA, *Portside News*, August 1960.

23. SFPA, *Portside News*, January 1963, 4.

24. Cyril Magnin, quoted in SFPA, *Portside News*, January 1958, 7.

25. Port activities directly created 23,000 jobs plus 52,000–67,000 indirectly created jobs, constituting 11 to 14 percent of San Francisco's employment at the time. Arthur D. Little, Inc. (ADL), *The Port of San Francisco, an In-Depth Study of Its Impact on the City, Its Economic Future, the Potential of Its Northern Waterfront* (San Francisco, 1966). One estimate calculated one of three San Francisco wage earners could trace their livelihood to the city's maritime industry. SFPA, *Portside News*, May 1959, 5.

26. State of California, *Ports of San Francisco Bay*, 20

27. Ibid., 22.

28. Eighty percent according to Ebasco, *Port of San Francisco Facilities Improvement Survey*.

29. Ibid.

30. Floyd Healey, "Ship Lines Blamed for Cargo Loss," *SFC*, November 29, 1950.

31. State of California, *Ports of San Francisco Bay*, 23.

32. San Francisco Chamber of Commerce, *Promotion and Improvement*, 21.

33. SFPA, *Portside News*, January 1958, 7.

34. Other ports were not so constrained, and a number of municipally owned ports in the bay Area and elsewhere benefitted from tax subvention or other local sources of income. For example, Long Beach/Los Angeles received royalties from petroleum production on harbor property. San Francisco Chamber of Commerce, *Promotion and Improvement*, 31.

35. San Francisco Chamber of Commerce, *Promotion and Improvement*, 42.

36. Mayor's Economic Development Advisory Council, *San Francisco Central Waterfront Economic Adjustment Strategy* (San Francisco, 1978), 9.

37. State of California, *San Francisco Bay*, 29.

38. Oakland and the East Bay had already been for decades the center of the region's industrial activities. For a wide-ranging account of the industrial relocation in the Bay Area, see Richard Walker, "Industry Builds the City: The Suburbanization of Manufacturing in the San Francisco Bay Area, 1850–1940," *Journal of Historical Geography* 27, no. 1 (2001): 36–57.

39. San Francisco Planning Department, *Studies in the Economy of Downtown San Francisco* (San Francisco, 1963).

40. San Francisco Planning Department, *Downtown San Francisco—General Plan Proposals* (San Francisco, 1963), 4, 7.

41. While numbers in Figure 205 are for San Francisco as a whole, a majority of the city's jobs were, and still are, found in the greater downtown.

42. As quoted in Chester Hartman, *The Transformation of San Francisco* (Totowa, NJ: Rowman & Allanheld, 1984), 9.

43. Chester Hartman, *City for Sale: The Transformation of San Francisco* (Berkeley: University of California Press, 2002), 11. In order to distance itself from what would become a much-maligned agency that pursued generally disastrous plans, SPUR changed its name to the San Francisco Urban and Research Association.

44. Such advisory committees are required for official redevelopment projects. However, rules regarding their composition and role in the redevelopment process have changed over the years, primarily to emphasize "real" citizen participation.

45. A full discussion of redevelopment agencies, their powers, and the process of redevelopment are beyond the scope of this book. For a thorough account of the fight against redevelopment, especially into the South of Market area of the city, see Hartman's, *City for Sale*, a story he first told in *Yerba Buena: Land Grab and Community Resistance in San Francisco* (San Francisco: Glide Publications, 1974).

46. While redevelopment plans are not technically subject to the San Francisco *Planning Code*, they must comply with the *General Plan*. In point of fact, the *General Plan* has often been amended to create conformance between it and a redevelopment plan.

47. SFPD, *A Report Recommending Designation of Two Redevelopment Areas under the Provisions of the California Redevelopment Act* (San Francisco, 1954), iii.

48. "Gateway Plan Lauded by Mayor," *SFC*, January 20, 1957.

49. Ibid.

50. A notable exception came from one Charles A. Christian. According to the *Chronicle*, he was a spokesman for an apartment-house association, and at the board of supervisors hearing, presciently bellowed, "What right does the city have to take that land and turn it over to real estate speculators from New York?" ("Supervisors OK Gateway Plan," *SFC*, October 10, 1958). Businesses did file lawsuits over the eminent domain proceedings but were not able to stop their forced relocation. Curiously, attorney and assemblyman Caspar Weinberger represented some of the affected businesses. He had been Mayor Christopher's choice to fill the position of chair of the agency's commission but a clear conflict of interest prevented the appointment. Instead, he was named to SPUR's executive committee (Hartman, *City for Sale*).

51. Michael Harris, "'Gateway' Plan May Start in 1958," *SFC*, January 18, 1957. Roger D. Lapham, Jr., was son of Roger Dearborn Lapham, a Republican mayor of San Francisco 1944–1948 and once president of the American-Hawaiian Steamship Company. He became famous for his proposal to scrap the city's cable car lines, and has been the only mayor subjected to a recall vote (which he survived).

52. Ibid.; and "Alioto Backs Gateway Development," *SFC*, January 23, 1957. Nat Owings was head of SOM's San Francisco office (the firm is based in Chicago). SOM has been, and continues to be, deeply involved in many of the city's planning and design issues, even as consultants for recent planning department efforts.

53. "Gateway Plans in High Praise," *SFC*, March 6, 1957.

54. "'Gateway' Plan May Start in 1958"; "City's Gateway Plan Ready for Big Test," *SFC*, July 4, 1958; and James Benet, "Winning Plan for Gateway Is Chosen," *SFC*, October 6, 1960.

55. As an example of how things often go in San Francisco planning, Jed Sullivan, a banker and member of the BZC, which as we have seen pushed the Golden Gateway process hard more or less behind the scenes, came forward to state publicly at the board of supervisors that he (and BZC members) thought the plan "'very worthy' of an approving vote" ("Supervisors OK Gateway Plan"). Such maneuvers lend a sense of legitimacy to the pronouncements of the business community because, in the eyes of the public, it seems as if its members are commenting on the issue as neutral observers when in fact they are not.

56. "Winning Plan for Gateway Is Chosen." Perini, of the titular Perini-San Francisco, owned the Milwaukee Braves. One of his partners in this venture was the Fleish-

hacker Company. Mortimer Fleishhacker became heavily involved in northern water-front issues, and would, by the mid-1960s, become a member of the city planning department and later a member of the board of supervisors. The deal did require a small amount of funding for community facilities and that about 1 percent of the cost of the project be spent on murals, statuary, and outdoor artwork. Very similar requirements for all downtown projects would be enacted as part of the city's 1985 *Downtown Plan*.

57. While initial concerns by the local downtown elite were that East Coast money might get the project away, it was the South that rose up to capture the biggest piece. Tramell Crow was a Texan investor responsible for the Dallas Trade Complex, Cloyce K. Box was president of Oklahoma Cement Company and an executive vice-president of George Fruller Company, two of the country's largest contractors at the time, and rising star John Portman was an Atlanta architect and developer. Temko described Herman's relationship with the team as one of "almost immodest devotion" (Alan Temko, "A Chance for Greatness," *SFC*, May 6, 1967).

58. In yet another example of the overly cozy relationships found in the development and planning world, Owings, of SOM, earlier had been engaged by Zellerbach to design his paper company's new Market Street headquarters.

59. "Gateway Land Sale Needs State OK," *SFC*, October 21, 1958.

60. "Port Told to Free Jam in Gateway Plan," *SFC*, June 1, 1962.

61. Editorial, "Real Leadership in Port Tangle," *SFC*, June 4, 1962.

62. Rich Jordon, "Port Bows, Will Sell Street for $24," *San Francisco Examiner*, June 8, 1962.

63. "$12 Million Hotel on Embarcadero," *SFC*, June 23, 1966.

64. Mitchell Thomas, "4 Gateway Highrise Towers Okd," *SFC*, March 31, 1973. The THD's president at the time, Robert Katz, was a sentinel of the waterfront. Note that the California Environmental Quality Act (CEQA) was passed while the Golden Gateway Redevelopment Area project was mid-course. It requires that development of nearly any size be evaluated for its potential impacts on the environment. The resulting documents are called "environmental impact reports." 'Environment' is a broad concept in CEQA, and covers topics that are not immediately related to what one might think of first, such as air quality and noise levels. Examples include views, historic and archeological resources, local ordinances, and population and employment.

65. Allan Temko, "The Long Shadow of Folly," *SFC*, May 8, 1967. His critique contrasted starkly with the Northern California chapter of the American Institute of Architects, which praised the project. In fact, Temko remarked that there had been "scarcely a murmur of criticism from any public official with the significant exception of the able new planning director, Allan B. Jacobs, who had some 'grave' problems with the slab-based design" ("A Chance for Greatness"). In fact, Jacobs requested that the planning department initiate a new study of the plan; he was flatly refused.

66. A next step in understanding the complex spatial ties that are part of such a development would be to examine office space leases and sales of housing units. A place like the Embarcadero is locally situated, but is home to branches or headquarters of transnational business, from corporate law offices serving an international clientele to global financial management services. It also leases space to local or regional business concerns. The leasing process itself, and building management, may be handled by local or national companies. Add to this a class structure characterized partly by white-collar office workers, including desirable internationals, and of blue-collar janitors and service workers who are largely ethnic immigrants, many struggling to acquire green cards. Housing units may be bought by locals or outside investors, and may be owner-occupied, leased, or used as vacation residences by the global elite. A complex like

the Golden Gateway/Embarcadero is a sort of microcosm of modern Western urban society.

67. Mike Davis, *City of Quartz* (New York: Vintage Books, 1990).

68. In the practice of contemporary planning in the United States, planners find themselves all too often in the difficult position of reacting to events rather than preparing the ground. The adage is that one should "plan in the down cycles." This painful irony is not lost on professionals, or many of their constituents.

69. Containerization began in Europe in the early 1950s, but it was ex-trucker Malcolm McLean who started commercial container shipping in the United States. with the *Ideal-X* in 1956. His innovation was the use of standardized containers that remained sealed until they reached the consignee. McLean founded the shipping line Sea-Land which was acquired by Maersk, the world's largest such operation, in 1999. The first fully containerized vessel was put into service in 1957 and sailed between Florida, Texas, and New York.

70. ADL, *Port of San Francisco.*

71. Ibid.

72. Henry S. Marcus, Nawal K. Taneja, and Paul O. Roberts, "The Impact of Changes in Transportation Technology on the Use of Land in Harbor Areas," in National Research Council, *Urban Waterfront Lands*, 163.

73. As calculated by ADL in *Port of San Francisco*. Note that not all goods can be containerized. Scrap metal, newsprint, bulk grains, and automobiles, for instance, must be moved traditionally. So, there has been and there will continue to be a need for breakbulk and other non-container facilities.

74. The army base and World War II demands contributed hugely to the development of the Port of Oakland's physical infrastructure, including piers, wharves, and sheds (State of California, *Ports of San Francisco Bay*, 116).

75. These included APL, mentioned earlier as the first to plan regular containership sailings, K Lines, Matson Navigation, NYK Lines, and Pacific Australia Direct (Mayor's Economic Advisory Council 1978). According to Don Delone, the Marine Terminal Company, which handled APL, "spent a lot of time going back and forth between Ben Nutter, the Oakland port director, and Rae Watts . . . , in effect playing off one side against the other." Oakland got the contract for a number of reasons, including better lease terms because of lower construction costs (Don DeLone to author, April 5, 2001, personal correspondence). According to DeLone, who was public relations director for the port from 1953 to 1960 and later manager of trade development. Watts was an aggressive director, who hated to see any business move across the bay.

76. Mayor's Economic Advisory Council, *San Francisco Central Waterfront Economic Adjustment Strategy*, 10.

77. Ibid., 27.

78. The rail lines were the Southern Pacific, the Atchison, Topeka and Santa Fe, and the Western Pacific (Mott, *Survey of United States Ports*).

79. ADL, *Port of San Francisco*. Another issue was that a tunnel through which trains heading south from San Francisco had to travel lacked sufficient clearance to allow double-stacked containers to pass, substantially limiting capacity and thus efficiency.

80. Ebasco, *Port of San Francisco Facilities Improvement Survey*, 132.

81. DeLone to author, February 5, 2001, personal communication.

82. ADL, *Port of San Francisco*, 119.

83. San Francisco Port Authority, *Ocean Shipping Handbook* (San Francisco, 1968), 17.

84. "Board Will Act on Port Takeover," *SFC*, January 7, 1967.

85. Quotations are from Don DeLone to author, January 8, 2001, personal communication.

86. DeLone to to author, April 5, 2001, personal communication.

87. Gruen and Gruen Associates, *Report of the Waterfront Committee* (San Francisco, 1970), 17. Note that Victor Gruen had worked for ADL and essentially authored their San Francisco waterfront reports.

88. ADL, *San Francisco's Maritime Future: Revolution and Response* (San Francisco, 1967); and San Francisco Port Authority, *Ocean Shipping Handbook* (San Francisco, 1966).

89. Donald Fitzgerald, "A History of Containerization in the California Maritime Industry: A Case History of San Francisco" (PhD diss., University of California, Santa Barbara, 1986). In 1969, only two years after the Army Street Terminal at Pier 80 was dedicated, the Port of Oakland would jump ahead of San Francisco in the amount of cargo moving across its docks.

90. ADL, *San Francisco's Maritime Future*, 1.

91. Ibid., 29.

92. Ibid., 3.

93. Ibid., 1.

94. The failure of LASH is well documented in Fitzgerald, "A History of Containerization." One crippling event was a loss in court to the ILWU, which contended that loading lighters (barges) was not part of its labor contract.

95. Fitzgerald, "A History of Containerization."

96. Ibid.

97. One exception was "Short and Long Range Program for Port Improvement and Development," released in 1955 (BSHC, *Ship via the Port of San Francisco* [San Francisco, winter 1956]). This title belies the focus of the document, which was primarily geared to improving operations, streamlining services, and making other changes intended to reduce costs to shipping lines.

98. Even while most of San Francisco's remaining industrial and heavy commercial uses retreated to the vicinity of the southern waterfront, not all shipping disappeared from the northern waterfront by the end of the 1960s. Rolls of newsprint paper, for instance, were off-loaded at Piers 27–29 until the end of the 1990s.

Chapter Three

1. Although in the late 1950s, there was a movement by the Bay Area Council and state senator John McCarthy to create the Golden Gate Authority, which was to be a regional agency coordinating transportation and infrastructure development for the area modeled after the New York New Jersey Port Authority. For an account of its origins and defeat, see Louise Nelson Dyble, "The Defeat of the Golden Gate Authority," *Journal of Urban History* 38, no. 2 (2008): 287–308.

2. STOL stands for "short takeoff and landing." As *Chronicle* writer Michael Harris described it in 1967, with San Francisco's airport moving one hundred passengers to every one brought by sea liner, the port was confronted with the jet age, not just containers. A certain nostalgia and a sense of displacement pervades his comment that "it is sad to realize that with the passing of the ferries there are thousands in this sea-faring city who have never set foot in a boat" ("A Look at Port's Future," *SCF*, February 13, 1967).

3. Only a few were trained as planners. Until 1940, there was no planning department, just the city planning commission. The commission was staffed by a stenographer, a secretary, and a draftsman, and did little other "than process routine zoning matters"

(San Francisco Planning Department, *Progress in City Planning: A Report to the People of San Francisco* [San Francisco, 1946], 4).

4. One impetus for creating a master plan came top-down, from the state. The 1945 California Community Redevelopment required that replacement of blighted areas had to be done according to a master plan.

5. San Francisco Planning Commission, *A Brief Summary of the Master Plan as Adopted by the City Planning Commission on December 20, 1945, with an Outline of the Task Ahead* (San Francisco, 1946), n.p. By contrast, the planning department today has about 120 staff members and the San Francisco *General Plan* includes more than twenty chapters.

6. This is not to say that there were no regulations on the port's activities. Federal and state laws regarding health, safety, the practice of commerce, and how the port functioned as a legal entity were in place.

7. State of California, *Ports of San Francisco Bay*, 115, emphasis added.

8. William Alonso, *Location and Land Use* (Cambridge, MA: Harvard University Press, 1964). Alonso also astutely pointed out that "when plans are statements of policies the emphasis shifts from the solution of particular problems through particular projects to a view of the city as a complicated system to be guided as well as corrected" (440).

9. SFPD, *Memorandum Report No. 61.2 to the City Planning Commission from James R. McCarthy, Director of Planning: Interim Report on Waterfront Development Plan and Height Control* (San Francisco, 1961), 5. McCarthy was the Director of Planning from 1958 to 1967.

10. California Department of Finance, *Management Survey*, 56.

11. Ebasco, *Port of San Francisco Facilities Improvement Survey*, 133.

12. An example is increased height limits, which make it desirable to replace structures that were home to chandler's offices or marine supply companies with office buildings.

13. The two agencies would find themselves more frequently having to deal with each other, especially after the port's transfer to the city. To this day, the vacillating relationship between port and planning staffs affects waterfront development and helps to form the kind of local condition that can impede investment from the outside or frustrate the ability of a place to establish goals and work toward them effectively.

14. BSHC, *World Trade Center in San Francisco* (San Francisco, 1946), 8. In actuality, the main force behind the concept of the WTC was none other than the San Francisco Chamber of Commerce, who named trustees to its governing board (the WTC was a nonprofit agency).

15. Ibid.

16. That the WTC and the port had offices in the Ferry Building reflected deeper connections. The governing boards of the port and the WTC were joined by two common members, B. J. Feigenbaum and Thomas C. Coakly (who was a member of the WTC authority and president of the BSHC), yet conflict of interest was only brought up in evaluating the legality of one state agency selling property to another and, in turn, leasing it ("40-Story World Trade Center Urged for Ferry Building," *SFC,* January 22, 1948).

17. They had neither the Blyth-Zellerbach Committee nor the SFRA to help. Nevertheless, Coakley suggested that "we could still move the (commission) district and develop that area into an extension of the financial district or a shopping center" ("Huge Terminal Suggested for Ferry Building Site," *SFC,* January 23, 1948). The commission district was another term for the Produce Market.

18. Editorial, "Where Our World Trade Begins," *SFC,* January 24, 1948.

19. SBHC, *Special Report of the Board of State Harbor Commissioners* (San Francisco, 1948, 4th Quarter).

20. Leland Cutler had, apparently, a penchant for splashy projects. He was president of the San Francisco Bay Exposition Company, the organization responsible for creating Treasure Island and the 1939 Golden Gate International Exposition, and had a hand in financing the Hoover Dam. He had also been president of the San Francisco Chamber of Commerce.

21. World Trade Center, prospectus (San Francisco, 1951).

22. "Huge Terminal Suggested for Ferry Building Site."

23. BSHC, *Progressive Port of San Francisco*, 1954.

24. The Blyth-Zellerbach Committee started a battle to build the freeway underground probably because they felt that otherwise it could jeopardize their pet project—clearing the Produce Market to make way for Golden Gateway. Afterward, various proposals and citizen initiatives to create park space near the Ferry Building (one of which included partial demolition of the Ferry Building) were put forth and rejected by either official committees or ballot-box measures.

25. Sally B. Woodbridge, "Visions of Renewal and Growth: 1945 to the Present," in *Visionary San Francisco*, ed. by Paolo Polledri (San Francisco: San Francisco Museum of Modern Art, 1990).

26. California Department of Finance, *Management Survey*, 48.

27. Ibid., 53, emphasis added.

28. Ibid., 54.

29. Ibid.

30. SFPA, *Portside News*, February 1959, 1.

31. Bolles was the president of the San Francisco Art Association, an organization that had contacted the port about the possibility of expanding onto one of the piers north of the Ferry Building (Michael Harris, "Waterfront 'City' Proposed by Port Authority," *SFC*, January 30, 1959; and Dan McClure, "Port Board Tells 'Dream City' Plan for Waterfront," *SFC*, February 3, 1959).

32. "Port Board Tells 'Dream City' Plan for Waterfront." This was an odd selling point in that many people already felt that San Francisco was as fair an urban place as any. It is perhaps a hint of hubris in its sponsors.

33. SFPA, *Portside News*, February 1959, 1.

34. Ibid., 8.

35. SFPA, *Portside News*, June 1959, 8. Senator McAteer was a development-minded man, or at least someone who wanted to "make progress." But he would later switch gears and, along with Senator Petris, author the bill which established the Bay Conservation and Development Commission. which was charged with preserving the bay.

36. The port's financial self-sufficiency was, and is still, a critical issue. Having to win voter approval for much of the money needed for capital projects subjected the port to the uncertainties of the political process.

37. At the time, this was a more real restriction than the application of the trust doctrine to specific land-use issues.

38. SFPA, *Portside News,* May 1959.

39. *California Harbors and Navigation Code* (San Francisco: Bancroft-Whitney Company, 1966), 3000(d). This code would no longer apply to the port after its transfer to city jurisdiction in 1969.

40. Models can be a form of spectacle—objects one considers for only a short time and which engage the imagination but in a fleeting, even ephemeral way. They can impart a sense of possibility or wonder and thus a subtle insubstantiality when in fact they represent a fixed form, a hardened vision of the future anchored in the built environment that if realized may not live up to expectations. Largely this derives from

the effect of scale, of viewing a three dimensional miniaturization from above, much like gazing on a town from a mountain top, which can make it seem toy-like and imaginary. So, when a model for something like Embarcadero City is made, it can be akin to putting a velvet glove on an iron fist. In creating this perspective, models can draw "oohs" and "ahs" from viewers, sometimes helping deflect focused scrutiny and appraisal. The rooted reality of trees gets lost in the abstraction of the forest.

41. Magnin quoted in SFPA, *Portside News,* February 1959, 7.

42. The report also suggested that existing cargo operations in the northern waterfront should be maintained as long as possible, and while new commercial activities should be encouraged, they should not be developed by the port itself—instead, they advised that the port should maintain ground leases.

43. Ebasco, *Port of San Francisco Facilities Improvement Survey,* 168.

44. The value of land for development is also a local condition to which external forces react. Land is valuable because it is on the water, has views, is accessible, and so on. Land value and use are filtered through socioeconomic lenses that reflects both top-down and local factors.

45. Quoted in Ebasco 1959, *Port of San Francisco Facilities Improvement Survey,* 167.

46. Ebasco, *Port of San Francisco Facilities Improvement Survey,* 134.

47. Ibid., 141, emphasis added.

48. Ebasco, *Port of San Francisco Facilities Improvement Survey, Summary Report* (San Francisco: San Francisco Port Authority, 1959), 36.

49. Ebasco, *Port of San Francisco Facilities Improvement Survey,* 133.

50. Ebasco, *Port of San Francisco Facilities Summary Report.* This is something that planning attempts to address by encouraging or restricting activities. Moreover, theoretically, planning policy goes beyond preparing the ground for capital investment, or the maximization of development potential for a given piece of land, to work for the public good or to respond to other societal values not embodied in the market and its mechanisms. In some contemporary contexts, however, it has become very important for planners to understand what interest and ability private capital has in developing a project in order to know what fees and exactions could be wrested from developers.

51. John S. Bolles and Ernest Born, *A Plan for Fisherman's Wharf* (San Francisco: San Francisco Port Authority, 1961), 6.

52. Ibid., 12. They use the term *carousel* in a curiously unabashed fashion. It is used in contemporary urban literature to deride, or impart a sense of scorn in relation to, the character of a place.

53. Ibid., 7.

54. "Drive Set to 'Save' Fisherman's Wharf," *SFC,* May 18, 1960.

55. "Fishermen Don't Like Wharf Plan," *SFC,* May 25, 1961.

56. Aquatic Park opened in the late 1930s as one of California's largest WPA projects. Its buildings were designed in the "streamline moderne" style, perhaps foreshadowing the waterfront development proposals to come in the 1950s. The San Francisco Maritime Museum Association was founded in 1950 and operated the Maritime Museum until its transfer to the National Park Service in 1978. The San Francisco Maritime National Park was designated a national historic park in 1989.

57. "Fisherman's Wharf Plan Protested," *SFC,* August 8, 1961; and "Mayor Finds Conflict on Wharf Plan," *SFC,* August 9, 1961.

58. It also attests to the power of the SFRA, which was, as we have seen, successful in transforming the Produce Market, an area and situation not entirely different from that of Fisherman's Wharf.

59. Consensus is sort of a holy grail in planning. Both in planning theory and practice there has been much discussion about how to achieve it, if it is even possible to achieve, and whether it should even be a goal. It seems obvious, though, that without some basic level of agreement among parties, to establish worthwhile policy would be very difficult outside of a more autocratic system.

60. Timothy A. Gibson, "The Trope of an Organic City," *space and culture* 6, no. 4 (2003): 429–48.

61. Perhaps the most well-known anti-growth campaign in San Francisco was launched in 1971 by Alvin Duskin, a clothes maker and activist who wanted to limit buildings in the city to seventy-six feet. He was not successful, but his efforts provided the foundation for a burgeoning anti-growth coalition.

62. Richard Walker has suggested that environmental activism fundamentally changed politics in the Bay Area. See *The Country in the City* for an excellent and generally uplifting account of the rise of Bay Area environmentalism and its impacts on the region (Seattle: University of Washington Press, 2007).

63. In a dense city like San Francisco, streets are an essential part of public space. Planners today even emphasize their importance in the development of networks of open spaces and, where sidewalks can be widened and streets closed off, as sources of open space themselves.

64. The last five or ten years, however, have seen a demographic shift in San Francisco. An influx of younger people has brought new attitudes toward development, at least in the downtown. The somewhat old-guard resistance to skyscrapers draws a quizzical response from many new residents; to them it seems a strange conservatism in a supposedly progressive city.

65. "Changes Urged in Zoning Laws," *SFC*, December 7, 1960.

66. Early fights over development in San Francisco did not necessarily start as populist grassroots actions. Some important urban planning decisions were the result of small cadres of residents maneuvering to protect their private self-interest. And it is a bit ironic that the first real encounters over these grand schemes were fought among the elite themselves, old wealth fighting the lieutenants of advanced capitalism—one form of private interest up against another.

67. "Changes Urged in Zoning Laws."

68. Planning director Allan B. Jacobs and the planning department would respond to buildings such as the Fontana Apartments in the pathbreaking *Urban Design Element*, adopted as part of the city's *General Plan* in 1971. This document put the San Francisco Planning Department squarely in the national urban planning limelight.

69. The city's definition of the northern waterfront included areas inland of the waterfront, outside of port jurisdiction.

70. "Russian Hill Group to Act to Block Apartment 'Wall,'" *SFC*, December 15, 1960. Caspar Weinberger was a former state assemblyman, reelected twice. He ran an unsuccessful campaign to become California's attorney general, but kept his hand in politics by becoming the chairman of the California Republican Party in 1962.

71. San Francisco Board of Supervisors, *Proceedings* 59 (San Francisco, February 3, 1964), 57.

72. "The Public Rises to Hail, and Assail, a Height Limit," *SFC*, October 25, 1963.

73. Mel Wax, "Don't Scrap Height Limit Proposal, Mayor Says," *SFC*, February 8, 1962.

74. Mel Wax, "Planners OK 40-Foot Height Limit," *SFC*, November 1, 1963.

75. Quoted in Francis Violich, "Intellectual Evolution in the Field of City and Regional Planning: A Personal Perspective Toward Holistic Planning Education 1937–

2010," working paper 2001–2007, Institute of Urban and Regional Development, University of California, Berkeley, 2001. For two important essays by practitioners that help remind us that planning is not (or should not be) just a rationalistic, technocratic endeavor, see Paul Davidoff, "Advocacy and Pluralism in Planning" and Allan Jacobs and Donald Appleyard, "Toward an Urban Design Manifesto," *Journal of the American Planning Association* 53, no. 1 (1987): 112–20.

76. *California Harbors and Navigation Code* '3000.7.

77. While not entirely clear, the port authority likely agreed to this change in part because it did not imagine that height limitations would be a real impediment. Furthermore, San Francisco was quite influential in state government, and local representatives in Sacramento may have lobbied to pressure the port to come to the table. It may also have been a way to mollify the city after a failed bid to transfer the port to the city a few years earlier.

78. San Francisco Board of Supervisors 3, *Proceedings* vol. 59 (San Francisco, February 3, 1964), 57, emphasis added.

79. Ibid.

80. Quoted from a staff report in Mel Wax, "A Plan to Save the View on S.F. Waterfront," *SFC*, October 5, 1963.

81. San Francisco Board of Supervisors, *Proceedings* vol. 59 (San Francisco, February 3, 1964), 60.

82. Mel Wax, "Supervisors Adopt Strict Height Limits," *SFC*, February 4, 1964.

83. Ibid. Jack Morrison served on the board from 1961–1969, and was later appointed as a port commissioner by Mayor Moscone. He was also an early and longtime member of the advocacy group San Francisco Tomorrow (SFT).

84. Save the Bay was instrumental in the creation of the Bay Conservation and Development Commission. SFT, founded in 1970, is an organization "dedicated to promoting environmental quality, neighborhood livability and good government in San Francisco. We concentrate on environmental issues because we believe a good environment is the necessary foundation upon which to build a good society. Our interests range from sewers to skylines" (http://www.sanfranciscotomorrow.org/#about). Note that many of the people active in San Francisco waterfront issues were also involved in the regional environmental movement, including Dorothy Erskine, Lawrence Livingston (of Livingston and Blaney), Richard Goldman, Jean and Karl Kortum, and William Evers.

85. "Land Syndicate to Aid S.F. Bay-Front Study," *SFC*, December 10, 1964.

86. Mayor Alioto quoted in Richard Reinhardt, "On the Waterfront: The Great Wall of Magnin," in *The Ultimate Highrise: San Francisco's Mad Rush to the Sky*, ed. Bruce Brugmann and Greggor Sletteland (San Francisco: San Francisco Bay Guardian, 1971), 108. Alioto refers to the Bolles plan for the northern waterfront, discussed later in this chapter.

87. "Ambitious Plan for Foot of Telegraph Hill," *SFC*, February 2, 1968.

88. Leonard Cahn, Letter to the Editor, *SFC*, July 15, 1968.

89. One of the several locally well-known members of THD was Dorothy Erskine. Heavily influenced by Telesis, Erskine was an influential planning advocate and one of the founders of the Bay Area environmental movement. She helped create the San Francisco Housing and Planning Association, which would later become SPUR.

90. Jacobs, *Making City Planning Work*; and "Compromise Reached on Waterfront," *SFC*, March 1, 1968.

91. This concept was formalized in the Urban Design Element of San Francisco's *General Plan*.

92. Karl Kortum, Letter to the Editor, *SFC*, July 9, 1968.

93. "New Blast in Embarcadero Row," *SFC* April 8, 1968; Ron Moskowitz, "Waterfront Height Limit Rejected," *SFC*, April 12, 1968; and "The Conflict over Waterfront Plans," *SFC*, April 17, 1968.

94. Keith Power, "Market Center Nears Approval," *SFC*, February 28, 1968.

95. "Big Market Plan Hits New Snags," *SFC*, December 30, 1969; and "Waterfront Mart Plan up in the Air," *SFC*, January 15, 1971.

96. Ron Moskowitz, "The 'Final' Market Center Plan," *SFC*, July 12, 1968.

97. David Harvey writes, "The right to the city is not merely a right of access to what already exists, but a right to change it after our heart's desire" ("The Right to the City," *International Journal of Urban and Regional Research* 27, no. 4 [2003]: 939–41, quotation on 939). His point, much more fundamental than the discussion here, is that we need to establish new political-economic practices that would allow the creation of a "new urban commons."

98. In a 1999 interview, Dorothy Erskine pointed out that planners such as Jack Kent, Mel Scott, and Frances Violich influenced and educated citizen groups ("An Interview with Dorothy Erskine," *SPUR Newsletter*, January 1999, http://www.spur.org/print/638).

99. Editorial, *SFC*, December 10, 1964.

100. Although a former trade union official and state representative, Shelly was considered an ineffective mayor, and was eventually urged to withdraw from his bid for reelection in 1967. He was not enough of a downtown man, and the Democratic machine feared that he would not be able to defeat Republican candidate Harold Dobbs (owner of the local Mel's Drive-In restaurants). Joseph Alioto was tapped to replace him and succeeded in winning the election. According to Hartman, Cyril Magnin was involved in the meeting that helped set the stage for Shelly's replacement by Alioto (*City for Sale*, 26).

101. Mel Wax, "Breathtaking Plan for S.F. Waterfront," *SFC*, November 30, 1966.

102. Ibid.

103. ADL based this on an analysis of types of trade classes (major, minor, inland, foreign), trade routes, and commodity trends. Their prediction was not entirely unreasonable as the port had seen increases in its cargo handling during the last few years before the study and the value of foreign goods it handled made it the sixth-ranked port in the nation. Furthermore, the direct income to the port authority from its operations was four times what Oakland received from its shipping activities. Nevertheless, growth at Oakland and elsewhere did create a relative decline as the port's share of total Bay Area cargo shrank.

104. ADL, *Summary of an In-Depth Study of the Port of San Francisco* (San Francisco: San Francisco Port Authority, 1966), 3.

105. ADL, *Port of San Francisco*, 35.

106. Peter Stack, "Port Leases Piers for Big Complex," *SFC*, September 4, 1969.

107. ADL *Summary of an In-Depth Study*, 4.

108. ADL, *Port of San Francisco*, 122.

109. "Breathtaking Plan for the Waterfront," *SFC*.

110. The report also stressed the importance of two major maritime projects underway at the time: the Army Street Terminal at Pier 80 and the revamped Pier 27–29. These two projects were considered significant because the capacity created by them would allow the port authority to retire eleven existing piers from cargo operations and to reuse them for other revenue-generating purposes. The remaining piers, it was predicted, would be sufficient as long as the "trend toward containerization is not accelerated." ADL, *Port of San Francisco*, 122.

111. Ibid., 164.

112. Ibid., 165.

113. Ibid.

114. Ibid., 166. They also express very unmistakably the interests of capital, and insofar as policy documents are expressions of public interest, they would not typically articulate so plainly the connection between government and capital.

115. Michael Harris, "Port's Seesaw—City and State," *SFC*, February 14, 1967.

116. Ibid.

117. SFPA, *Hearing Notes of the San Francisco Port Commission* (San Francisco, December 14, 1966), 17.

118. "Board Will Act on Port Takeover," *SFC*, January 7, 1967. Blake also complained that "railroad tracks foul up traffic on the Embarcadero," a clear indicator of the how much that part of the waterfront had changed, as had certain attitudes toward it.

119. Ibid.

120. Ron Moskowitz, "Waterfront Plan's Hot Reception," *SFC*, April 2, 1968.

121. Ibid. In fact, the Citizen's Advisory Committee included an array of waterfront-related groups and agencies, including the Crab Boat Owners Association, the ILWU, San Francisco Beautiful (a progressive nonprofit founded by Friedel Klussman, a resident of Telegraph Hill, in 1947), RHIA, and Northern Waterfront Associates (real estate developers).

122. Mel Wax, "Hard Look at Plan for Waterfront," *SFC*, December 14, 1966, referring to the Bolles report.

123. "A Look at Port's Future."

124. Ibid.

125. Jerry Burns, "Ambitious Ideas for Waterfront," *SFC*, September 1, 1967.

126. Scott Blakey, "20-Year Plan for S.F.'s Northern Waterfront," *SFC*, November 21, 1968.

Chapter Four

1. After the disappointing defeat, members of the Telegraph Hill Dwellers split to form San Francisco Tomorrow.

2. SFPD, *The Northern Waterfront Plan* (San Francisco, 1969), 1. This is quite different from the contemporary San Francisco *General Plan*, wherein elements, or chapters, consist entirely of policy statements. There are no specific proposals and no implementation sections.

3. Ibid., 2.

4. Ibid., 5.

5. Scott Blakey, "Waterfront Plan Adopted," *SFC*, June 20, 1969.

6. Ibid.

7. SFPD, *Northern Waterfront Plan*, 1969, 17.

8. Ibid., 37.

9. Ibid, 38. The discussion of urban design in this plan was a precursor to what would become the Urban Design Element, see Chapter Two, note 91.

10. SFPD, *Northern Waterfront Plan*, 41.

11. Ibid.

12. An SUD is the designation given to an area the character of which does not fit one of the typical land use types, for instance residential, commercial, or industrial, and to which special rules may apply. In this case, the SUD included floor-to-area

ratio restrictions (FAR, a way to control building bulk), established land-use restrictions, parking requirements, and required conditional use (CU) approval for non-maritime development on port property in the SUDs. The special requirement for CUs was removed in the process of creating the *Waterfront Land Use Plan* (see Chapter Eight).

13. When an element of the *General Plan* is changed, or a new one is added, it can carry much more weight if it generates changes or additions to the *Planning Code*. At minimum, such changes serve to codify aspects of planning policy. Typically, plans were not (and are not) intended to create new development, rather, they guide the character of proposed development. However, over the last several decades a range of planning tools have evolved, such as California's "specific plan," that are intended to foster development, if not actually to identify funds and carry out capital projects, or to more directly force certain results through exactions from developers and similar mechanisms.

15. "Supervisors to Study S.F. Port Problems," *SFC*, August 13, 1951. Later, as mayor, Christopher would appoint Justin Herman as head of the SFRA. He fully supported Herman's Golden Gateway project. Christopher was without doubt a "development-oriented" mayor.

16. SFPD, *Memorandum Report No. 61.2 to the City Planning Commission from James R. McCarthy, Director of Planning: Interim Report on Waterfront Development Plan and Height Control* (San Francisco, 1961), 5. This concern predates adoption of height limits and changes to the *Harbors and Navigation Code* discussed earlier.

17. "A Suggestion for Port Land," *SFC*, December 1, 1966.

18. "Magnin Defends Port Facility Sale," *SFC*, December 2, 1966.

19. Editorial, "Waterfront Control," *SFC*, December 5, 1966.

20. William Chapin, "A Rowdy Standoff at Board Meeting," *SFC*, January 31, 1967.

21. "All-Out S.F. Drive to Regain Control of Port," *SFC*, March 21, 1968.

22. San Francisco Planning and Urban Research Association, *San Francisco Port . . . Asset or Liability?* (San Francisco, 1968), 5.

23. Ibid., 8.

24. Some of SPUR's roots extended from the BZC. Unsurprisingly, there was a crossover between SPUR's board and some of the power elite in San Francisco. For instance, Fleishhacker, hotelier Ben Swig, and James Zellerbach were members of the same social clubs and shared an interest in supporting the arts. And Ben Swig, Mortimer Fleishhacker, and Cyril Magnin were together largely responsible for bringing one of San Francisco's most prominent theaters, the American Conservatory Theater, to the city.

25. "Port's Seesaw—City and State."

26. "All-Out S.F. Drive to Regain Control of Port."

27. One insider has speculated that state officials believed that the new Bay Conservation and Development Commission might make development difficult, and thus viewed the transfer as a way to get rid of what could become a liability.

28. Reinhardt, "On the Waterfront," suggests that the $100 million requirement was arbitrary, and not definitively traceable to any person or agency.

29. Dick Hallgreen, "Port Authority Wants Better Hyde Pier Offer," *SFC*, August 15, 1968.

30. Editorial, "Restore the Port to City Control," *SFC*, October 14, 1968.

31. Charles Howe, "Mellon Backs Port Issues," *SFC*, October 24, 1968.

32. Reinhardt, "On the Waterfront," 100.

33. Some years later, this condition was removed from the act, but not from the Transfer Agreement or city's charter, creating difficulties in reconciling priorities, especially with respect to the often conflicting goal of providing public amenities.

34. The agreement also required legislative approval for expenditures over $2.50

million and two gubernatorial appointees out of seven port commissioners, conditions that would later be rescinded. When it was realized that commercial development along the northern waterfront would be difficult to achieve, the spending requirement was reduced to $25 million.

35. Reinhardt, "On the Waterfront," 101. Reinhardt was one of the founders of the *San Francisco Bay Guardian*, a very left-leaning free local paper.

36. Ibid., 104.

37. This addition was championed by Quentin Kopp, a lawyer and member of the board of supervisors, later to be a state senator. He took issue with leasing practices after the transfer that favored Fisherman's Wharf restaurants, including the Alioto family businesses, and some of the deals made at Pier 39 for friends and family of port officials. Many leases are month-to-month, and such terms can avoid the need for review by the board of supervisors,

38. Quoted in Reinhardt, "On the Waterfront," 108.

39. Esther Gulick, "Saving San Francisco Bay: Past, Present, and Future," Horace M. Albright Conservation Lectureship, University of California, Berkeley, Center for Forestry, April 14, 1988, http://www.cnr.berkeley.edu/forestry/lectures/albright/1988gkm.html.

40. Walker, *Country in the City*. Walker also points out the rapid transformation of the movement to protect the bay from its elite origins to a truly populist endeavor.

41. Michael Wilmar, "The Public Trust Doctrine," *SPUR Newsletter*, November 1999, X.

42. SFPD, *Port of San Francisco Waterfront Land Use Plan, Final Environmental Impact Report*, 96.

43. If, for instance, a project required additional piles to be driven, then the area supported by those piles was considered new fill and could not be used for housing or office.

44. Scott Blakey, "Waterfront Hotel Project Plans Presented to Port," *SFC*, August 14, 1969. Ten years earlier, Ebasco rated Piers 1 and 7 to be in good condition, Pier 3 to be in poor condition, and Pier 5 had already been condemned.

45. Ibid.

46. Scott Blakey, "Ford Foundation Joins in Project," *SFC*, February 12, 1970.

47. "Hotel, Ferry Park Plaza Proposed for Waterfront," *SFC*, June 20, 1970.

48. "Angry Throng Attends Waterfront Hearing," *SFC*, September 4, 1970.

49. Maitland Zane, "Plan to Fight U.S. Steel's Big Project," *SFC*, September 16, 1970.

50. "Chronicle Makes a Big Mistake," *SFC*, September 19, 1970.

51. "Alioto Hails U.S. Steel's Bay Project," *SFC*, September 18, 1970

52. Gar Pill, "Alternate Plan to Ferry Port Plaza," *SFC*, October 12, 1970.

53. Bill Workman, "Architects Defend the Ferry Port Plaza Plan," *SFC*, October 15. 1970.

54. Bill Workman, "A Setback for Ferry Port Plaza," *SFC*, December 4, 1970.

55. Ibid.

56. William L. Pereira and Associates, "*Planning Study: Ford Urban Dealership San Fran-cisco*, San Francisco, 1969.

57. According to Reinhardt, the port did not so much "receive" a proposal from U.S. Steel as it actively solicited it, using real estate kingpin Walter Shornstein as local "muscle" to work the project through San Francisco's approval process. He also points out what he considered questionable relationships between Magnin, his son-in-law (who sat on the planning commission), hotelier Ben Swig, and Mayor Alioto. A potent mixture of purpose and circumstances, but in this case not enough to allow unfettered transformation of the built environment by capital.

58. Alioto, who had relied on organized labor to bolster his campaign, paid back some of his political debts with appointments to city commissions. One of these was the appointment of ILWU leader Harry Bridges to the port authority commission.

59. "Board Tackles Waterfront Building Rules," *SFC*, March 4, 1970.

60. In the decades to follow, justifying the inclusion of non-maritime uses in a project to support maritime ones (here, office supporting a new cruise terminal) would evolve into a complex game to attempt to satisfy the public trust requirements in proposals for development. Arguments may be made, for instance, that to save historic buildings, a trust goal, requires that they be leased as office space to pay for their preservation.

61. Bill Workman, "A 550-Foot Waterfront Height Okd," *SFC*, September 11, 1970.

62. Maitland Zane, "Plan to Fight U.S. Steel's Big Project," *SFC*, September 12, 1970.

63. Jerry Burns, "City Hall Clash on Steel Site," *SFC*, September 29, 1970.

64. "Praise for U.S. Steel Tower," *SFC*, October 6, 1970.

65. Jerry Burns, "S.F. Supervisors Block the U.S. Steel Tower," *SFC*, February 17, 1971.

66. Herod, *Labor Geographies: Workers and the Landscapes of Capitalism* (New York: The Guilford Press, 2001), 67.

67. The strongest union support for development came from the building and construction trades, affiliated with the AFL-CIO. The ILWU might typically have pushed against anything that hastened the demise of the working waterfront, but it was back on its heels. Although the Modernization and Mechanization Agreement had been ratified in 1960, troubles plagued the union and its rank and file, leading to a major strike in 1971.

Chapter Five

1. The port could still issue revenue bonds and could request money from the city's general fund, although the latter was unlikely to be granted.

2. New San Francisco conflict of interest laws led the city attorney to advise port commissioners Cyril Magnin and Michael Driscoll to step down from their posts, which they did in August 1974 (Jerry Carroll, "Whole Board to Probe Port," *SFC*, September 7, 1974). A few years later, Mayor Moscone appointee Richard Goldman also resigned because his wife, Rhoda Goldman, was a Haas family member. The Haas family controlled Levi-Strauss, which was building an office development across from Pier 27, a project that included several small parcels of port land.

3. Ralph Craib, "Blistering Critique of S.F. Port," *SFC*, December 14, 1972.

4. The board of supervisors can decide to intervene in the mayor's selection of port commissioners. Once it decides to takes such an action, a two-thirds vote is required to reject a nominee.

5. "The Port Had a Good Year despite Strike," *SFC*, December 15, 1972. The 135-day strike of 1971 shut down all of the West Coast's ports until a Taft-Hartley injunction was imposed. See Donald Fitzgerald, "A History of Containerization in the California Maritime Industry: The Case of San Francisco," report produced under the National Seagrant College Program, Department of Commerce, grant number NA 80AA-D-00190, project number R/MA-23, 1986. The fiscal issues discussed here pertain to the port's regular operating budget. One positive aspect of the transfer was that the port could ask San Francisco voters (as opposed to statewide election) to approve general obligation bonds, although this would not happen until 2007.

6. Craib, "Blistering Critique of S.F. Port."

7. Alioto's connections to the port were being called into question at the same time. The Alioto family was in the restaurant business in Fisherman's Wharf and the mayor had interest in a firm bought by shipping line PFEL, which his son ran. Furthermore, Alioto's law firm worked for shipping firms with connections to the port and to Cyril Magnin (Jerry Carroll, "Board to Try Again on Port Probe," *SFC*, September 5, 1974).

8. "City 'Finds' More Money for Port," *SFC*, May 3, 1975.

9. Ibid.

10. Marshall Kilduff, "Forecast on Port's Loss—$ 1.9 Million," *SFC*, January 22, 1976.

11. Marshall Kilduff, "Port Wants State to Cancel Bond Debt," *SFC*, April 14, 1977.

12. "Moscone Asks the State to Take Over Port Debt," *SFC*, August 27, 1977.

13. Marshall Kilduff, "S.F. Port's $172,000 Foul-up on Rents," *SFC*, November 27, 1975; and "Port Tenant Lags in Rent—Quake Job," *SFC*, December 10, 1976.

14. Larry Liebert, "Jury May Order a Port Probe," *SFC*, October 2, 1974.

15. Robert Hollis, "The Port's Dead Beat Tenants Owe $661,000," *SFC*, December 17, 1976.

16. Ibid.

17. "S.F. Port Expects Big Profit," *SFC*, December 7, 1979.

18. Much of the same friction and uncertainty could also be found in the port commission chambers. Even members of Mayor Moscone's commission, comprised largely of his own appointees, found themselves at opposites sides of the table. For instance, insurance executive and Citizens' Waterfront Committee member Richard Goldman, appointed by Moscone in 1976, envisioned development from Fisherman's Wharf to the Bay Bridge—but development "with dignity" ("New Port Official Asks End to Oakland Rivalry," *SFC*, December 29, 1976). His ideas were quite different from that of his fellow commissioner Jack Morrison, also a Moscone appointee, who was concerned primarily with resuscitating the port's maritime activities, and not with pursing real estate ventures.

19. Craib, "Blistering Critique of S.F. Port."

20. Fitzgerald, "The History of Containerization in the California Maritime Transportation Industry: The Case of San Francisco." Wolff was vocal in her support of the U.S. Steel proposal because it meant money for developing the port's maritime businesses.

21. Larry Liebert, "Alioto Aide to Run Port for 3 Months," *SFC*, August 22, 1974.

22. Larry Liebert, "S.F. Port Has a New Director," *SFC*, January 16, 1975.

23. Don Fortune, "The Port after Soules: Fuzzy Future Full of Problems," *SFC*, November 20, 1977.

24. Marshall Kiduff, "Port Director Fired—Reacts Bitterly," *SFC*, November 16, 1977.

25. Ibid.

26. Ibid.

27. Nevertheless, Soules managed to get a good bit of work done during his tenure, including removing old piers; completing substantial work on a new terminal in the southern waterfront; and initiating the massive retail/entertainment project at Pier 39.

28. This can go both ways. Because policy language can be less than rigorous and policies themselves can be inconsistent, it is sometimes possible to support both sides of the same argument using different parts of a general plan.

29. Brugmann and Slettleland, *Ultimate Highrise*.

30. Bill Workman, "New Group Joins Waterfront Fight," *SFC*, November 12, 1970.

31. Ibid. Goldman was a former insurance magnate who became known worldwide

for his philanthropy, and especially for being the founder of the Goldman Environ-mental Prize.

32. Ralph Craib, "A Citizens Plan for Waterfront," *SFC*, September 23, 1971.

33. Lawrence Livingston and John A.Blayney, *What to Do about the Waterfront* (San Francisco: San Francisco Citizens' Waterfront Committee, 1971). The main author of the CWC report, Lawrence Livingston, was influenced by Christopher Tunnard from whose *Taming Megalopolis* he quoted: "Our urban waterfronts can be treated as a new resource for the economy of leisure. But there must be safeguards, or they will be despoiled all over again in the very name of the public" (quoted in Ibid., 8). Livingston was a colleague of landscape architect Lawrence Halprin and was known in the regional environmental movement for his reports on the impacts of sprawl, eventually earning him the sobri-quet "Mr. Open Space."

34. Maitland Zane, "A 'Tivoli' Plan for the Embarcadero," *SFC*, April 10, 1973.

35. Michael Grieg, "New Details of Waterfront Plan," *SFC*, February 7, 1974.

36. "A 'Tivoli' Plan for the Embarcadero." Why this is the case is a little unclear. Most likely is that it would have been difficult to pay for. Advocates from S.F. Tomorrow later claimed that business interests allied with Mayor Alioto were trying to keep the area for their own development ideas. Port of San Francisco (PSF), *Special Meeting of the San Francisco Port Commission, Thursday, April 3, 1975*. Regardless, it would likely have run into difficulty with BCDC restrictions to do with building over the water. It gained new life when its cre-ator, architect, and one-time president of SFT Richard Gryziec, brought his vision to the so-called South of Market area (often called SoMa), where Mayor Moscone and Roger Boas (the city's new chief administrative officer) were trying to land a redevelopment project. The Tivoli Gardens concept would fade away here too, overshadowed by the Moscone convention center and other pieces of what would become the Yerba Buena Center. See Hartman, *City for Sale*.

37. Greig, "New Details of Waterfront Plan."

38. Concurrent planning efforts also forestalled the proposal; indeed, many ideas were held in abeyance (often until they evaporated) until BCDC completed its *Special Area Plan*.

39. "Group on Developing S.F. Port," *SFC*, March 15, 1972. Goldman would later become a port commissioner, appointed by Mayor Moscone. After circumstances forced him to step down, he was appointed to the Northeastern Waterfront Advisory Com-mittee, an influential group formed as part of the multiagency planning effort for the Northeastern Waterfront Survey, described later. See Chapter Five, note 2.

40. "Jobs and Scenery on the Waterfront," *SFC*, May 12, 1972.

41. Ibid.

42. Mayor's Port Committee, "Report of the Mayor's Port Committee: Findings and Conclusions" (San Francisco, 1972), 9.

43. "Group Named to 'Save' the Wharf," *SFC*, May 22, 1973.

Chapter Six

1. Geese in the world of planning seem to be particularly vulnerable. Even minor modifications to existing codes or land use regulations can be threatening. Sometimes, it is even claimed that failing to grant special exceptions may have dire results not just for a particular project, but the city's economy. This, of course, is a logic found more generally as part of urban governance and economic policy. For example, there may be

a push to suspend payroll tax to attract businesses in certain sectors or to make public land available for private development. Such strategies are especially prevalent in the climate of neoliberal urbanism, wherein city governments may be forced down the entrepreneurial path in response to intensified inter-urban competition. See David Harvey, "From Managerialism to Entrepreneurialism: The Transformation in Urban Governance in Late Capitalism," *Geografiska Annaler* 71, no. 1 (1989): 3–17; and Jasper Rubin, "San Francisco's Waterfront in the Age of Neoliberal Urbanism," in *Transforming Urban Waterfronts: Fixity and Flow*, ed. Gene Desfor, Jennefer Laidley, Dirk Schubert, and Quentin Stevens (New York: Routledge, 2011).

2. The broadened concerns caused some rifts in the activist community. For instance, one group split from SFT to become San Franciscans for Reasonable Growth. The new group was unhappy with what they felt to be SFT's nearly singular attention to views, aesthetics, and other "elitist" concerns.

3. Well-known attorney-activist and SFRG member Sue Hestor was a master of this strategy.

4. The genesis of the Downtown Plan and Proposition M, and more generally the politics of downtown development in San Francisco have been well covered elsewhere. See, for example, McGovern 1998, DeLeon, *Left Coast City* and Hartman, *City for Sale*. There is a tendency, however, to credit activists with coming up with all of the ideas and strategies employed to battle the excesses of downtown development. To some degree, this is true. Many planners were not attuned to the social and economic issues so critical to activists. But once the standard was raised, planning staff responded creatively and produced a flawed but tremendously valuable document in the Downtown Plan. What is missing in such accounts is a more nuanced exploration of the relationships between planning staff, the agency director, and the planning commission; a bureaucracy is a complex creature, not a single-celled organism. Certainly, many members of the planning bureaucracy accepted growth relatively unquestioningly, at least at first, including the planning director (Dean Macris from 1980–1992) and members of the planning commission. Or they believed that the market for office construction would shrink of its own accord, which in essence it did after a couple of years. At the staff level, reactions to growth issues were a little more diverse. But it is very difficult for staff, or a director, to push for a progressive agenda if the mayor is pro-development, as was Diane Feinstein, mayor from the 1978 to 1988. Until 2000, the mayor appointed all planning commissioners and even now the director serves at their pleasure. Thus to counter the hegemony of capitalistic interests in development politics, anti-growth forces must help enable planners. And there is reason to do so because, despite the negative stereotype of the technocrat, planners do have useful and sometimes uncommon skills, knowledge, and connections, and are paid for the time to use them. Planners can have a unique perspective on problems because of their centrality in the process; planners are in the position, depending on the larger political context, to address multiple constituencies and varied sets of issues. The result of doing so may mean that what planners propose is somewhere in the middle. Albeit, to some, especially progressive activists, the middle means failure (and is sometimes rightly interpreted as so). That is why activists are so important to the planning process. Planners can only advocate effectively if there is political support for them to do so. Short of sub-rosa and possibly subversive actions on the part of staff, pressure applied from the outside on officials and appointees may be the only way planners acquire the capacity to advance a progressive cause. Planning staff (and perhaps directors) may be happy to be coerced into changing their agenda or pushed into finding a new subject for their technical expertise. Indeed, thinking around an issue may already have occurred, planners waiting only for the right political breath of life to bring it to light.

5. According to *County Business Patterns* 1970 and 1990, U.S. Bureau of the Census.

6. The 1985 Downtown Plan included policy to *constrain* development to certain parts of the SoMa in order to protect light industry.

7. SFPD, *Environmental Impact Report: Amendments to the Comprehensive Plan Proposed by the Fisherman's Wharf Action Plan* (San Francisco, 1983).

8. PSF, *Port and Shipping Handbook 1988–1989* (San Francisco, 1989).

9. As discussed by John Logan, "Cycles and Trends in the Globalization of Real Estate," in *The Restless Urban Landscape*, ed. Paul L. Knox (Englewood Cliffs: Prentice-Hall, Inc., 1993), though he points out that the process of doing business in globalized real estate actually relies on local actors with local knowledge and connections, which reduces the power of global forces to alter landscapes on their own.

10. Sasia Sasken, *The Global City: New York, London, Tokyo* (Princeton, NJ: Princeton University Press, 1991).

11. See, for instance, Jason Hackworth, *The Neoliberal City: Governance, Ideology, and Development in American Urbanism* (Ithaca, NY: Cornell University Press, 2007); Gordon MacLeod, "From Urban Entrepreneurialism to a 'Revanchist City?' On the Spatial Injustices of Glasgow's Renaissance," *Antipode* 34, no. 3 (2002): 602–24; Neil Brenner and Nik Theodore, "Cities and the Geographies of 'Actually Existing Neoliberalism,'" *Antipode* 34, no. 3 (2002): 349–79; and Rubin, "San Francisco's Waterfront in the Age of Neoliberal Urbanism."

12. It is not possible to cover every plan produced during this time. Among those omitted or discussed only cursorily are the *South Bayshore Plan*, an "area plan" of the *General Plan*, and the *San Francisco Bay Area Seaport Plan*, a regional plan adopted by the Metropolitan Transportation Committee and BCDC in 1982.

13. PSF, *Port and Shipping Handbook*, 1989.

14. Although they have been amended and updated over the years, all of the plans discussed in this chapter still exist as of this writing.

15. The *Northern Waterfront Plan* is an "area plan" of the *General Plan* and as such, it is more targeted and specific in nature. However, the goals and policies therein are based on the more general goals and policies in the "elements"; policies from the "elements" not refined or incorporated in an "area plan" may still be applicable to development in the particular area covered.

16. SFPD, 1971, 3.

17. Bay Conservation and Development Commission, *Total Design Plan* (San Francisco, 1980), ii.

18. Here, "the public's interest" refers both to what members of the public said was important and to the general benefit of the polity.

19. One of the most important parts of creating policy, as presented in a planning document, is vetting it with the public, a process that has evolved to include many approaches (and a subject of much discussion in planning circles). A properly created plan typically reflects some level of involvement by other agencies, citizens, or interest groups. It is the result of engagement among parties, albeit with more or less influence, in a political process. Of course, what often happens is that no group is completely happy with the results. But as Planning Director Dean Macris was given to saying (and I paraphrase here), "if everyone is a little pissed-off, you've done your job." Even so, if one can demonstrate that a proposal complies with established policy, the process can be less contentious because, theoretically, it represents some form of prior agreement among active participants. This can prove difficult if, as in San Francisco's *General Plan*, there are conflicting policies. Regardless, policy documents provide an important framework for

publicly informed decision making and evaluation, making them an essential part of the democratic process.

20. SFPD, *The Plan for the Northeastern Waterfront* (San Francisco, 1977), v. The plan's overall goal was to "create a physical and economic environment in the Northeastern Waterfront area which will use the area's resources and potential in the manner which will best serve the needs of the San Francisco community" (Ibid., 1).

21. Ibid., 11. These policies support the "Urban Design Objective: To develop the full potential of the northeastern waterfront in accord with the unusual opportunities presented by its relation to the bay, to the operating port, fishing industry, and downtown; and to enhance its unique aesthetic qualities offered by the water, topography, views of the city and bay, and its historic maritime character" (Ibid.).

22. The emphasis on open space an access was expressed in the "Recreation and Open Space Objective: To strengthen and expand the recreation character of the northeastern waterfront and to develop a system of public open spaces and recreation facilities that recognizes its recreational potential, provides unity and identity to the urban area, and establishes an overall waterfront character of openness of views, water and sky and public accessibility to the water's edge" (Ibid., 4). Of course words like *feasible* are subject to interpretation and therefore debate.

23. Ibid., 2.

24. Ibid.

25. Ibid., 2, 4. Emphasis added.

26. SFPD, *Northeastern Waterfront Plan*, 13.

27. As a temporary use, parking on piers did not require BCDC approval and complied with the *Northern Waterfront Plan*.

28. PSF, *Special Meeting*, 25.

29. It is possible for developers to argue over particular policies; the outcomes of such engagements depend partly on the members of the BCDC and the port commission at the time, the importance of the project, and its characteristics. Developers, sometimes in coordination with other city agencies, can occasionally negotiate the relaxation of some policy restrictions because their proposal may include elements that are particularly desirable to the public or the commissions, and which would not be provided without the project. Of course, this can also create scandal.

30. "City Loses Plea on Waterfront," *SFC*, March 9, 1974. Jacobs had been at odds with BCDC since its staff made decisions that were not supportive of the Planning Department's newly amended 1971 *Northern Waterfront Plan*.

31. PSF, *Special Meeting*, 14. As noted earlier, the public trust was not yet considered a serious impediment, and the SLC had yet to assert itself in enforcing trust principles.

32. Larry Liebert, "S.F. Port Rejects Waterfront Plan," *SFC*, April 16, 1975; and Dale Champion, "Port Blueprint Wins Approval," *SFC*, April 18, 1975.

33. PSF, *Special Meeting*, 29. SFT had no love for Alioto. The organization had called for Alioto's removal six months earlier, based partly on his purportedly illegal appointment of Bernard Orsi as interim port director, and because of his family's financial connections with PFEL. They were not happy with his appointments to commissions, either ("S.F. Tomorrow Calls for Alioto's Removal," *SFC*, October 24, 1974).

34. PSF, *Special Meeting* 24.

35. "Port Blueprint Wins Approval." Although Feinstein had campaigned against U.S. Steel, she was not anti-development.

36. Ibid.

37. PSF, *Special Meeting*, 38.

38. Ibid., 30. Note that port staff did not necessarily agree with their commission's stance.

39. Liebert , "S.F. Port Rejects Waterfront Plan."

40. PSF, *Special Meeting*, 8. Debate also ensued over requirements for 50 percent walkable open space for any proposed projects in the Ferry Building area.

41. This was based partly on the committee's conclusion that city restrictions on height would render any office or housing development too small to generate rent to the port. Therefore, it was not worth revisiting state legislation for something already restricted by the city (hiding behind the Planning Department's skirts, it seems).

42. BCDC, *San Francisco Waterfront Special Area Plan* (San Francisco, 1975), 2.

43. Larry Liebert, "Bold New Plan for Port Development," *SFC*, December 21, 1974.

44. Livingston and Blayney, *What to Do about the Waterfront*.

45. Inclusion of these policies probably helped broker her support for the *Special Area Plan*.

46. It is also possible to swap land—that is, exchange a piece of land burdened with the public trust for another piece that is not, so that development can be undertaken. In order to allow such a swap, it has to be shown that the land to receive the burden of the trust be of equal value to the land taken out of the trust. The process by which decisions regarding the public trust are made is arcane. Suffice it to say that to argue that a piece of land no longer serves trust purposes has been exceedingly difficult.

47. Allan Temko, "A Great Plan to Transform the Waterfront," *SFC*, October 8, 1979.

48. San Francisco Redevelopment Agency (SFRA), *Northeastern Waterfront Survey Summary Report* (San Francisco,1979), n.p.

49. "A Great Plan to Transform the Waterfront." Temko was referring to the 1969 *Northern Waterfront Plan*.

50. The first substantial housing affordability requirement, that at least 20 percent of tax increment income be set aside for low and moderate income housing, was enacted in 1979.

51. PSF, *Maritime Strategy: Maritime and Commercial Land Use Objectives* (San Francisco, 1979), 1.

52. Ibid., n.p..

53. In some places, the port is required to preserve areas for existing or future maritime operations, especially cargo handling, to support the needs of the Bay Area, in accordance with the *San Francisco Bay Area Seaport Plan*.

54. BCDC, *Total Design Plan*, i.

55. In fact, the NEWAC comprised the same familiar people from the same citizens groups and public and private agencies and organizations. This could cause one to wonder exactly how representative they really were, or who they really represented.

56. BCDC, *Total Design Plan*, 1.

57. Ibid., viii.

58. Ibid., 3.

59. Mayor's Economic Advisory Council, 1978. By the late 1980s, the central waterfront had become home to many light industrial businesses displaced by the growth of the Financial District into SoMa. Blue-collar workers still outnumber residents in the area by about six to one.

60. SFPD, *Central Waterfront Plan* (San Francisco, 1980), 2.

61. Ibid., 16.

62. Ibid., 19.

63. A host of other technical and regulatory requirements overseen by agencies such as the U.S. Army Corps of Engineers and the U.S. Coast Guard are not discussed here.

64. PSF, *The Port of San Francisco Waterfront Land Use Plan* (San Francisco, 2000), 47.

65. How this works, for instance, is that a *General Plan* policy may state that heights must be lower as buildings approach the water. The *Planning Code* would then include specific height designations, such as the current 40-foot limit that applies to most of the northern waterfront.

66. PSF, *Port and Shipping Handbook 1988–1989*, 4.

67. *San Francisco Business Times*, August 1987

68. While the planning process provides information and tools that can empower citizens and activist organizations, as well as encourage growth, it goes without saying that institutions vary in their outlook over time, and are sometimes sources of conservative, if not reactionary, approaches to issues. San Francisco's planning bureaucracy has certainly exhibited distinctly unenlightened qualities, as have organizations and individuals in the wider community. See also Chapter Six, note 4.

69. Local jurisdictions have a fair amount of flexibility in how CEQA standards are established and how projects are assessed against them. San Francisco has developed a particular "way of doing things" in this regard. In most cases, the San Francisco Planning Department is the "lead agency" responsible for implementing CEQA.

70. Some types of plans, such as the "specific plan" legislated by the State of California or redevelopment agency plans, can implement development programs.

Chapter Seven

1. Williams was quoted in Marshall Kilduff, "S.F. Port Commission Loses a Project and a Top Aide," *SFC*, February 26, 1976.

2. While the Burton Act was amended to remove the requirement to seek development that would generate the most profit to the port, that stricture was not removed from the city's charter. Such inconsistencies only add to the difficulty of getting things done, partly because decisions are made more subjective in light of them.

3. Niels Erch, "Tangled Priorities at Fisherman's Wharf: What's the Catch?" *San Francisco Business Times* 22, no. 8 (August 1987).

4. While wringing exchange value out of the wharf affected much of its character, it nevertheless became a place used by many and continues to serve a wide public. This is largely because Fisherman's Wharf is not functionally separated from the adjacent San Francisco Maritime National Historic Park, which includes the unmistakable curved seawall, a large open park and sand beach, the historic ships at Hyde Street Pier, and the Maritime Museum. The wharf is also connected to the rest of the city by its most evocative public transit lines: the F-line, which runs the world's largest collection of historic streetcars, and the Powell-Hyde Street cable car line. That much of the park was a Works Progress Administration project also lends to the wider area a sense of publicness.

5. SFPD, *Northern Waterfront Plan* (San Francisco, 1969), 5.

6. BCDC, *Special Area Plan*, 8.

7. Allan Temko, "S.F. Port's Architectural Disaster," *SFC*, October 30, 1978.

8. BCDC, *Special Area Plan*, 19.

9. Generally, the *Special Area Plan* allowed fill for only a limited set of non-maritime industrial uses, few of which have the potential to generate much rent to the port, as well as marinas, bay-oriented commercial recreation, and bay-oriented public assembly. These uses are defined as "facilities specifically designed to attract large numbers of people to enjoy the bay and its shoreline, such as restaurants, specialty shops, and hotels" (BCDC, *Special Area Plan*, 8).

10. Ibid., 20.

11. SFPD *Plan for the Northeastern Waterfront*, 15. How general commercial recreation and retail is water-oriented remains open to debate. It may just require painting buildings blue and grey, dressing them up with life preservers, fishing nets, and stencils of anchors and sea birds, and selling fish and chips and fake pieces of eight.

12. David Johnston, "Dispute over Pier Tourism Project Churns up S.F. Bay," *Los Angeles Times*, October 5, 1978.

13. Larry Liebert, "Big Waterfront Complex Wins Preliminary OK," *SFC*, May 15, 1975. According to the *Los Angeles Times*, Simmons saw the dilapidated Pier 39 and thought it would be a good place for a Tia Maria restaurant. The site was huge, though, and so his scheme grew to fill it. Initially, his ideas met resistance, but boat owners said that they would support his project if he included a marina, which he did, and so they did ("Dispute over Pier Tourism Project Churns up S.F. Bay").

14. Liebert, "Big Waterfront Complex Wins Preliminary OK."

15. For instance, improvements to the Hyde Street Pier were required as part of any development of Pier 45, as discussed later in this chapter.

16. Ralph Craib, "Big Waterfront 'Village' Approved," *SFC*, August 4, 1977.

17. "Waterfront Developer Meets Foes," *SFC*, July 30, 1976. Both men were members of the committee that authored BCDC's *Special Area Plan*.

18. "Waterfront Developer Meets Foes."

19. Alfred Frankenstein, "Ironing Out the North Point Project," *SFC*, March 12, 1978. Other issues would arise later, including charges that several commissioners who voted to approve the project were granted large restaurant concessions.

20. Craib, "Big Waterfront 'Village' Approved."

21. Allan Temko, "The Latest Dip at the Waterfront," *SFC*, August 29, 1977.

22. Temko, "S.F. Port's Architectural Disaster."

23. The port's revenue from restaurant leases in the wharf is substantial, so such businesses are well protected.

24. ROMA worked with a civic advisory committee composed of representatives from area businesses, neighborhood groups, and many local agencies. The plan was intended as a refinement of existing BCDC and city plans for Fisherman's Wharf.

25. ROMA Architecture and Design, *Fisherman's Wharf Action Plan* (San Francisco, 1981), 1.

26. SFPD, *Northeastern Waterfront Plan* (San Francisco 1980), 25.

27. Peter Grenell and Associates, *Fisherman's Wharf Community Action Plan* (San Francisco: Telegraph Hill Neighborhood Center, 1985), 3.

28. Some of these improvements were part of a package funded by a voter-approved bond measure in 1984; but most of the money was directed to cargo operations in the southern waterfront.

29. SPUR, *SPUR Report No. 177*, (San Francisco: SPUR, 1981). It should be noted that by the 1980s, SPUR was motivated by a more catholic membership and administration, and its opinions on policy and development were much more varied in orientation.

30. "Port OKs Development of Pier 45," *SFC*, April 11, 1974.

31. Ralph Craib, "Barbagelata Hits Income of Pier 45," *SFC* December 24, 1974. Supervisor John Barbagelata attacked the proposals because he felt they would not generate enough income.

32. "Lively Hearing on Waterfront," *SFC*, December 11, 1974.

33. Larry Liebert, "Realtors Assail Pier 45 Project," *SFC*, January 11, 1975. These restrictions were being negotiated in light of efforts then underway to complete BCDC's *Special Area Plan*. The *Chronicle* described them as "the rigid restrictions placed on devel-

opment during negotiations with waterfront conservationists" (Ibid.).

34. There was particular sensitivity to this issue as voters had just passed a tough conflict-of-interest measure in June 1974. SPUR actually defended the port, denying criticisms that the agency was wheeling and dealing sub-rosa, and contended that pursuit of development was being fully disclosed and that the process "could not be faulted" ("Lively Hearing on Waterfront").

35. As noted earlier, at the time the planning department's Northern Waterfront Plan did not support housing on the pier, contrary to Jacobs' general feeling about the benefits of residential development at the waterfront. A change to the policy would have been necessary to allow any project to move ahead.

36. Globalization cold-war style reared its head briefly when the *Chronicle* reported that even the Soviets wanted in on the Forty Five Associates proposal. Their interest was in building a cultural center that would "be used for showing the achievements of the USSR in the field of oceanography, shipbuilding, and fishing, as well as the cultural life of the Soviet people." "Bid for Soviet Center at the Wharf," *SFC*, September 6, 1974.

37. Notably, some opposition to the project was based on the feeling that it would not earn enough money for the port.

38. Hines was only the last to pull out. Before them, Gordon Bakar withdrew from consideration citing obstructionist anti-development waterfront types, and Amfac dropped out (it was involved in two proposals) because of conflict of interest issues. Larry Liebert, "Two Pier 45 Plans Pull Ahead of the Field," *SFC*, December 12, 1974.

39. Larry Liebert, "Port OKs No-Bid Lease," *SFC*, July 18, 1975.

40. Allen Temko, "Projects Revived," *SFC*, January 30, 1985.

41. Nancy A. Saggese, "Commercial Office Building Use of Tidelands," memorandum from the Office of the Attorney General, Los Angeles, December 1, 1982, 12. Saggese's analysis authoritatively dissected the lease agreements, which were written to allow the developer maximum flexibility. She concludes, for instance, that "this second amendment . . . does not insure that non-maritime related uses will be incidental to the main purpose of the office buildings. Indeed, it does not even insure that 'qualified tenants' as therein described will be trust tenants" (12).

42. New fill is severely restricted. Even current legal interpretations of public trust restrictionson state lands are not as limiting. For instance, the California attorney general has advised the port that repairs and improvements to existing structures that may extend their useful life (this includes seismic retrofitting) constitute fill. The implications of this interpretation are still being worked out. It could mean that if a pier needed repair, any existing, non-water-oriented uses would have to be removed.

43. John K. Van De Kamp, California Attorney General, to Alan R. Pendleton, "Request for Informal Opinion Concerning BCDC Jurisdiction Over Piers that Predate the Establishment of BCDC," California Department of Justice, October 8, 1986. In particular, "proposed development upon a pier that does not involve any additional coverage of Bay waters *and that does not involve any work on the pier itself or its substructure* may be treated as coming within the Commission's shoreline band jurisdiction; that is, the uses supported by the pier need not be water-oriented as long as the area has not been designated for water-oriented priority land uses" (Ibid., 2, emphasis added). The shoreline band jurisdiction is somewhat distinct from BCDC's bay water jurisdiction, and typically allows a more flexible range of uses.

44. Jim Burns, letter to the editor, *SFC*, July 6, 1987.

45. David Dietz, "Wharf Hotel Plan Due More Study," *SFC*, July 9, 1987.

46. Erch, "Tangled Priorities at Fisherman's Wharf: What's the Catch?"

47. Feinstein was in general a supporter of maritime activity in the port, partly

because it was a source of blue-collar jobs. She pushed hard for the successful passage of a $42 million bond that paid for upgrades to Piers 80 and 94. Unfortunately, two years after completing those projects, container shipments slowed to a trickle.

48. "Wharf Plan Looks Promising," editorial, *SFC*, August 10, 1987.

49. Dawn Garcia and David Dietz, "Obstacles Facing Feinstein Plan for Fisherman's Wharf," *SFC*, August 8, 1987.

50. Dawn Garcia, "Squabbling Perils Wharf Overhaul," *SFC*, October 9, 1987.

51. "Squabbling Perils Wharf Overhaul."

52. Ingfei Chen, "Money Woes Sink Fisherman's Wharf Plan," *SFC*, November 28, 1991.

53. Agnos' political career was that of a fairly principled man, as evidenced by his support for health and human rights issues. He stopped police sweeps of Golden Gate Park as part of a "rights for homeless" policy, for instance. He was also instrumental in pushing for the removal of the Embarcadero Freeway, a position that cost him reelection (he lost by about 3,000 votes) because it alienated his Chinatown allies.

54. Dale Champion, "Wharf Hopes For 'Fishing Center,'" *SFC*, April 5, 1986.

55. The center was not an original notion of his, as the 1982 *FWAP* had called for a "marine research center" at the end of Pier 45.

56. PSF, *Annual Report* (San Francisco, 1990). In 1989, it was estimated that 750 full-time-equivalent jobs could be associated with fishing and the seafood industry, with gross sales impact exceeding $60 million (PSF, *Shipping Handbook 1988–1989*).

57. Recent attempts to improve this space drew interest from a developer who wanted to construct a neo-museum called "the San Francisco Experience" and a non-profit organization that hoped to build a research and educational complex focused on the bay. Public outcry squelched the former and the latter had apparent difficulty with funding.

58. San Francisco Port Commission *Minutes* (San Francisco, October 9, 1968), 248–49.

59. Ibid., 252–53.

60. Allan Temko, "Ferry Building Threatened by Tacky Plans," *SFC*, March 26, 1979. Temko was quite incensed that the port chose CDC partly because of their original architecture partner, the fast-growing M. Arthur Gensler Jr. & Associates. He described their proposal as "cheap-o design" and bemoaned the port's inability to keep the Rouse Company interested in the project.

61. Carl Nolte, "Port OKs New Plan for Ferry Building," *SFC*, December 10, 1981.

62. Continental Development Corporation, "Continental Development Corporation's Proposal for the Restoration and Adaptive Re-Use of the Ferry Building, Pier One, and the Agricultural Building" (San Francisco, 1980).

63. Ibid.

64. Susan Ward, "Developer's New Move in Ferry Building Feud," *SFC*, February 5, 1986.

65. George Marshall, "S.F. May Settle With Developer for $3 Million," *SFC*, February 9, 1991. By this time, the SLC had started to impose restrictions on development not consistent with the public trust, which had not been the case when the project was first proposed in 1980. So, by the time the CDC project was weighed down in court battles, the results may have been moot as the imposition of trust restrictions could have halted CDC and the port in any case even if the project complied with other policies and regulations.

66. Allan Temko, "Project for Piers Appears To Be Full of Promise," *SFC*, August 20, 1985.

67. Diane Oshima, Port planner, to author February 4, 1999.

68. For projects like Pier 7 and other public improvements, as well as some upkeep, the cash-strapped port has used revenue bonds (paid for primarily by commercial leases) and a variety of grants from state and federal programs.

69. PSF, *Wharfside* (San Francisco, April 1978).

70. Carl Nolte, "S.F. Port Reveals Plans for a Bold Expansion," *SFC*, January 14, 1982.

71. SFRA, *San Francisco Redevelopment Program, 1995–1996* (San Francisco, 1996). The project produced 2,800 units, with about 26 percent affordable to people with low and moderate incomes. See page 194 for discussion of the plan's origins.

72. The stories of the ballpark and the Embarcadero Roadway are for the most part beyond the scope of this discussion. The former is covered by Richard E. DeLeon, though his account is now out of date, and the latter is mentioned briefly in Chapter Eight of this book (*Left Coast City* [Lawrence: University of Kansas Press, 1992]).

73. The Rincon Point-South Beach project has the distinction of being the first San Francisco urban renewal project sponsored by the agency that did not require direct use of eminent domain. Instead, it used "owner participation agreements" "backed by the threat of eminent domain" (David Habert, "Fifty Years of Redevelopment" *San Francisco Planning and Urban Research Association Newsletter* [San Francisco: SPUR, March 1999, no page.], http://www.spur.org/publications/library/article/50yearsredevelopment03011999, last accessed 1/14/2011).

74. Largely built by its residents, the Delancey Street housing complex is part of a multifaceted program that helps people who have fallen through society's cracks. The organization also runs several businesses, including a restaurant and moving company, all staffed by members of the program. While Allan Temko was cool toward its somewhat ersatz Italian architectural style, he described Delancey's project as "a masterpiece of contemporary social design" ("Italian Look for Delancey Street Complex, *SFC*, December 28, 1989).

75. Gerald Adams, "4 Piers to Become Yacht Harbor," *San Francisco Examiner*, October 25, 1979.

76. Ibid.

77. Editorial, "Rincon Project," *SFC*, December 24, 1980.

78. Marshall Kilduff, "A New Neighborhood for S.F.," *SFC*, December 16, 1985.

79. This condition was, initially, an obstacle for the new baseball stadium. It was difficult for the owners of the Giants baseball team and their partners to commit to a project that could be confiscated, essentially, by the State of California if it was deemed the land was needed for trust purposes in the future.

80. Involved in the production of the Rincon Point-South Beach built environment were a combination of firms from San Francisco and other parts of California, as well as engineering firms from Japan and a stable of American architecture, design, and construction companies of national and international status from outside California..

81. Jim Doyle and Steve Massey, "Development Plans Stir Debate," *SFC*, October 16, 1989.

82. Thom Calandra, "On the Waterfront," *SFC*, February 18, 1990.

83. In the mid-1980s, the port's activities and administration were scrutinized by another grand jury, which was created to investigate accusations of sweetheart deals, poor lease management, and charges that director Gartland had conflicts of interest. He was later cleared of those charges.

84. His appointment was welcomed by many observers because he was financially astute. Moreover, for three years, he was a commissioner for New York City's Department of Ports, International Trade, and Commerce and, as one of his ex-colleagues said of him, "he knew a ship from a boat" ("On the Waterfront").

85. Ibid.

86. "Development Plans Stir Debate."

87. Ibid.

88. Steve Massey, "Panel OKs Plan for Hotel on S.F. Waterfront," *SFC*, December 12, 1989.

89. Ibid.

90. Jim Doyle, "Rebuilding the S.F. Waterfront a Mandate for Port Director," *SFC*, February 17. 1990.

91. Allan Temko, "S.F. Hotels Could Block Bay Views," *SFC*, December 11, 1989.

92. Editorial, "Shipping Center May Cruise Away," *SFC*, March 25, 1988.

93. Jim Doyle, "Why S.F. Port's Plan to Build Cruise Terminal Irks Experts," *SFC*, May 25, 1990.

94. Ibid.

95. Steve Massey, "Port Panel Approves Second Hotel Plan," *SFC*, May 31, 1990.

96. Many planners and planning organizations decry "ballot-box planning" and insist that planning problems are complex and cannot readily be reduced to the short statements found on voter information pamphlets. As planners are also at the center of negotiations among parties, and thus are often plunged into a world colored by shades of gray, the idea that a decision can be made in a simple yes/no fashion can be disquieting. Some professionals also believe that planning is an educational process, and that making decisions at the ballot box does not allow information exchange and deliberation that can resolve issues in an iterative fashion. Nevertheless, the ballot initiative has proven to be a powerful tool for citizens and coalitions frustrated by a politics of planning that can favor business and development.

97. "Development Plans Stir Debate."

98. Opposition to the initiative was led by Mayor Agnos and included Jimmy Herman who, despite his opposition to the Sailing Center felt that the port would be too restricted by a plan. The campaign included a specious slogan: "Save the Waterfront for Blue Collar People. Yuppies can work everywhere else" (Thomas G. Keane, "A Vote on Waterfront's Future," *SFC*, October 25, 1990).

99. Steven Schwartz, "S.F. Ship Terminal Plan Granted an Extension," *SFC*, October 29, 1992.

100. DeLeon, *Left Coast City*, 132.

Chapter Eight

1. Dennis Bouey as quoted in Tibbet L. Speer, "Waterfront Revival," *San Francisco Business Times*, April 4, 1994.

2. Tibbet L. Speer, "Waterfront Revival," *San Francisco Business Times*, April 4, 1994.

3. PSF, *Annual Report, 2004–2005* (San Francisco, 2005).

4. Gerald D. Adams, "S.F. Port's Tunnel Vision Gets Blaster," *San Francisco Examiner*, May 10, 1995.

5. Recently, San Francisco has also been able to capture "special shipment" business, which includes transshipment of art exhibits and large scientific and research equipment, and has been trying to lure automobile shippers to its facilities.

6. Gerald D. Adams, "Port Abandons Plan to Renovate 2 Cargo Tunnels," *San Francisco Examiner*, February 2, 1995.

7. John King, "S.F. Port Veers from Shipping to Shopping," *SFC*, January 23, 1995. King also quoted Jordan as saying "Pier 39—I like that . . . .It's one of the top retail devel-

opments in the country." Compared to his predecessors Jordan was quite conservative, and was notorious for his strong-arm approach to dealing with the homeless.

8. PSF, *Annual Report, 2004–2005*.

9. PSF, *Annual Report, 2000*. The increase in bulk shipping is strongly connected to the building and recycling industries; the latter has been particularly vibrant, at least until the economic downturn of 2008.

10. Notably, the board vote was close—six to five. Chinatown merchants and political agitators pushed for the freeway's reconstruction, arguing that tourism and trade would suffer without the easy automobile access. Their fears were never realized.

11. Planning for the Waterfront Transportation Projects, also called the Embarcadero Transportation Projects, had actually begun before the earthquake, and assumed the presence of the freeway. The earthquake caused a complete reevaluation of the WTP, especially for the mid-Embarcadero segment running from Folsom to Broadway (PSF, *Waterfront Land Use Plan*, 24).

12. *Mid-Embarcadero Open Space Project*, Chief Administrative Officor's Waterfront Transportation Projects Office (San Francisco, 1994), 5.

13. PSF, "Information Presentation on a Ten-Year Review of the Waterfront Land Use Plan," staff memorandum to the port commission, San Francisco, December 3, 2008, 15.

14. Dan Levy, "Dean of Renaissance at Ferry Plaza," *SFC*, October 9, 1995.

15. Ibid.

16. PSF, "Information Presentation on a Ten-Year Review of the Waterfront Land Use Plan."

17. Retired fireman Don Beck whose boat was moored at Pier 40, quoted in John King, "Waterfront Potential S.F. Deal Buoys Hopes at Port Potential," *SFC*, January 13, 1997.

18. "S.F. Port Veers from Shipping to Shopping."

19. PSF, "Quarterly Update to Port Commission," memorandum from staff to the port commission, San Francisco, October 25, 2001.

20. PSF, "Information Briefing on the Waterfront Land Use Plan," staff memorandum to the port commission, San Francisco, August 7, 2008.

21. According to Diane Oshima, assistant deputy director of planning and development at the port, staff at the SLC, the attorney general's office, BCDC, various city agencies, as well as project sponsors themselves, together worked out how to be more flexible in deciding what kinds of projects would be allowable while respecting the values and objectives that the public trust was designed to protect and advance. This effort resulted in agreement that historic preservation should be a trust objective that could be supported by office development and general retail (personal communication with Diane Oshima, December 16, 2008).

22. One significant change was to amend the *Special Area Plan* to replace the "50% rule" with pier-specific open space and public access requirements in the northern waterfront. In general the "Replacement Fill Policy (50% Rule) in the *San Francisco Bay Plan* provides, in part, that BCDC can permit fill on publicly owned land for Bay-oriented commercial recreation and Bay-oriented public assembly, provided that the fill is a replacement pier that covers less of the Bay than was being uncovered, and the amount of Bay-oriented commercial recreation or Bay-oriented public assembly uses cover no more than 50% of the area of the Bay uncovered and the remainder (50%) of the replaced pier must be used either for public recreation, public access or open space, including open water" (BCDC, *San Francisco Waterfront Special Area Plan* [San Francisco, 2000], 7).

23. Jenny Stasburg, "Deal on Waterfront Development," *San Francisco Examiner*, July 21, 2000.

24. PSF, *Waterfront Land Use Plan*, 23.

25. Ibid., 4.

26. PSF, "Informational Briefing on Status of Port Planning and Development Projects," memorandum from Douglas F. Wong, Executive Director, to the port commission, San Francisco, 1999, 1.

27. PSF, *Annual Report* (San Francisco, 2001), 4.

28. Port staffers surely winced a little at John King's quip that the space is "so industrially chic it makes you wish you were a bureaucrat." John King, "15 Seconds that Changed San Francisco," *SFC*, October 17, 2004.

29. Ibid.

30. Carl Nolte, "3 Neglected Piers Taking on New Life," *SFC*, November 16, 2006, quoting the port's project manager Jennifer Sobol.

31. The idea of a historic district was not universally appreciated. Some members of the development community, architect Jeffrey Heller, and SPUR felt that historic status would limit the potential to encourage new uses along the waterfront and would place another layer of bureaucracy on the port. Their fears so far have proved unsubstantiated, especially given that the SLC has indicated historic preservation to be a trust goal.

32. Developers' fears were eventually allayed by language in the Burton Act. Essentially, the act indicated that should the transfer be revoked, the state would honor any leases already entered into legally (in other words, that supported the public trust). This led the project sponsor to request a letter from the SLC confirming that the project, because of its various public trust features, would be protected. Just about every other developer involved with projects on the waterfront now requests similar letters. This has made the SLC into a very powerful agency, with developers in the position of becoming tenants of the state. The SLC can request that nearly any condition be met before they will provide letters asserting that leases were "lawfully entered into." In the opinions of some, this has been carried to heights of ridiculousness. For instance, in one recent project that involved the historic preservation of a bulkhead building, the occupants of the rehabilitated space (used for offices) were required to raise their blinds during certain times of day so that passers-by would be able to see the building's interior structural elements.

33. Dan Levy, "Panel OKs Vision for S.F. Port," *SFC*, June 25, 1997. While entertainment uses such as amusement parks are allowed in certain places, his fears have so far been baseless.

34. The board of supervisors actually placed a measure on the 2000 ballot, Proposition R, that asserted a preference for the Bay Center project over Marlite's museum; although nonbinding, it won with 73 percent of the vote.

35. Lend/Lease's local representative was Paul Osmondson, one time director of planning and development at the port. Environmentalists, however, were critical of the project; cruise ships do not float lightly on the planet. Even in port, their diesel engines idle.

36. According to city officials, Lend/Lease was also scaling back its North American operations. J. K. Dineen, "Cruise Ship Terminal in Hot Water," *San Francisco Business Times*, May 12, 2006.

37. The Chelsea project, which had scored higher in the evaluation process than Mills, was recommended by staff to the commission. The commission rejected staff's advice, and ignored the votes of advisory groups in making its decision. Reportedly, a series of phone calls from the mayor's office to commissioners heavily influenced the outcome.

38. Aaron Peskin, an attorney and member of THD, has been a powerful voice in waterfront development issues. He termed out as a member of the board of supervisors,

but as chair of the San Francisco Democratic Party continues to be influential.

39. Supervisor Aaron Peskin also made things difficult by getting legislation passed at the board that required the projects to be reviewed for its fiscal feasibility; Mills' project was found to be unsound.

40. PSF, "Information Presentation on a Ten-Year Review of the Waterfront Land Use Plan," 12.

41. SPUR, *The Urbanist* (San Francisco, August 2007), 10–11.

42. This is not news to planners, whose essential training includes how to wield the fairly blunt tool of zoning as a way to influence the market. The effectiveness of such tools comes partly in how they are implemented (or not), leading some critics to accuse planning of being a conservative force that reproduces the power of the state, especially in its conspiratorial relationship with capitalism.

43. Walker, "Another Round of Globalization in San Francisco."

44. Don Mitchell and Lynn A. Staehelii have described the removal of homeless in downtown San Diego as part of a "Clean and Safe" business improvement district program as replacing the traditional regulation of private property with "a privatized set of rules of exclusion, and a form of violence—perhaps potential—that while retaining state sanction, is nonetheless left in the hands of private individuals" ("Clean and Safe? Property Redevelopment, Public Space, and Homelessness in Downtown San Diego," in Low and Smith, *Politics of Public Space*, 165.)

45. One small exception is the sea-creature-themed anti-skate-board features placed into low walls. They are a sign of the obvious, that even use value has its contestations—in this case, the decision was to reduce maintenance costs and, in some places, ensure seating is not co-opted by one group. Then again, no skate park yet exists on the waterfront.

46. David Harvey, "The Political Economy of Public Space," in Low and Smith, *Politics of Public Space*.

47. Harvey, "The Right to the City." Harvey borrows from Robert Park to make this point.

Index

Numbers in *bold* indicate pages with illustrations